AF400898

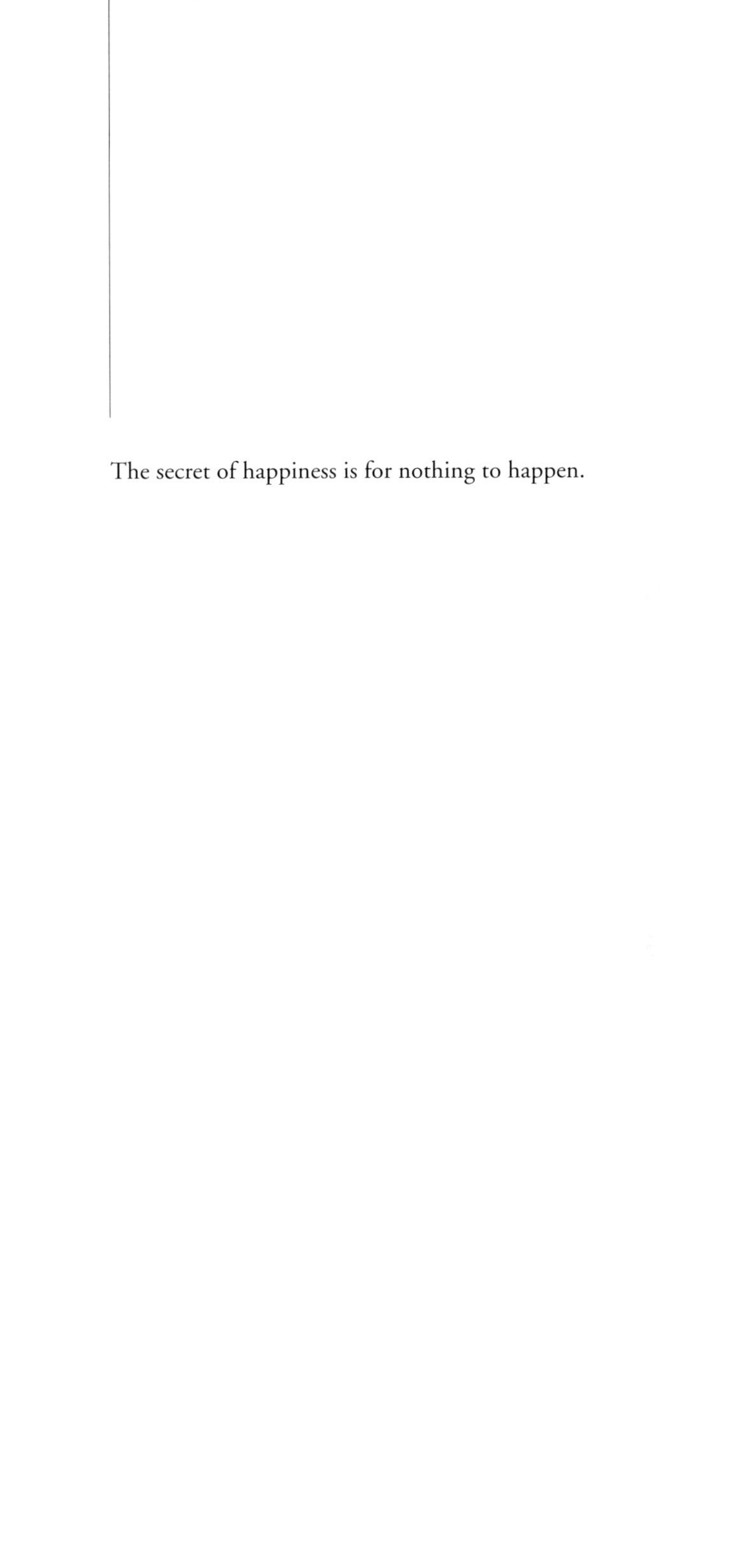

The secret of happiness is for nothing to happen.

All About Saul Leiter

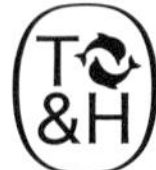

Contents

6   **Gallery**

274   **The Painter in Saul Leiter**
Margit Erb

276   **The New York Nabi**
Pauline Vermare

282   **Photographs that creep up behind you and tickle your left ear**
Motoyuki Shibata

291   Sources of Saul Leiter quotations

292   Saul Leiter chronology

295   Acknowledgments

I had the hope that the result would look like a photograph
rather than a fashion photograph.

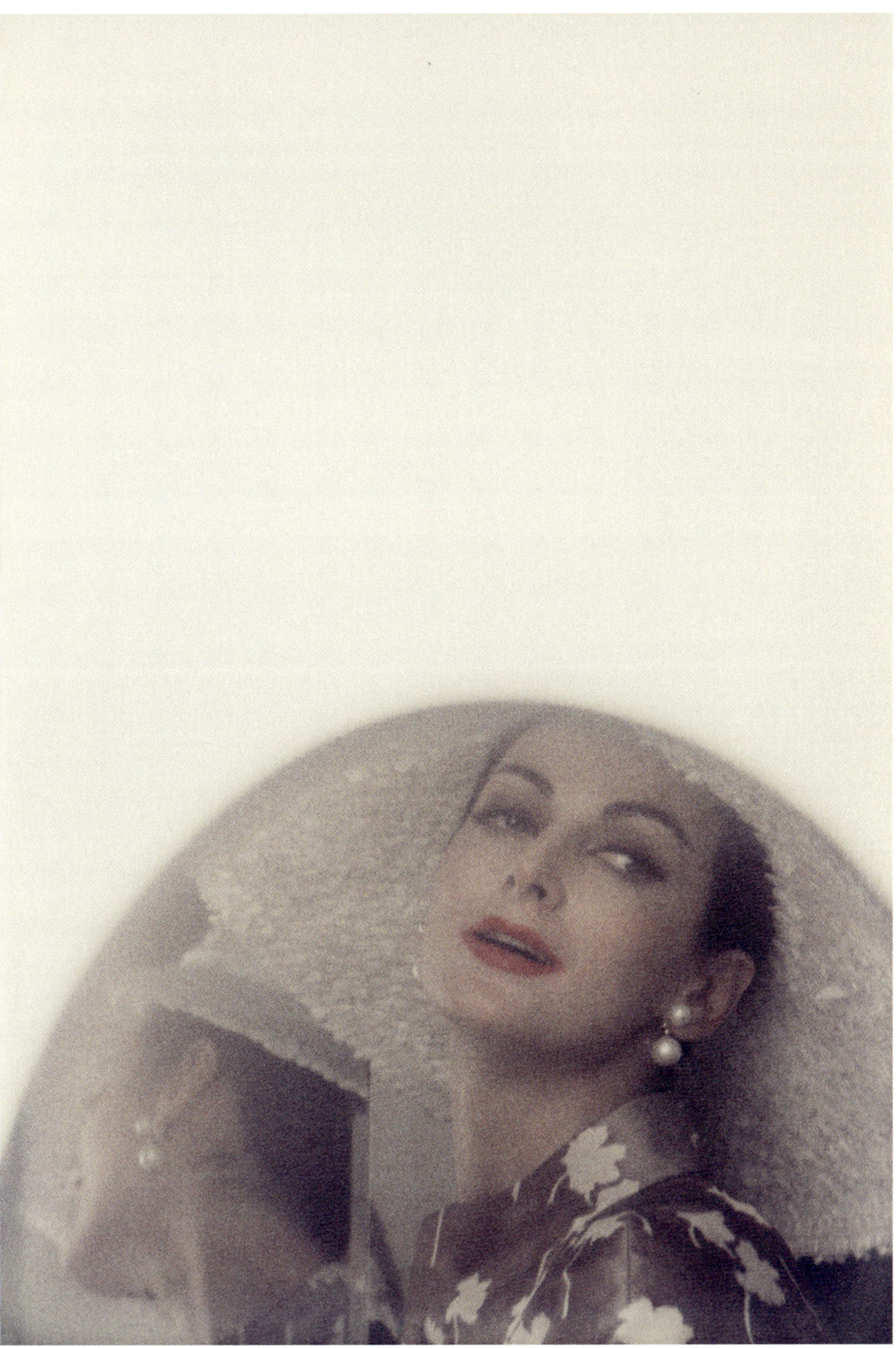

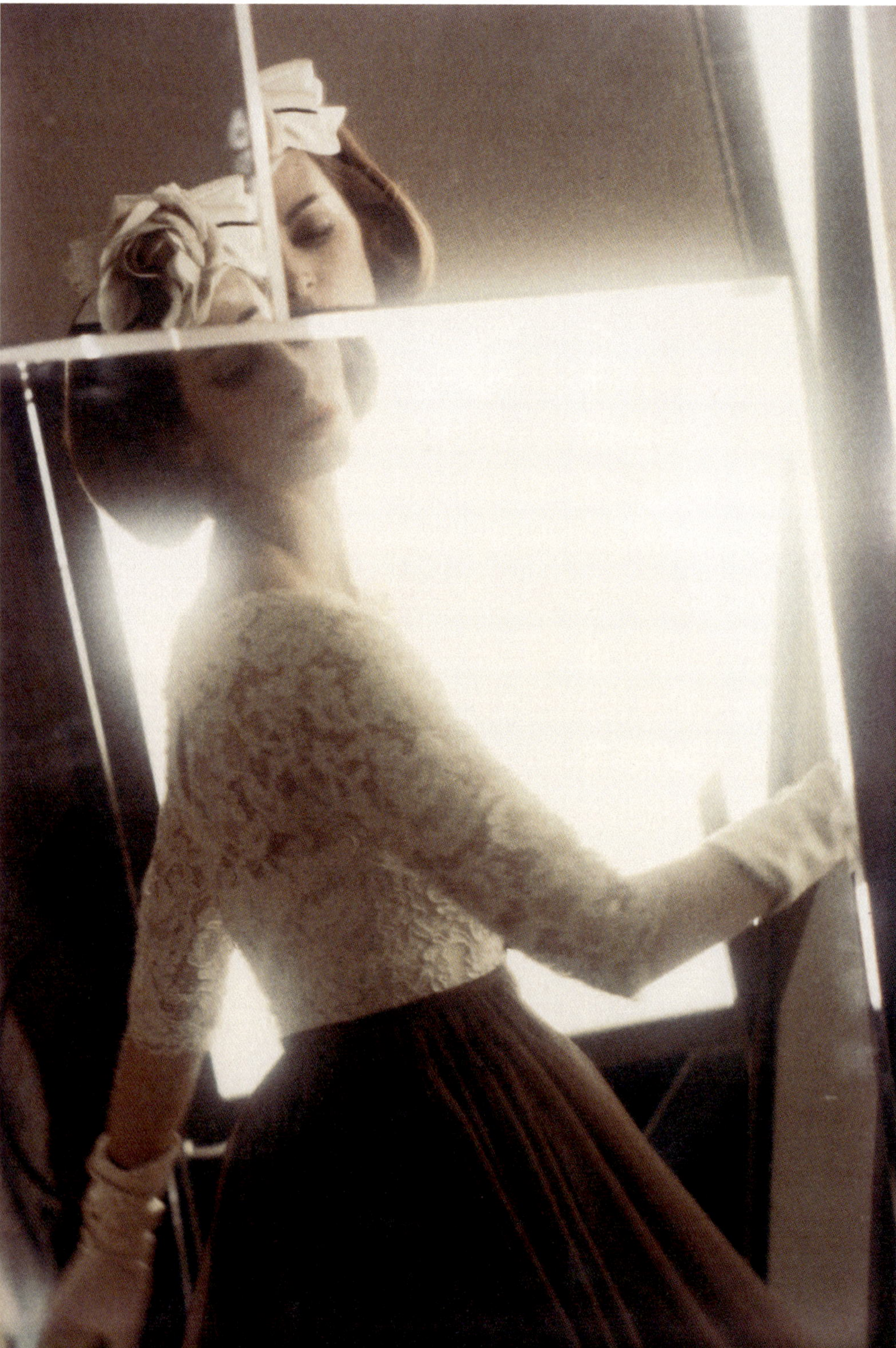

Carmen, *Harper's Bazaar*, 1959

There is a tremendous advantage of being unimportant.

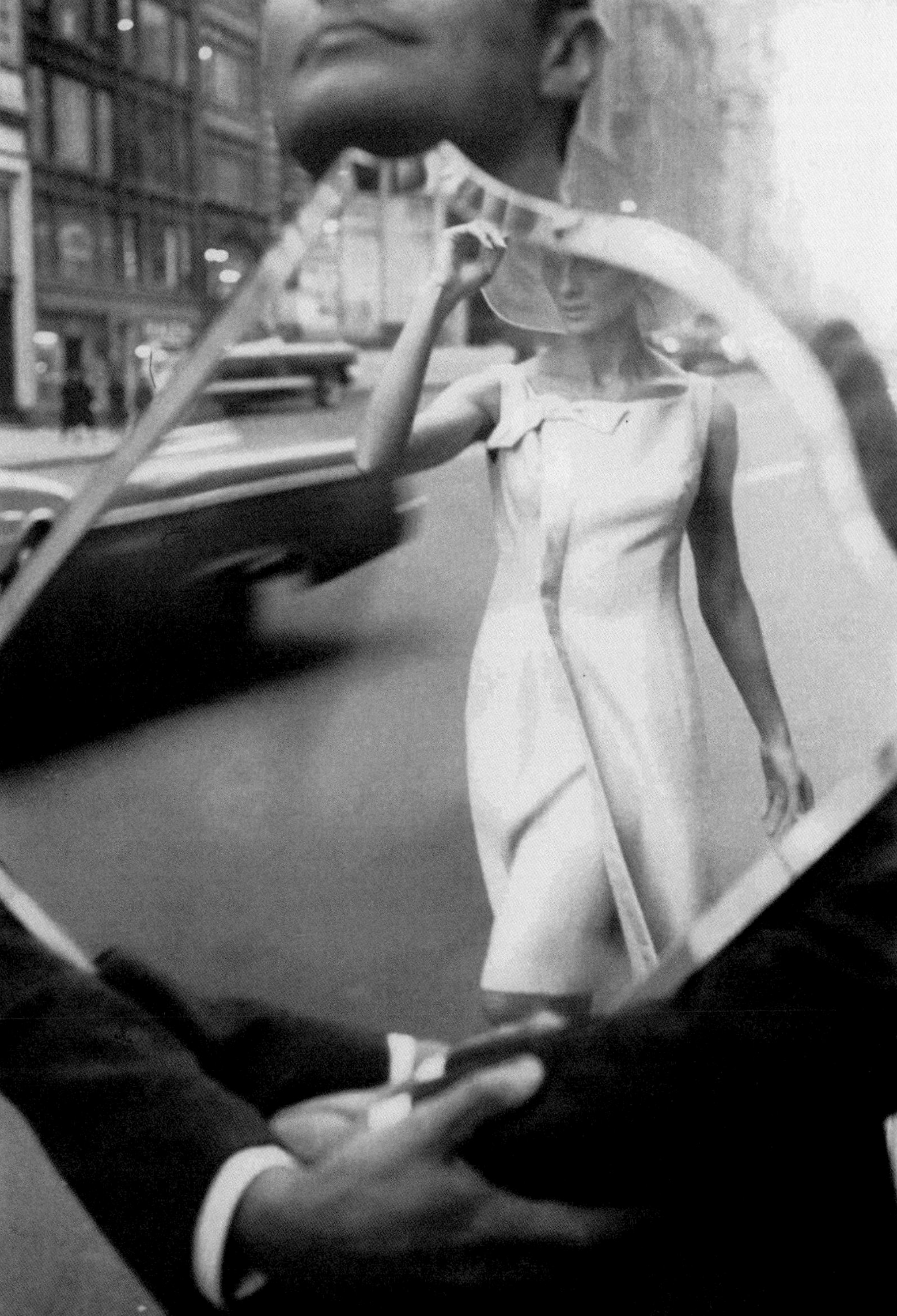

There's just too much.

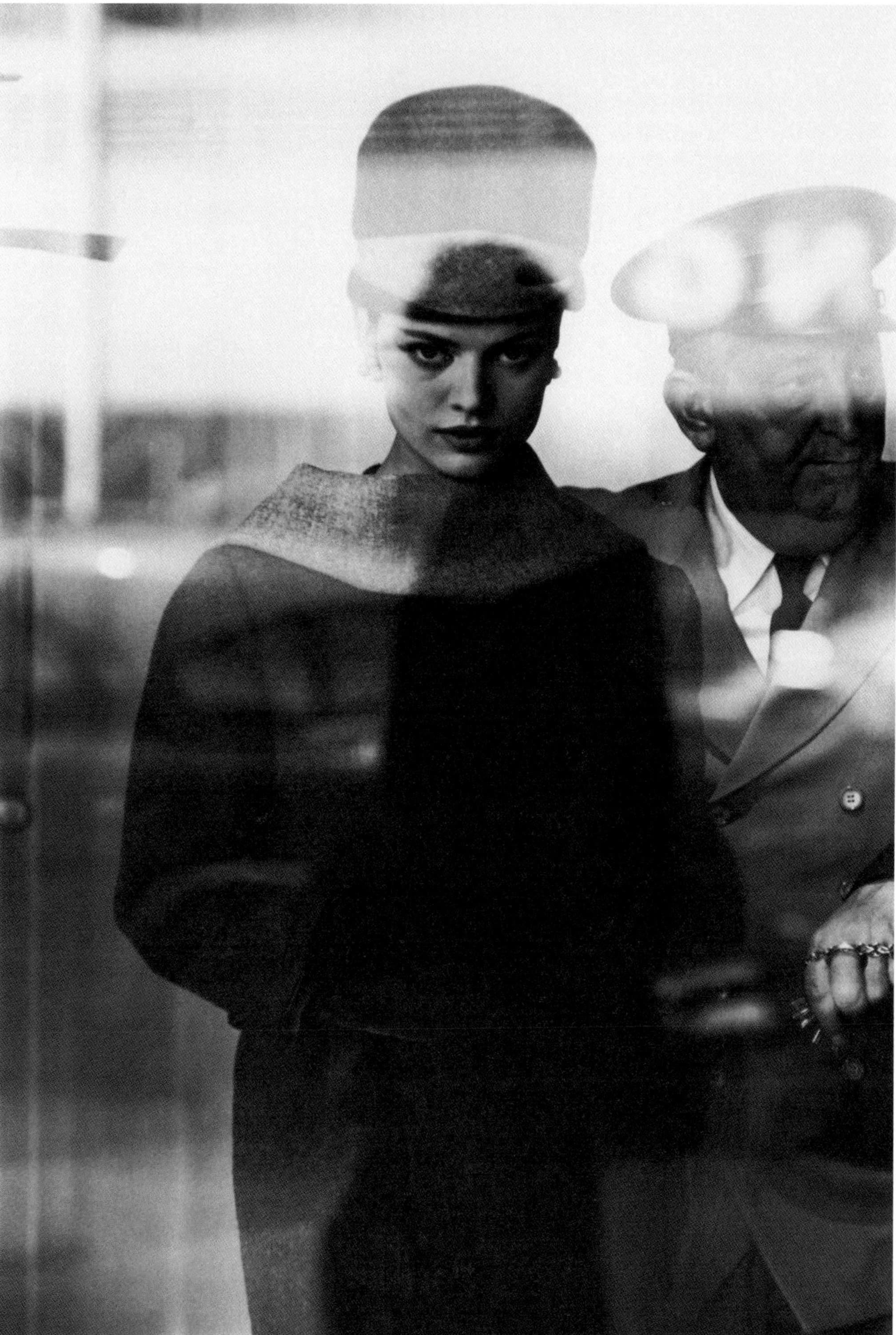

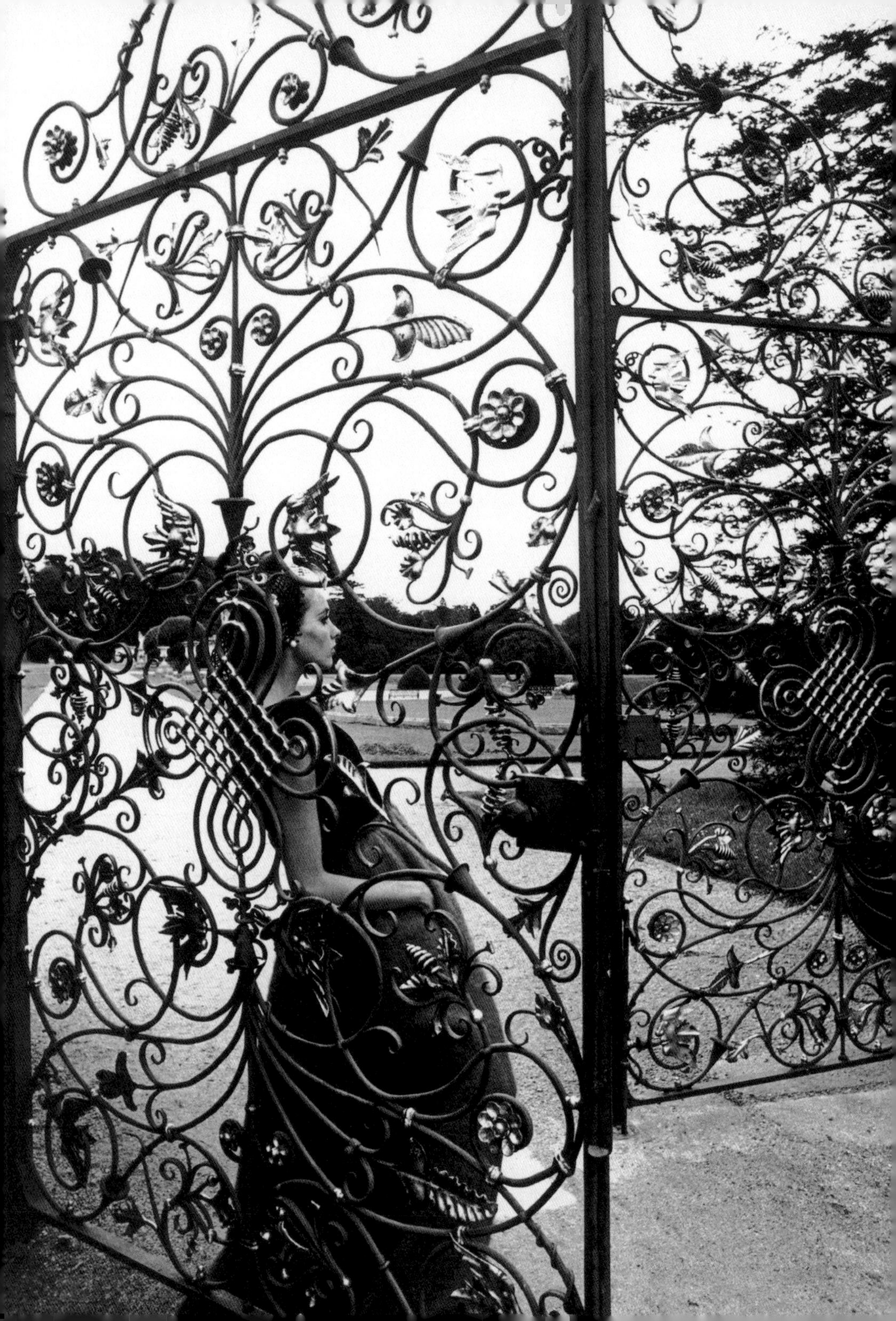

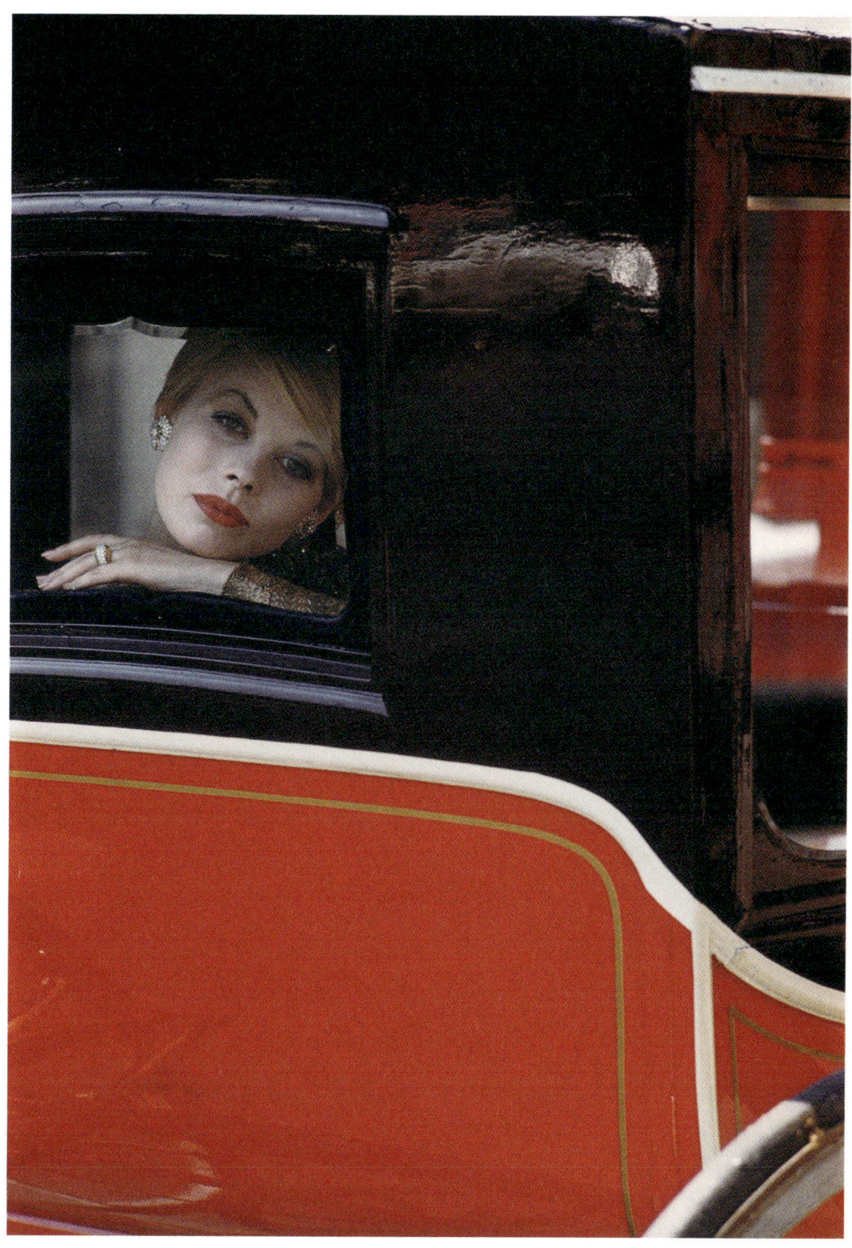

Untitled, c. 1965   Carriage Series, *Harper's Bazaar*, October 1960

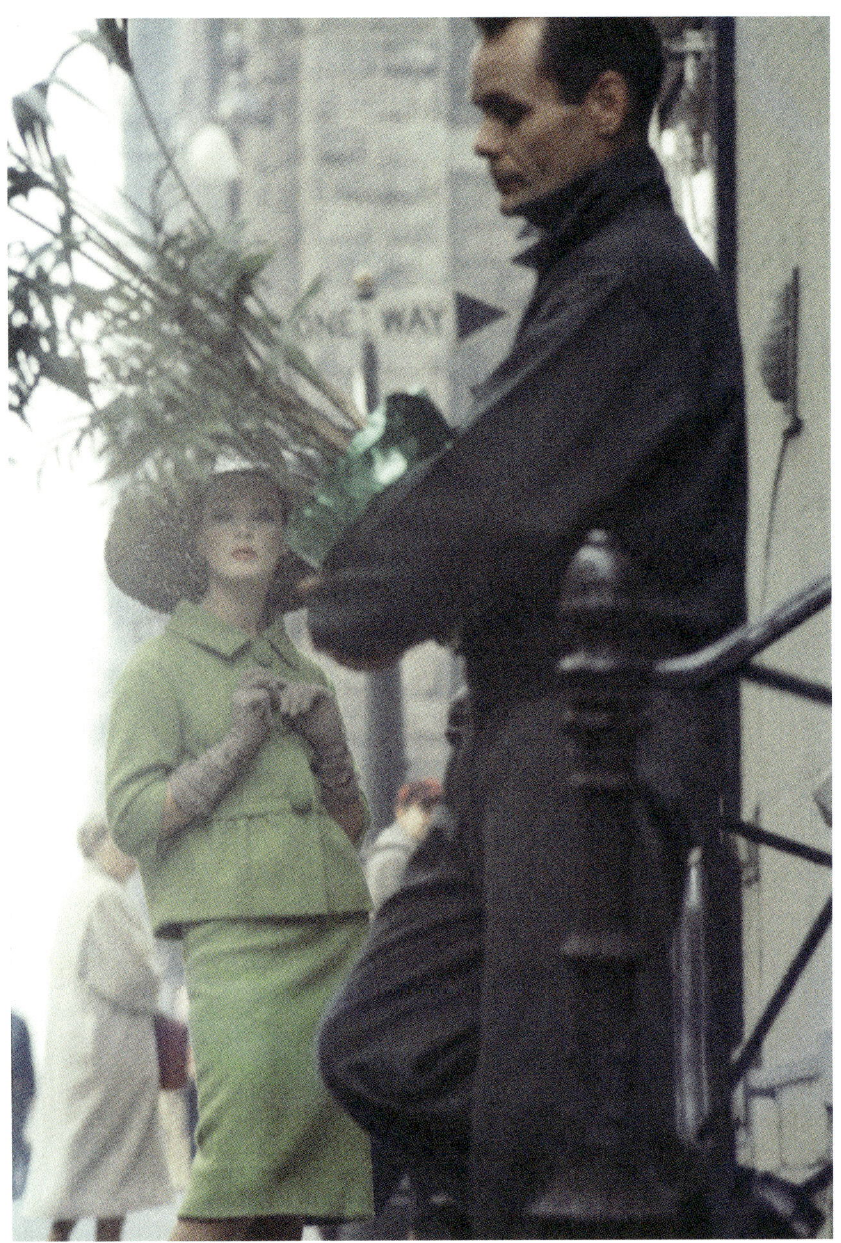

Harper's Bazaar, February 1959

Lily Moore, *Harper's Bazaar*, c. 1963

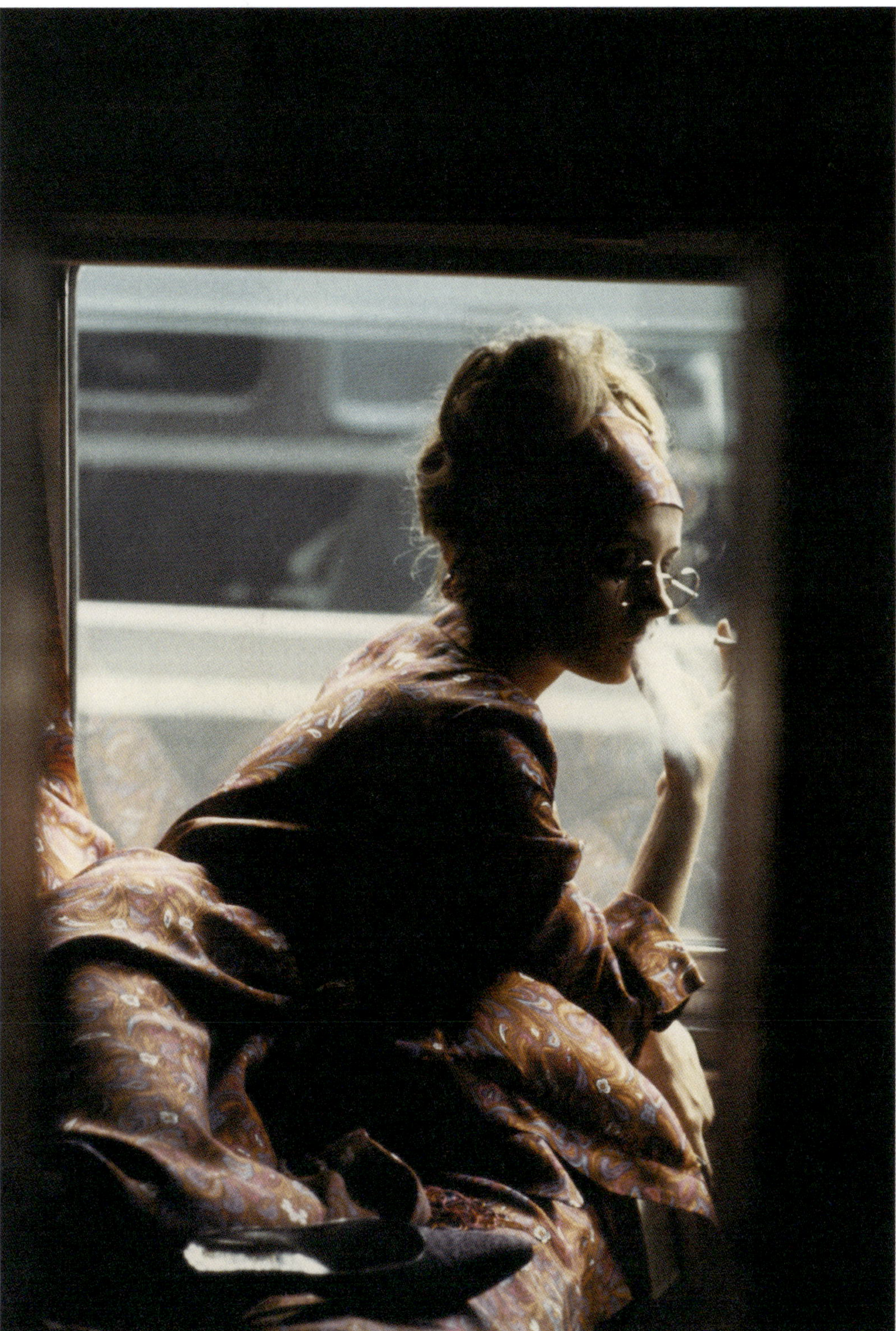

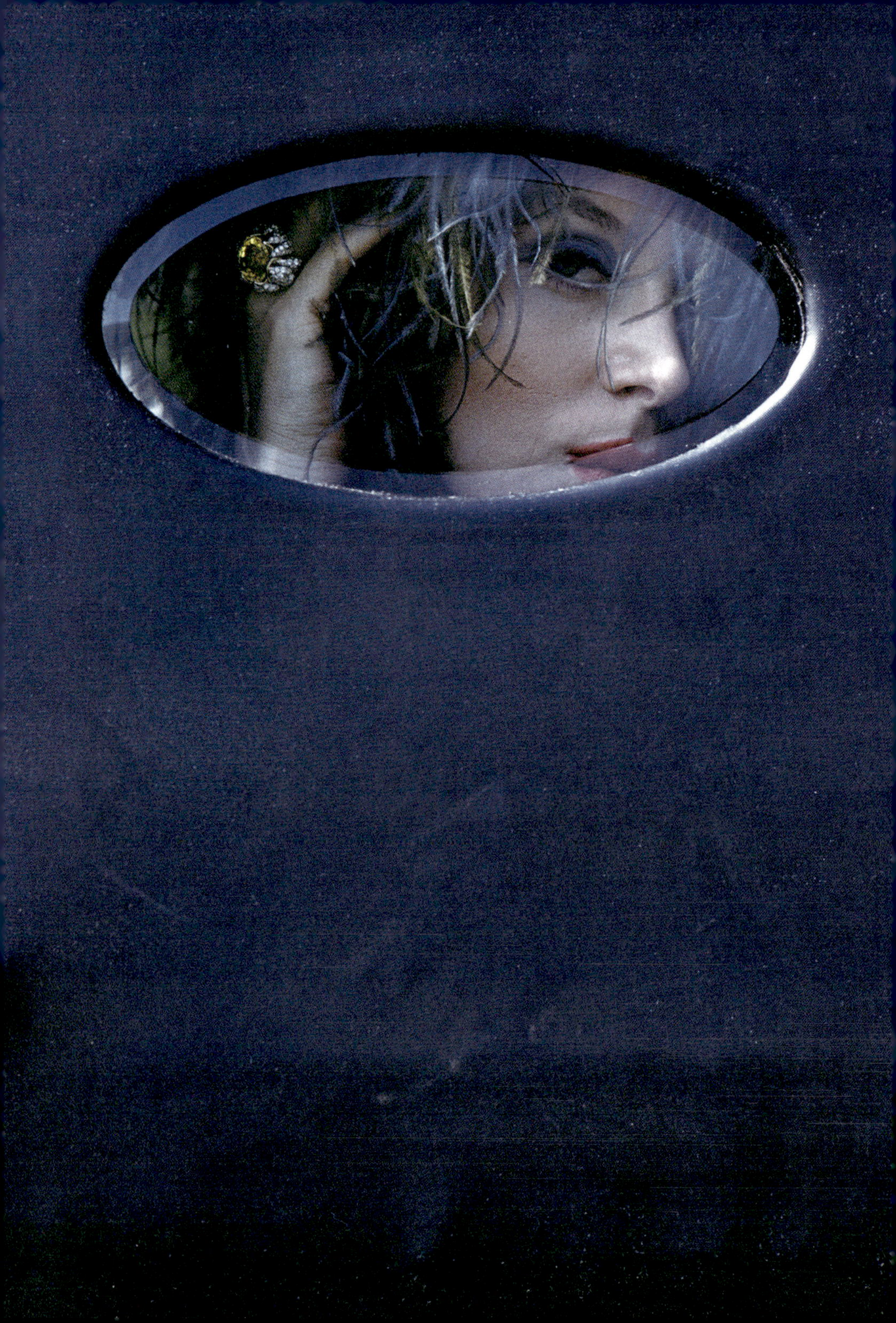

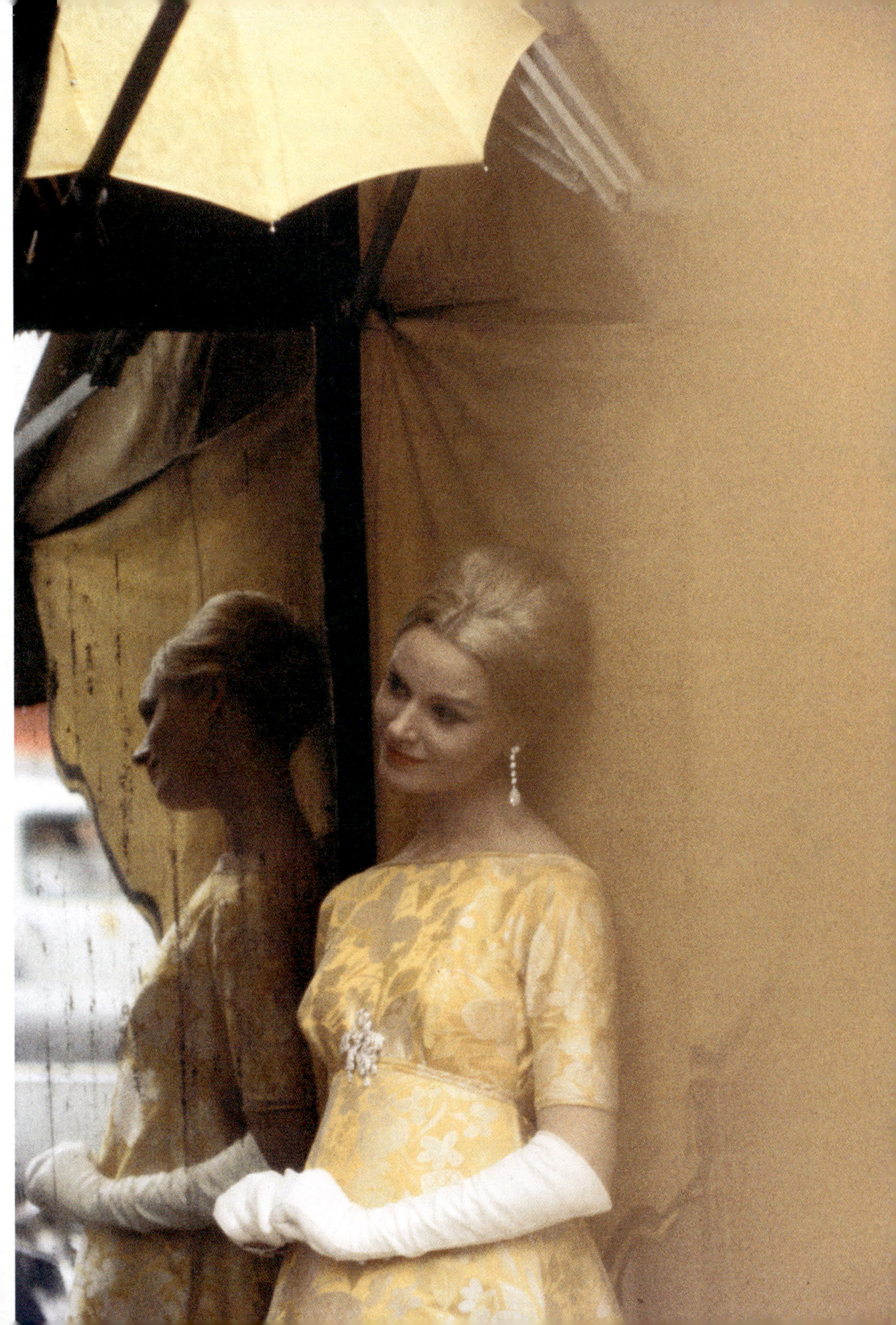

p. 18 Soames Bantry, *Harper's Bazaar*, c. 1963
p. 19 *Harper's Bazaar*, c. 1958

Shoe advertisement, 1957

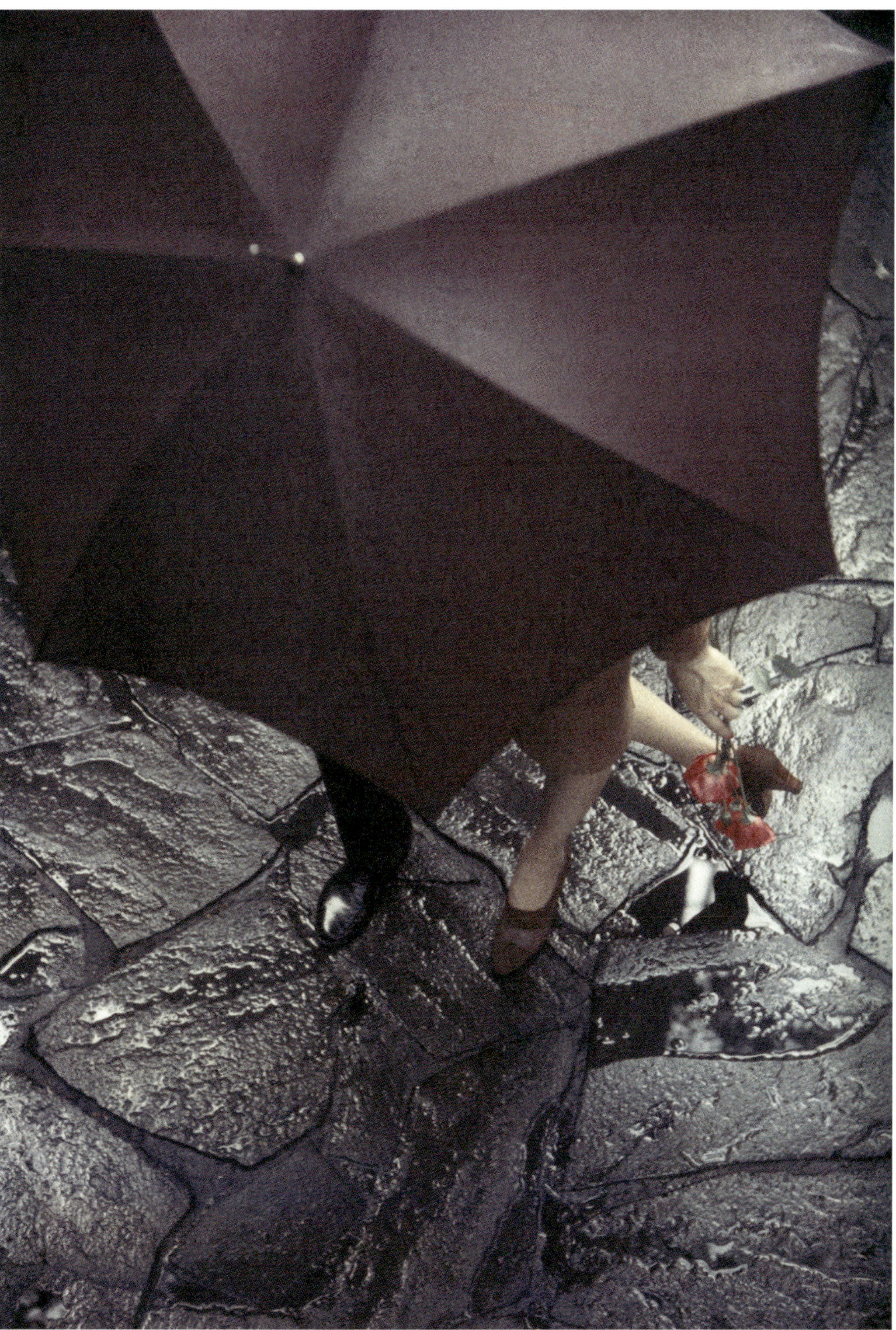

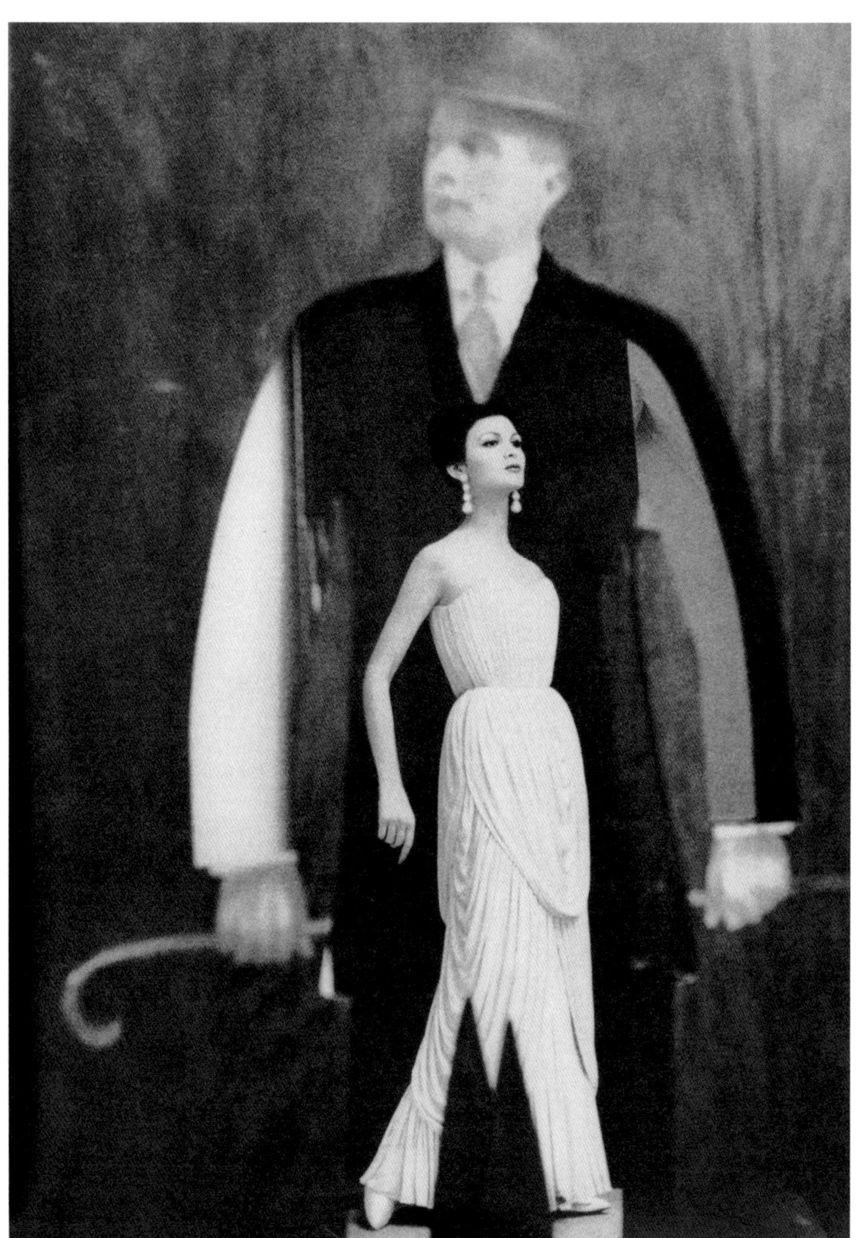

Harper's Bazaar, c. 1960

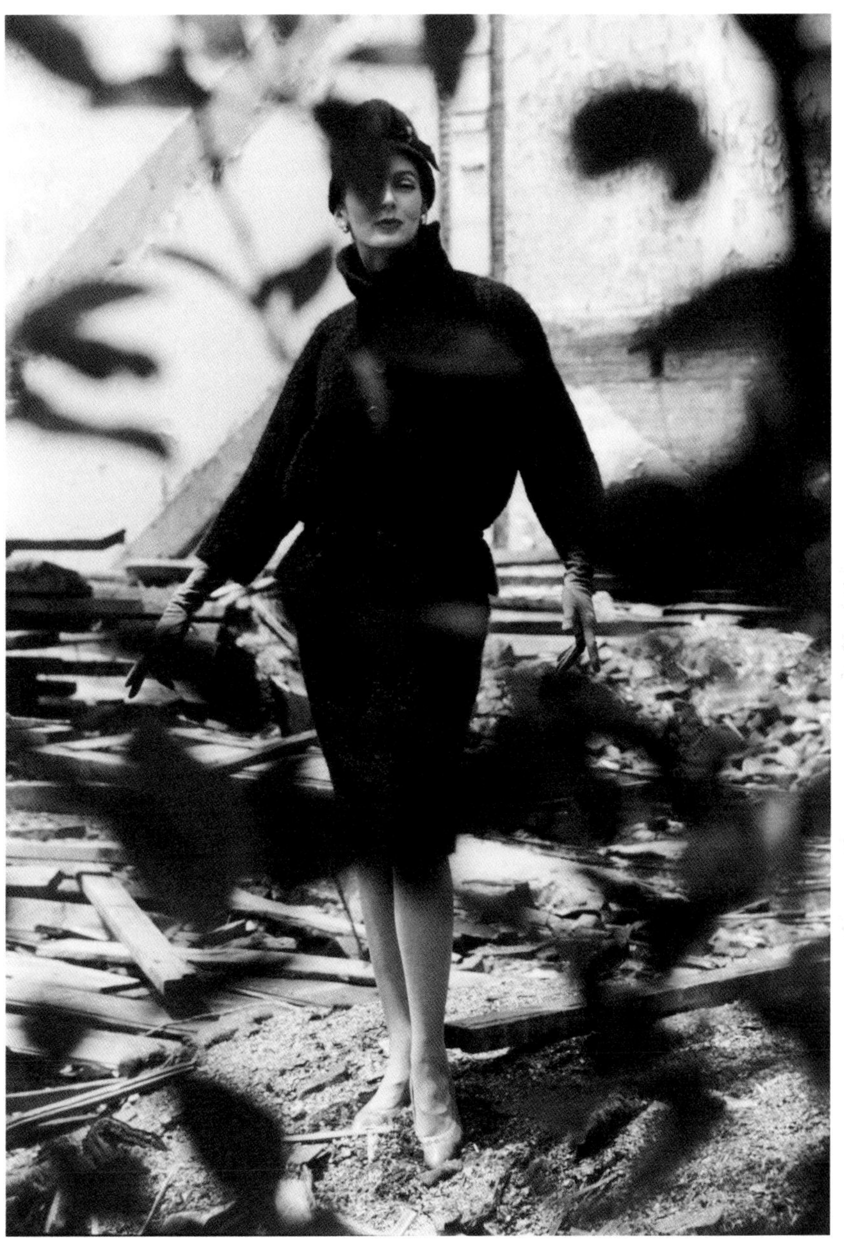

Harper's Bazaar, c. 1960

I once said to the editor at the magazine
that a drawing by Bonnard meant more to me
than a whole year of *Harper's Bazaar*.
And she looked at me in complete horror and total disgust.

Harper's Bazaar, 1950s

p. 26 *Harper's Bazaar*, c. 1960
p. 27 *Harper's Bazaar*, c. 1965

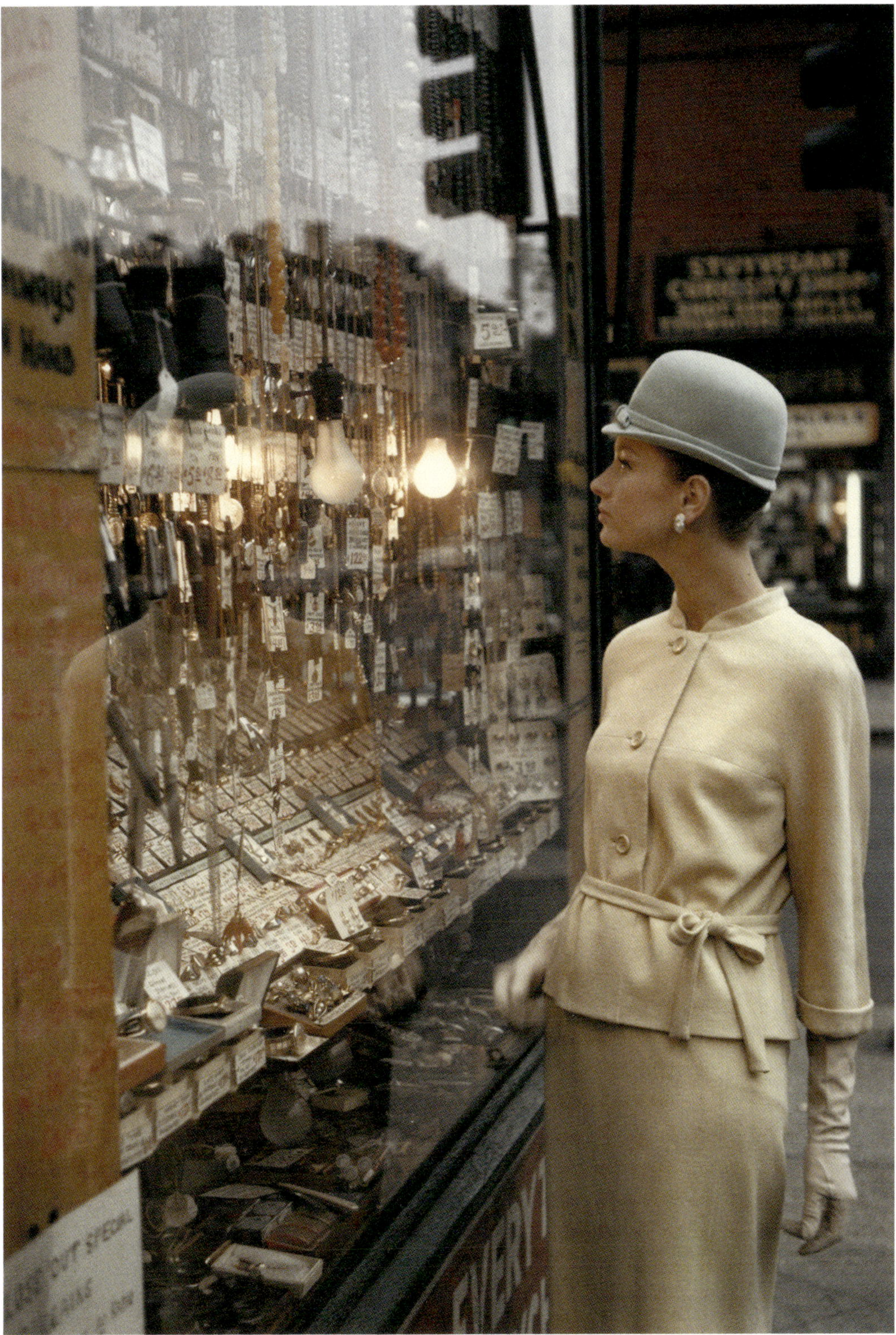

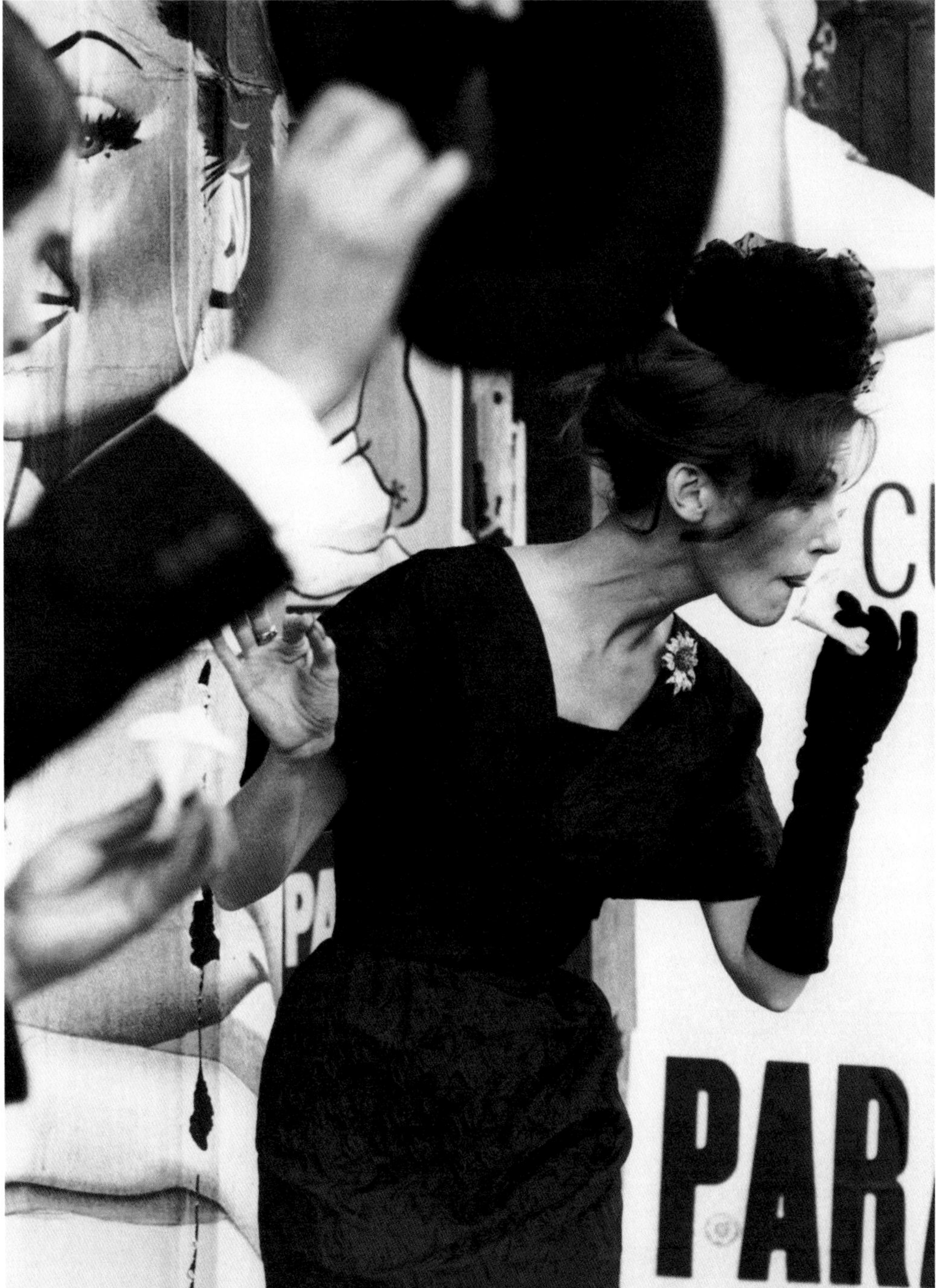

PAR
THEATR

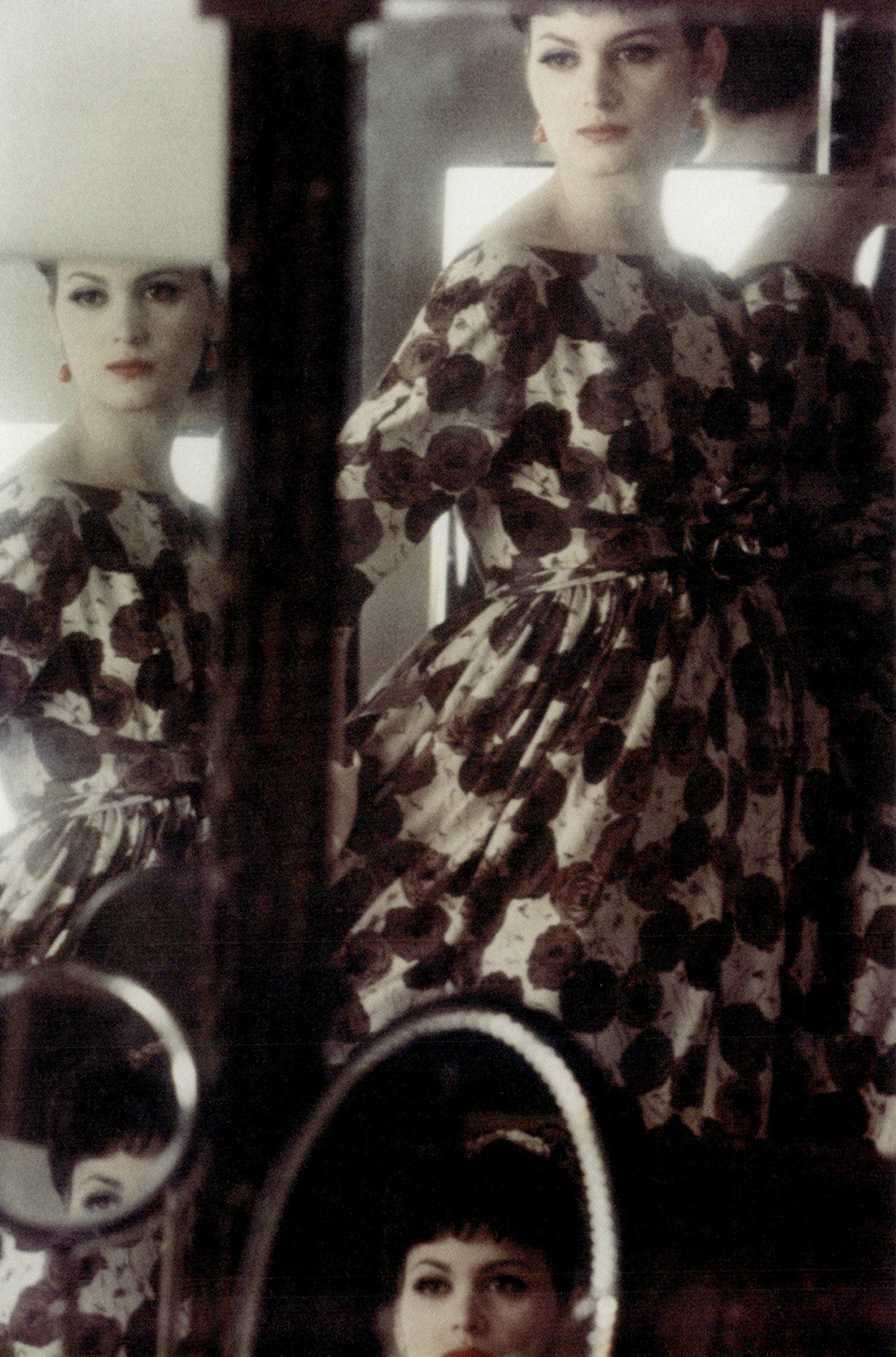

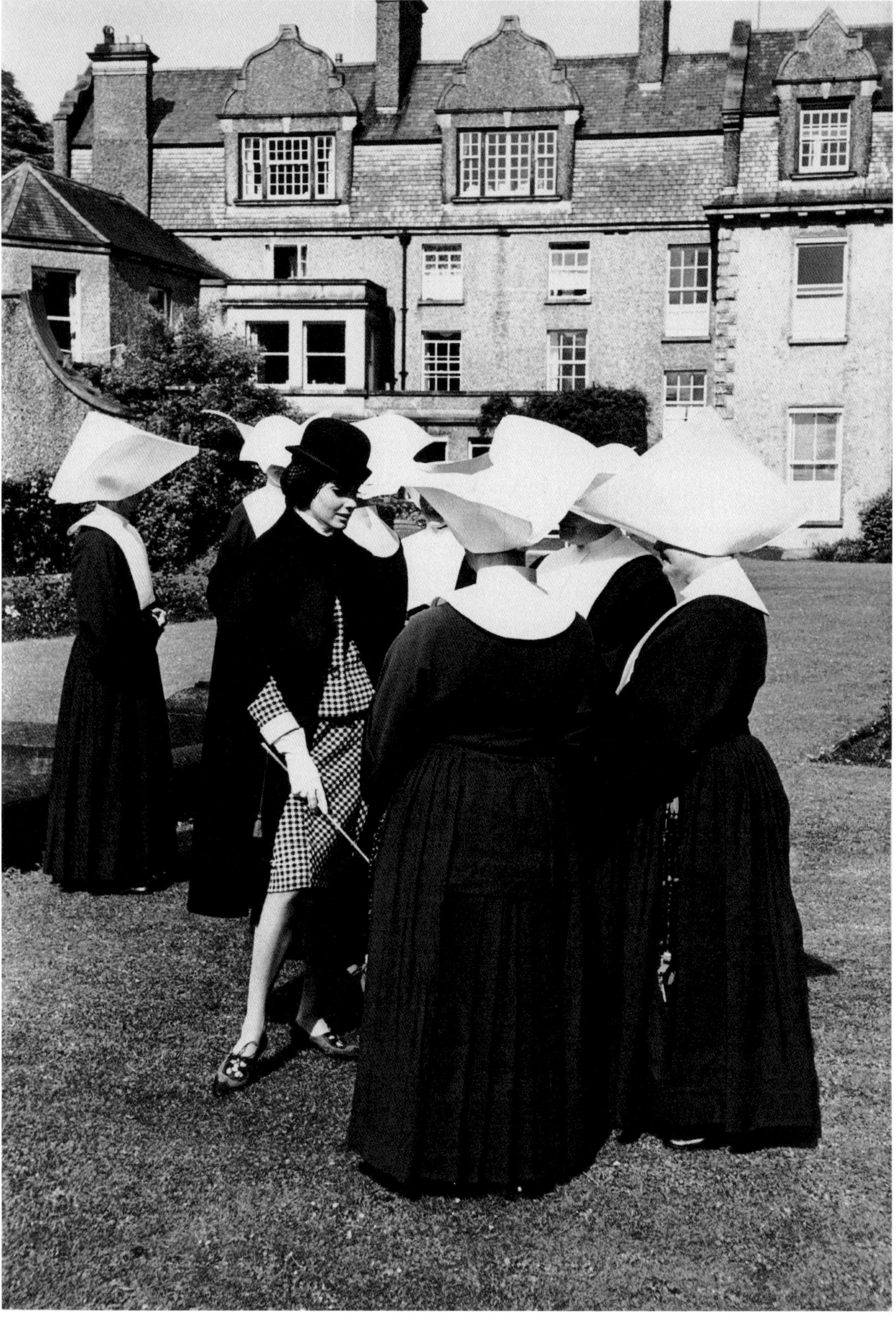

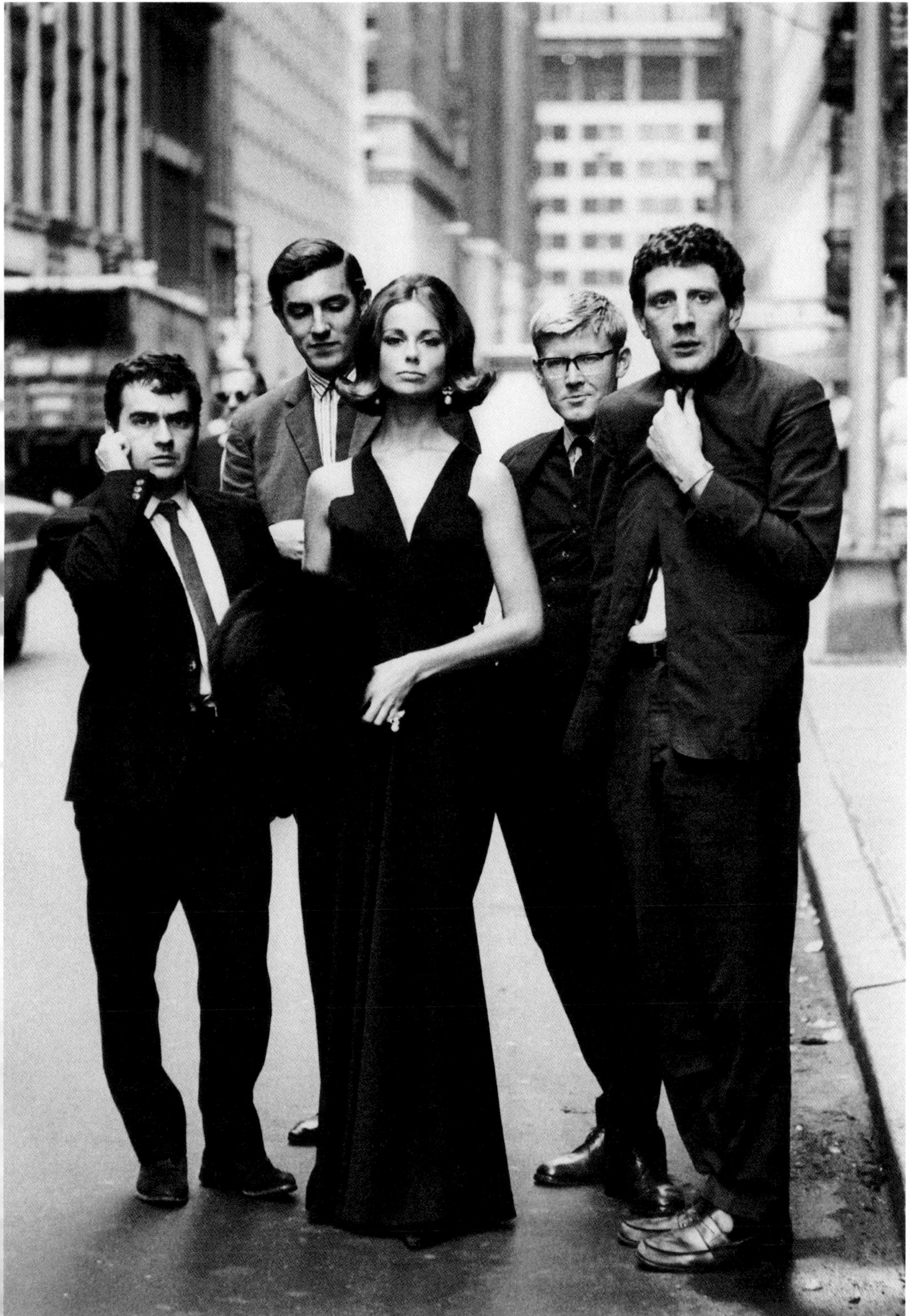

p. 28 *Harper's Bazaar*, c. 1965
p. 29 Model with the cast of *Beyond the Fringe* (Dudley Moore, Peter Cook, Alan Bennett, and Jonathan Miller), *Esquire*, c. 1962

I worked with editors who liked studio sessions.
They were comfortable in the studio
because they could make luncheon appointments there.
You can't do that when you're out in the street,
and I liked working in the street.

Harper's Bazaar, c. 1960

pp. 32–33 Untitled, c. 1965

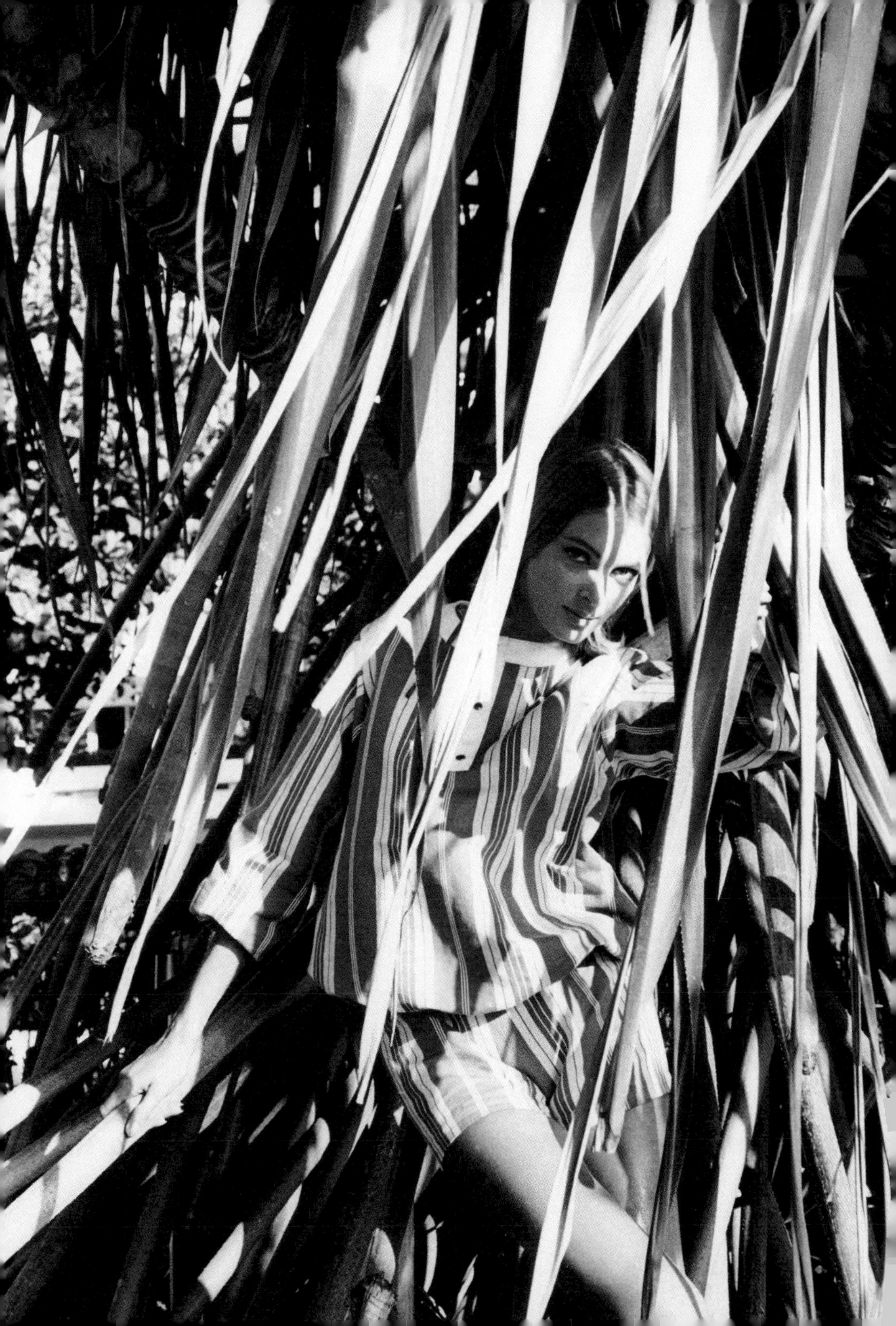

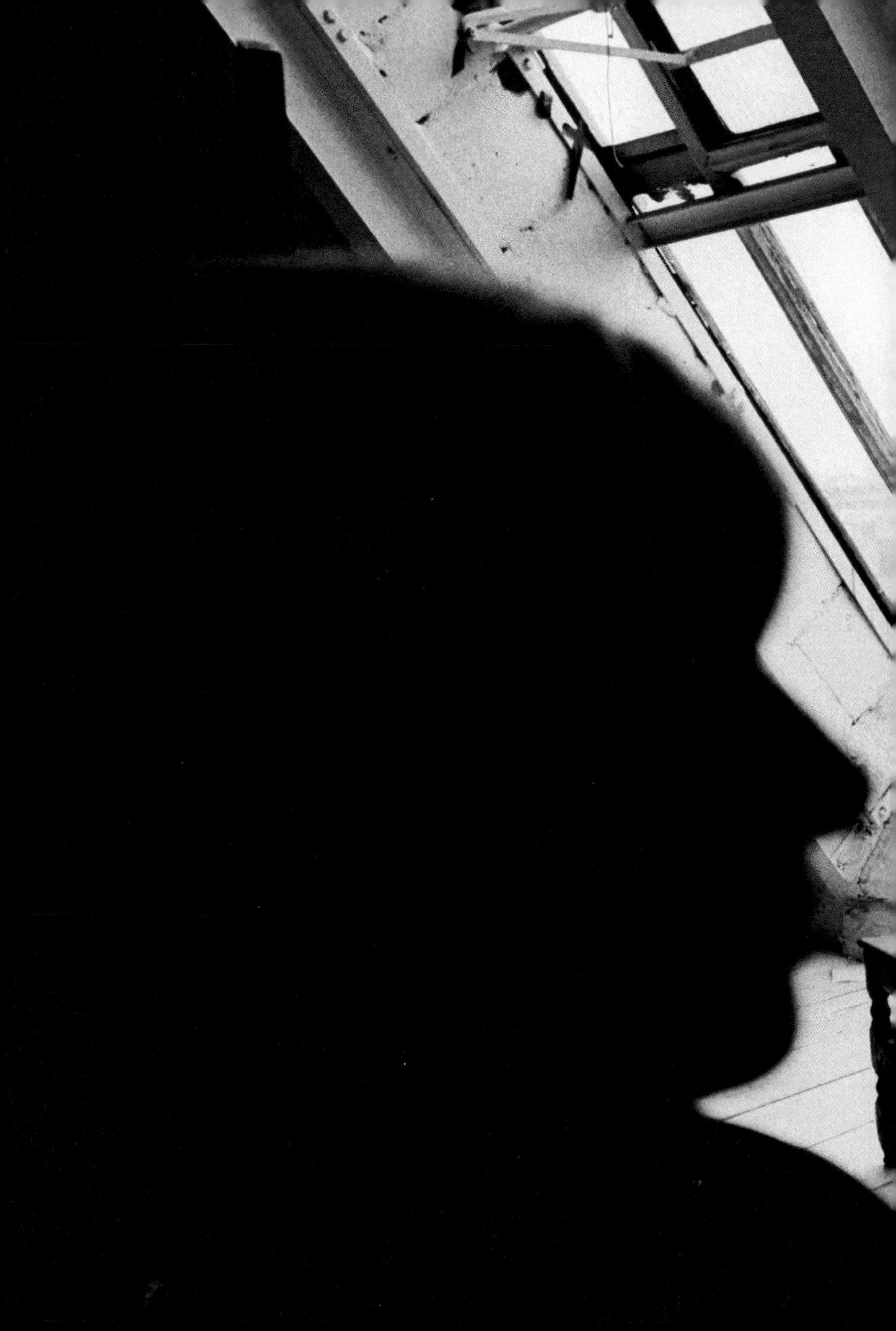

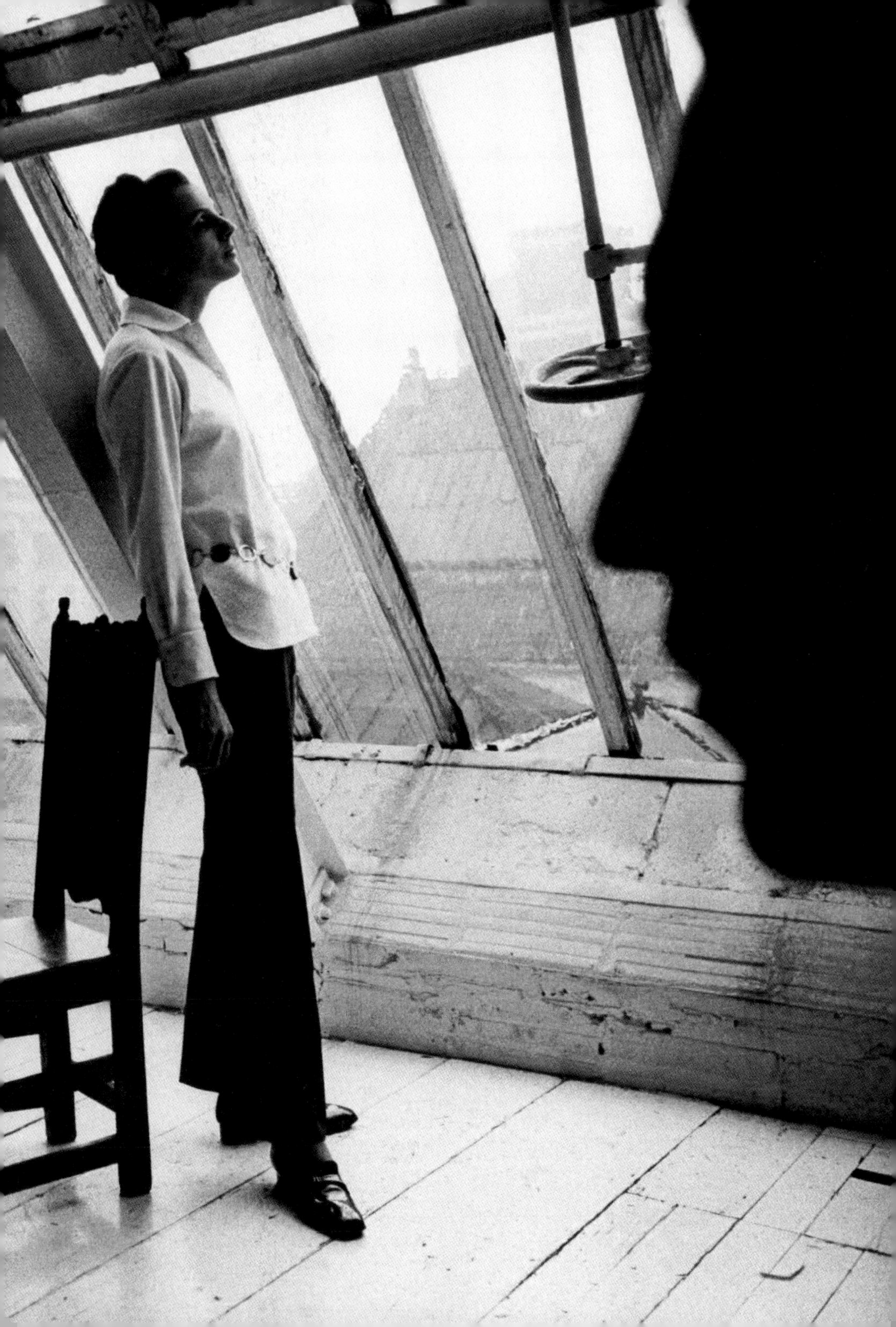

I take photographs in my neighborhood.
I think that mysterious things happen in familiar places.
We don't always need to run to the other end of the world.

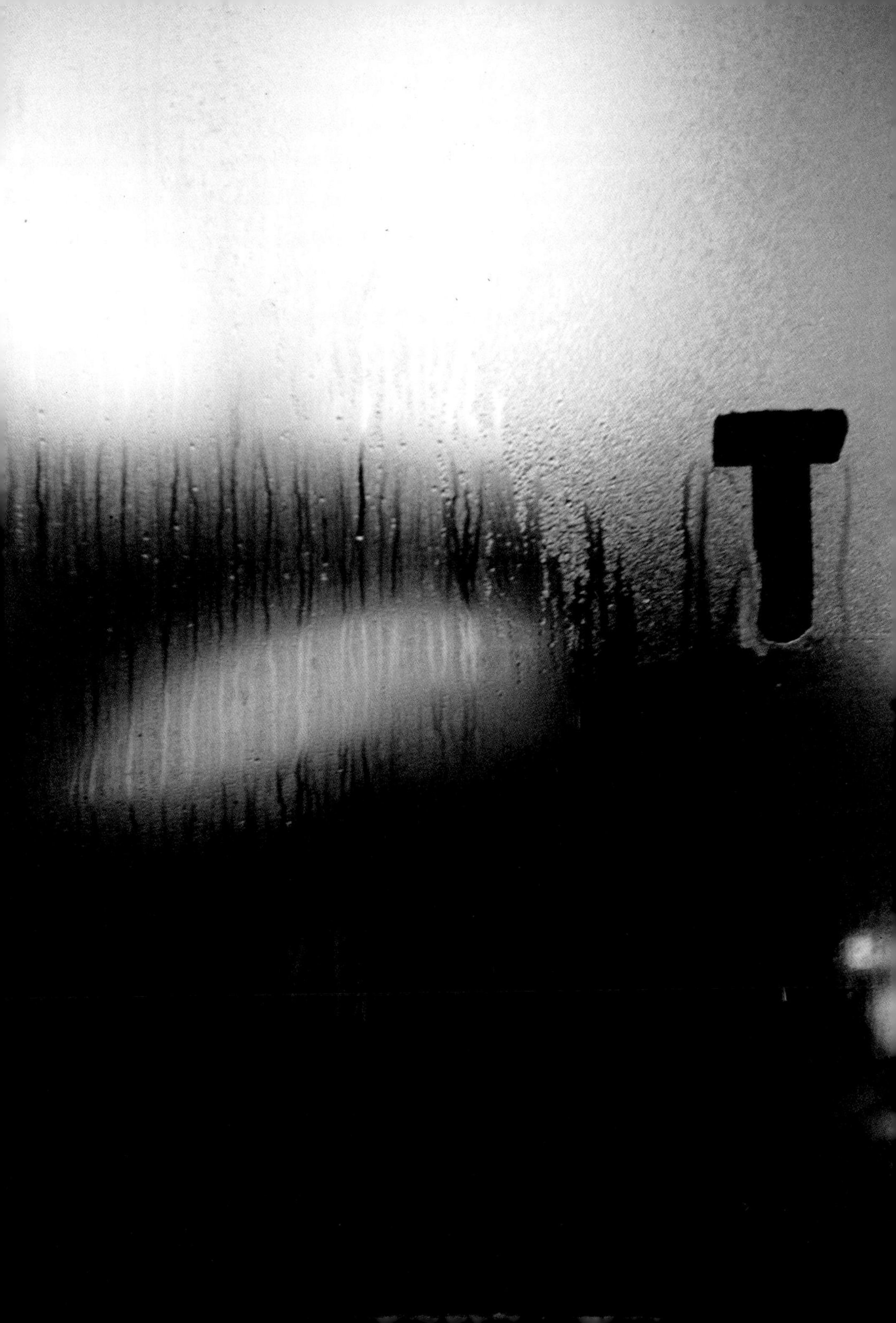

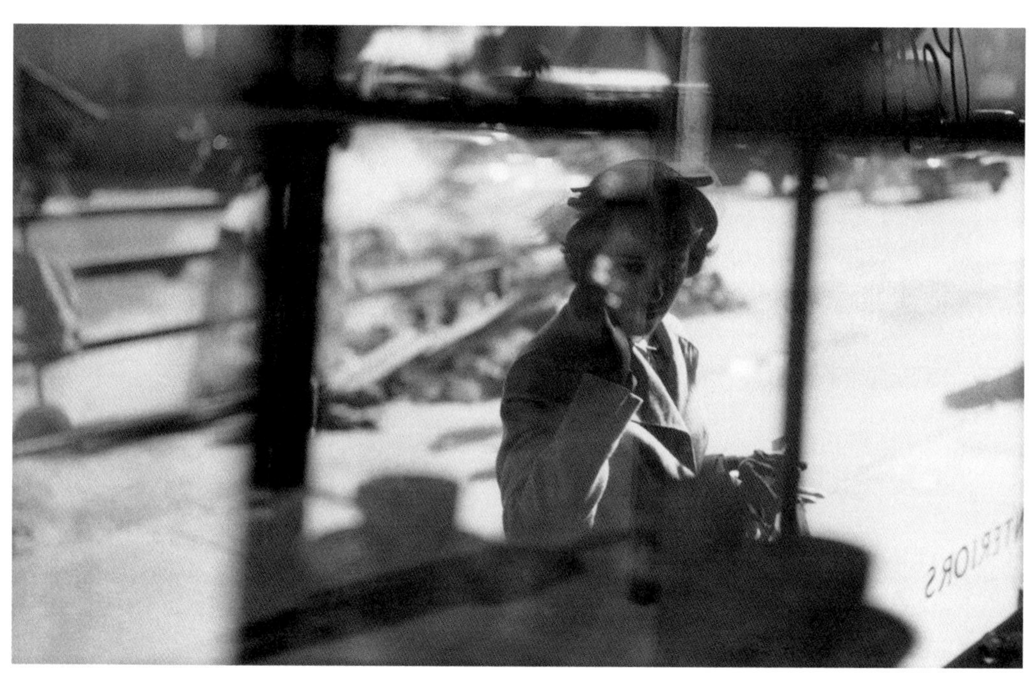

Exacta, 1948

Coachman, 1957

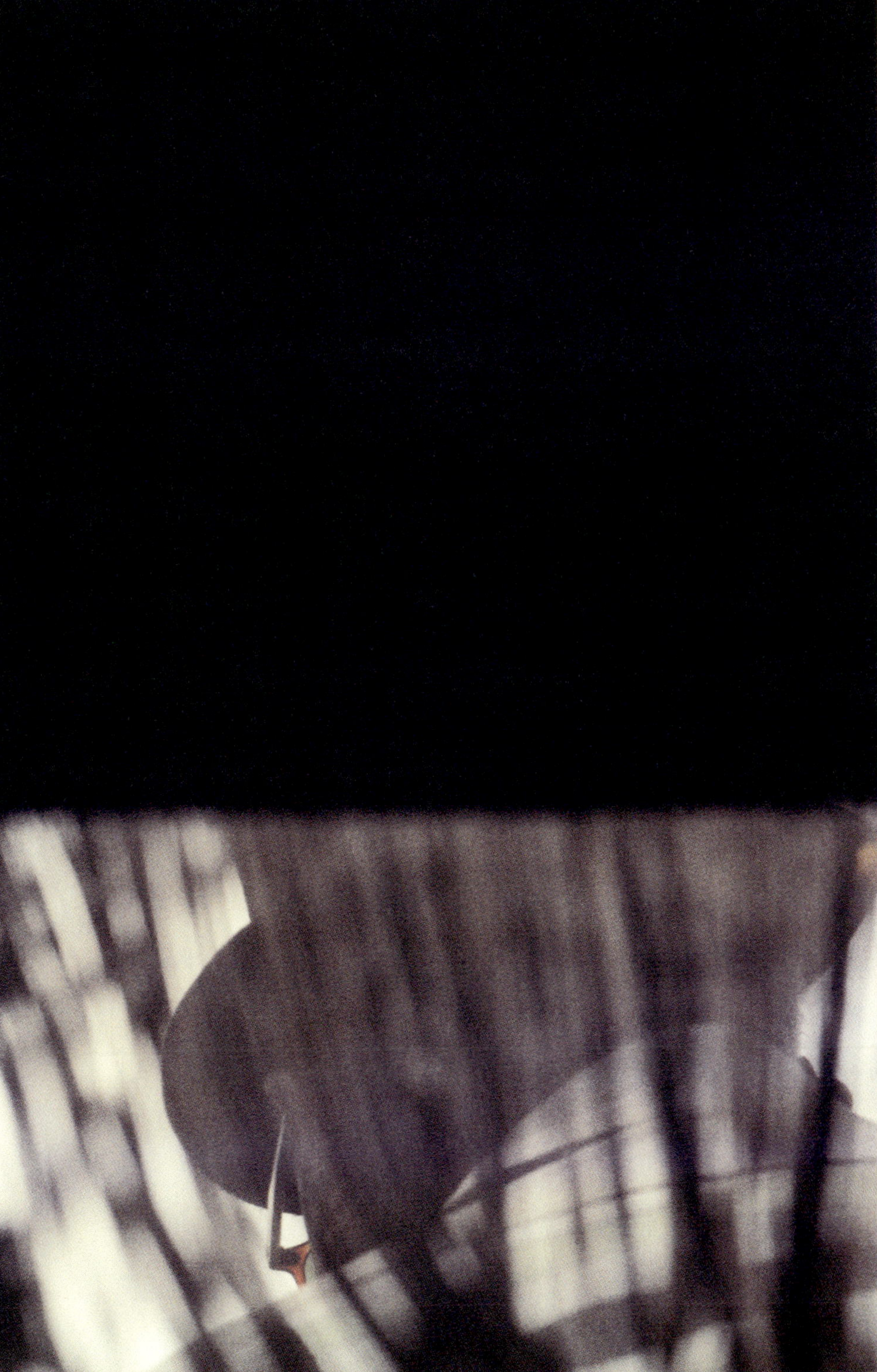

I have a great respect for people who do nothing.

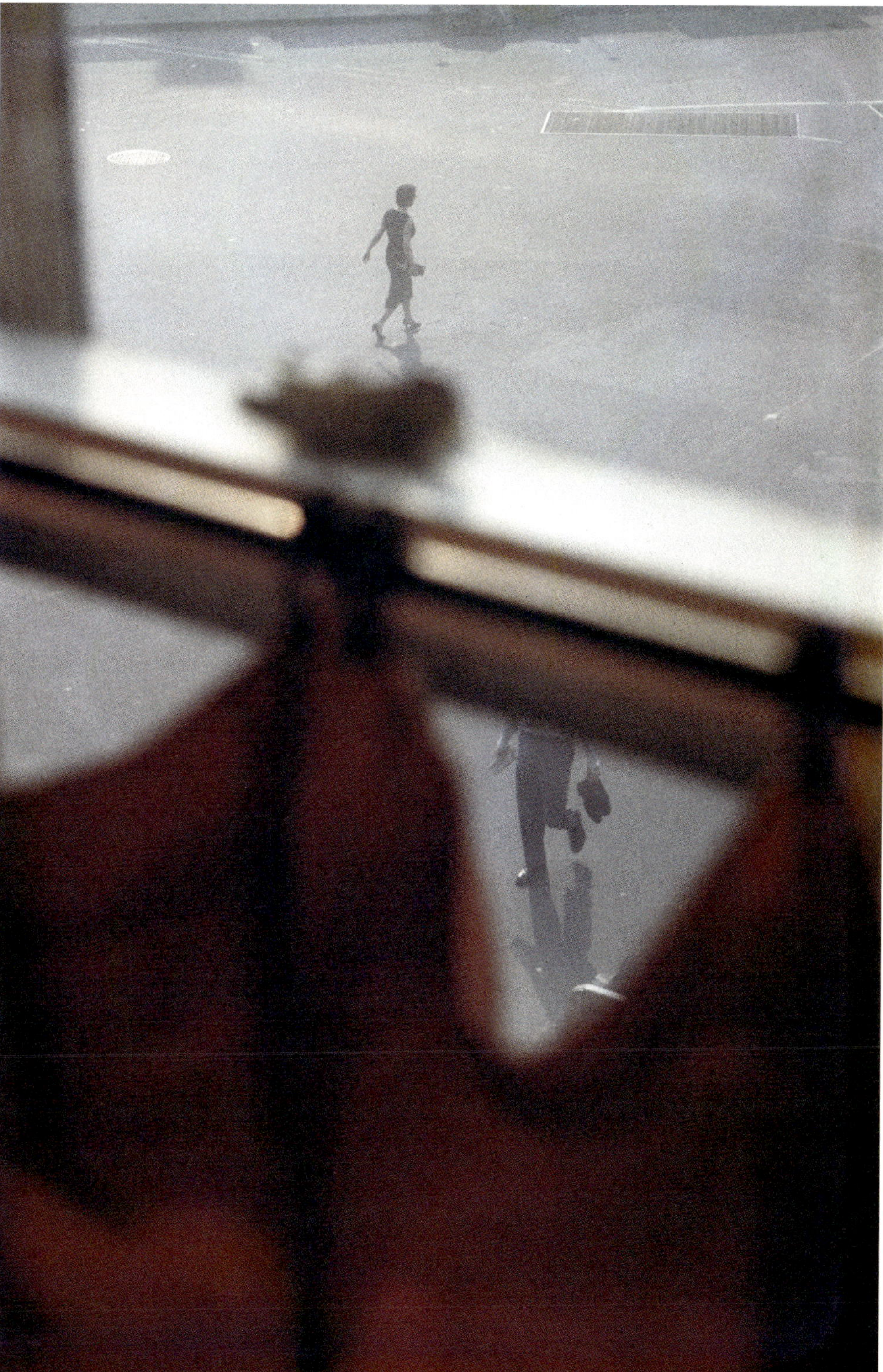

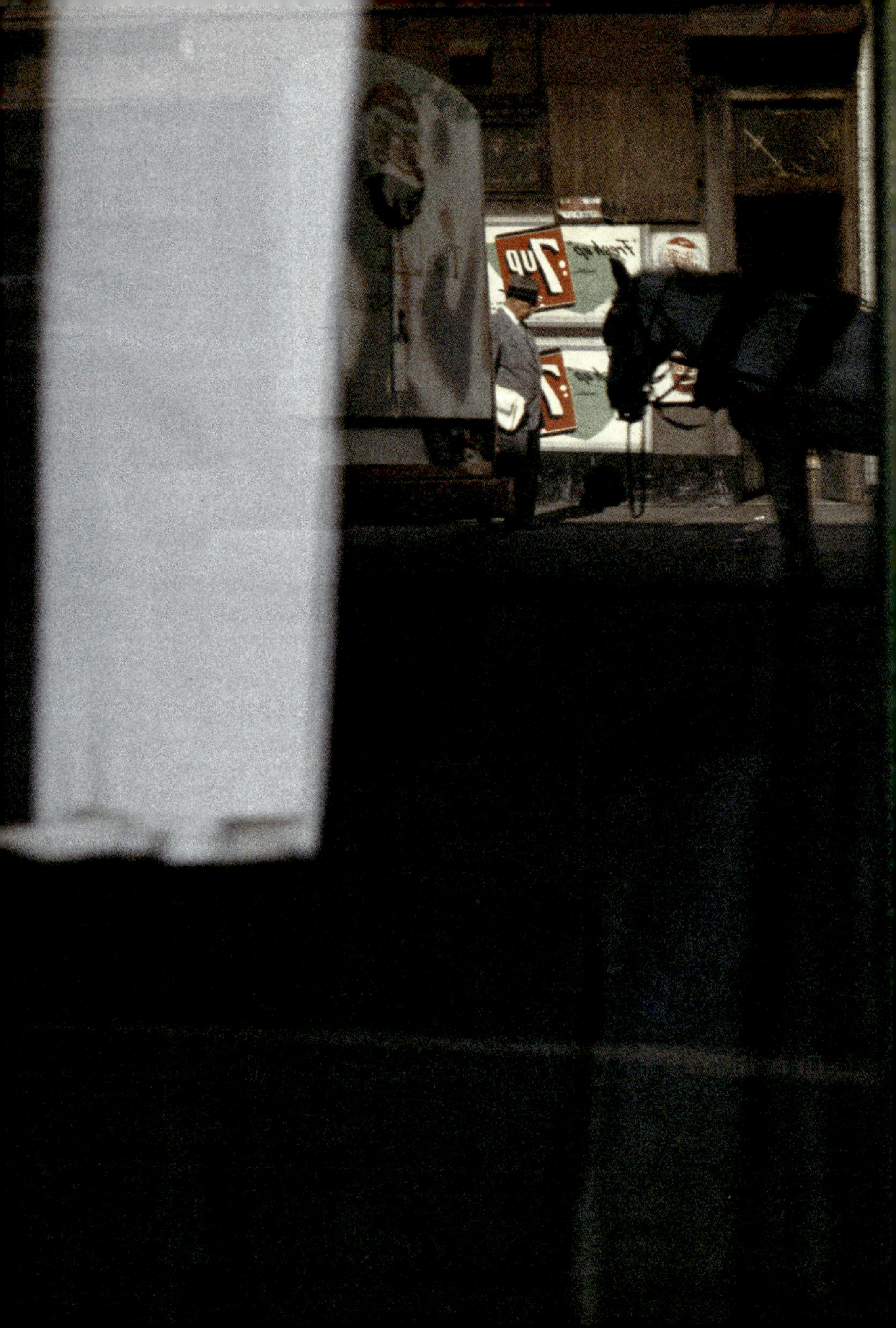

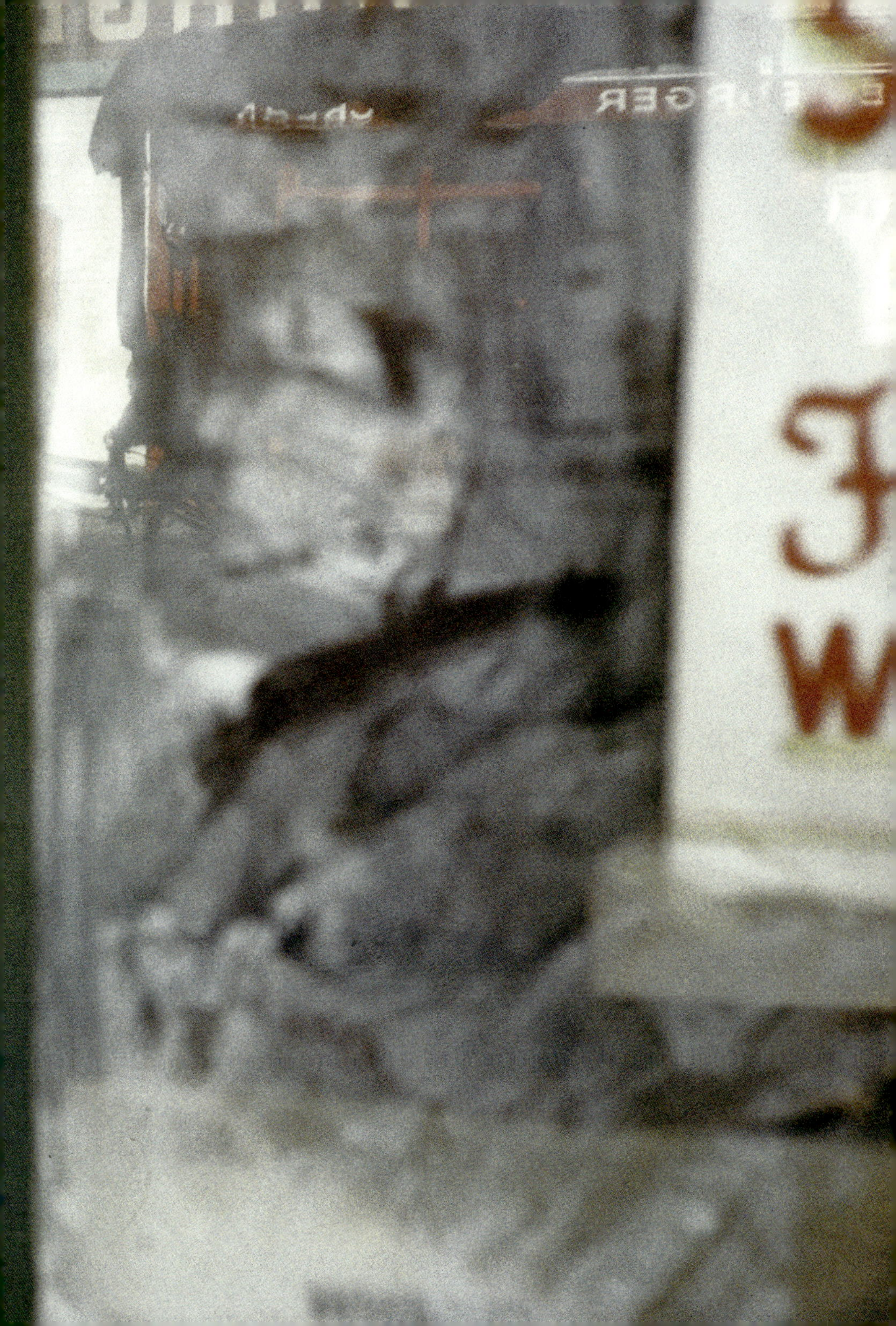

A window covered with raindrops interests me
more than a photograph of a famous person.

Snow, 1960

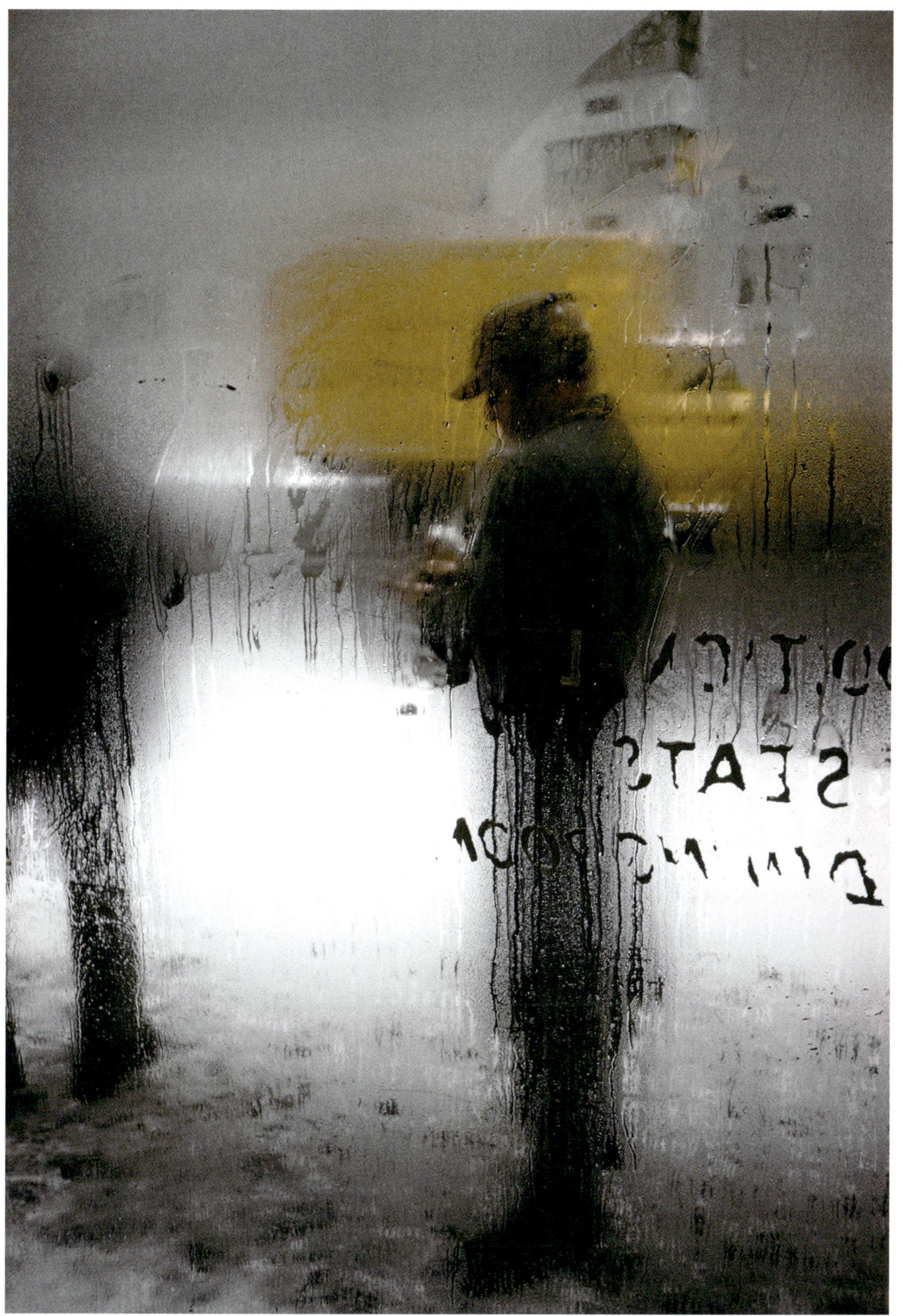

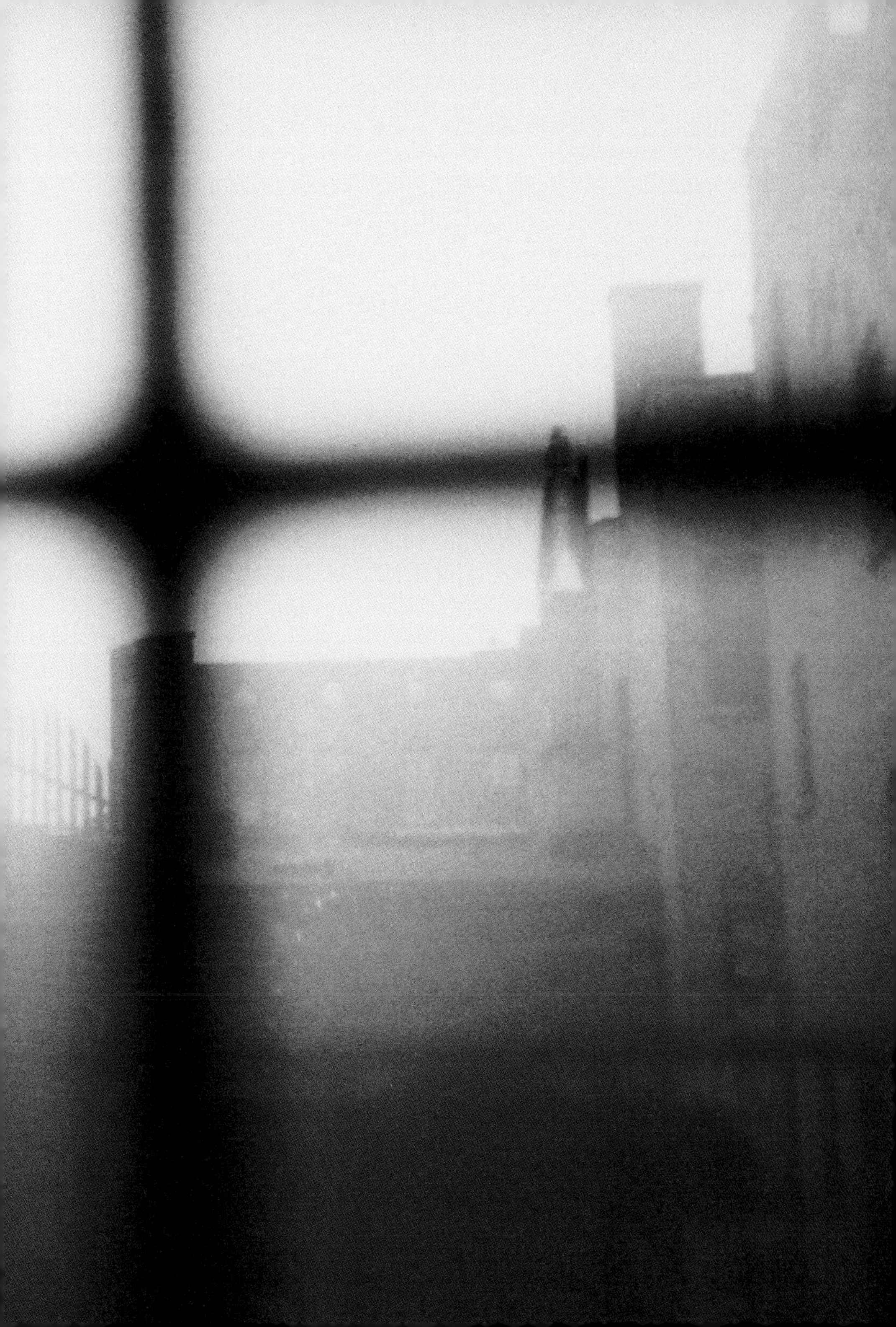

48 | 49

I didn't walk around feeling that I was important…
I had not spent my life feeling important.

Near the Tanager, 1954

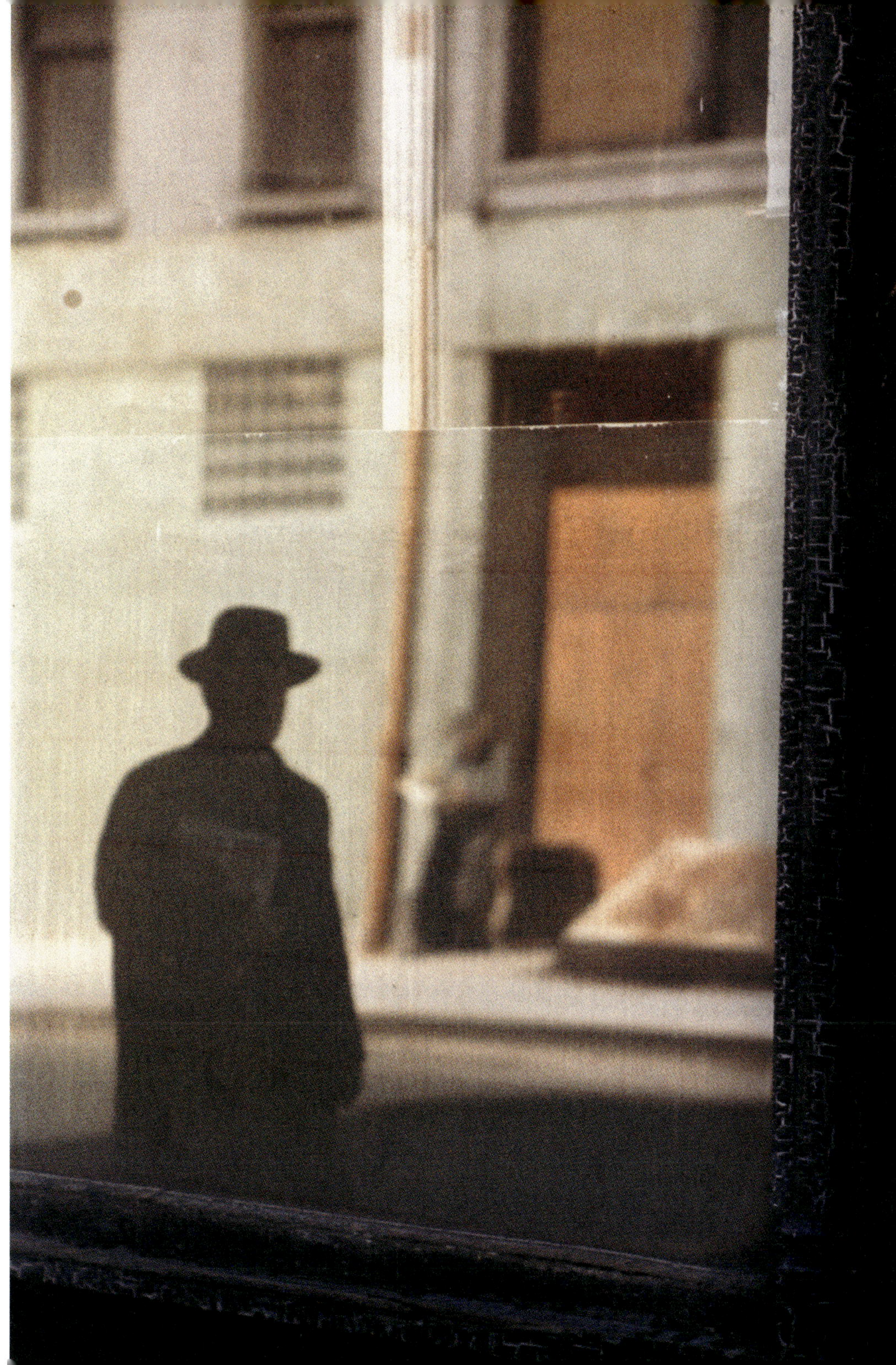

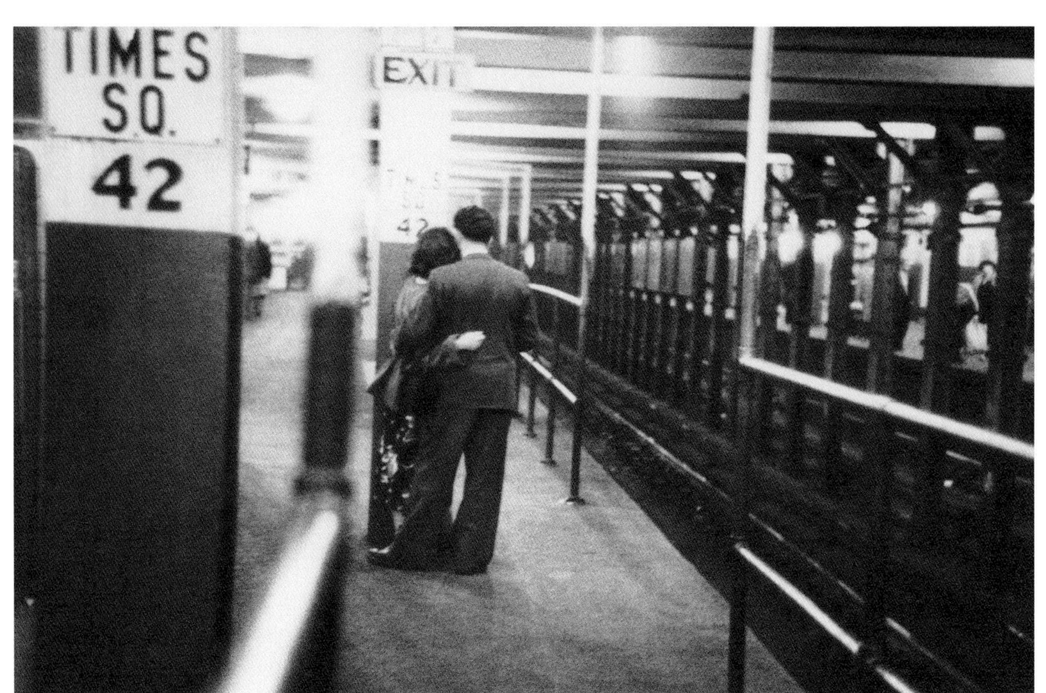

Untitled, 1950s

From the El, c. 1955

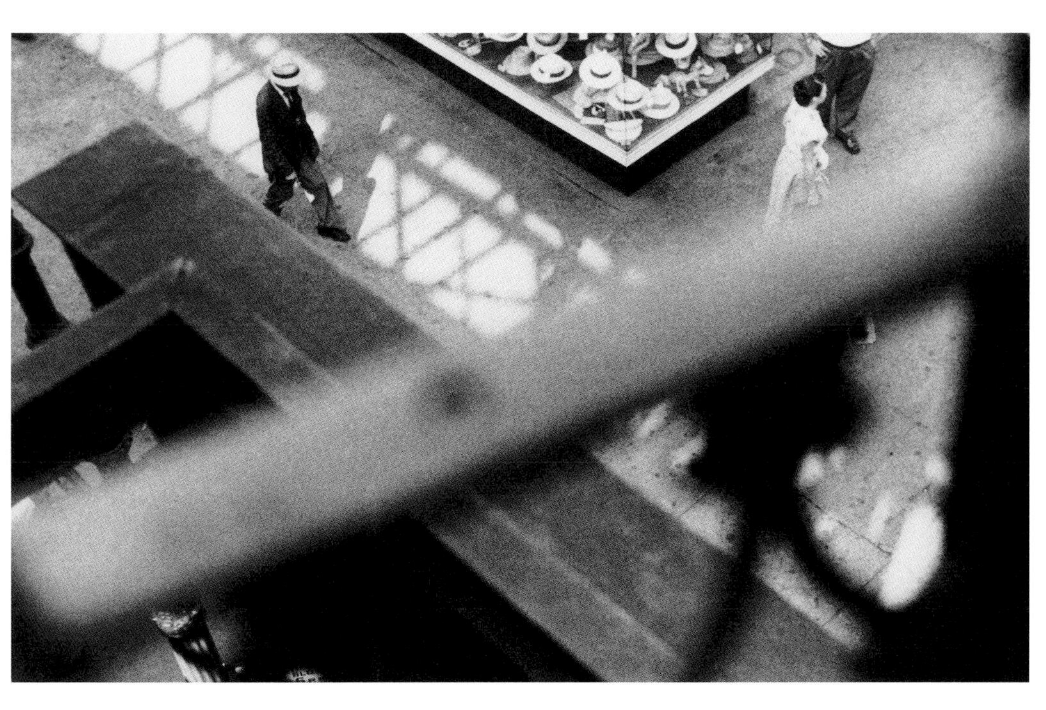

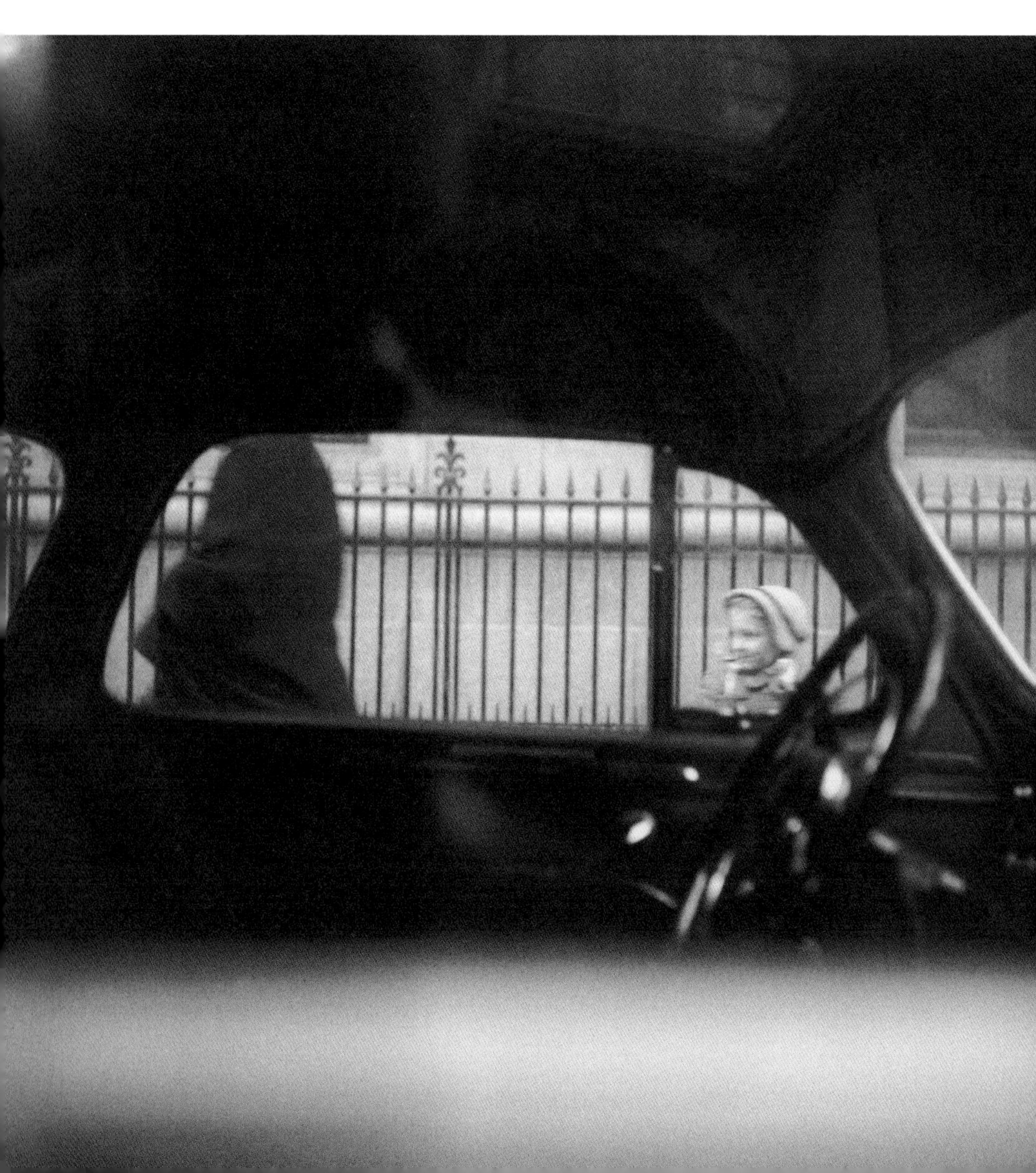

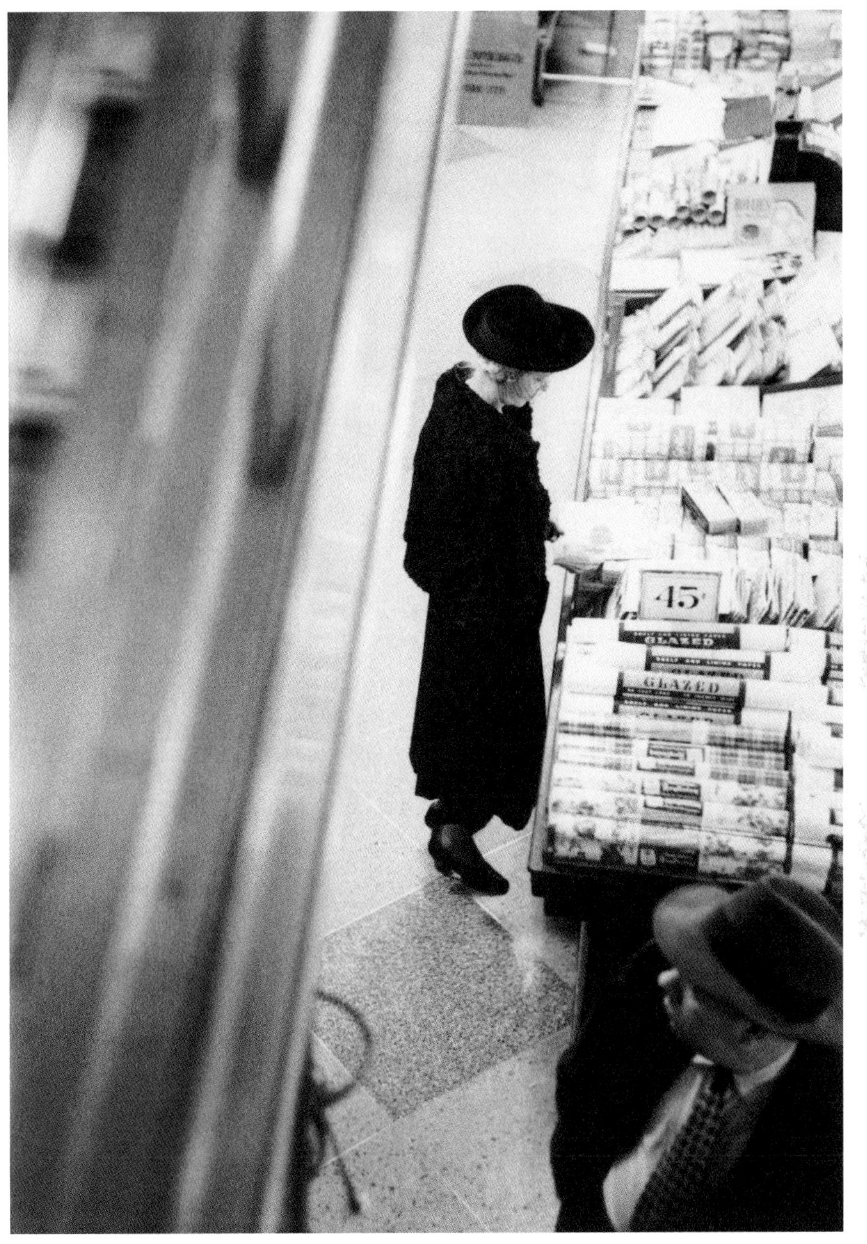

Bonnet, c. 1950   45 Cents, c. 1948

Everything is a photo…
we live in a world today where almost
everything is a photograph.

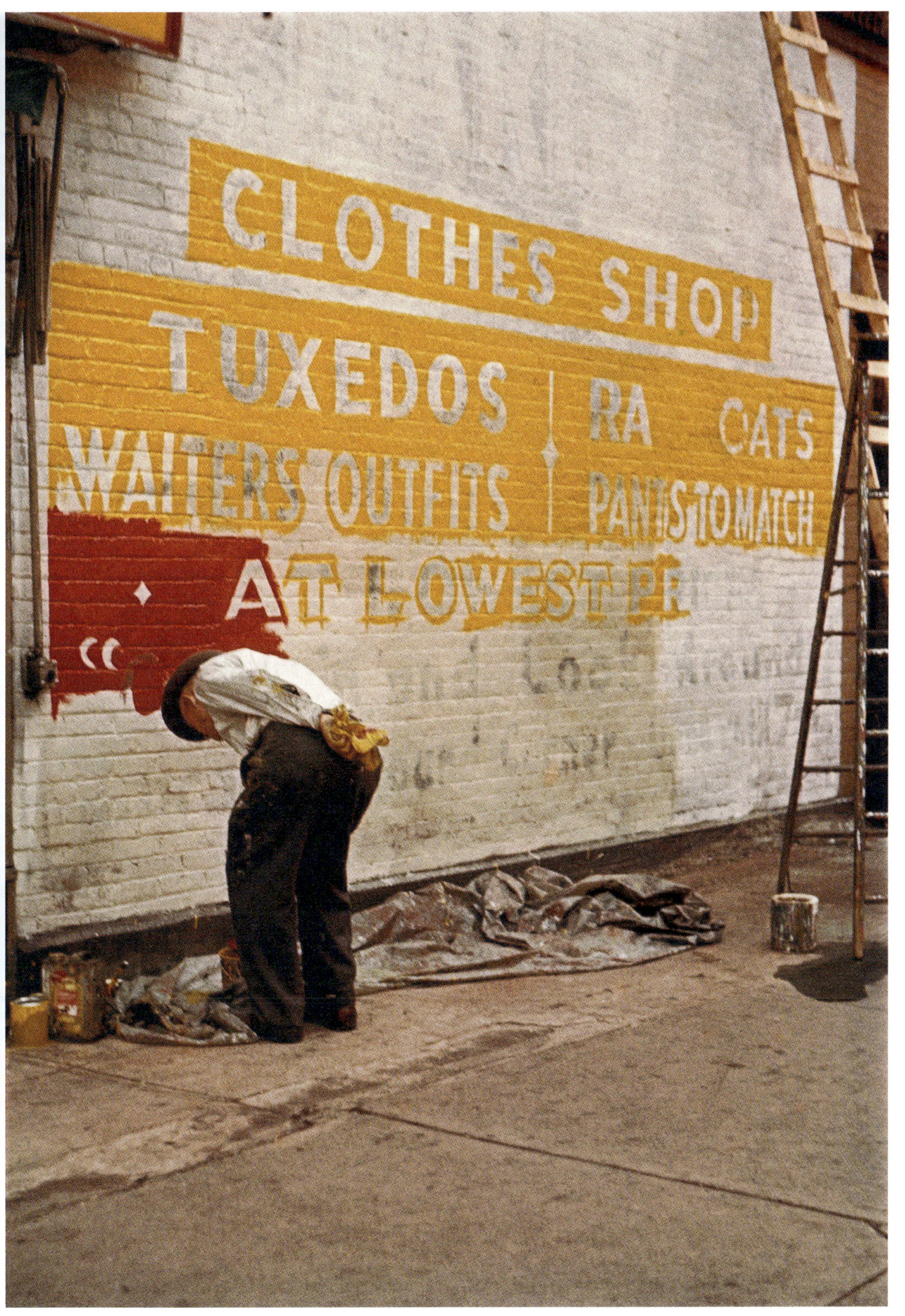

CLOTHES SHOP
TUXEDOS | RA CATS
WAITERS OUTFITS | PANTS TO MATCH
AT LOWEST PR

The important thing in life is not what you get
but what you throw out.

Dog in Doorway, Paterson, 1952

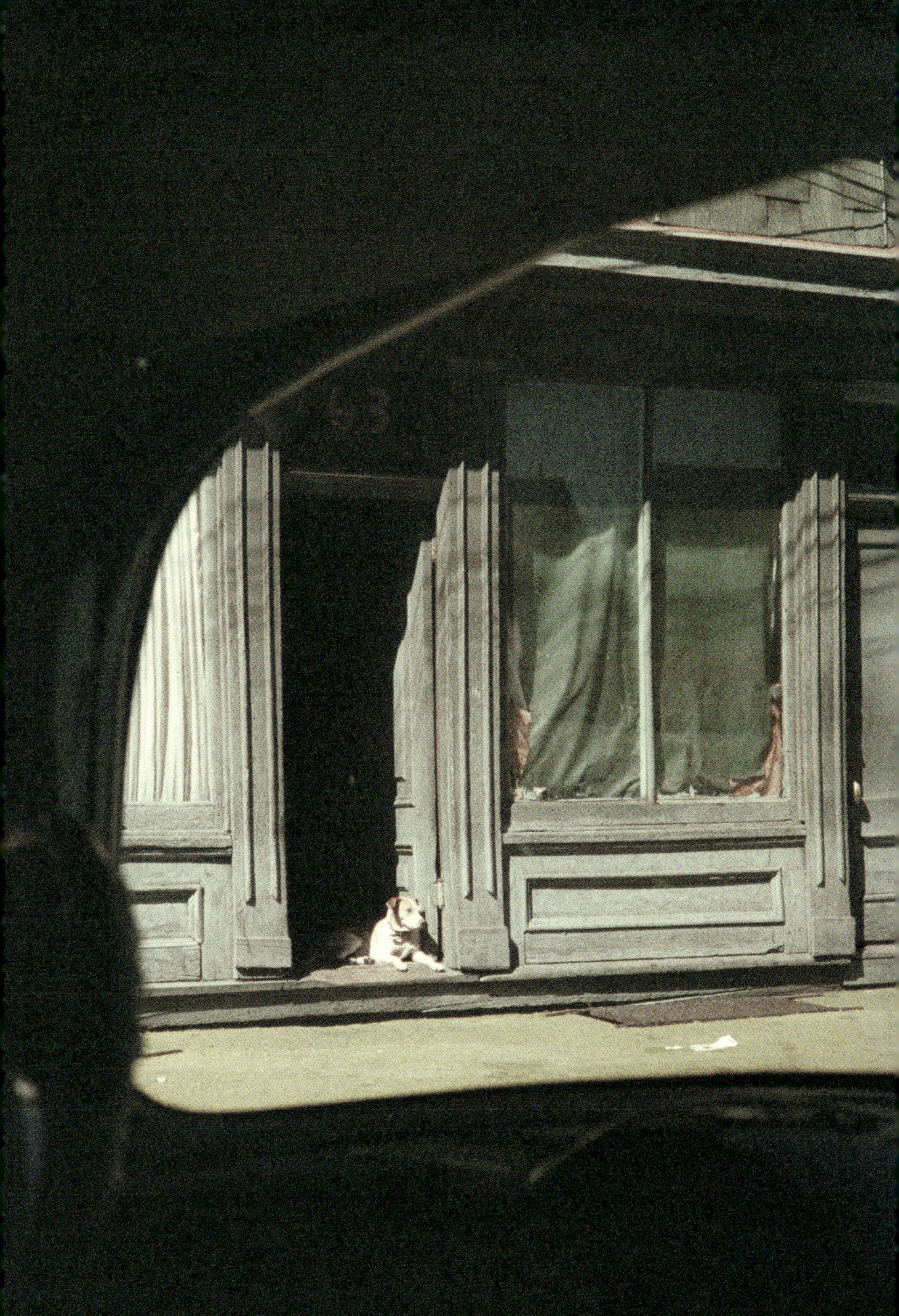

Canopy, 1958

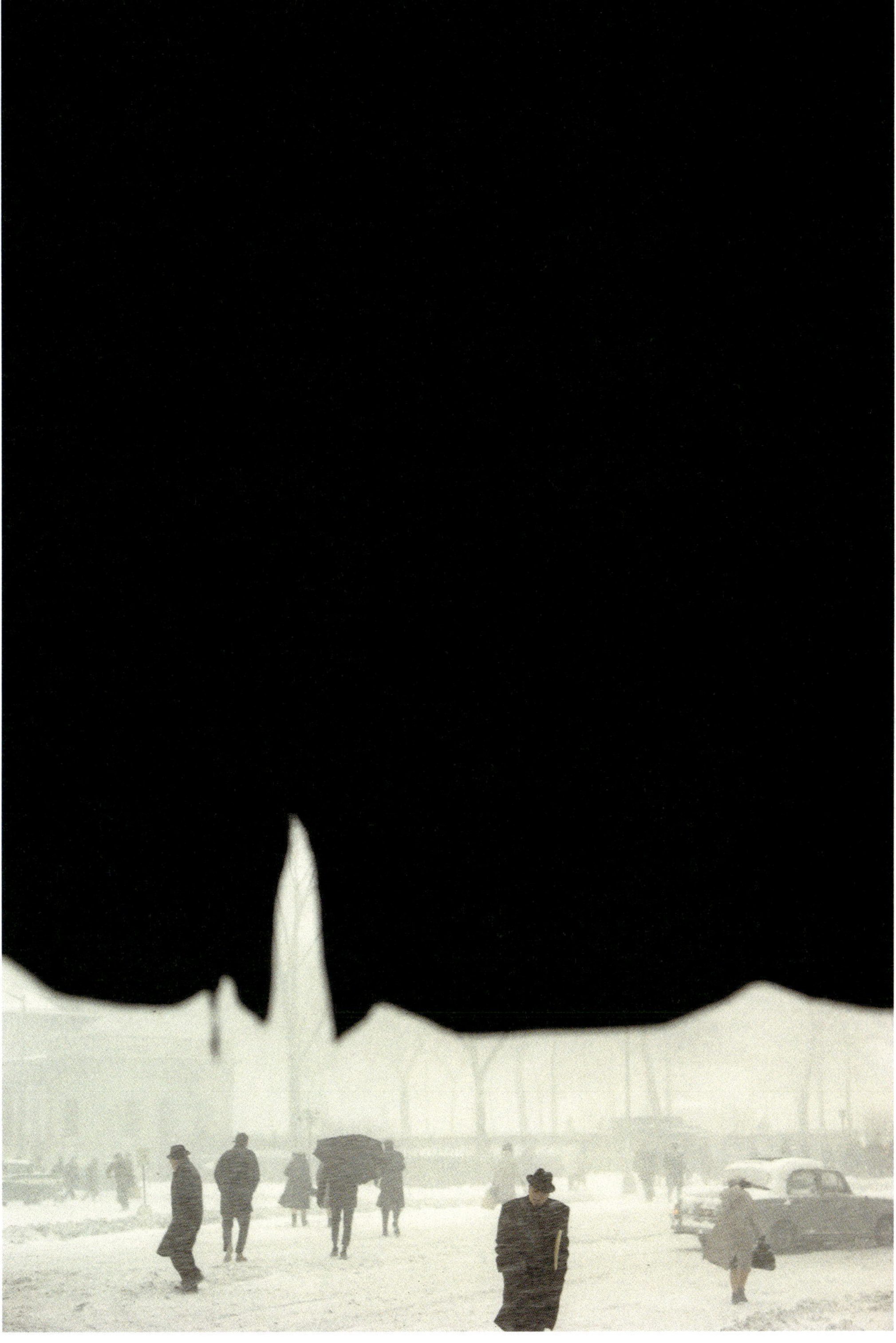

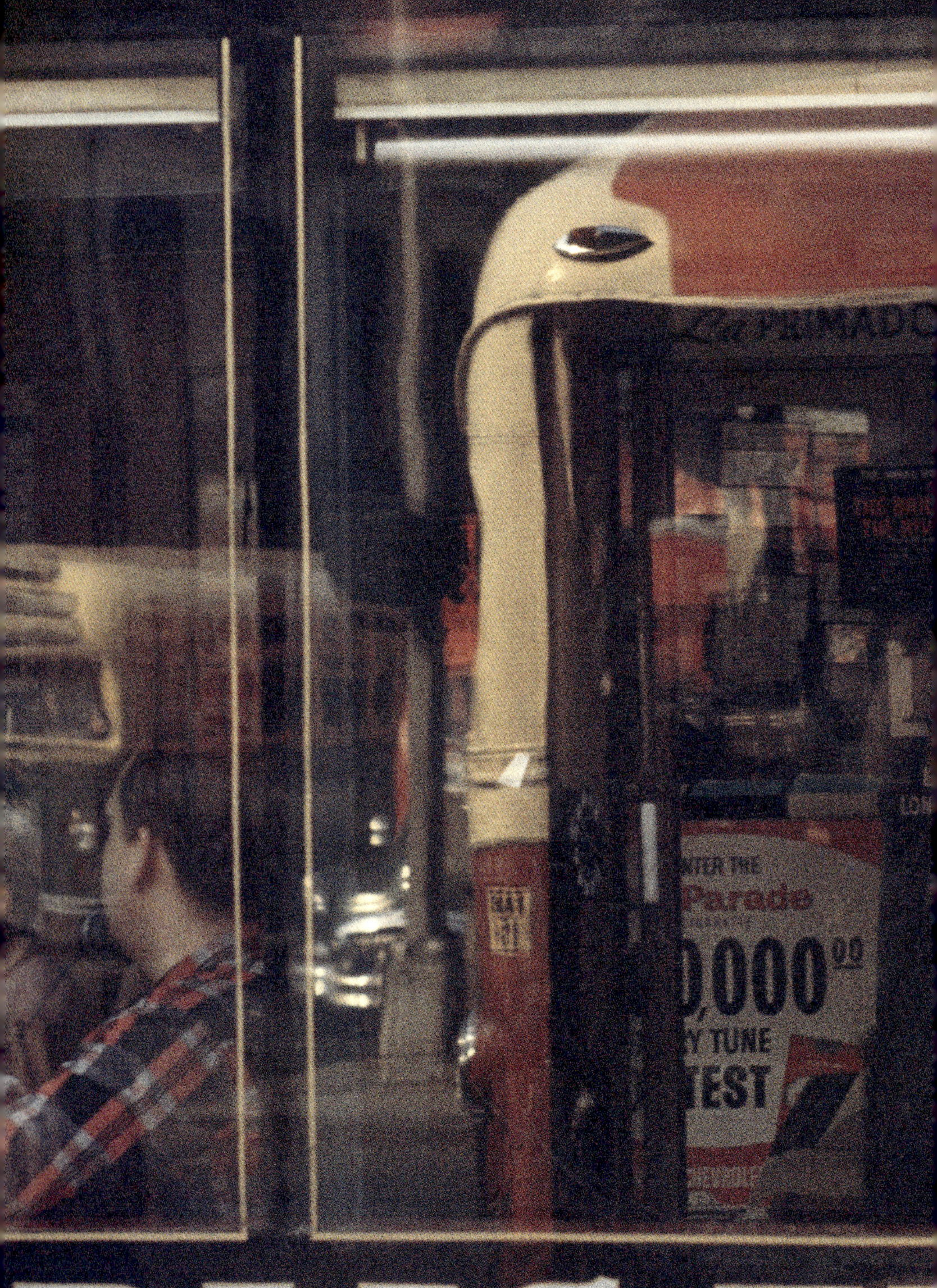
La PRIMADO
ENTER THE
Parade
0,000.00
Y TUNE
EST
BLIC T

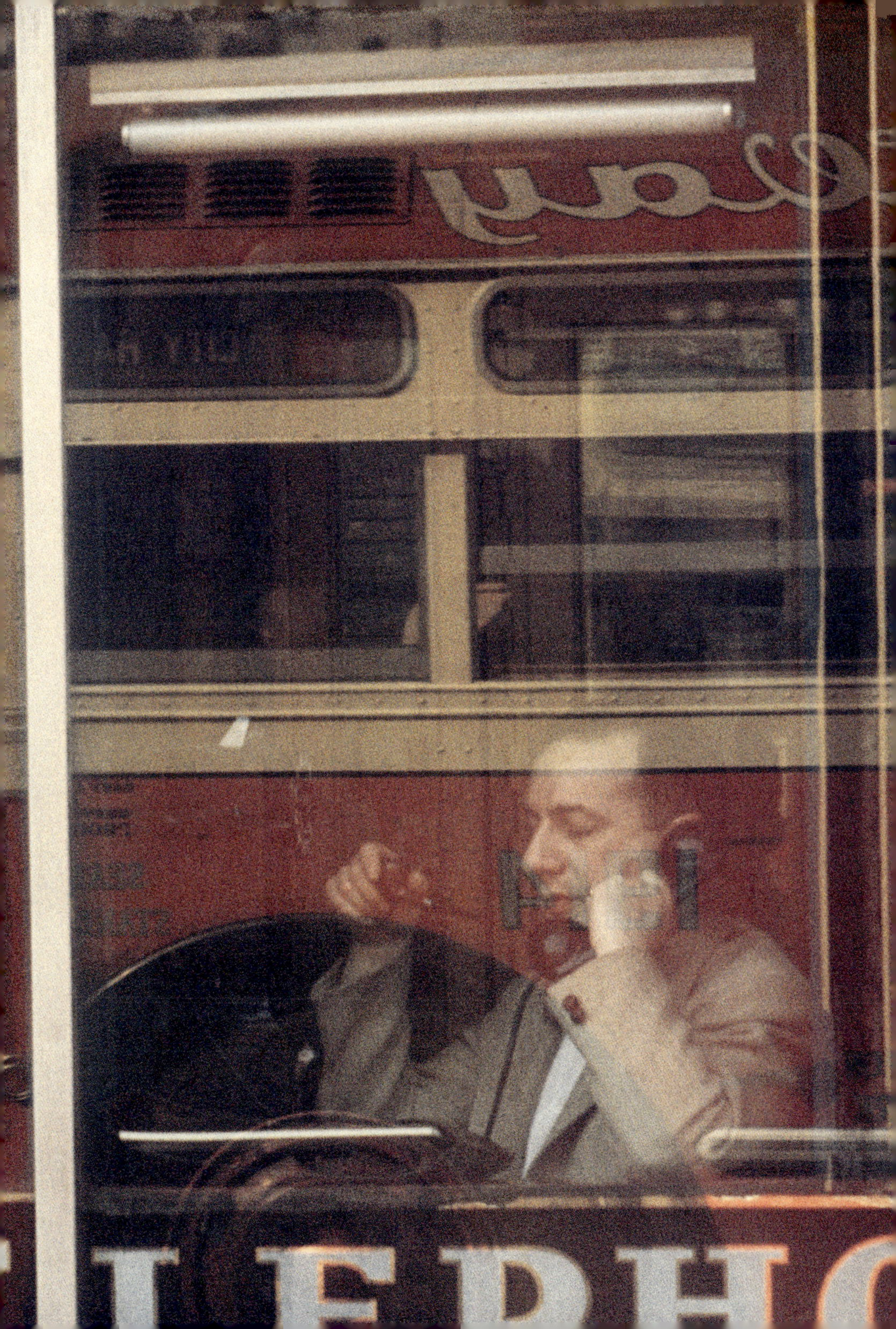

TELEPHO

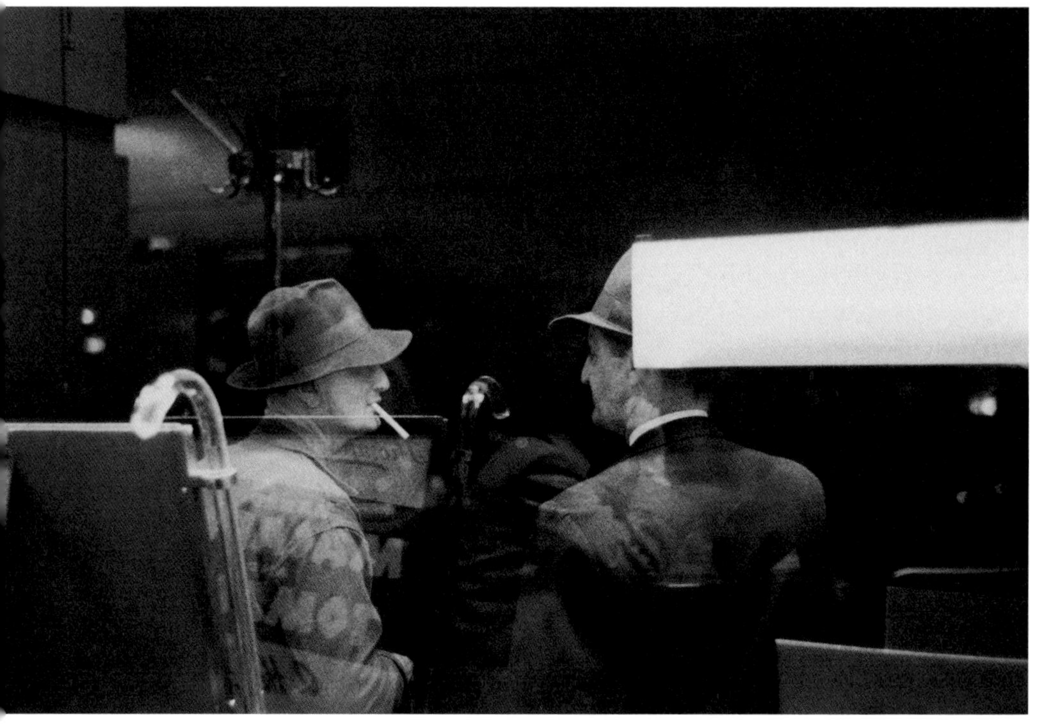

Hats, c. 1958

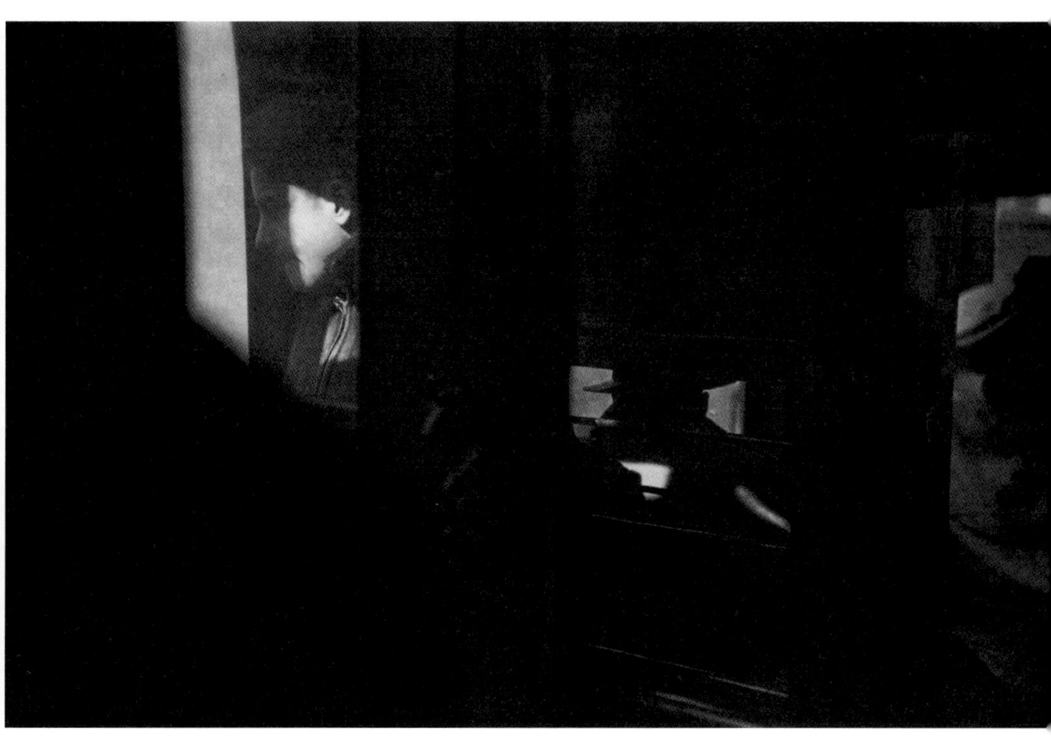

On the El, 1950s

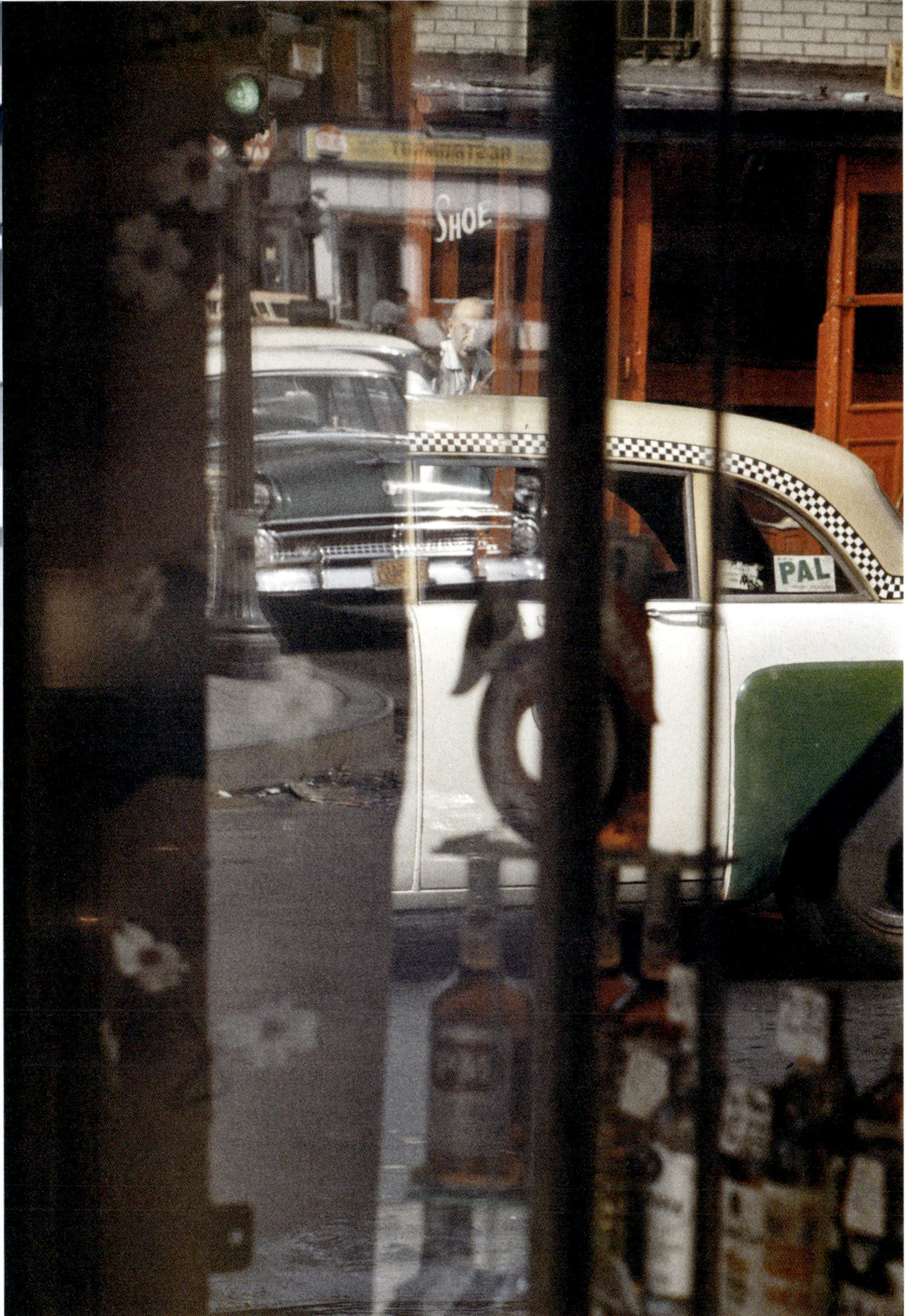

SHOE
PAL

In the 19th century someone was very lucky.
He or she acquired a Vermeer for $12.

Driver, 1950s

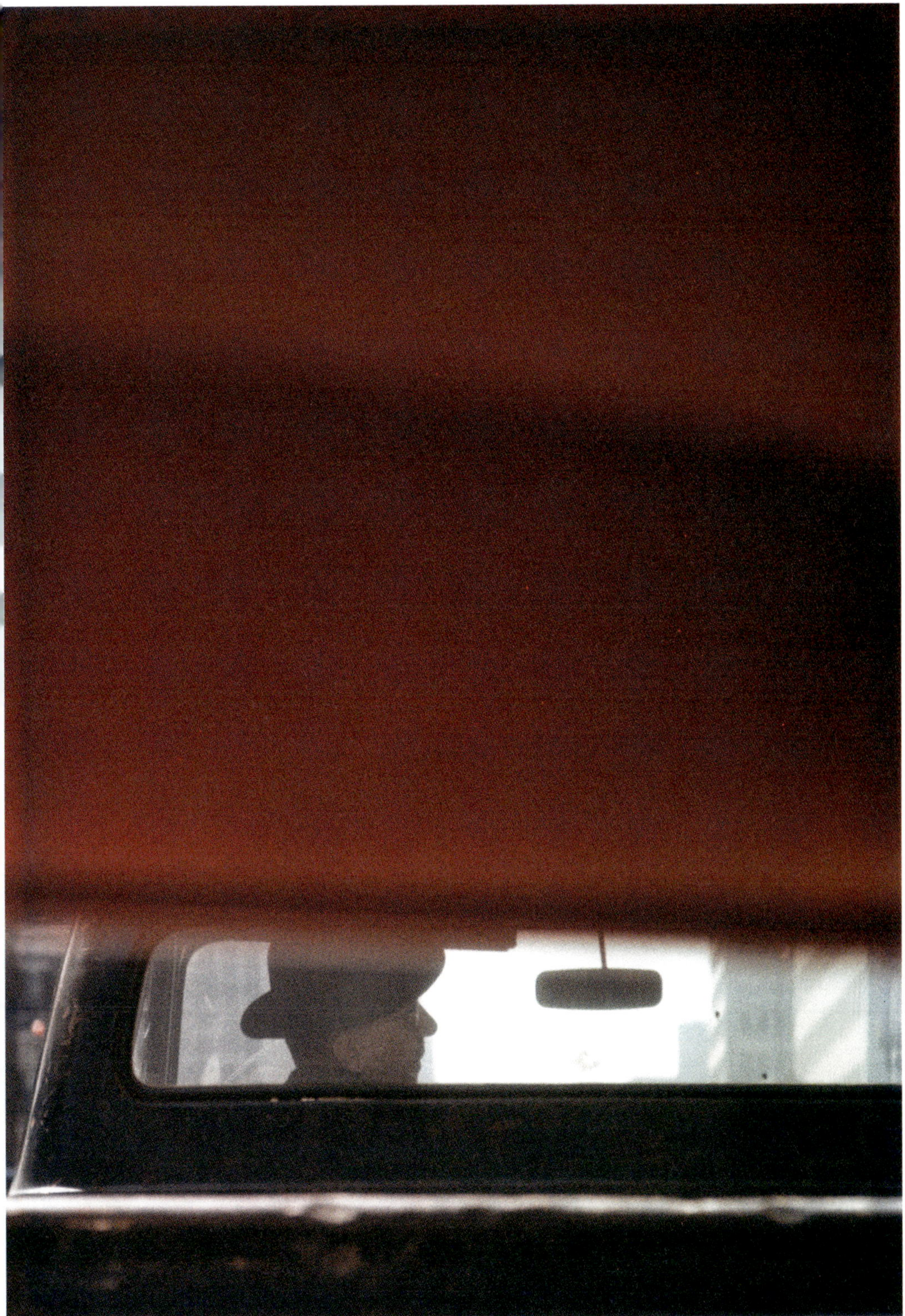

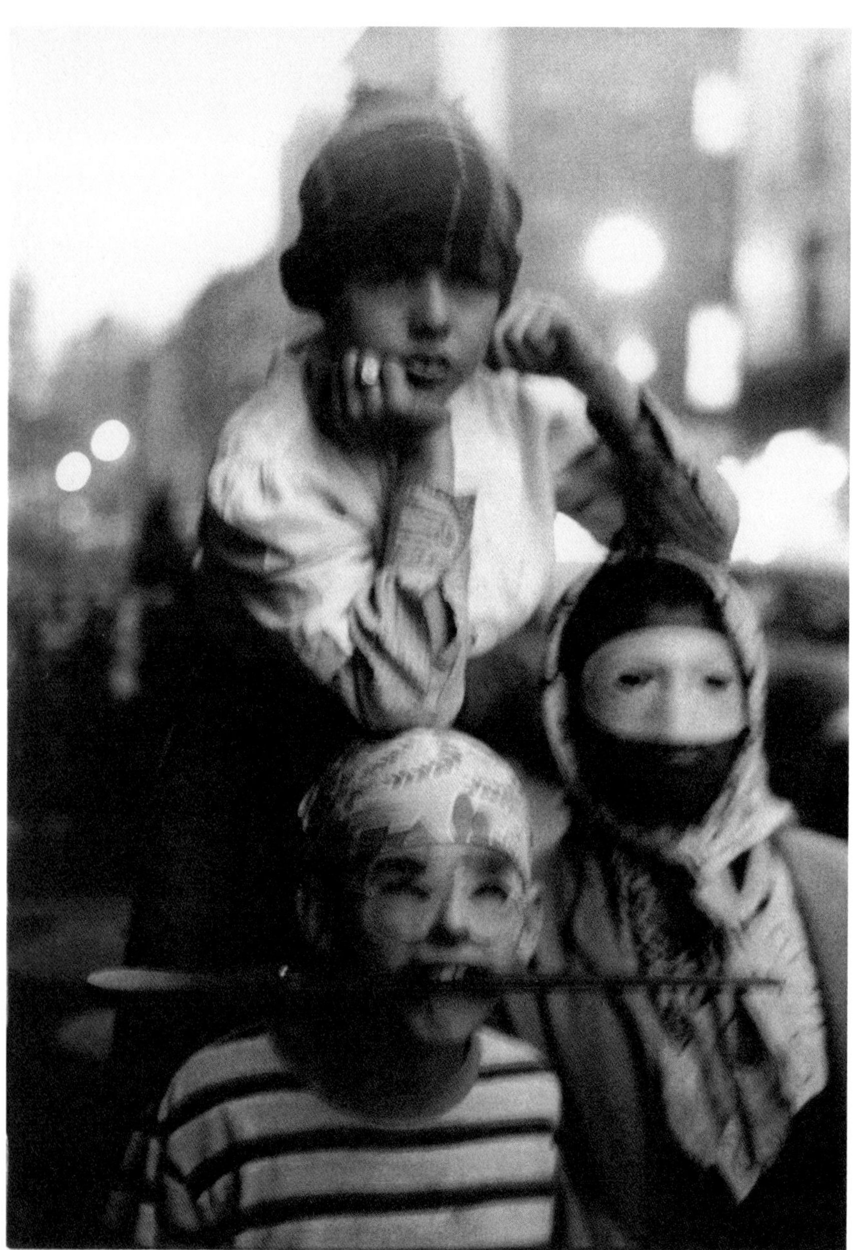

Halloween, 1952

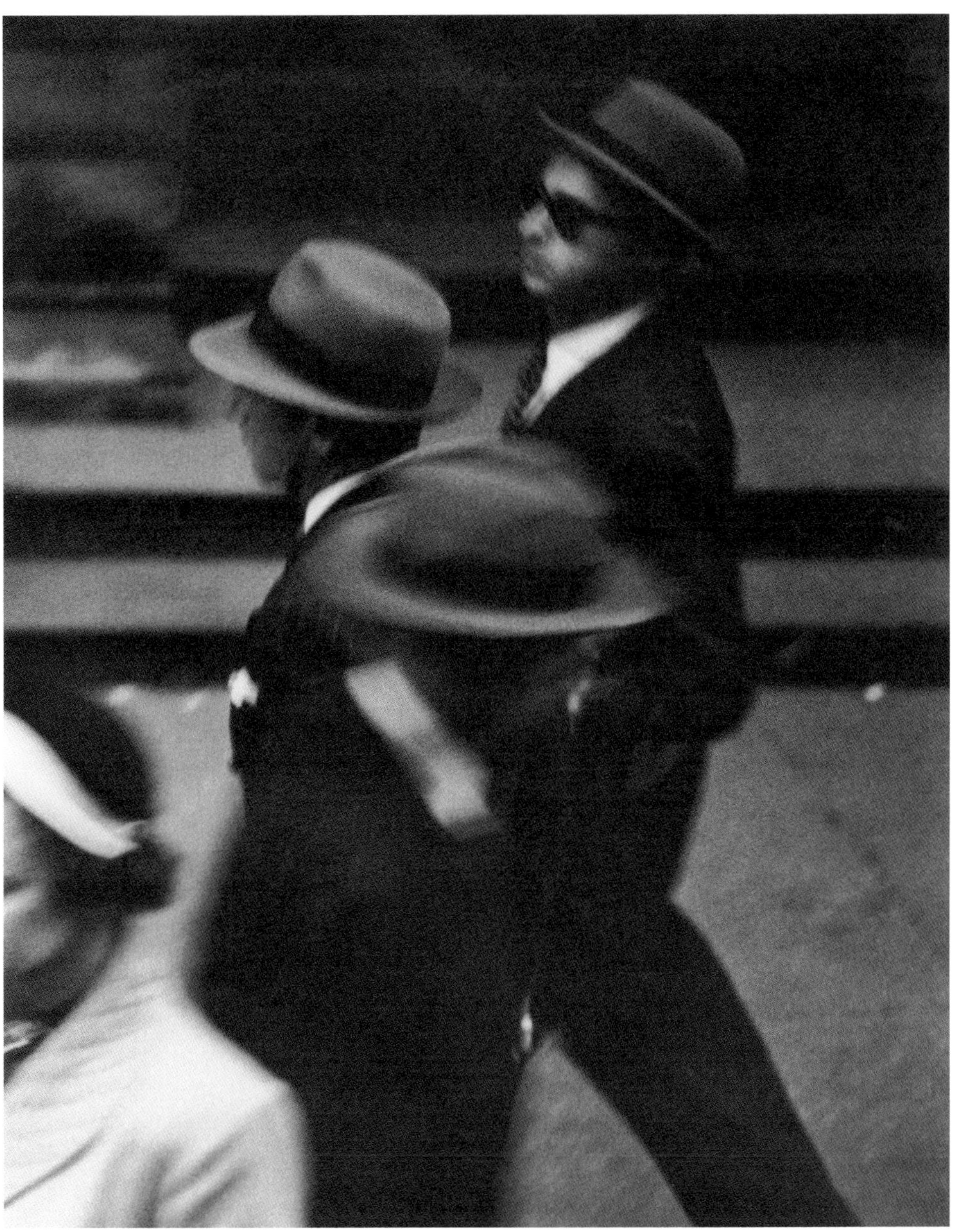

Hats, c. 1948

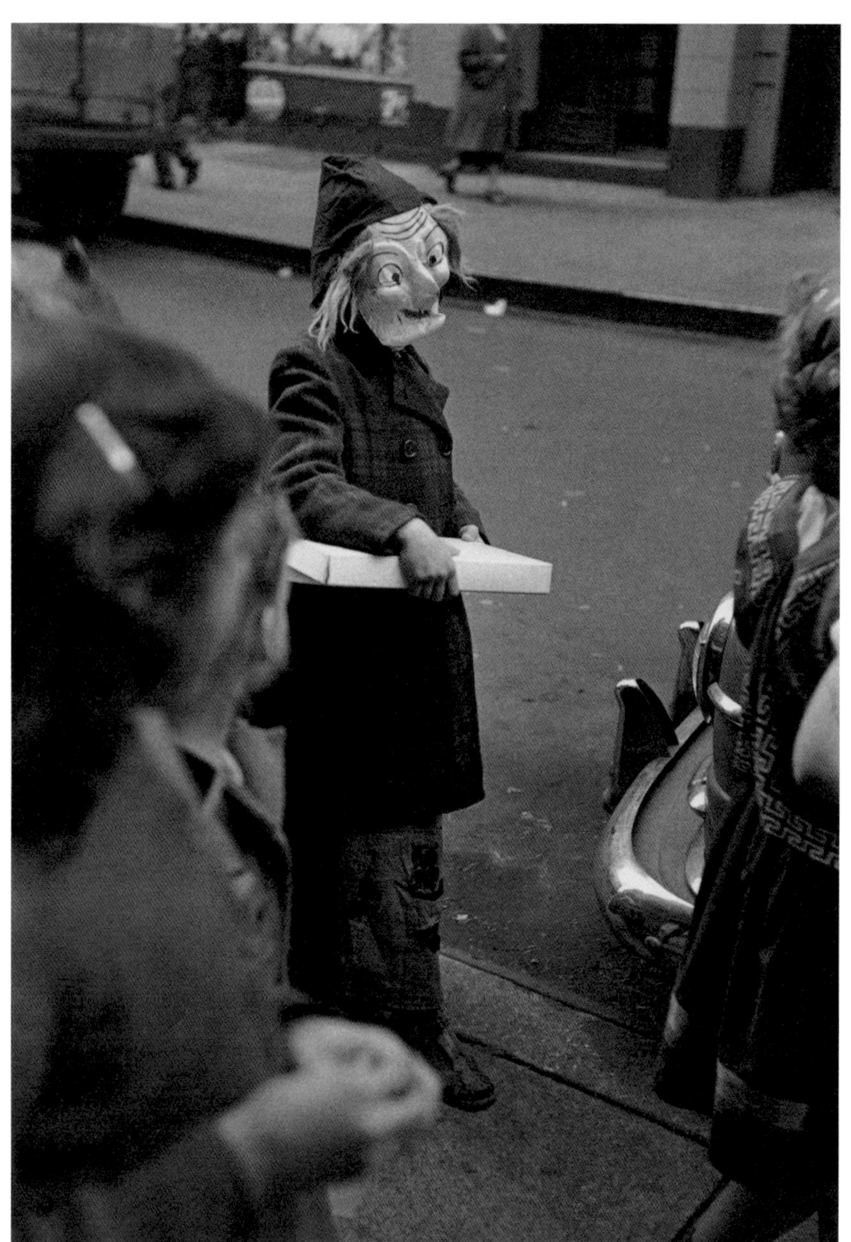

Halloween, 1952

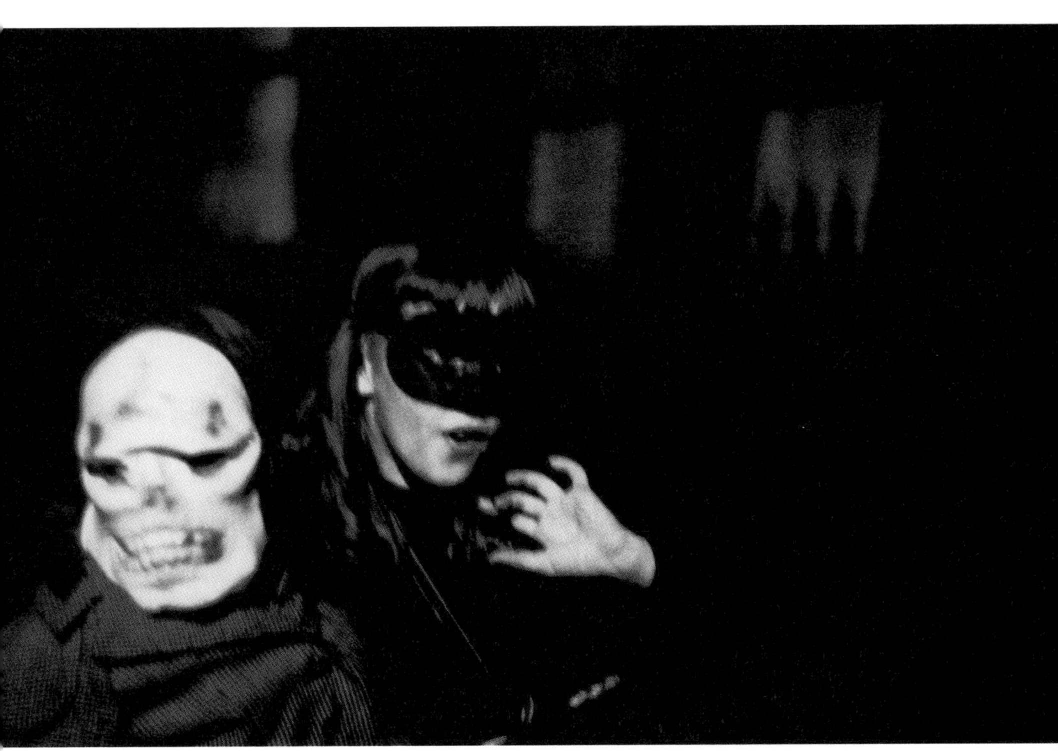

Halloween, 1952

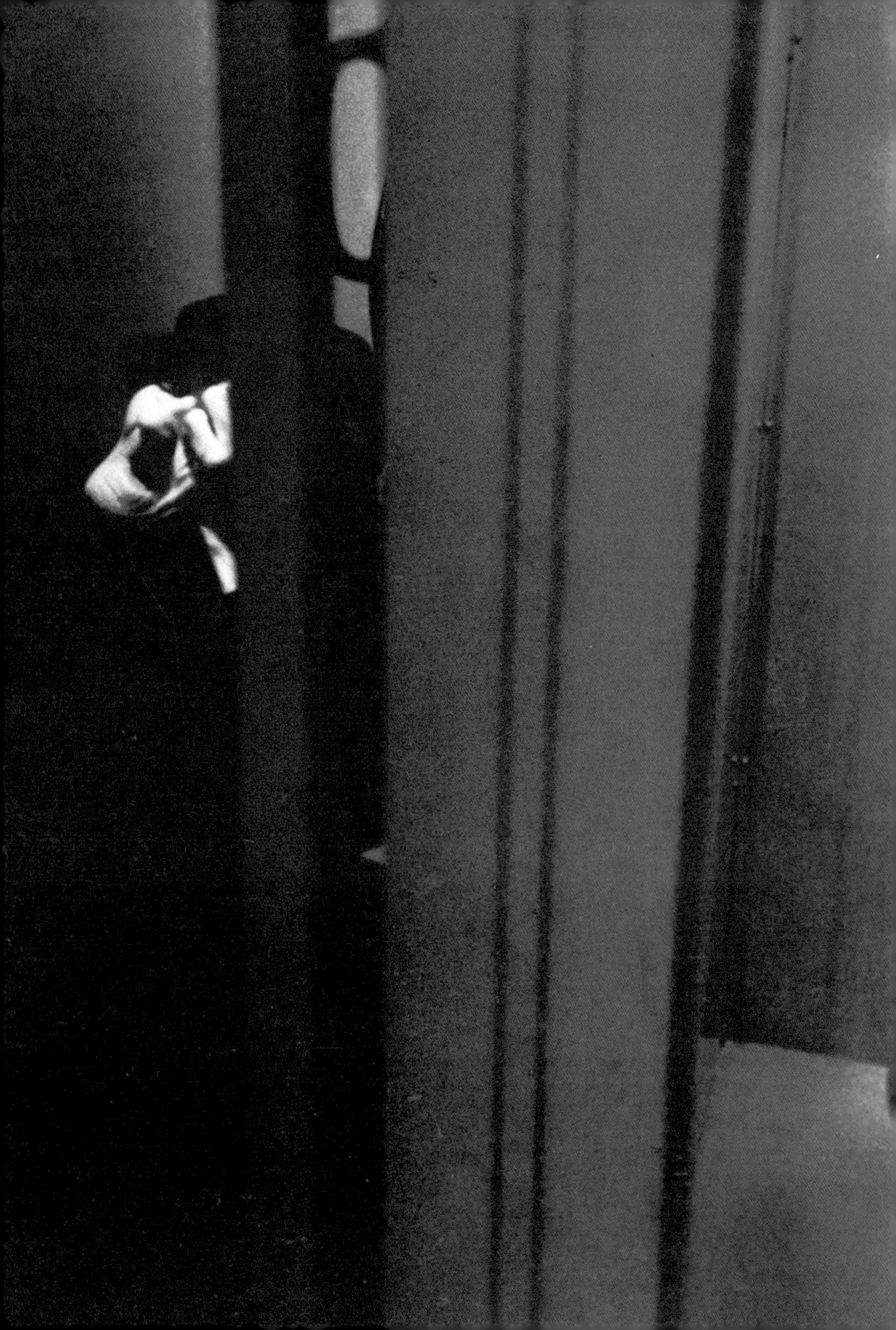

The cream does not always rise to the surface. The history of art is a history of
great things neglected and ignored and bad and mediocre things being admired.

Mannequin, c. 1952

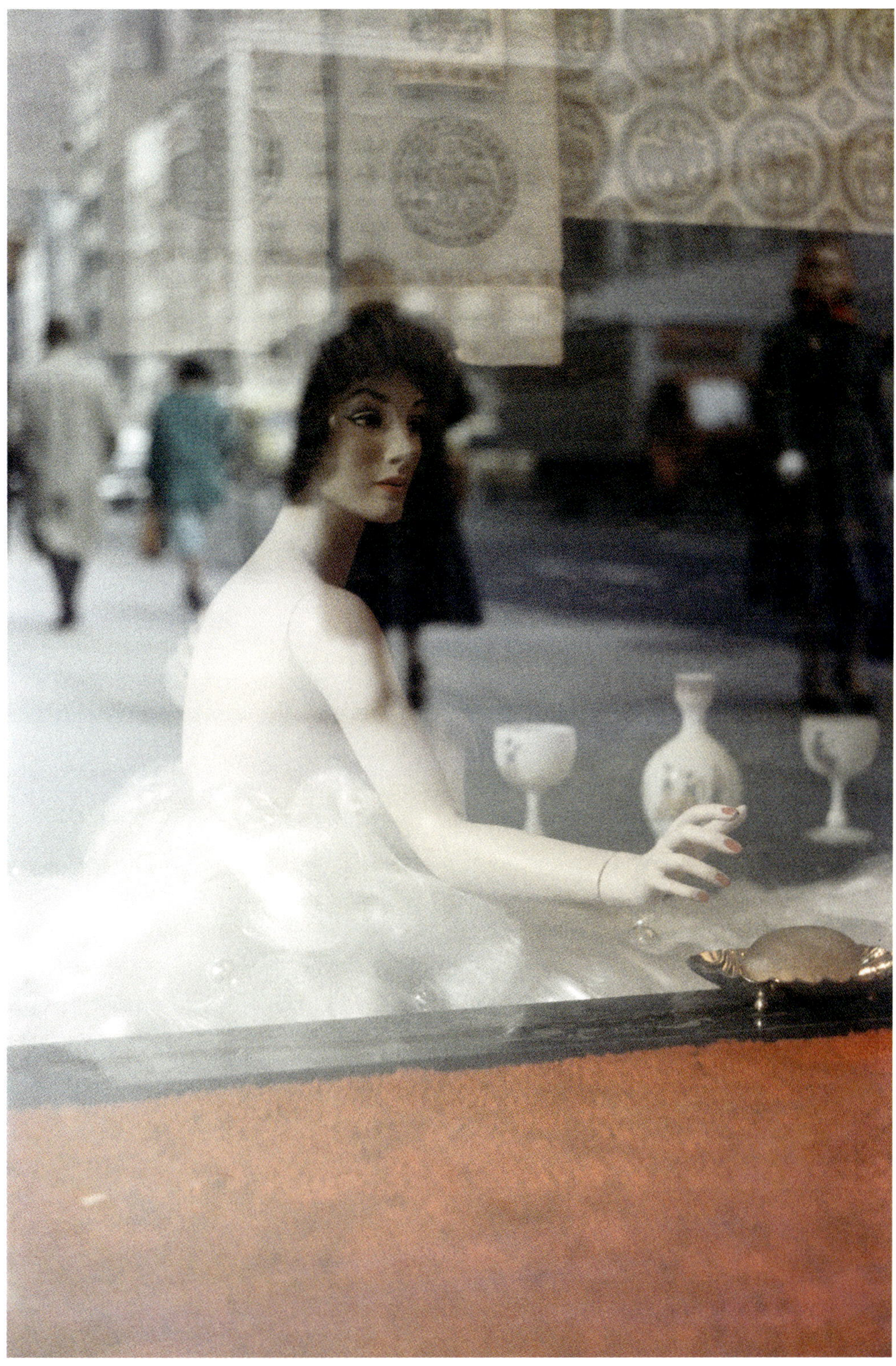

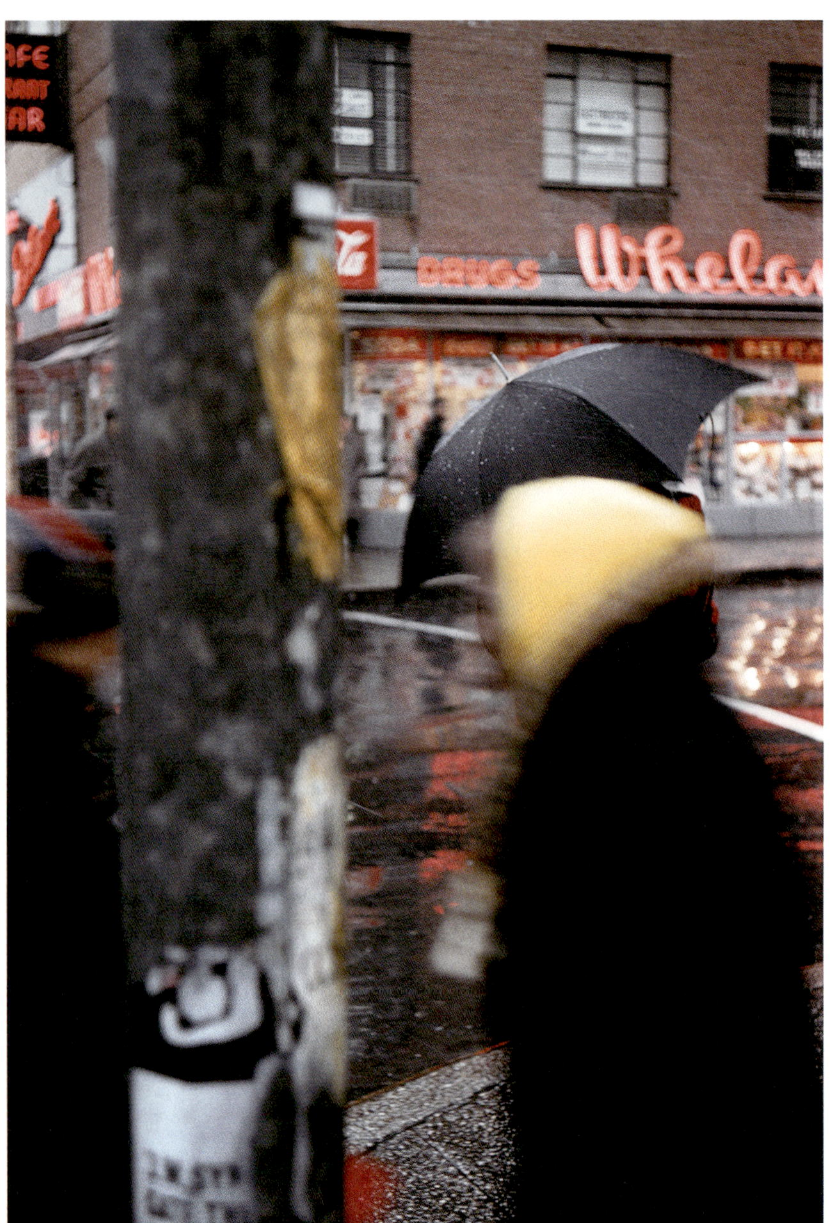

Yellow Scarf, 1956

Horn & Hardart, c. 1959

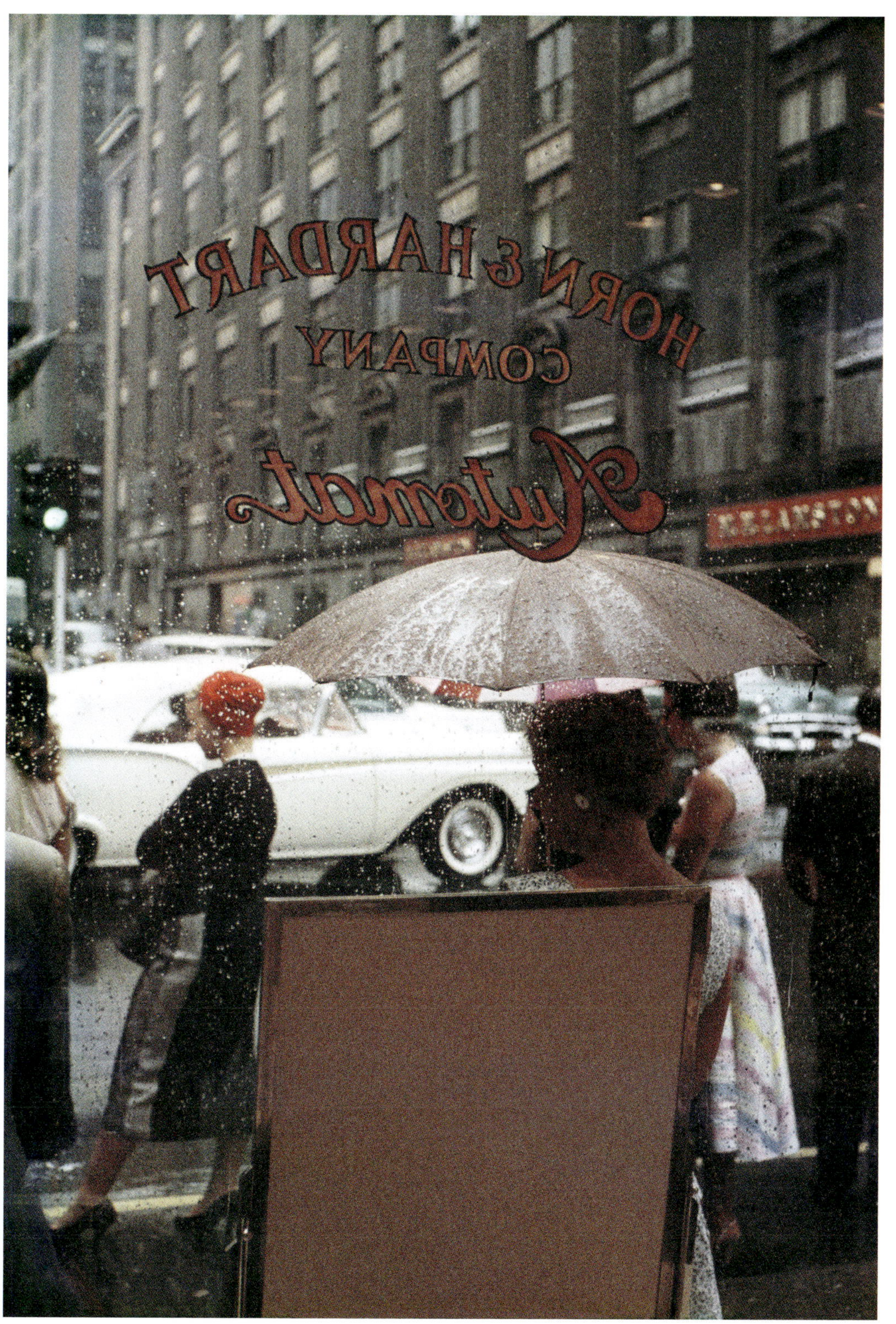

Walk with Soames, 1958

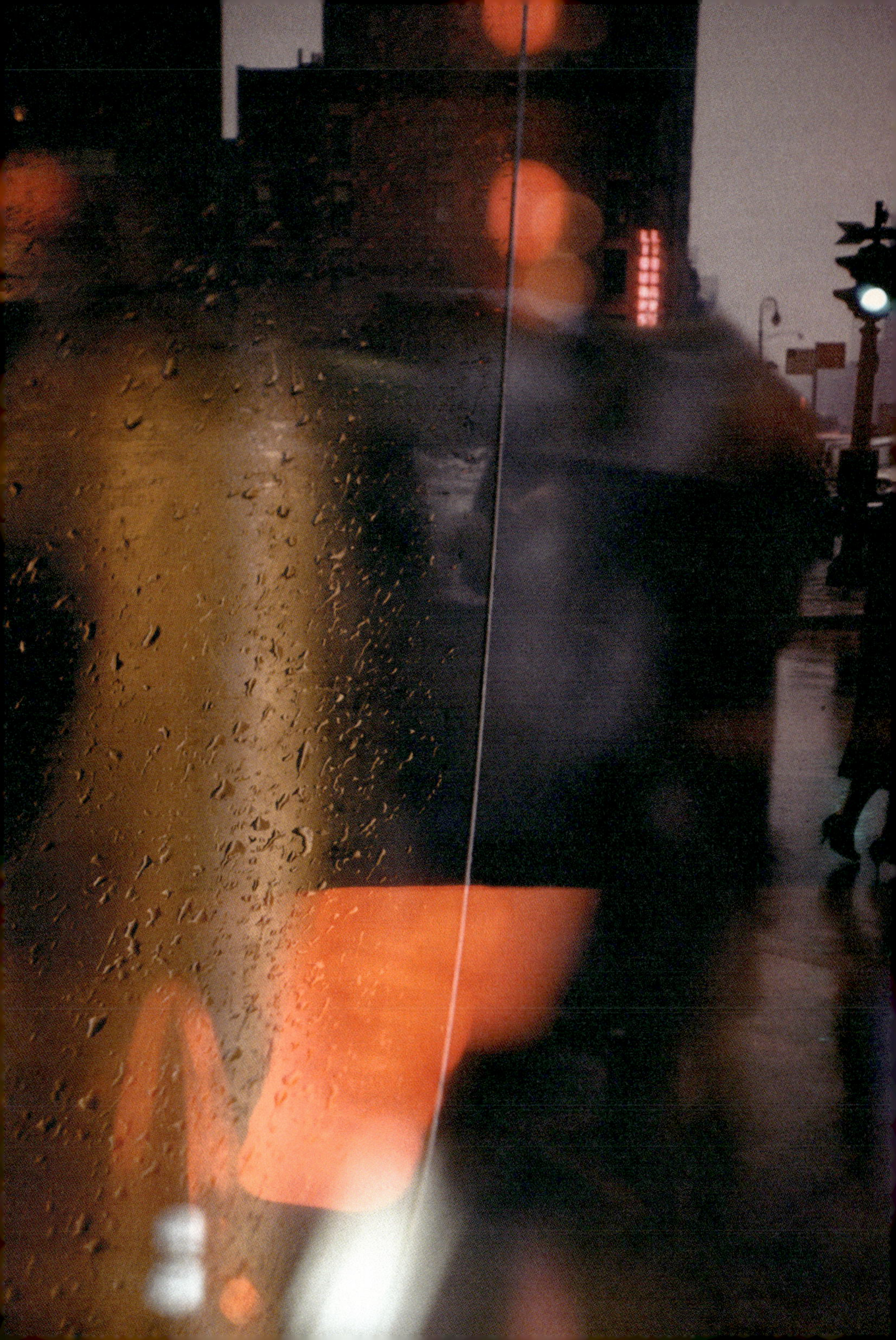

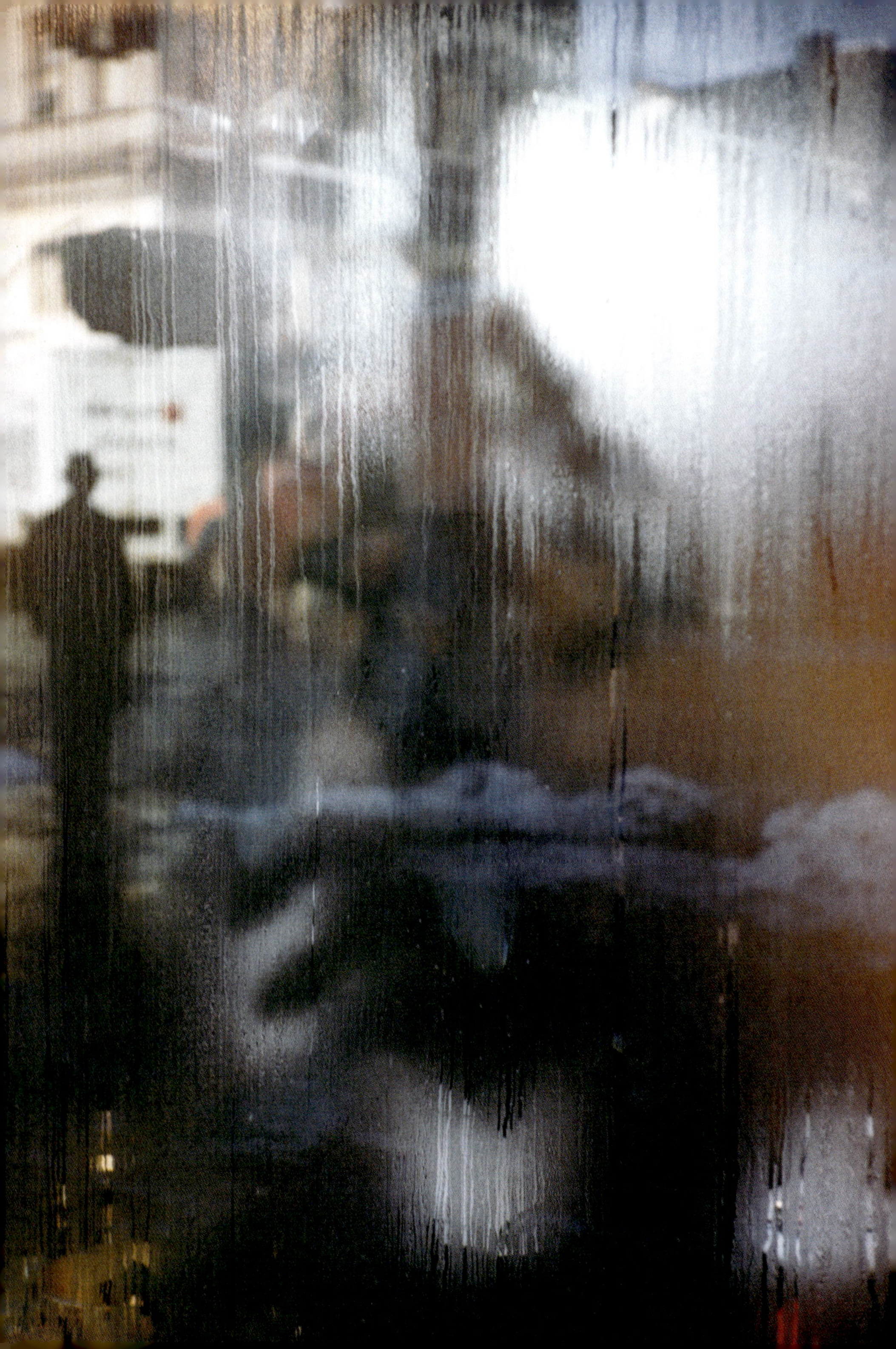

I had collections of Japanese prints, I owned Bonnard, Vuillard…
it was a time when you could buy things [like that] cheap, and when
I needed money I would sell them. Soames, I think, was unhappy about that.

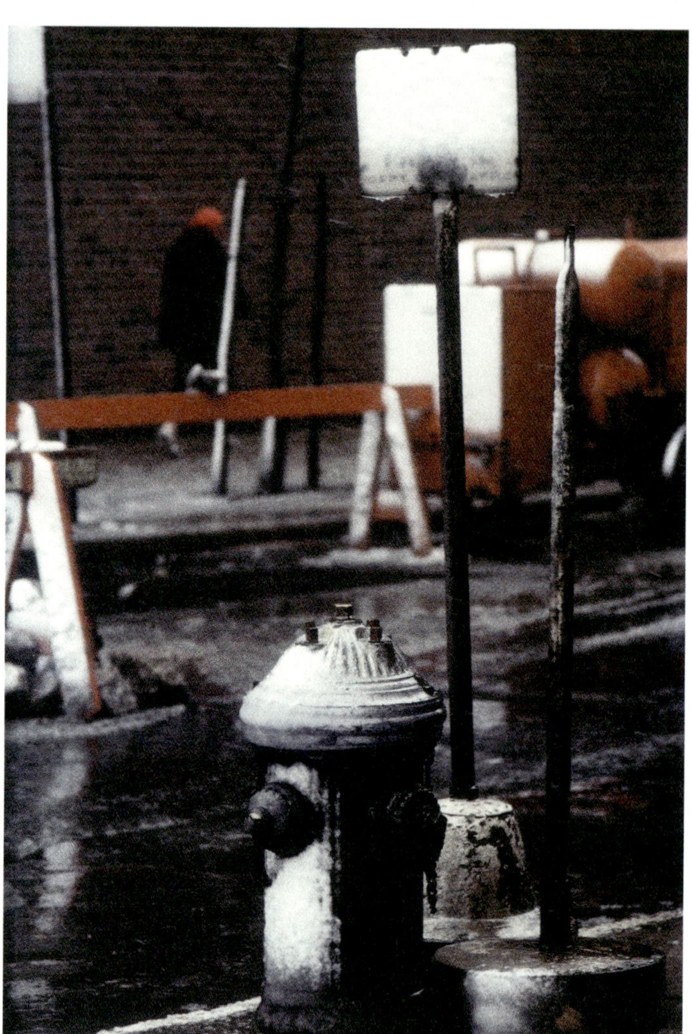

Fire Hydrant, 1957

463, 1956

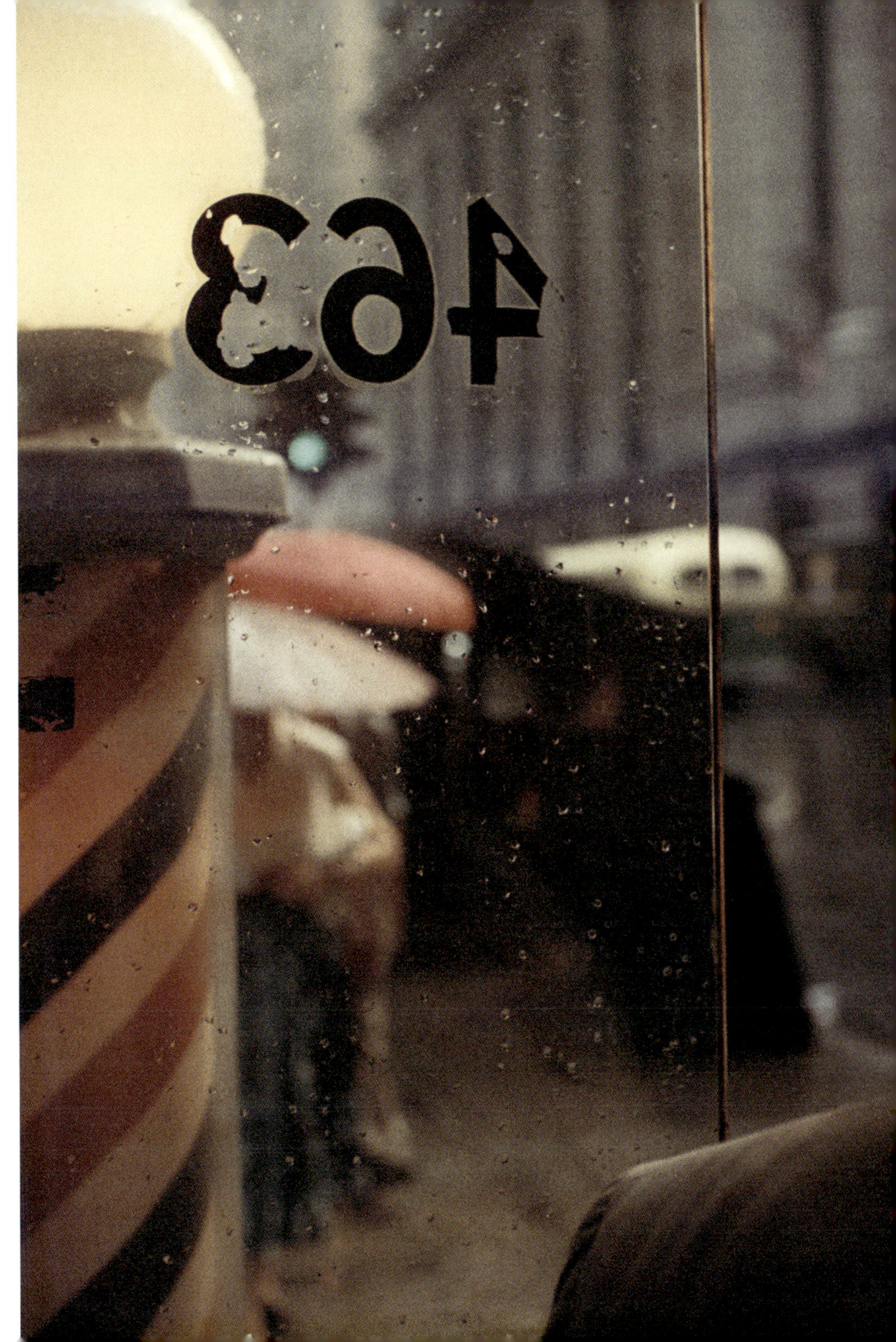

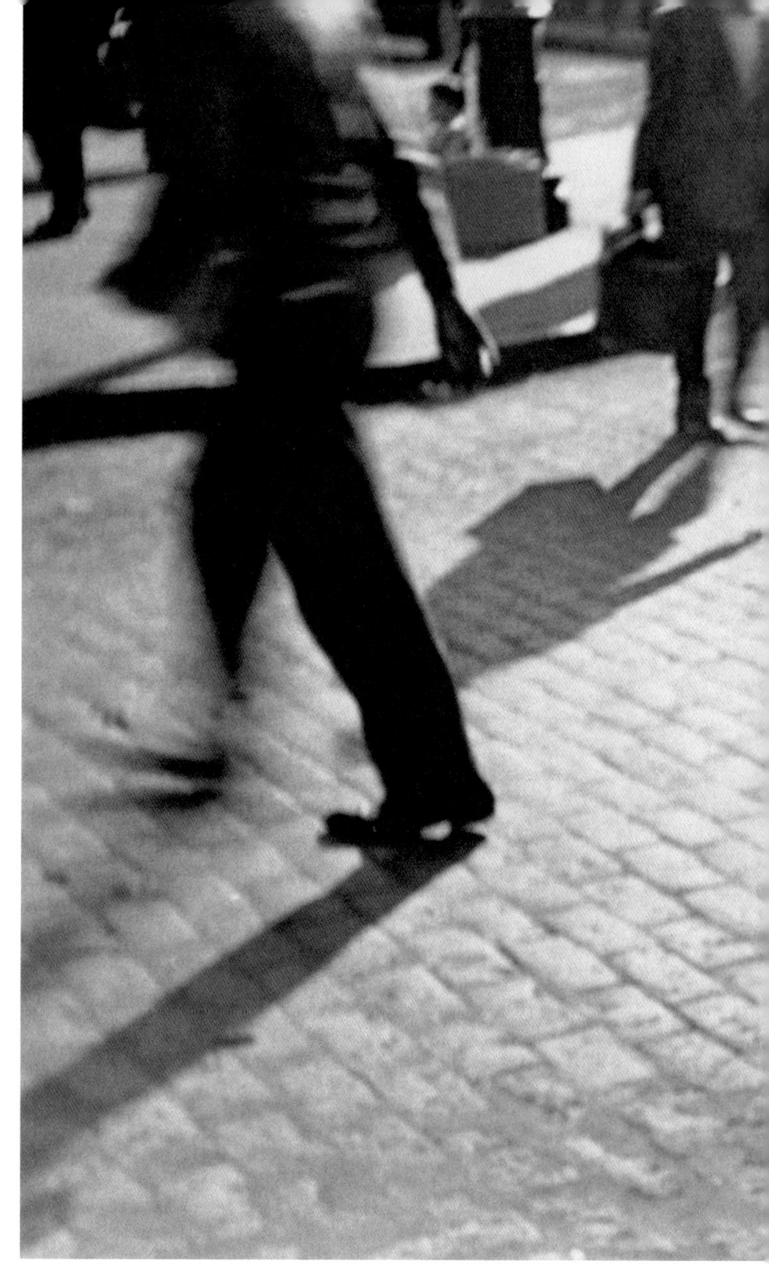

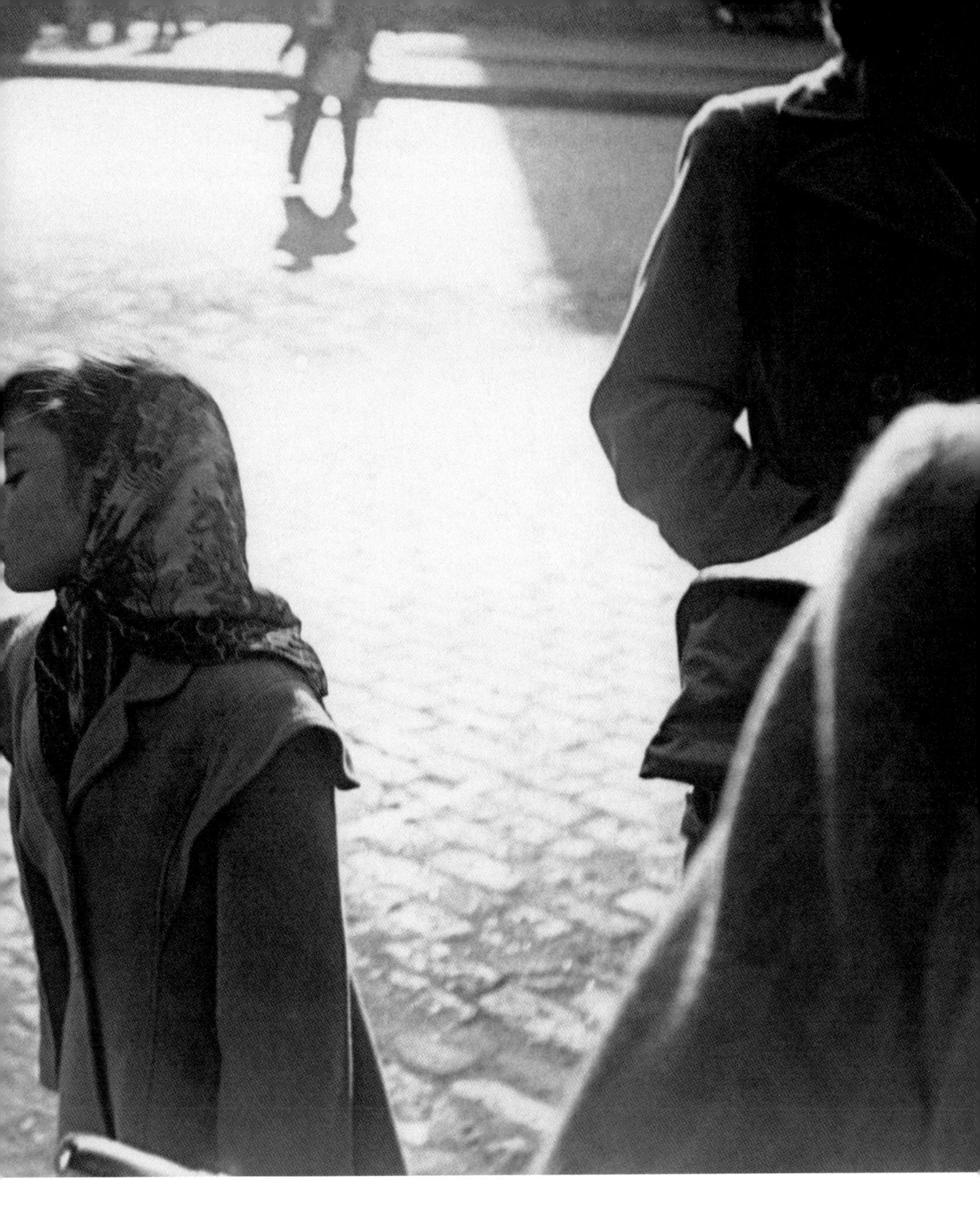

Scarf, c. 1948

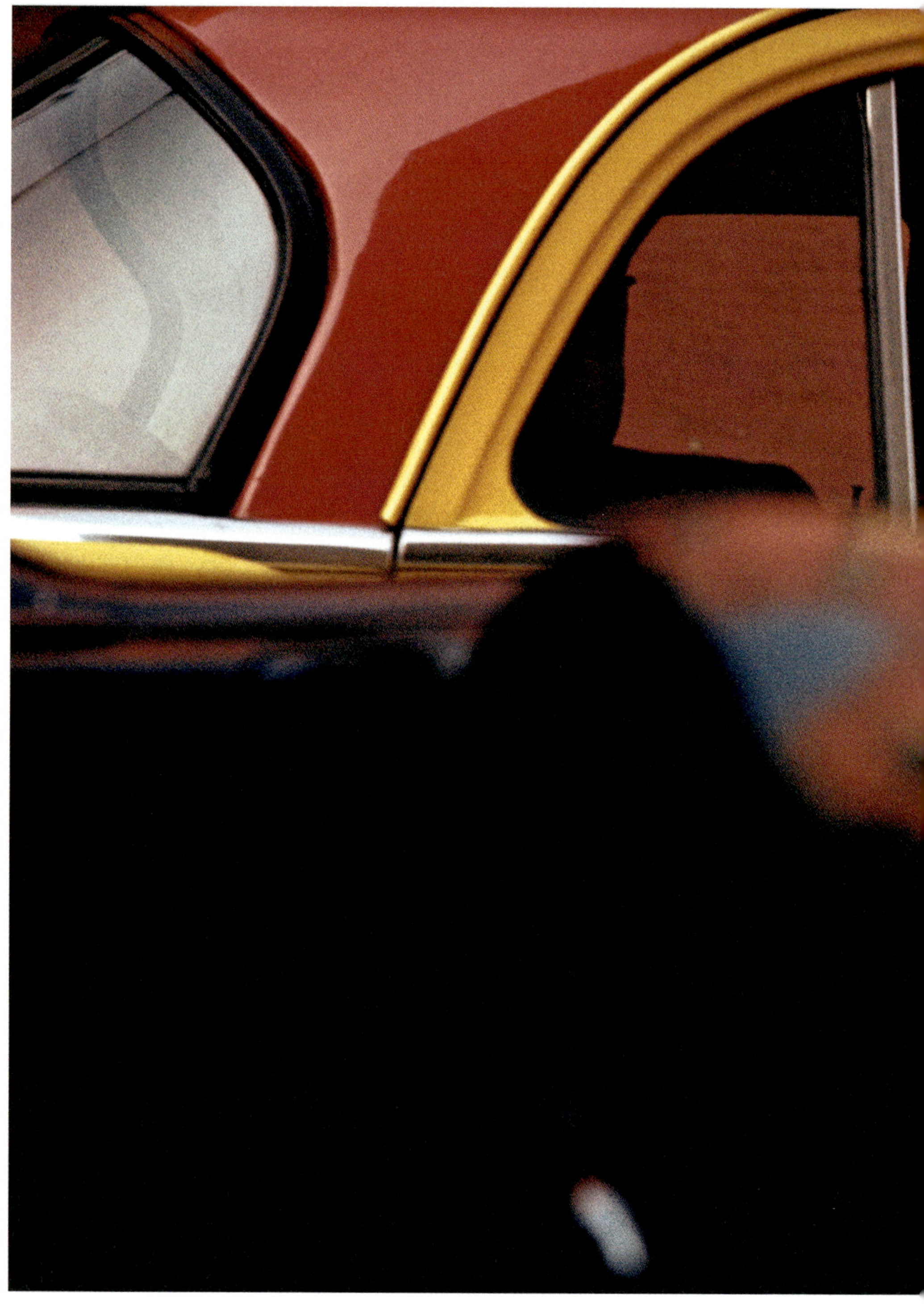

Taxi, 1957

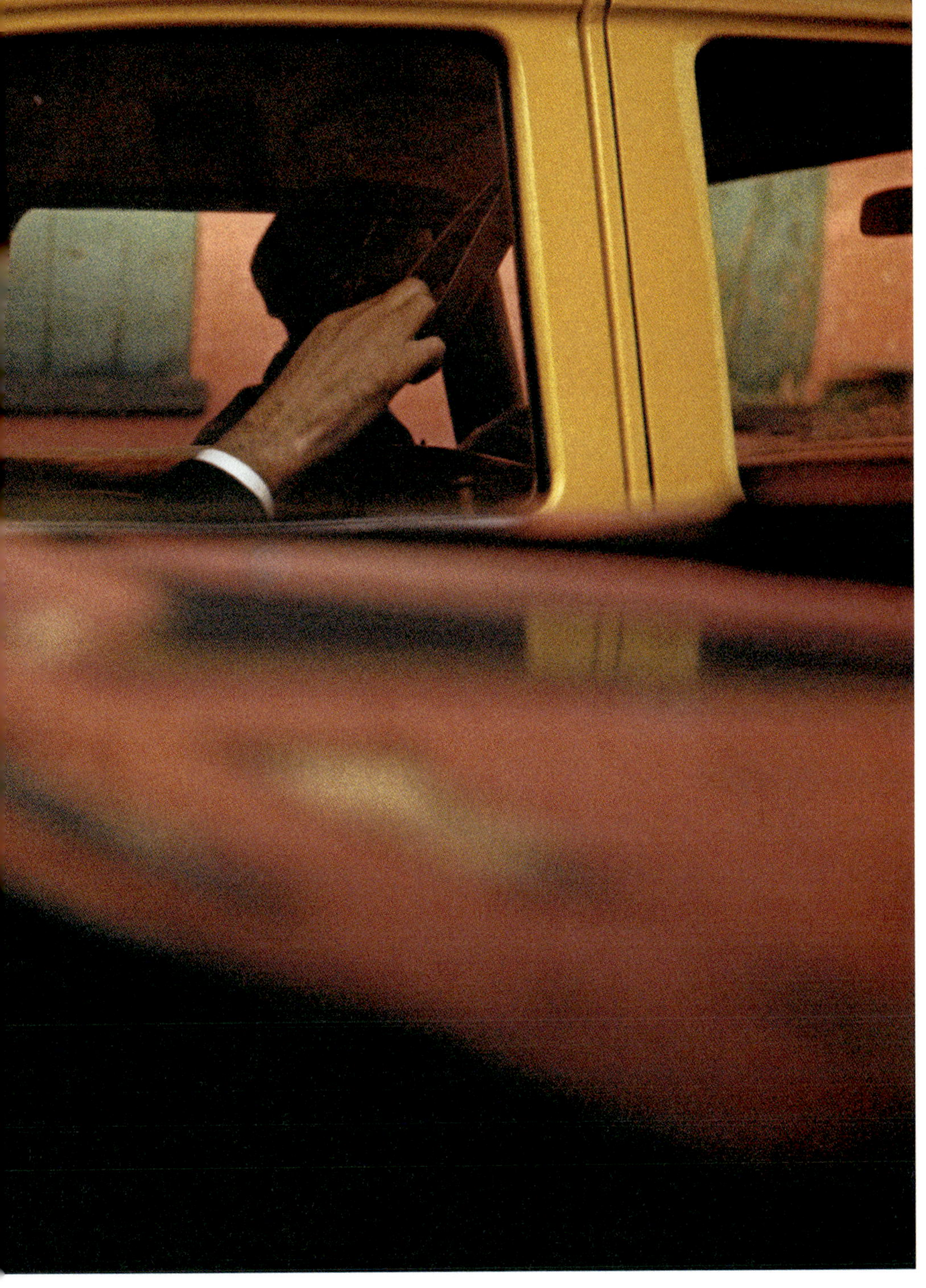

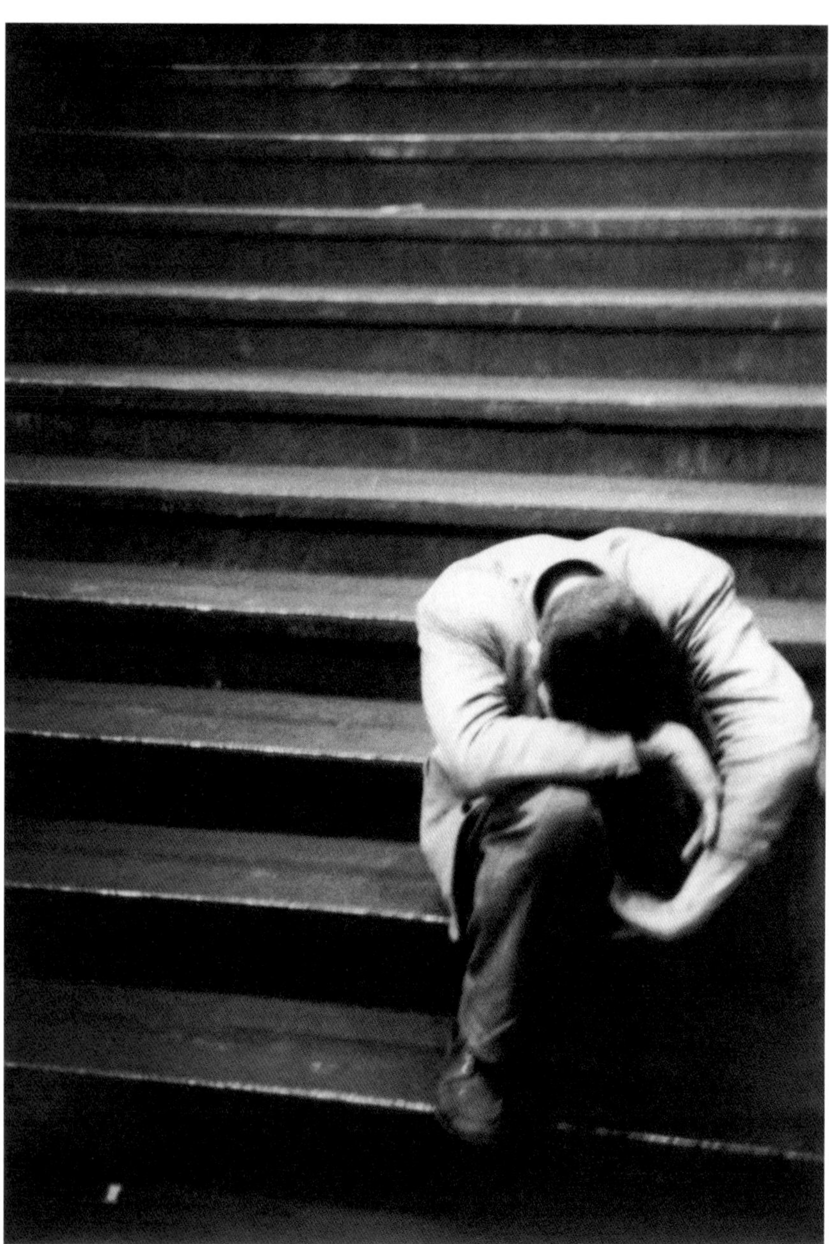

Subway, late 1950s

Untitled, 1950s
Sweeper, c. 1950

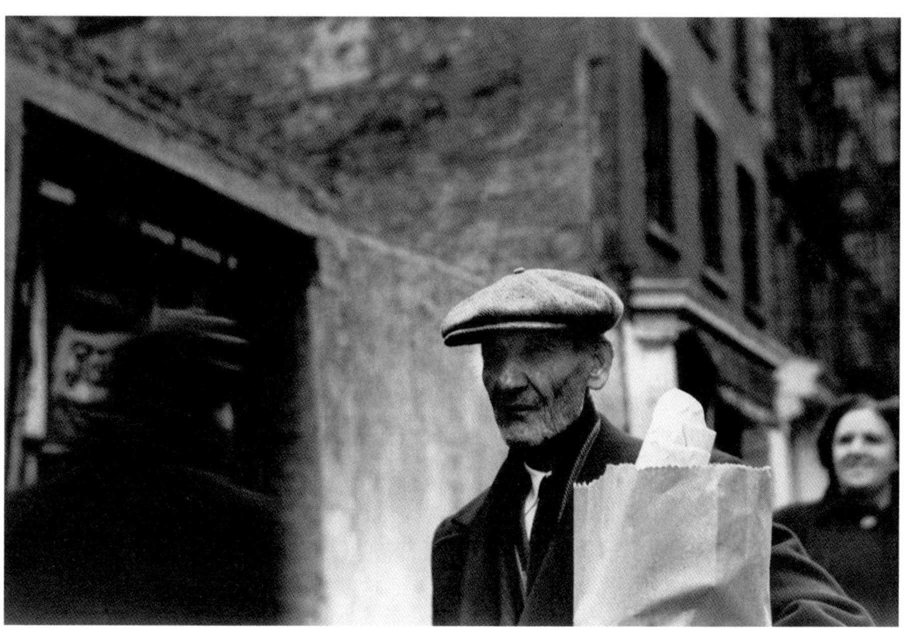

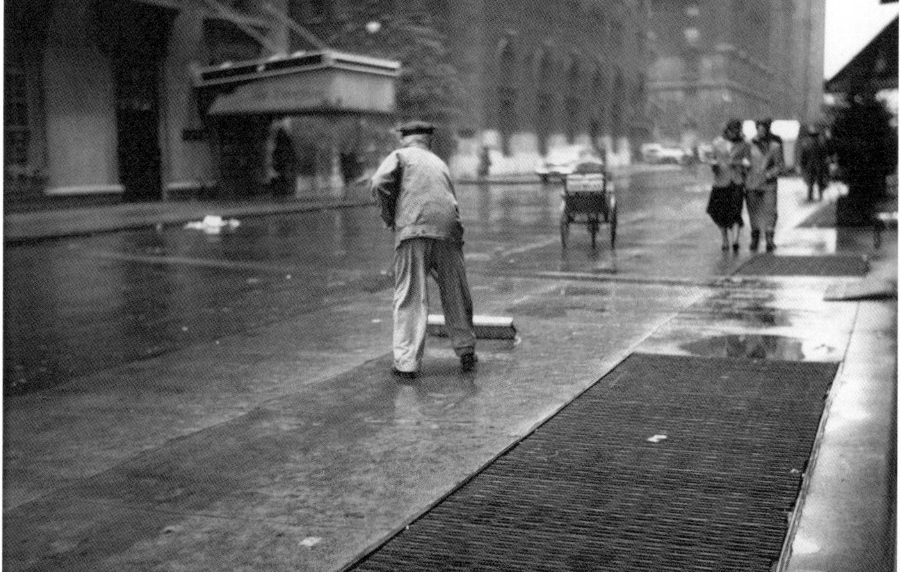

It is not where it is or what it is that matters but how you see it.

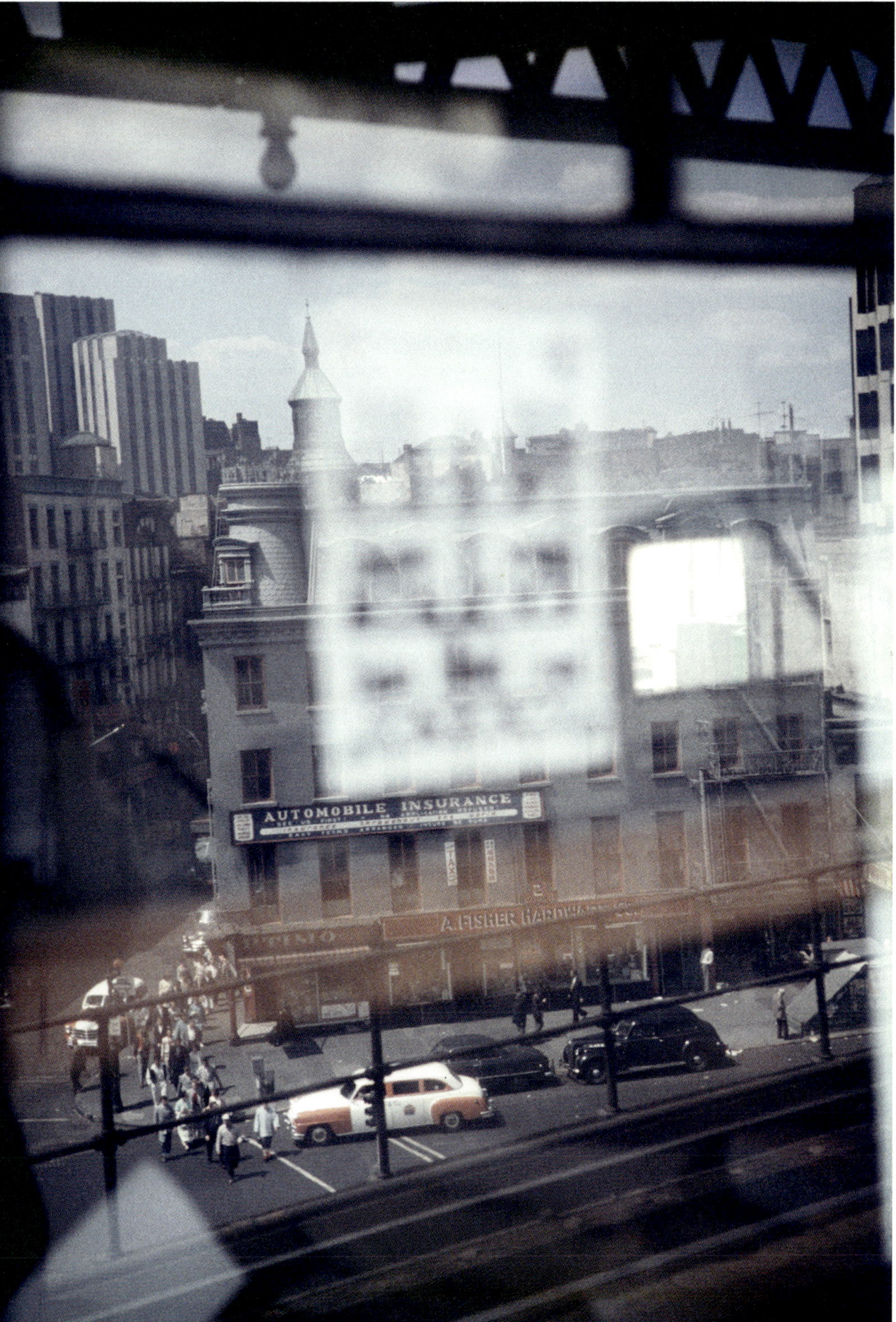

AUTOMOBILE INSURANCE
A. FISHER HARDWARE

A person's back tells me more than the front.

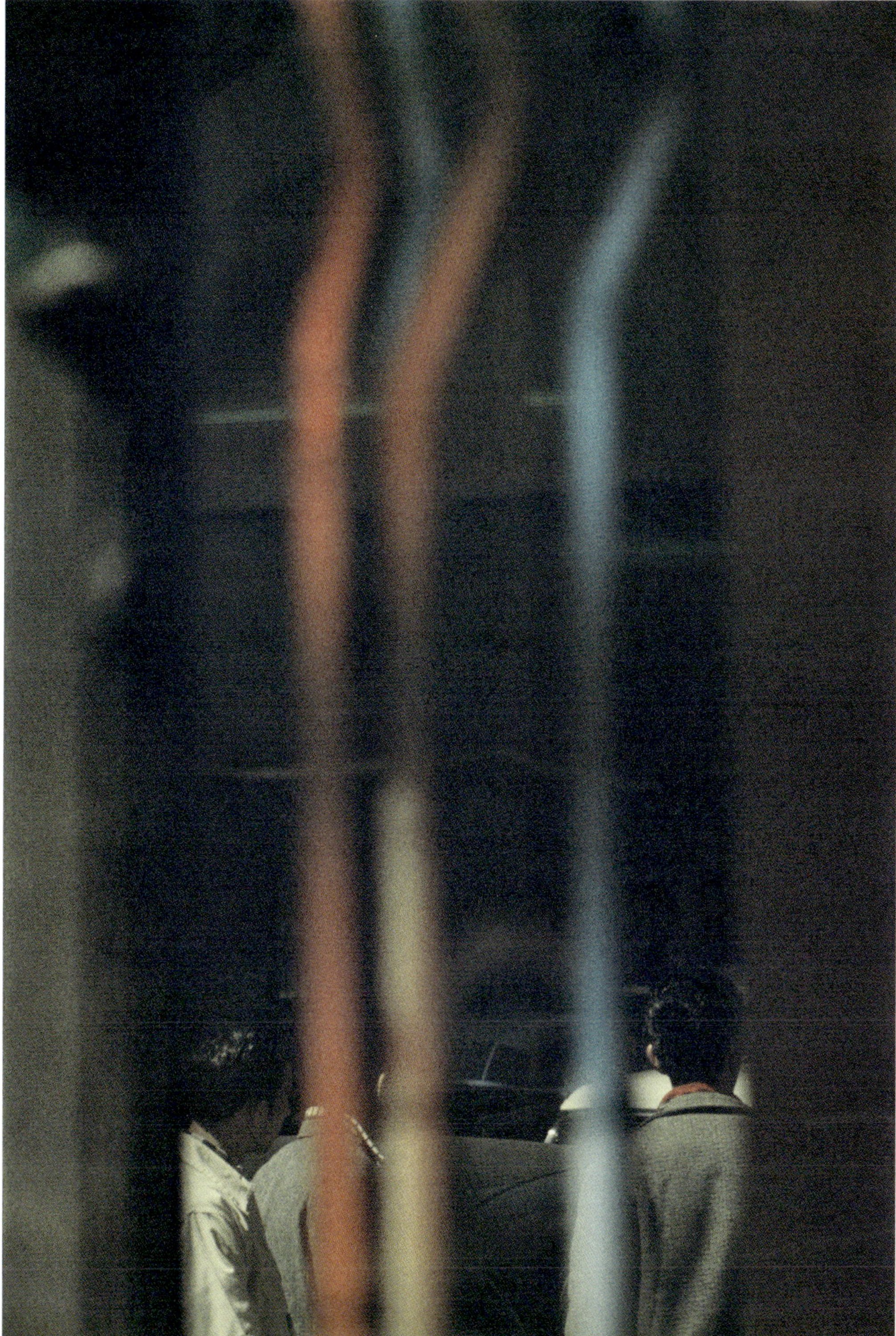

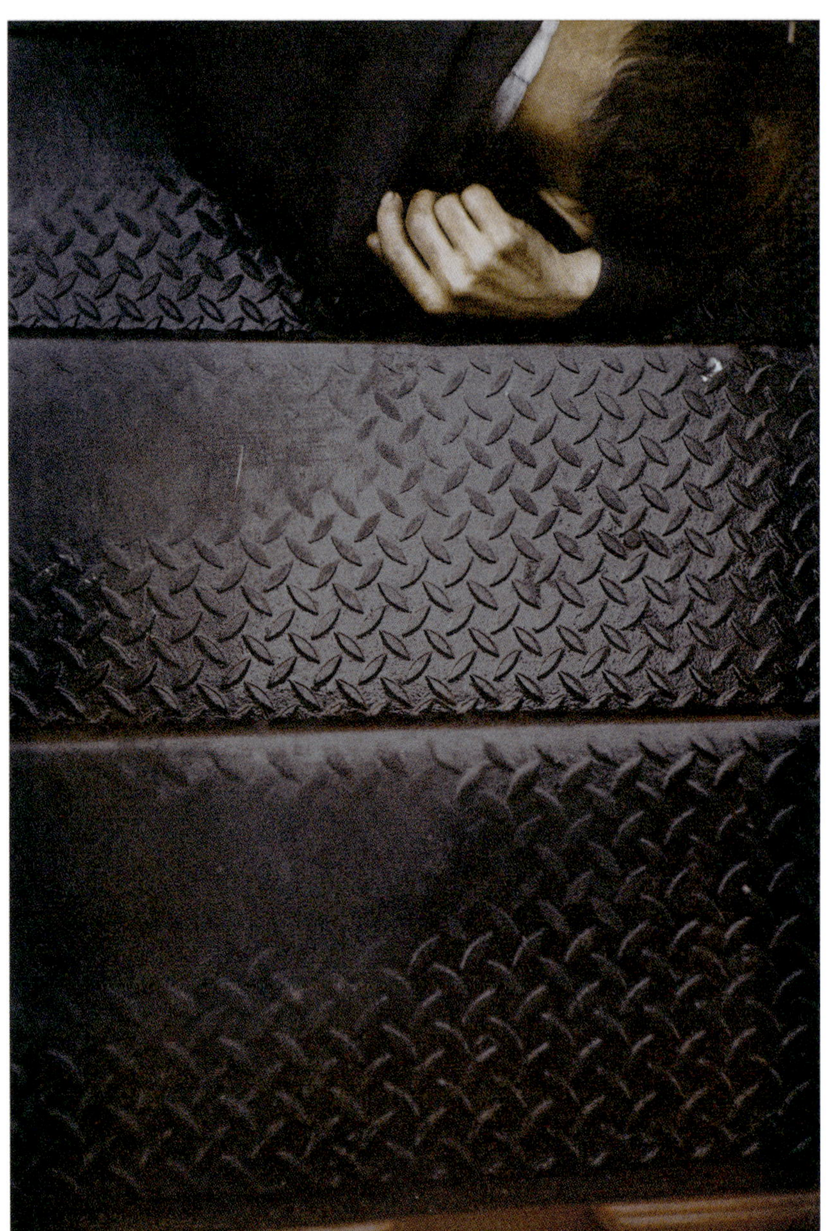

Tanager Stairs, c. 1954

From the El, c. 1955

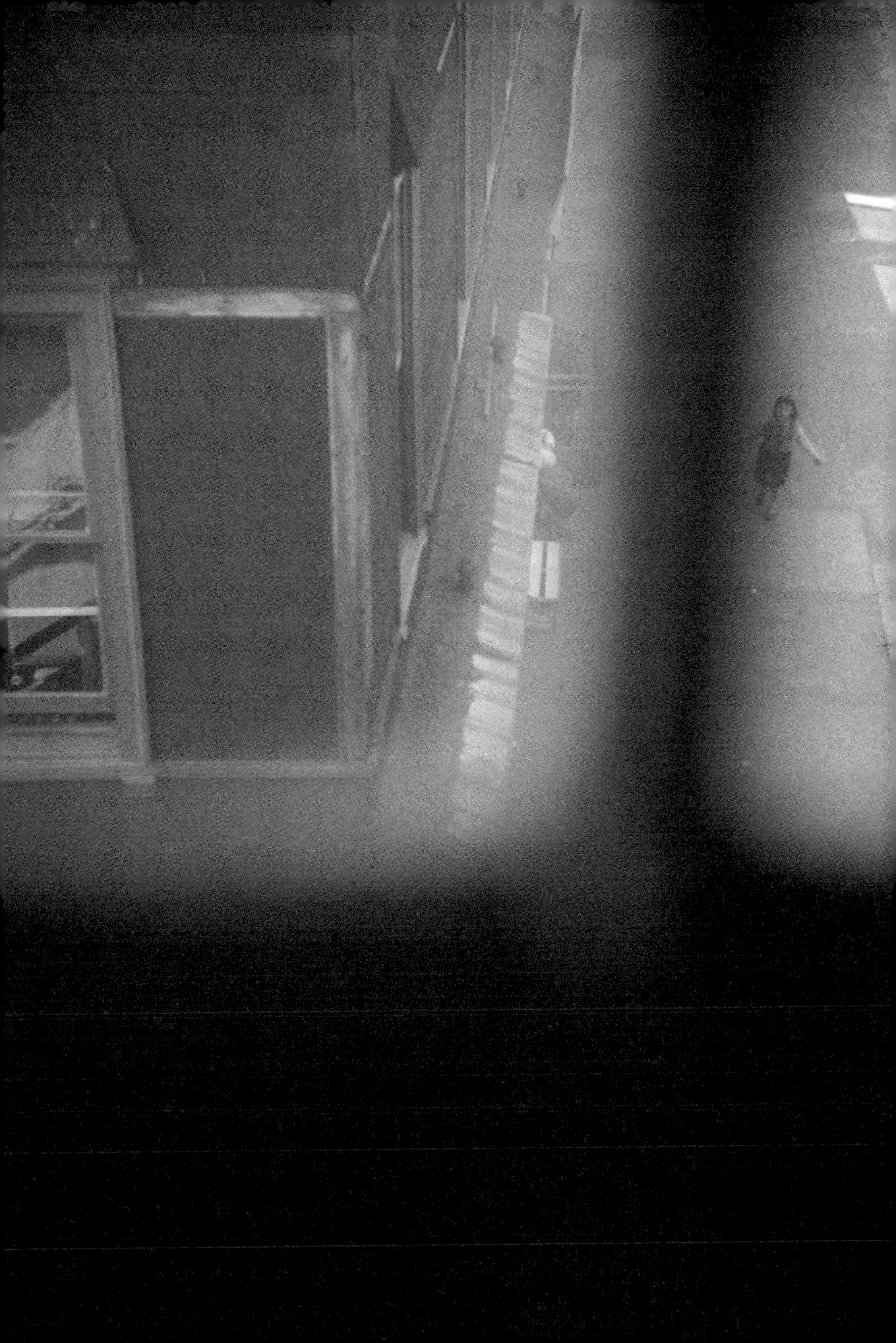

Photographs are often treated as important moments
but really they are little fragments and souvenirs of an unfinished world.

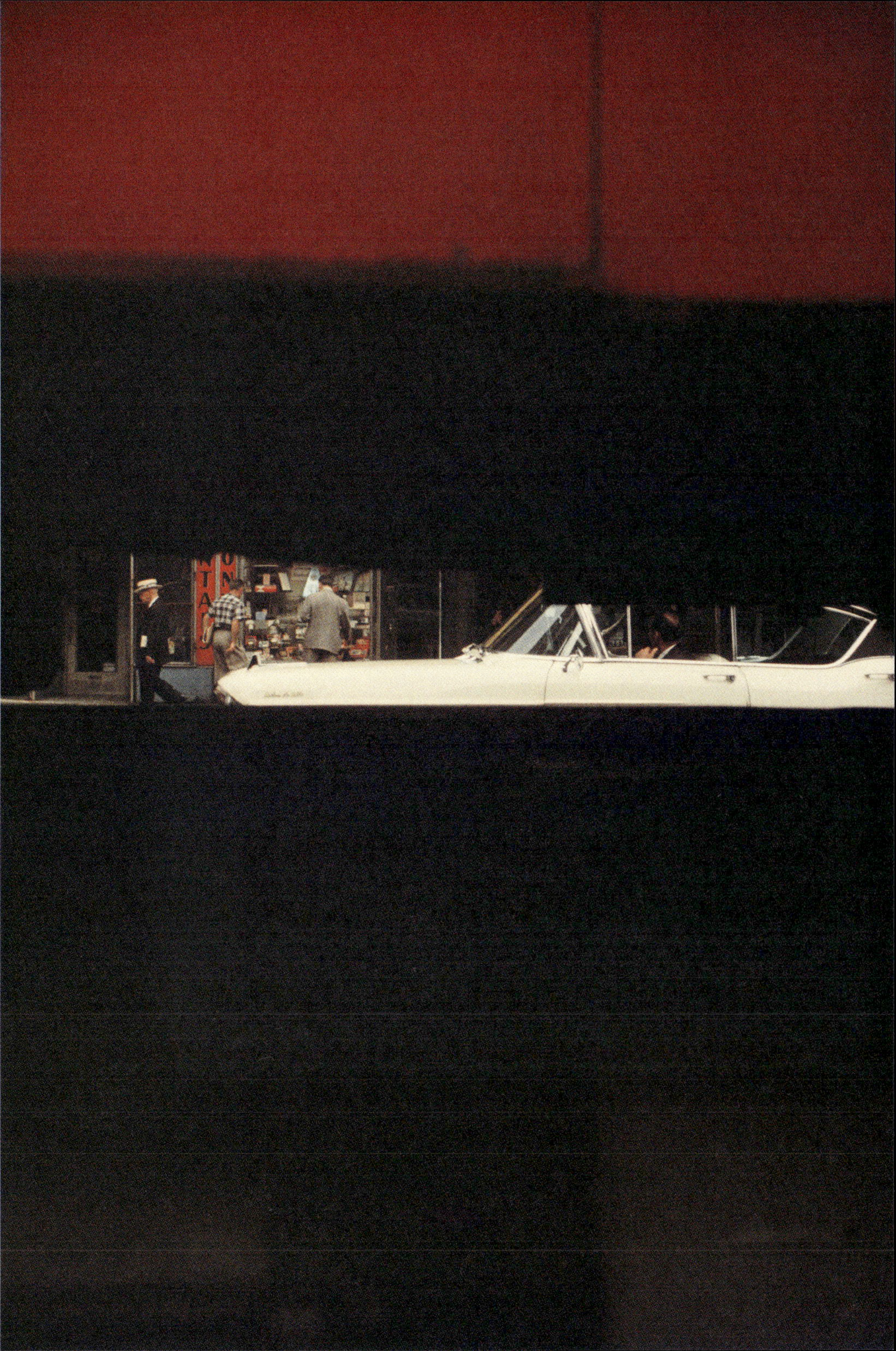

Parade, 1954

Don't Walk, 1952

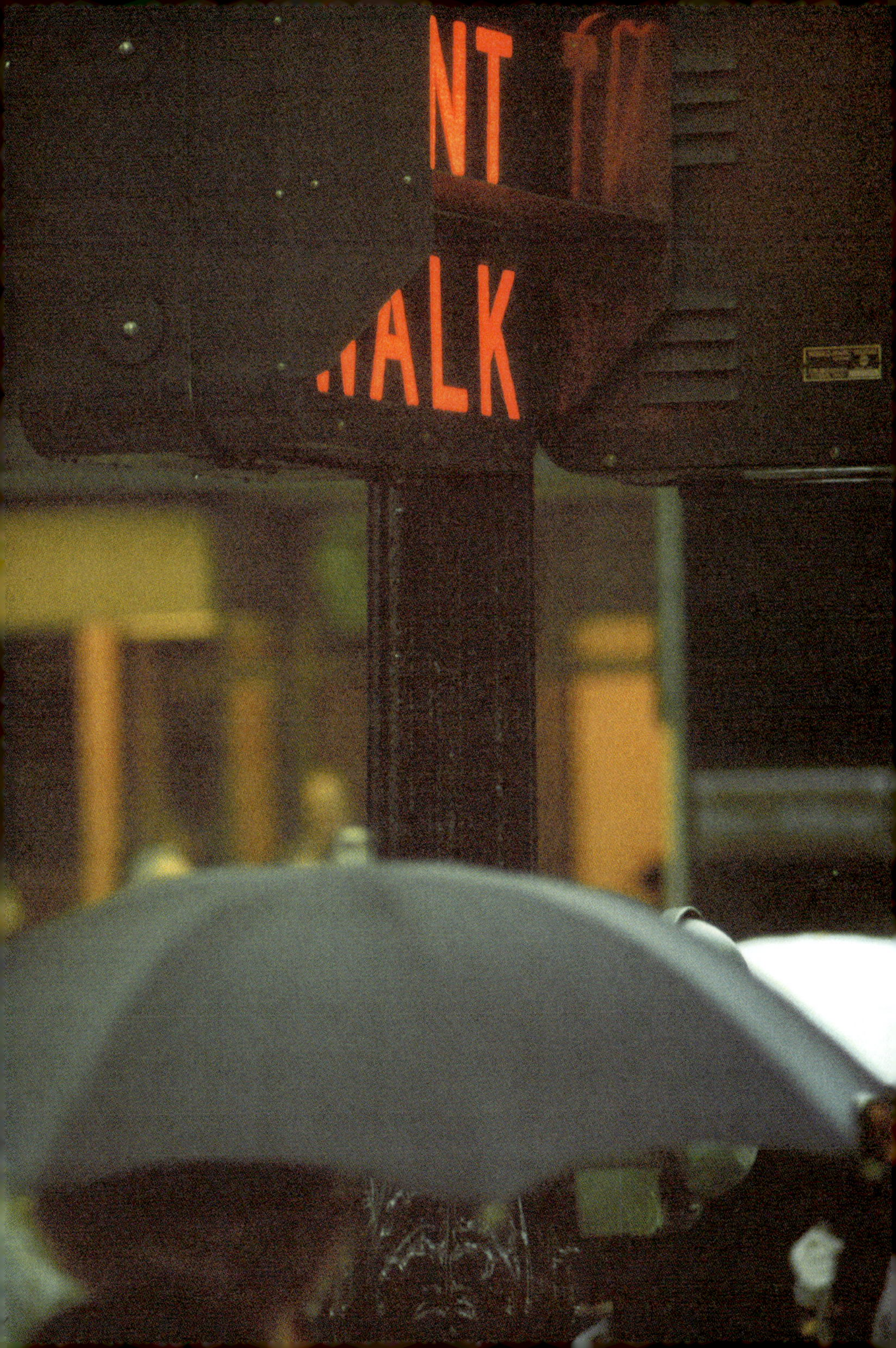
NT
HALK

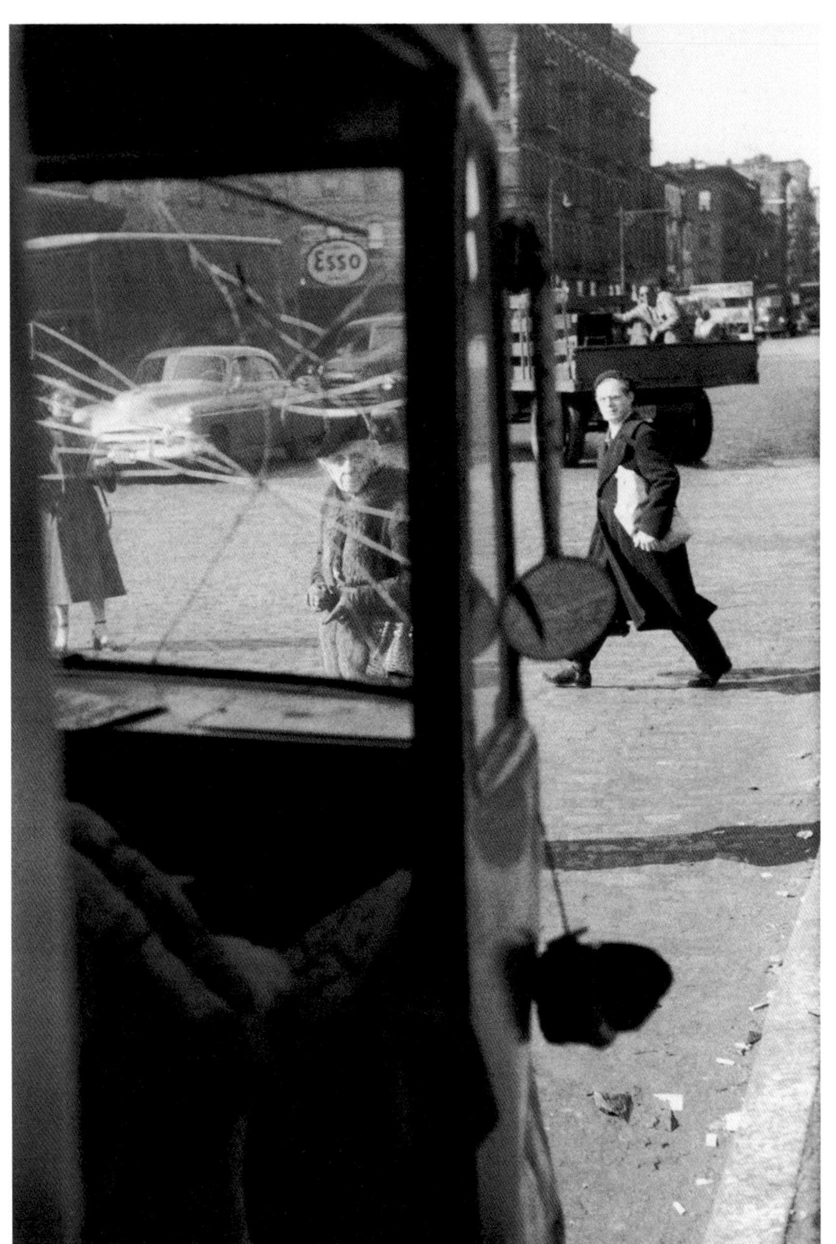

Cracked, c. 1948

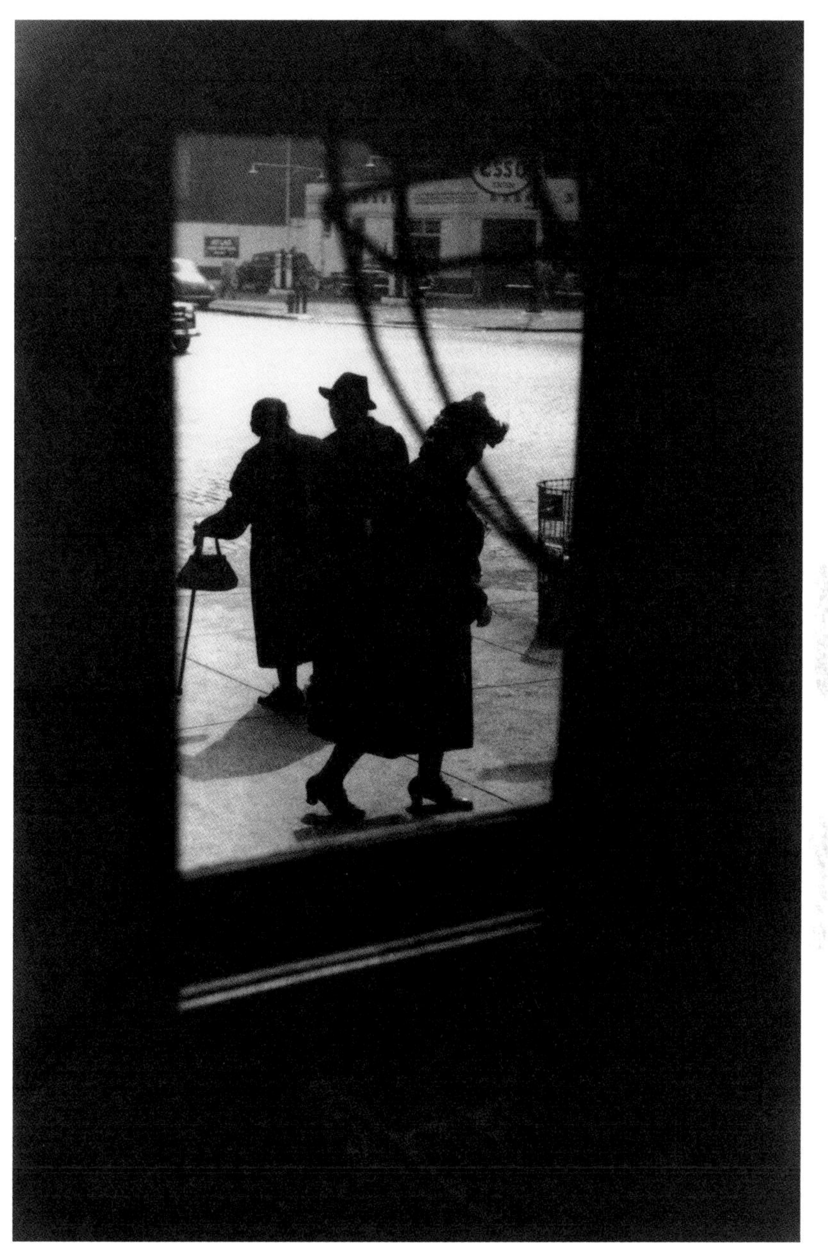

Three Ladies, c. 1948

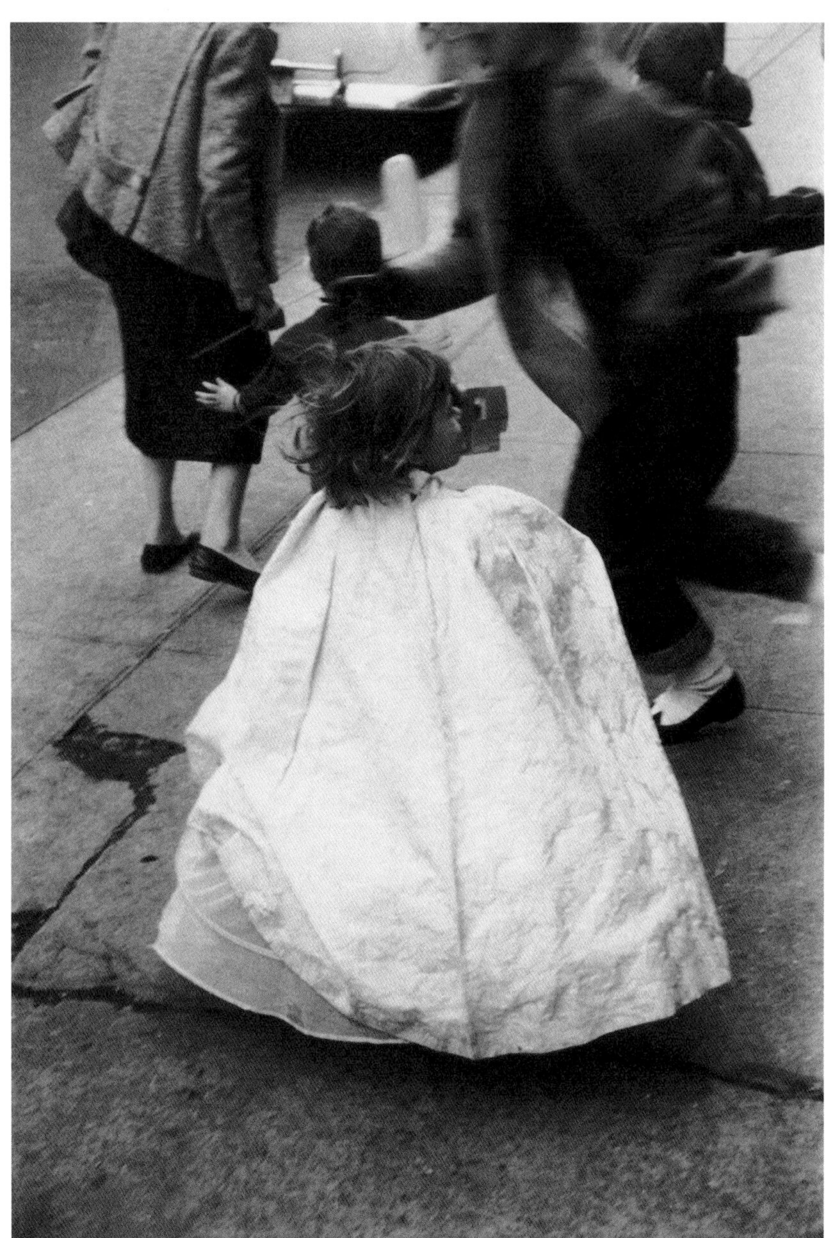

Rebecca, 1968

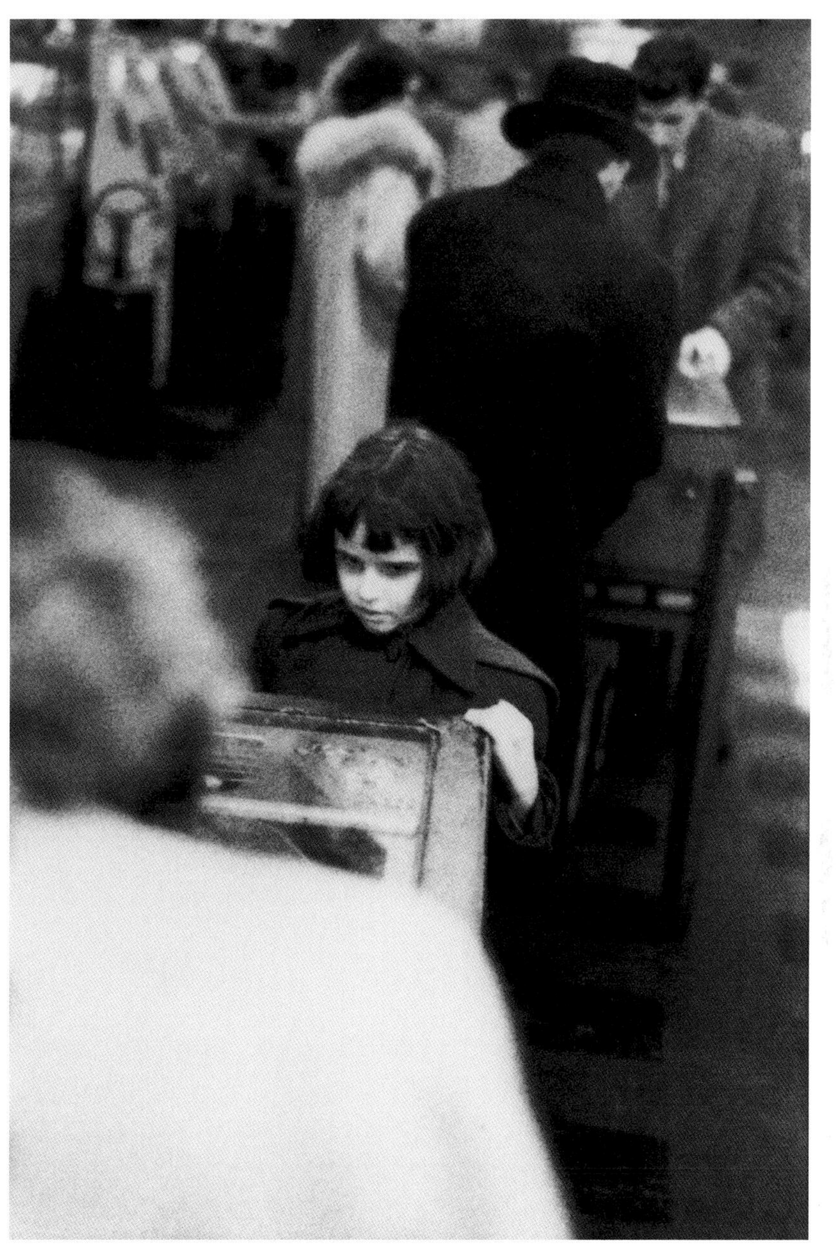

Pinball, c. 1950

A photographer's gift to the viewer is sometimes beauty in the overlooked ordinary.

Footprints, c. 1950

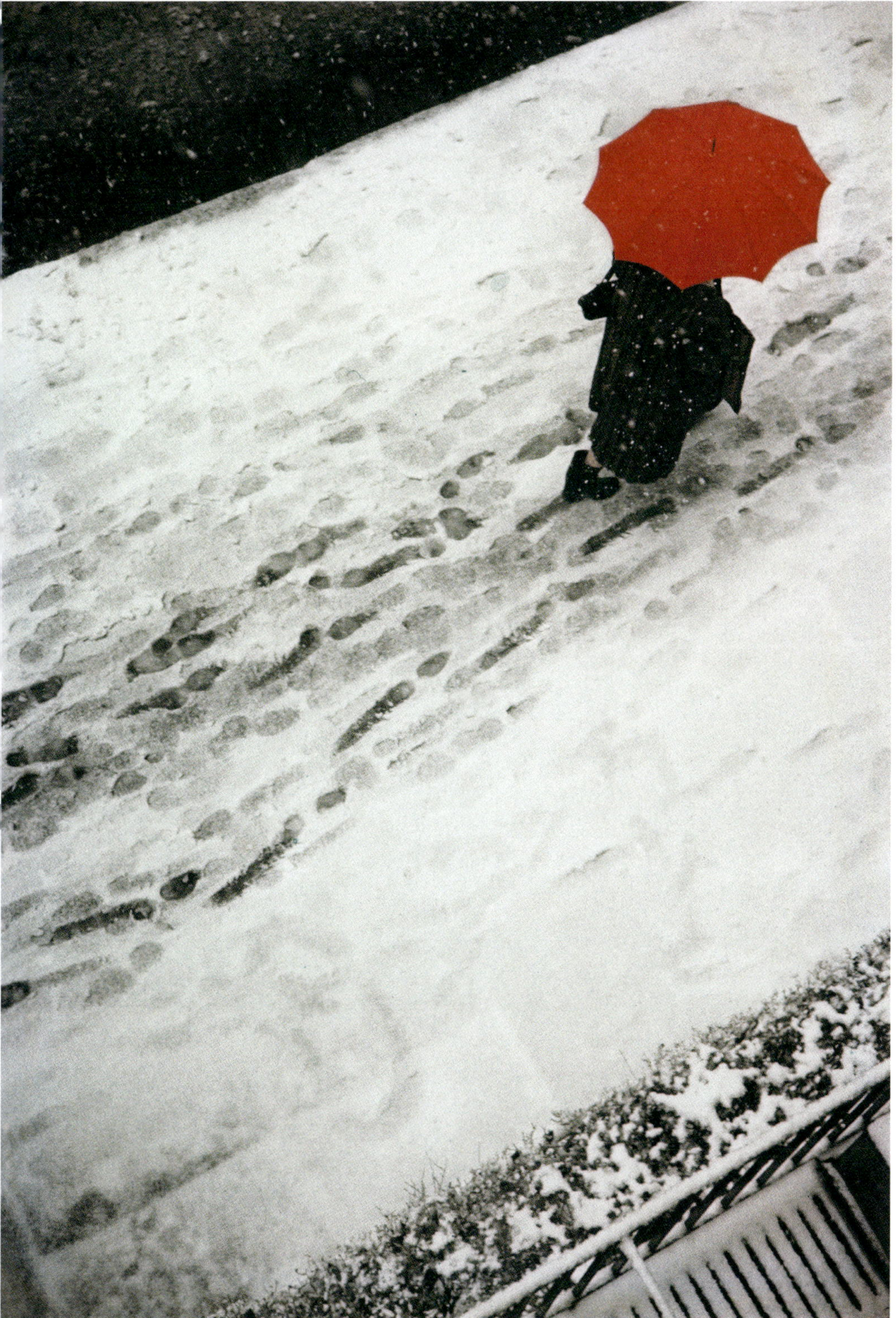

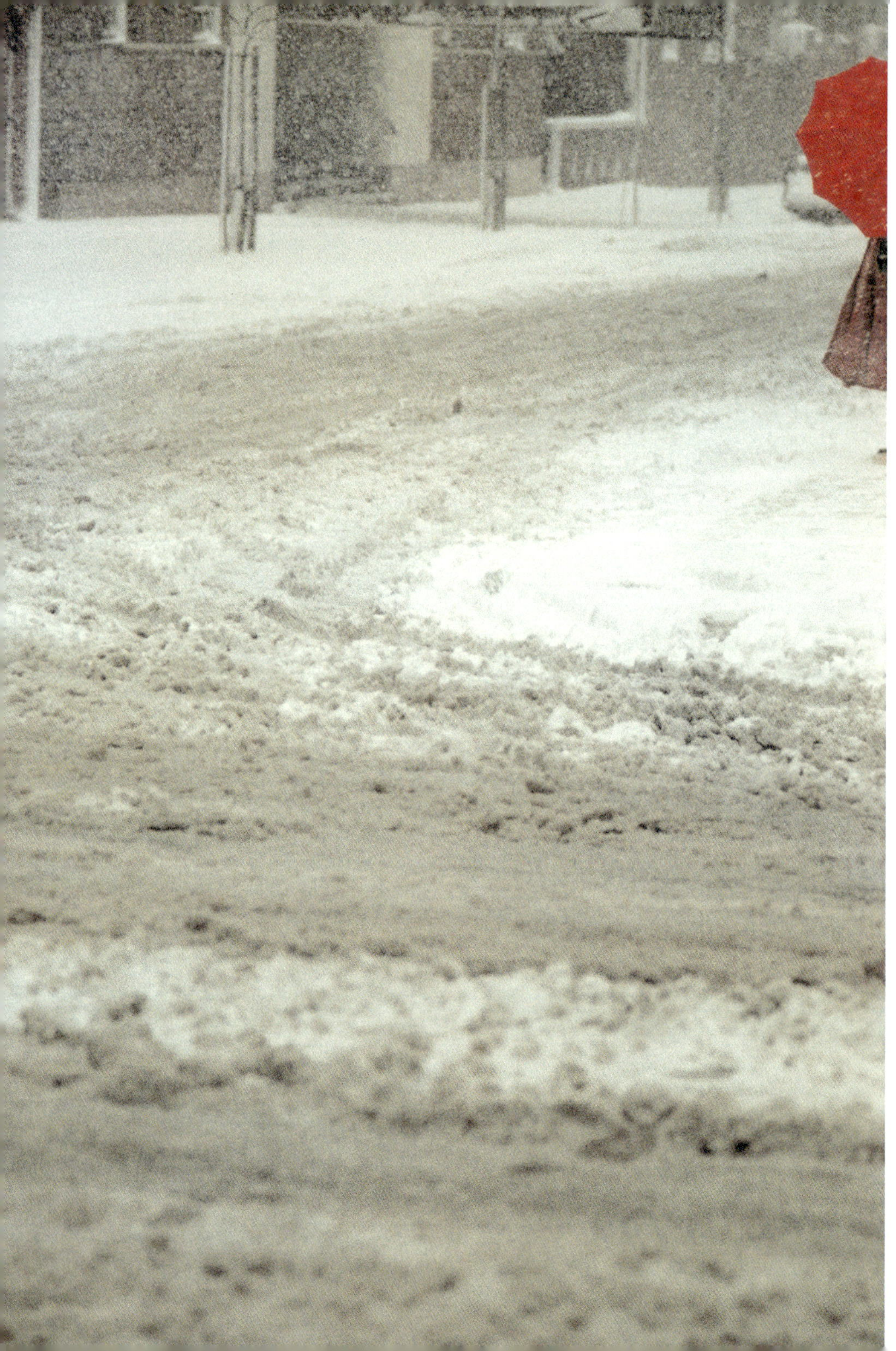

Red Umbrella, 1957

Green Light Against Grey, New York, c. 1950

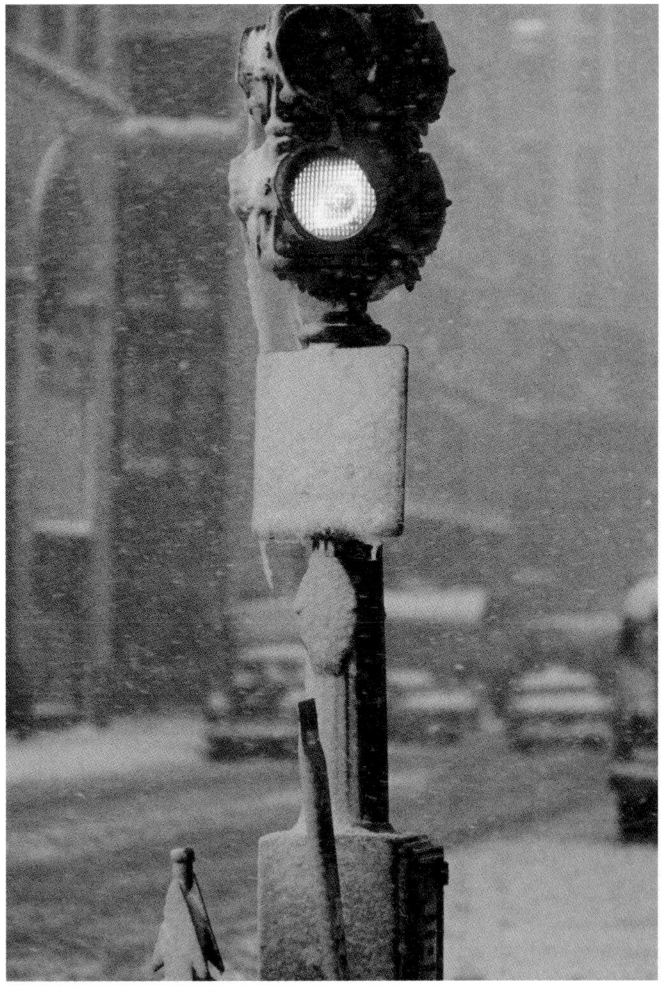

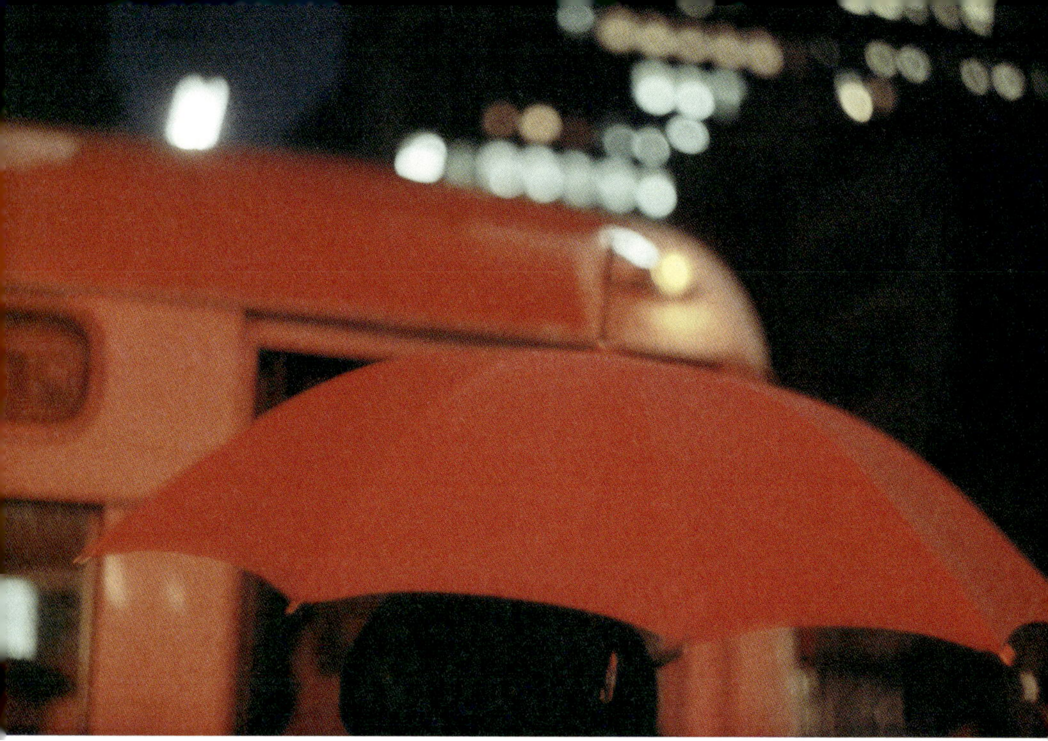

His lab assistant once remarked in boredom: "Not umbrellas again!"
to which Leiter simply replied: "I love umbrellas!"

Red Umbrella, 1951

Grey Umbrella, c. 1954

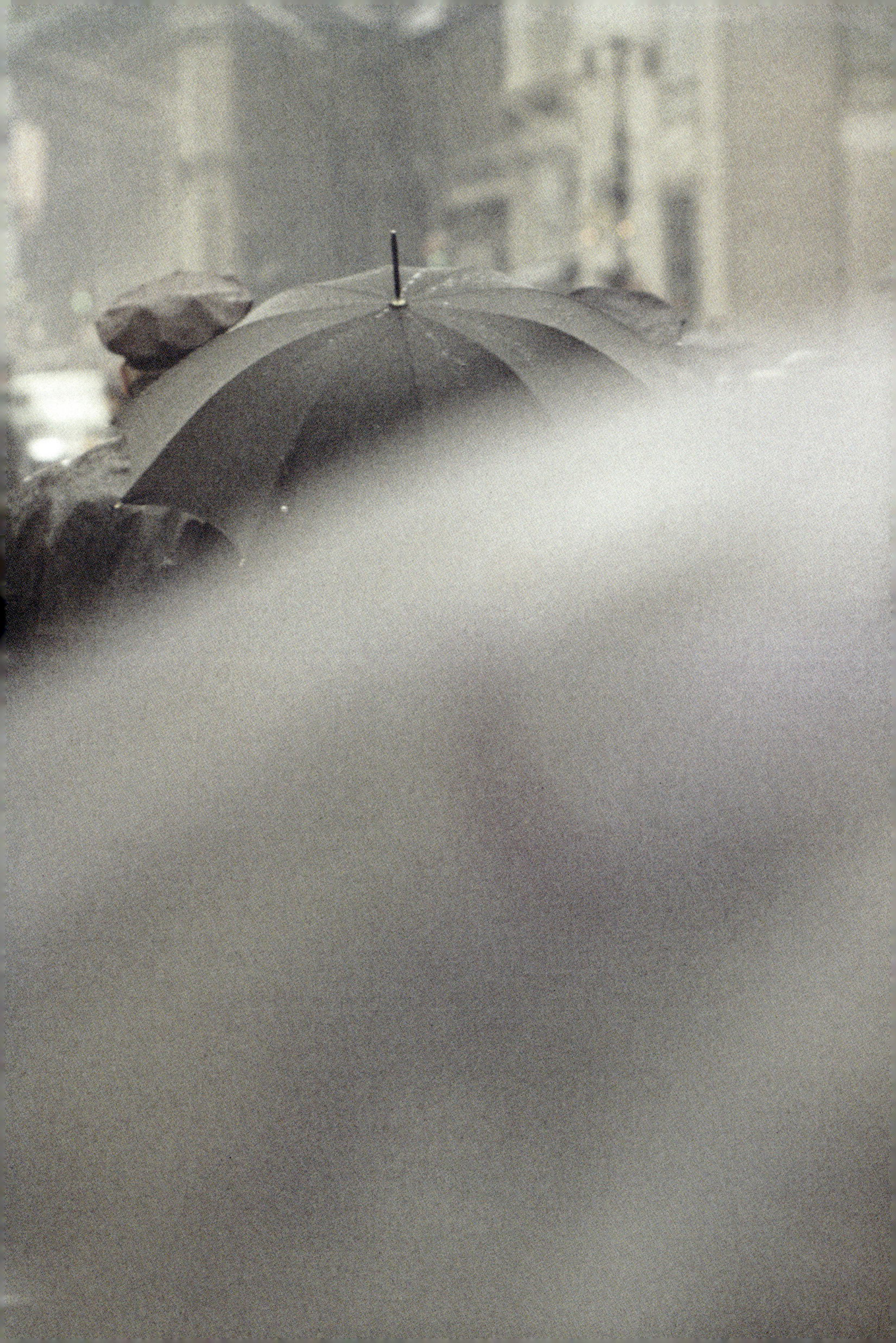

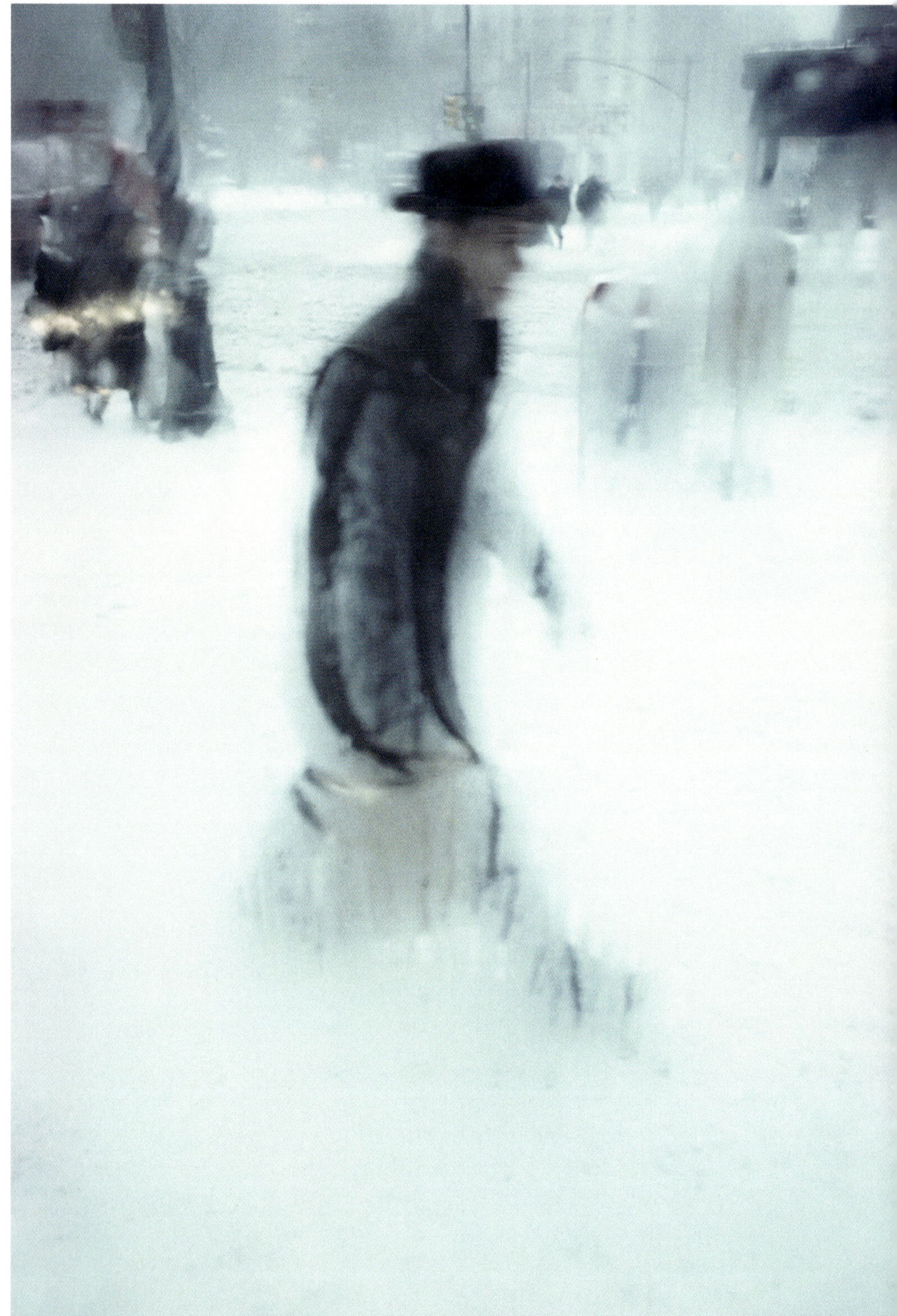

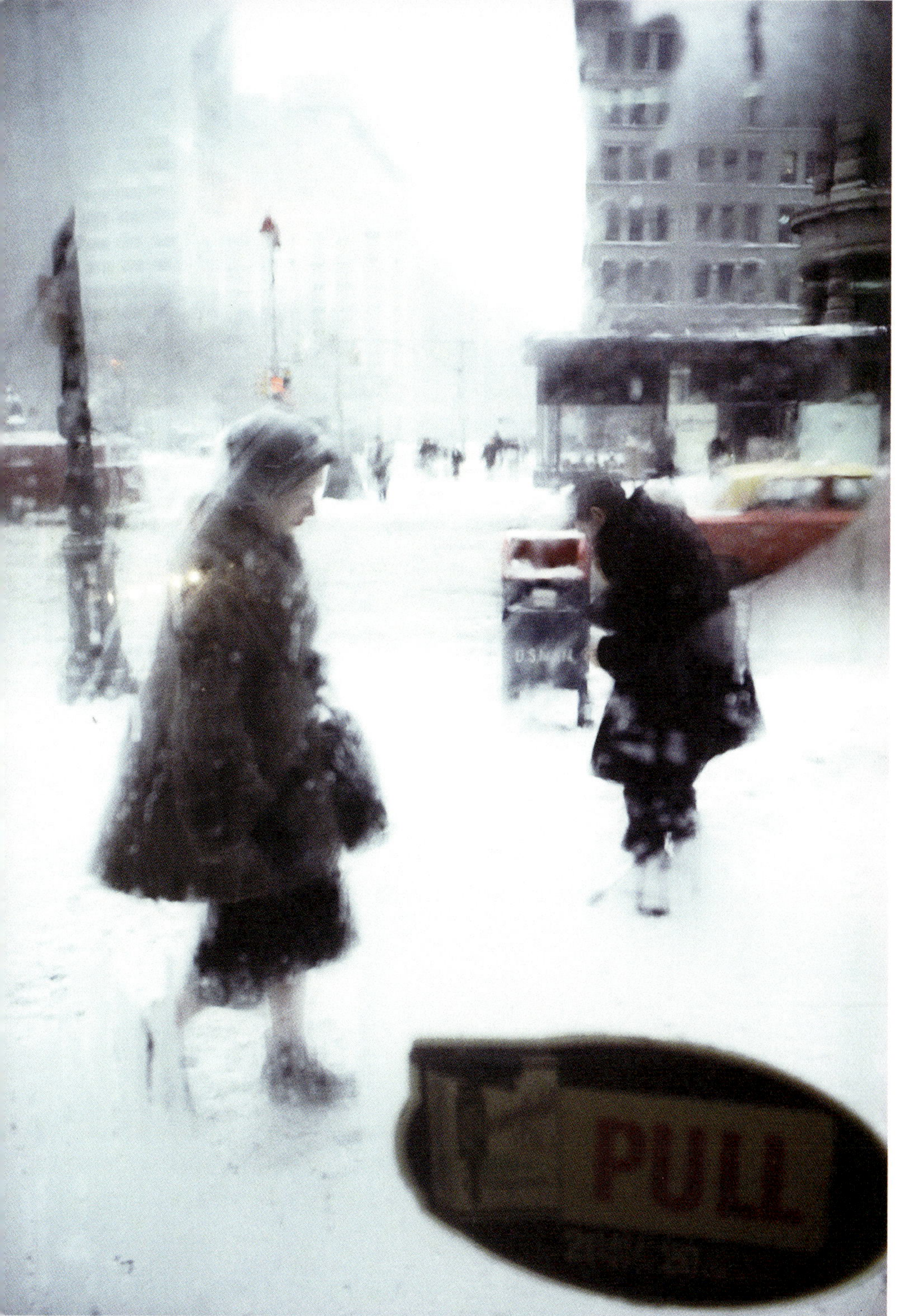
PULL

p. 110 Package, c. 1960
p. 111 Pull, c. 1960

pp. 114–115 Red Umbrella, c. 1955

L&L Dairy, c. 1949

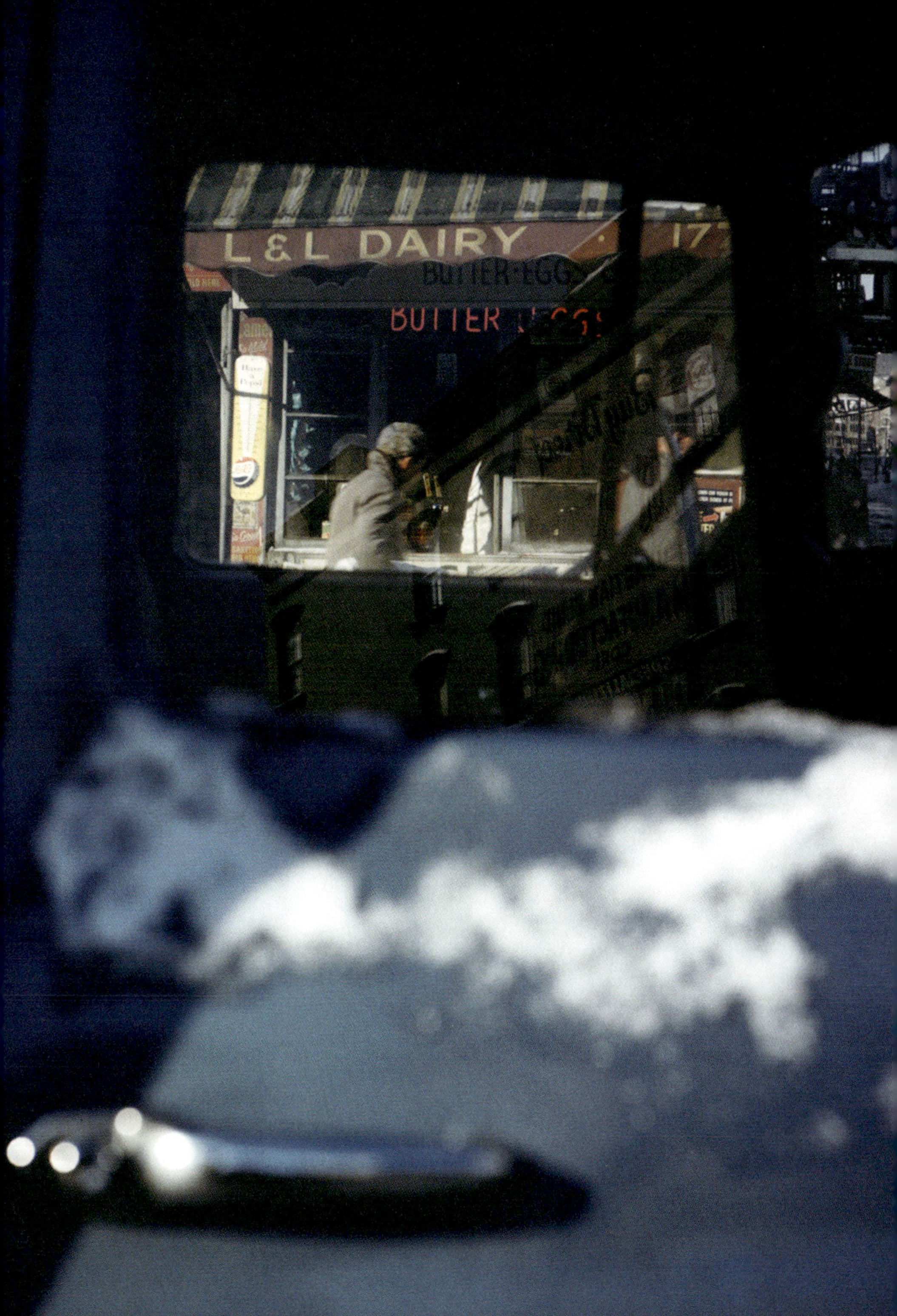
L & L DAIRY
BUTTER·EGG
BUTTER EGGS
Pepsi

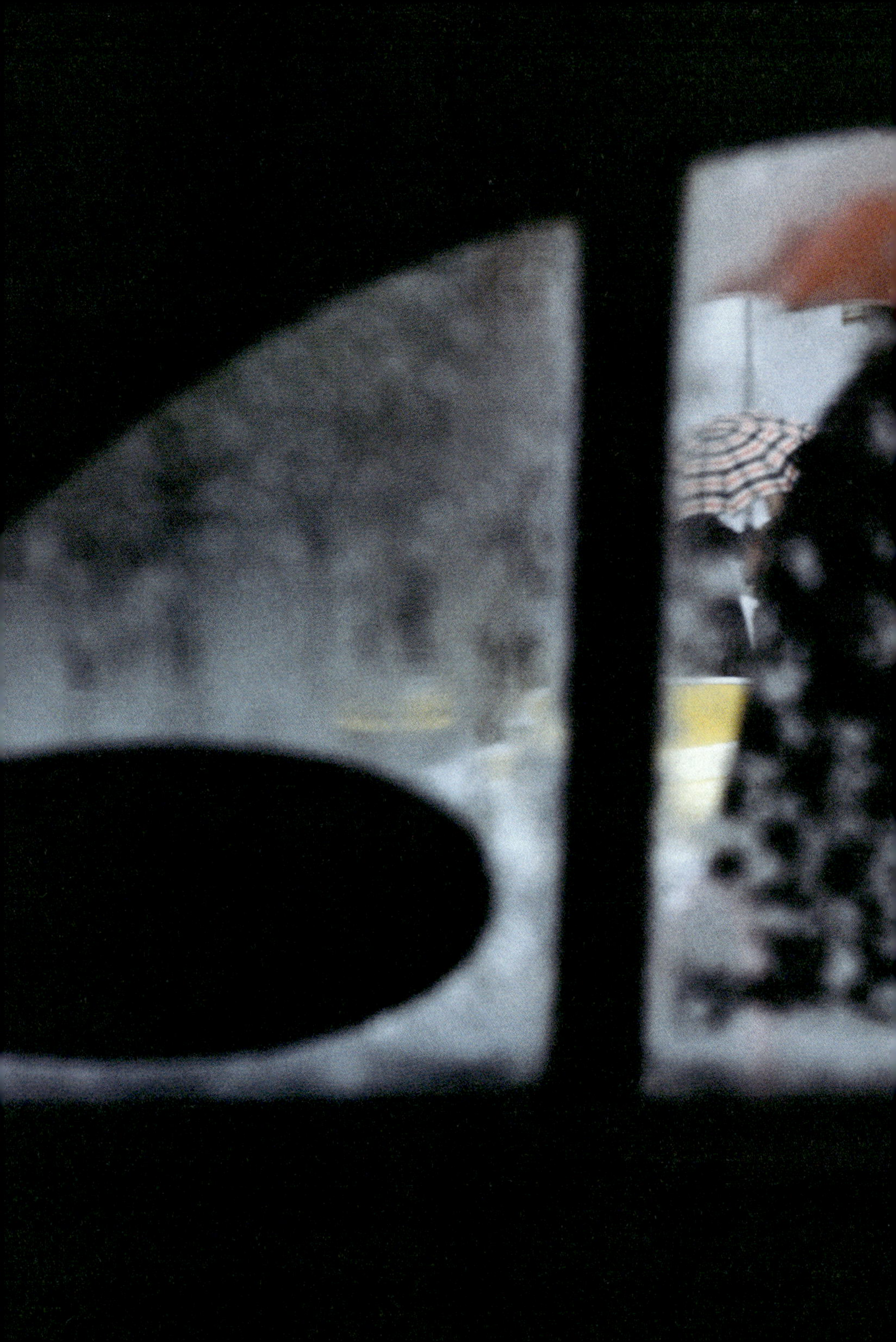

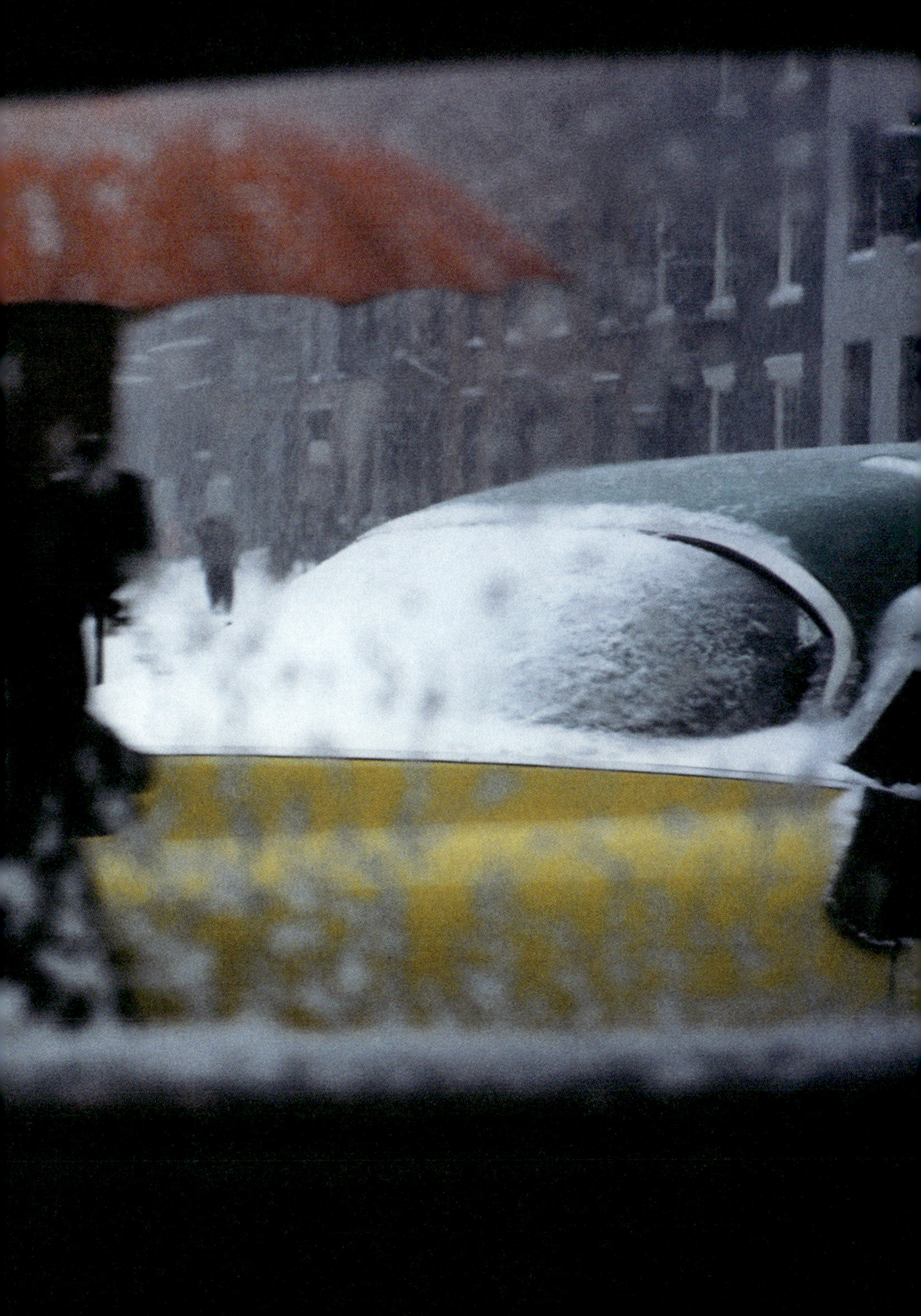

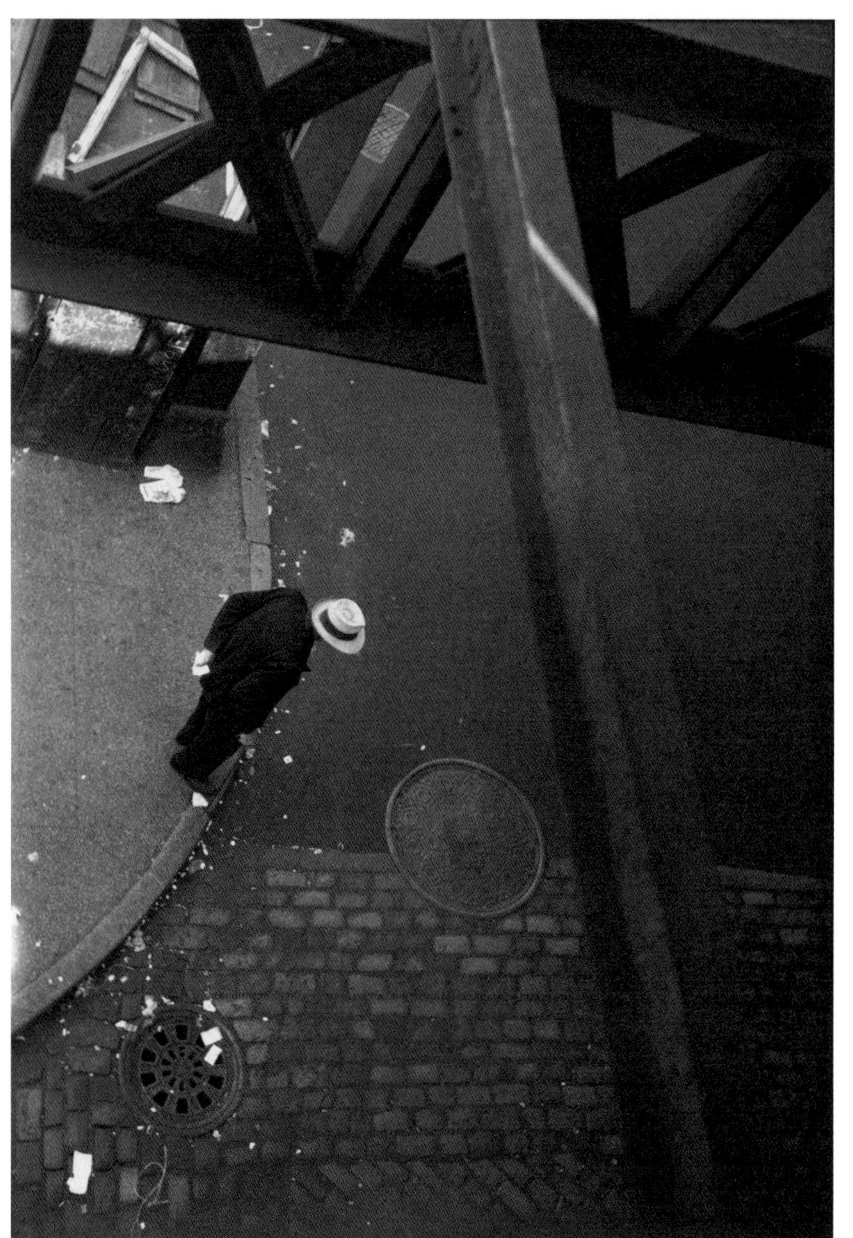

From the El, c. 1955

Rain, 1950s
Untitled, 1950s

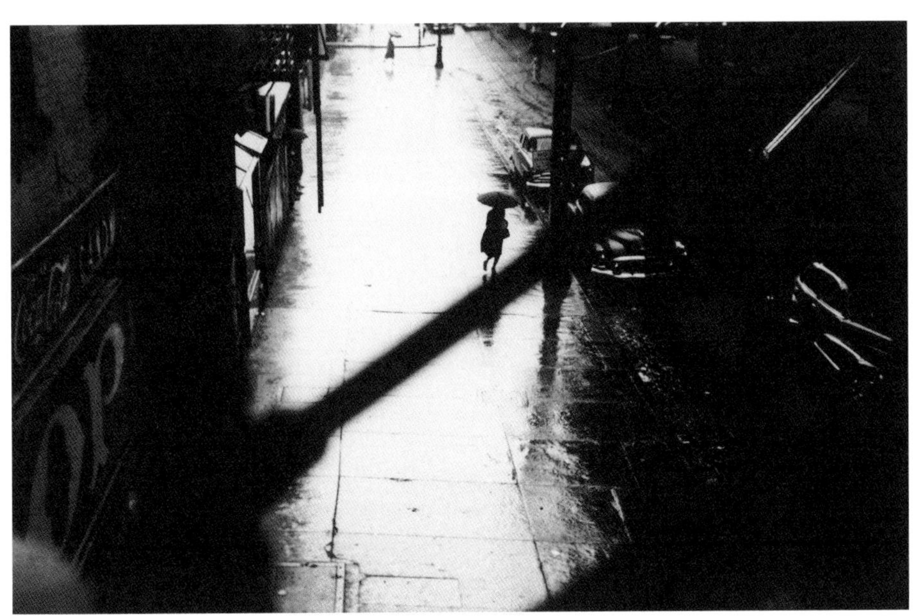

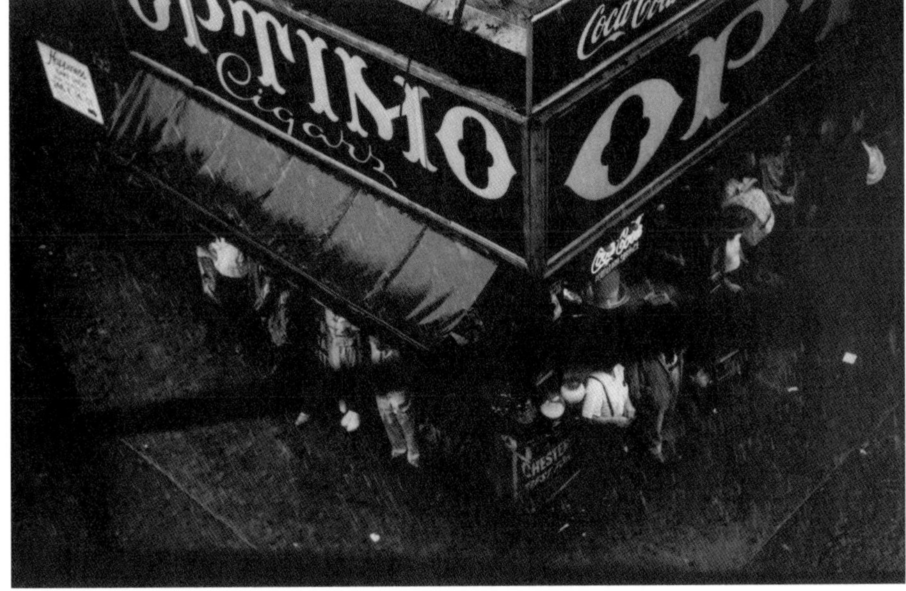
OPTIMO
Coca-Cola
OP
CHESTER

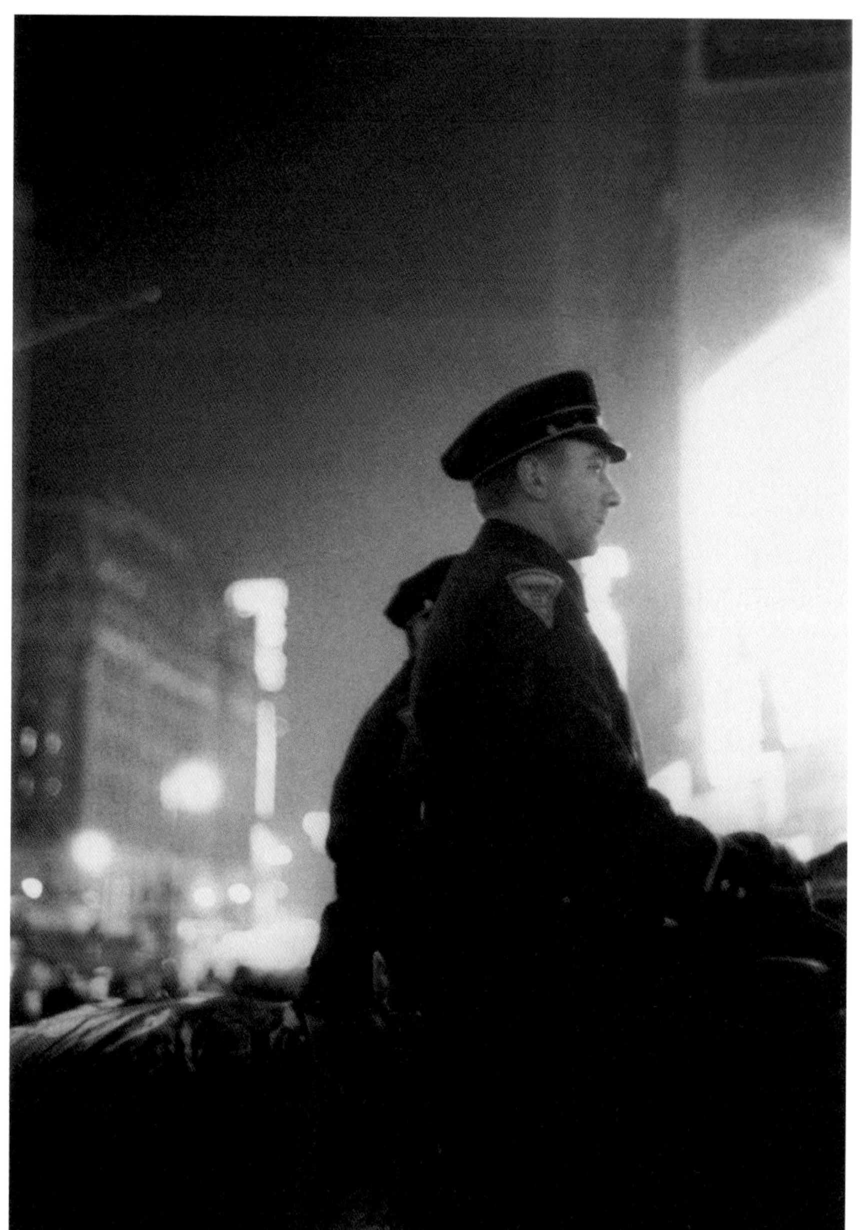

New Year's Eve, 1952–53   Freckles, c. 1958

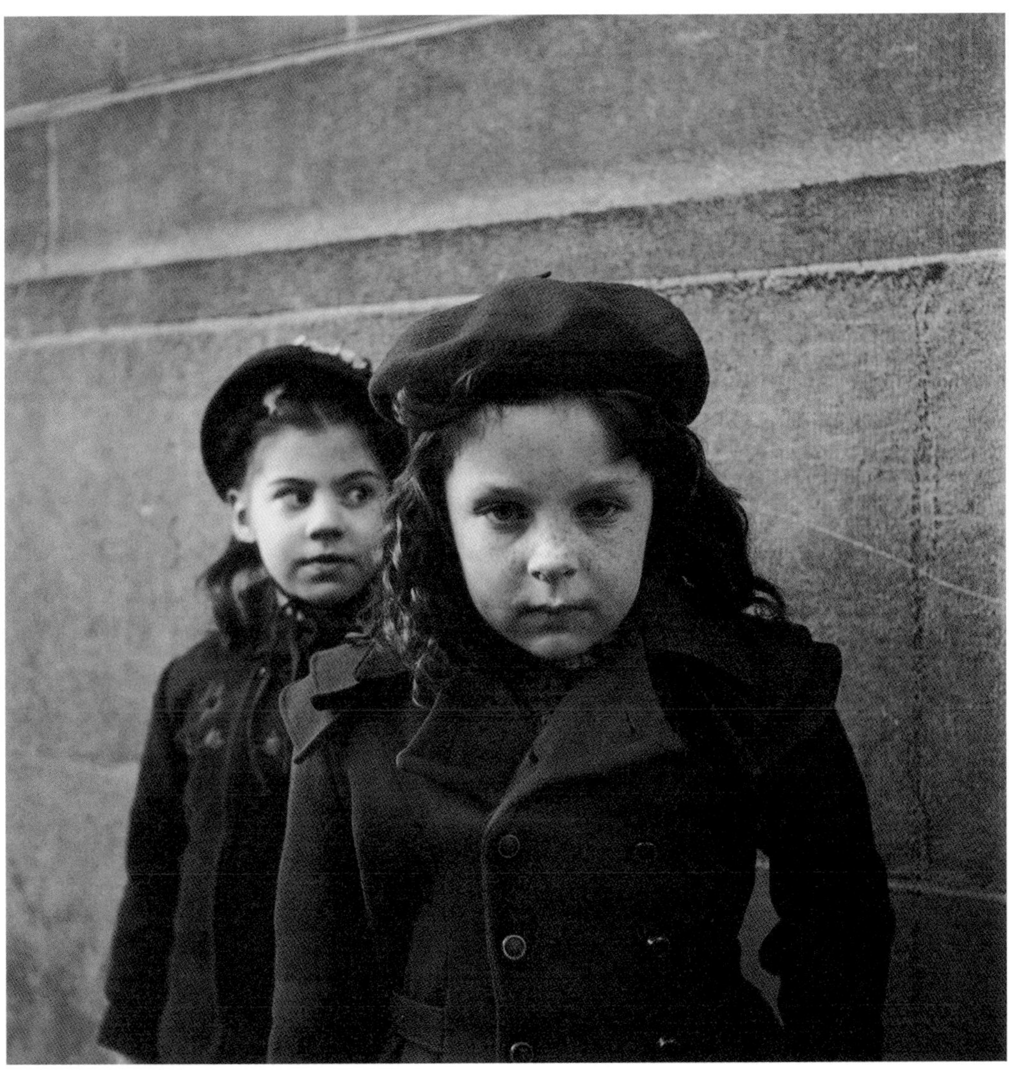

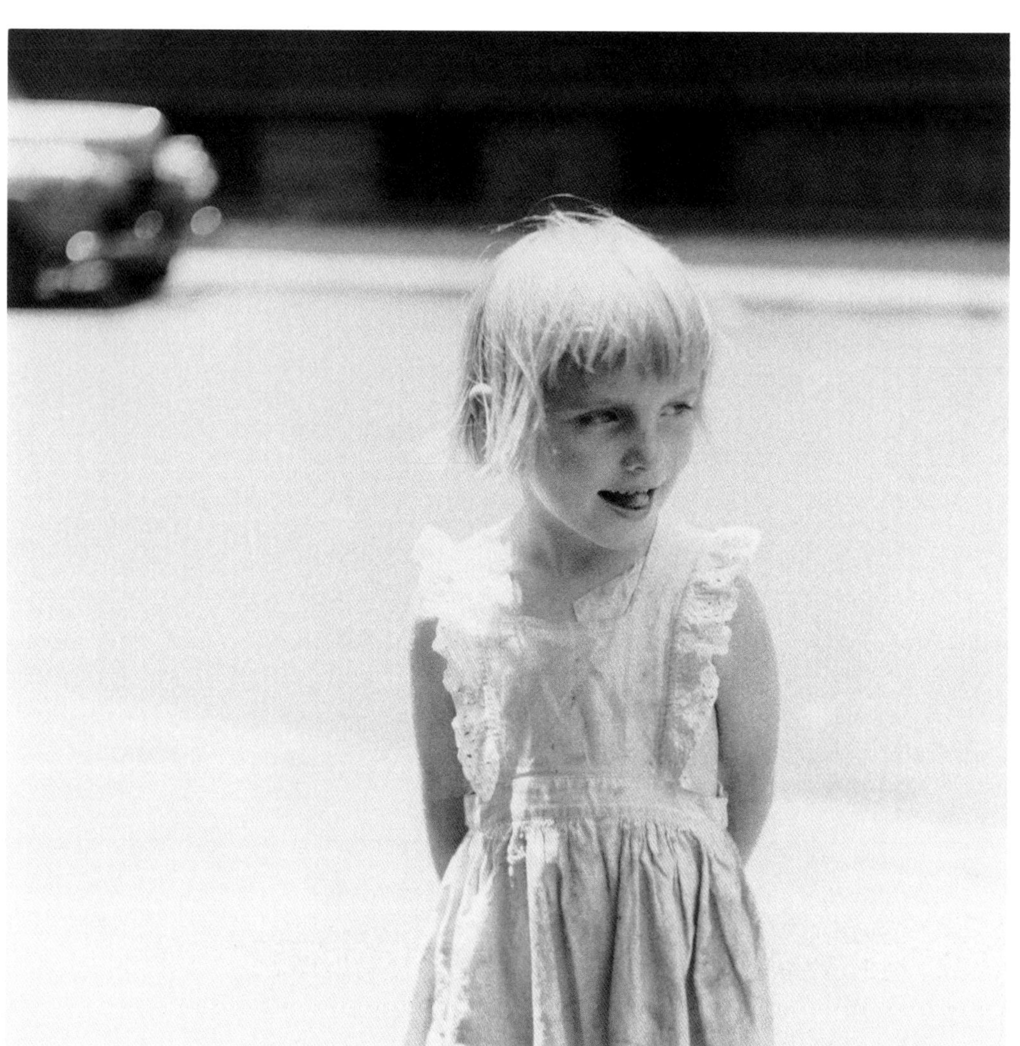

    Untitled, c. 1950   Shoes of the Shoeshine Man, c. 1951

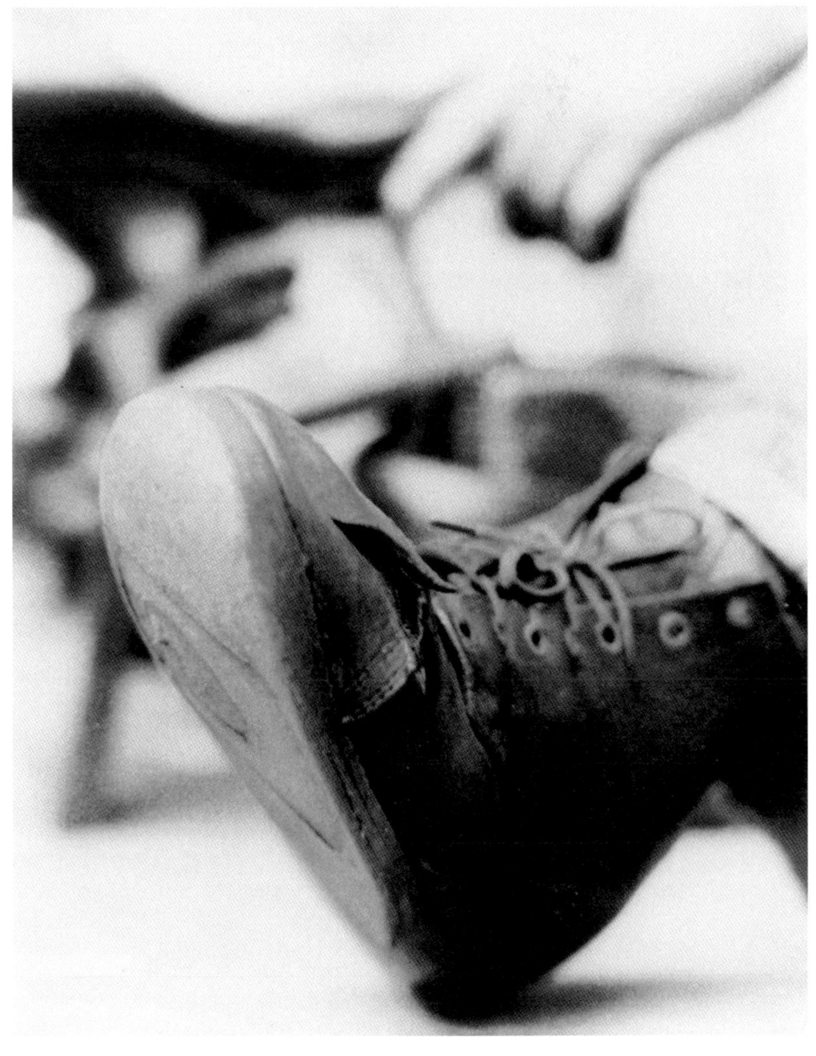

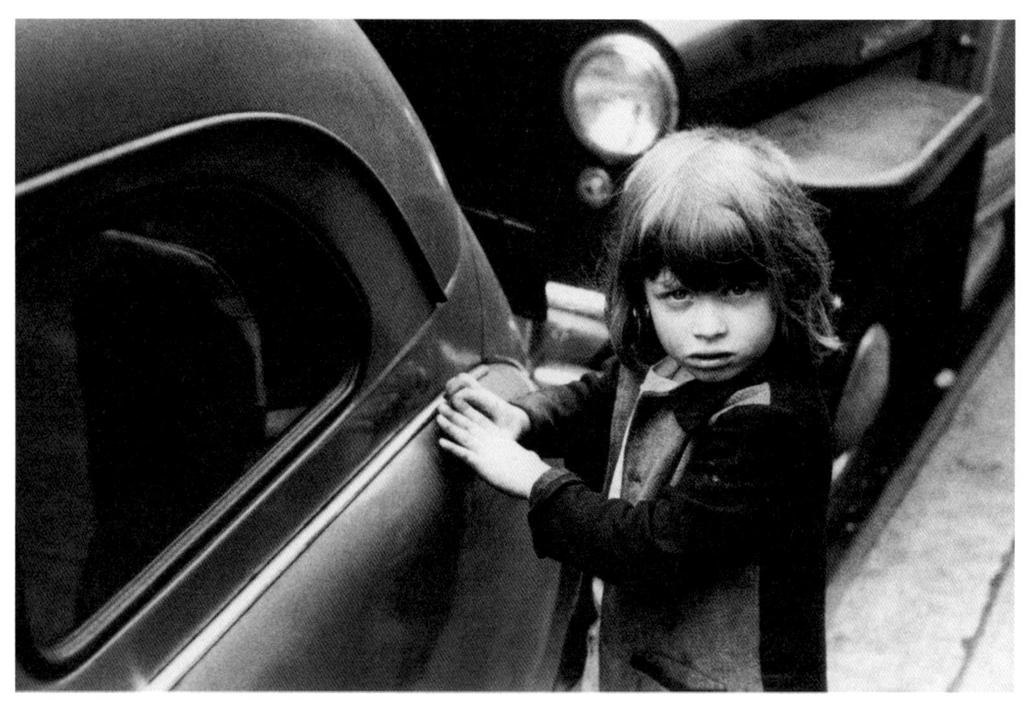

Children seemed to like me and I got along with them—not all of them—and I enjoyed it a lot.

Girl, c. 1953

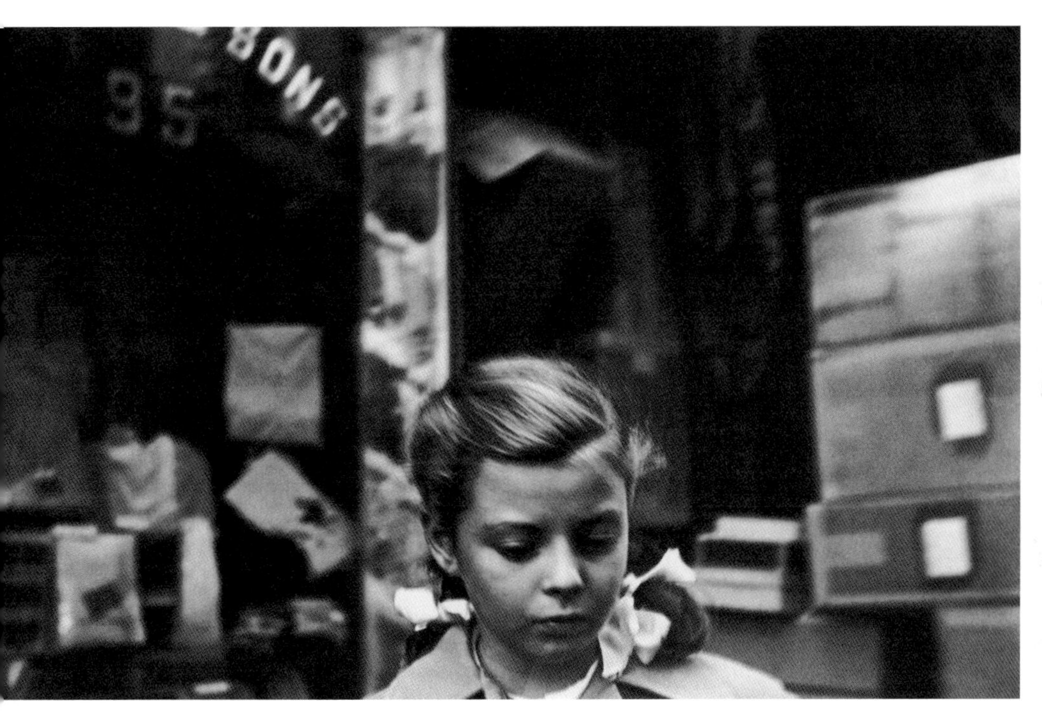

Ribbons, c. 1962

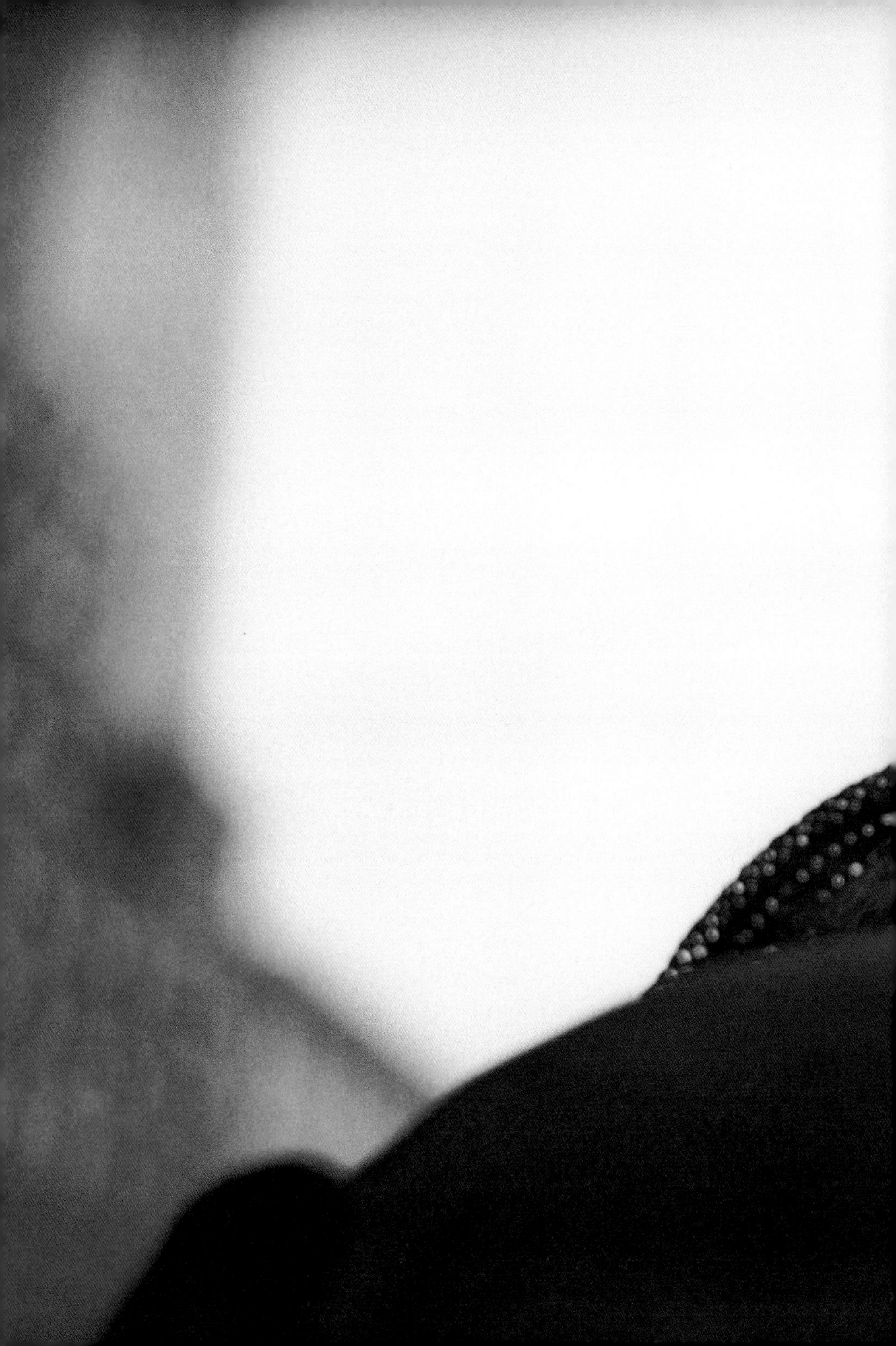

pp. 124–125 Back, c. 1948

Postmen, 1952

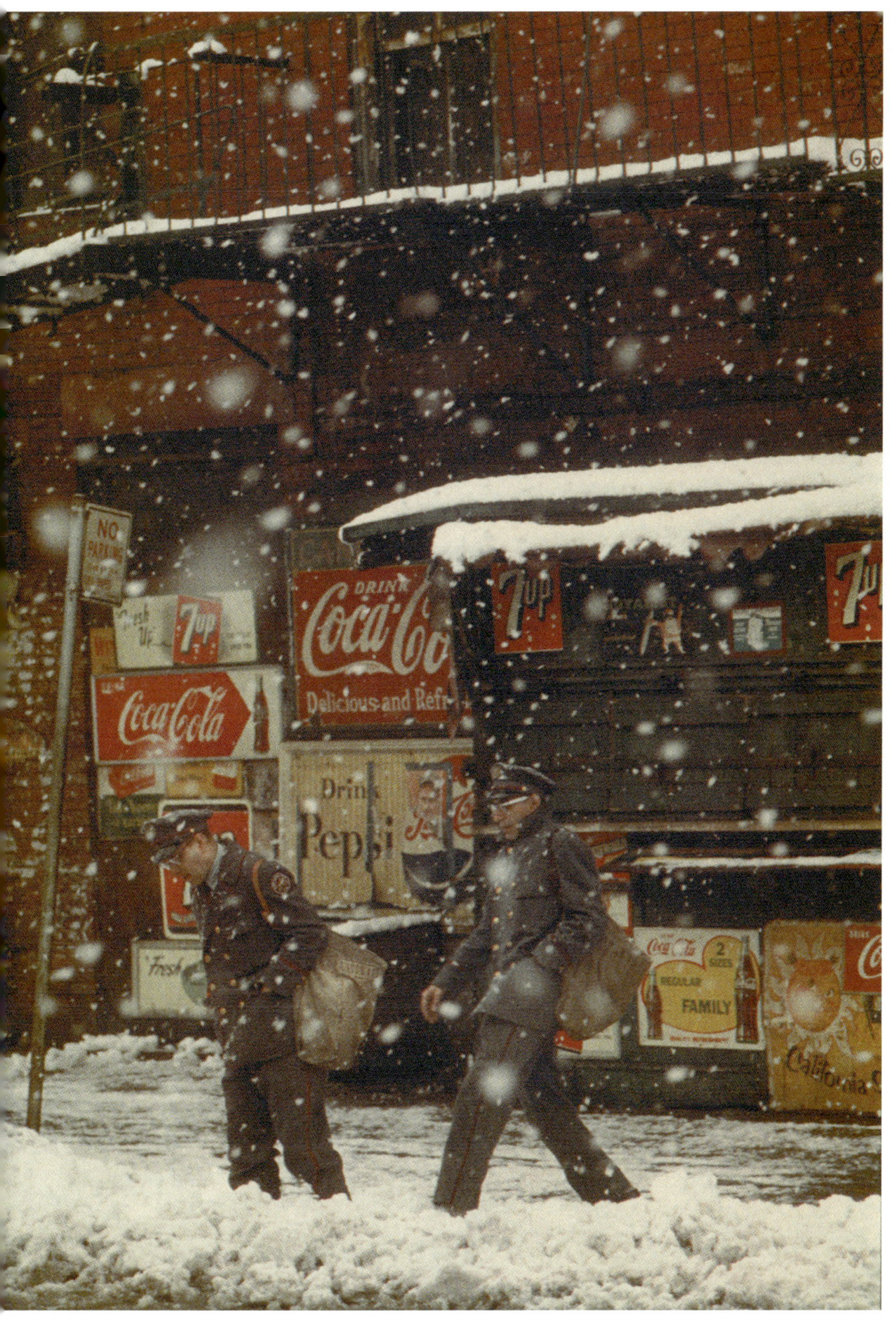

NO PARKING
Fresh Up 7up
DRINK
Coca-Cola
Delicious and Refr
Coca-Cola
Drink
Pepsi
7up
7up
Fresh
Coca-Cola
2 SIZES
REGULAR
FAMILY
California

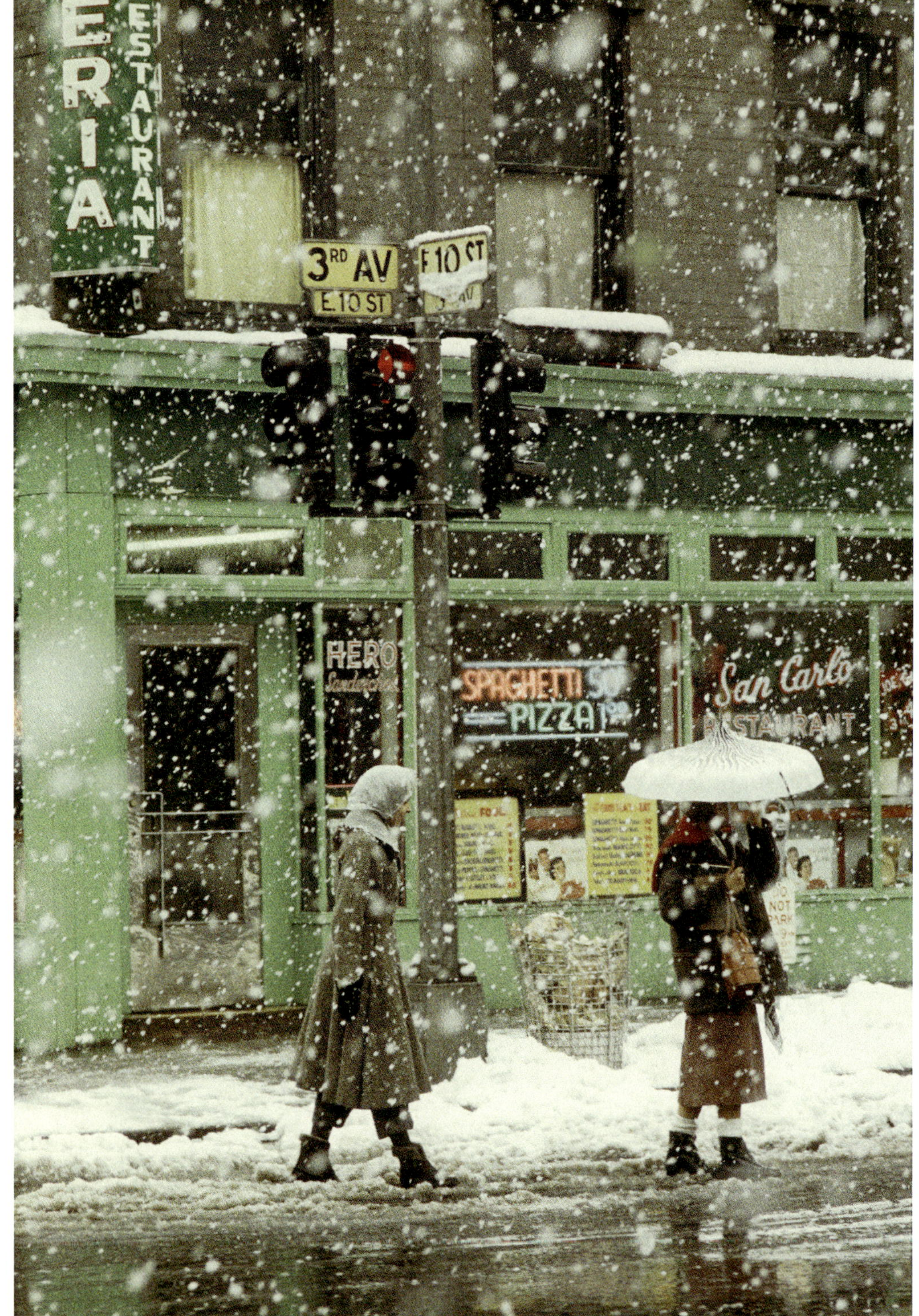
ERIA
RESTAURANT
3RD AV
E 10 ST
E 10 ST
3 AV
HERO
Sandwiches
SPAGHETTI 90
PIZZA 1.00
San Carlo
RESTAURANT
DO
NOT
PARK

I like it when one is not certain of what one sees.
When we do not know why we are looking at it,
all of a sudden we discover something that we start seeing.
I like this confusion.

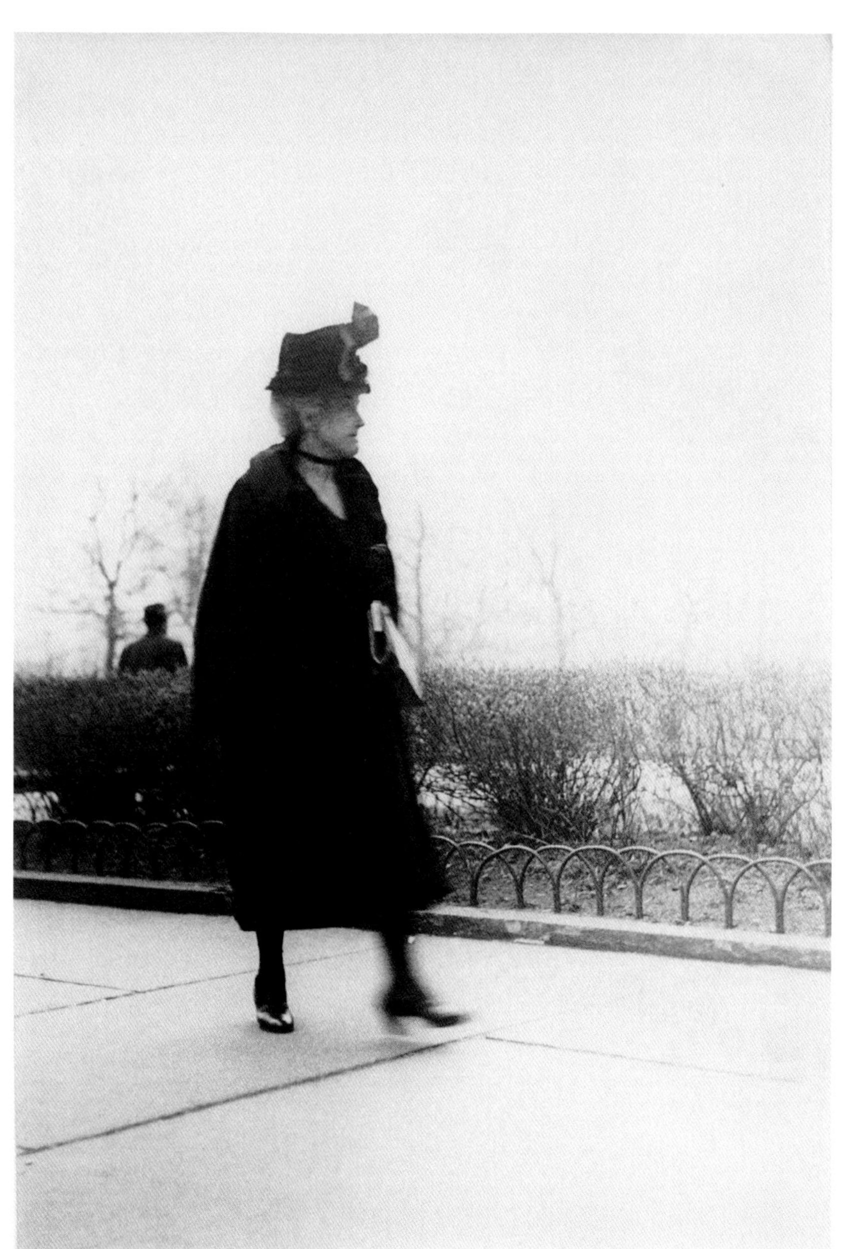

Foot, c. 1948

Halloween, c. 1952
Dick and Adele, 1947

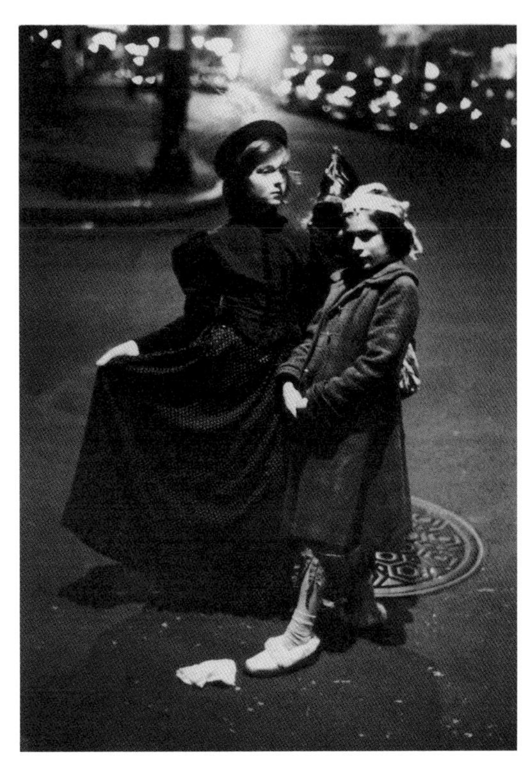

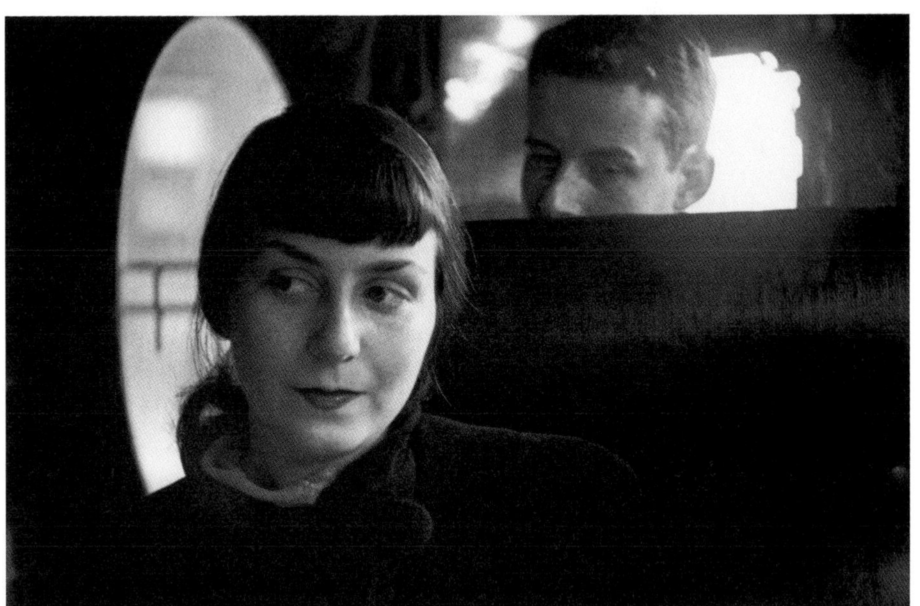

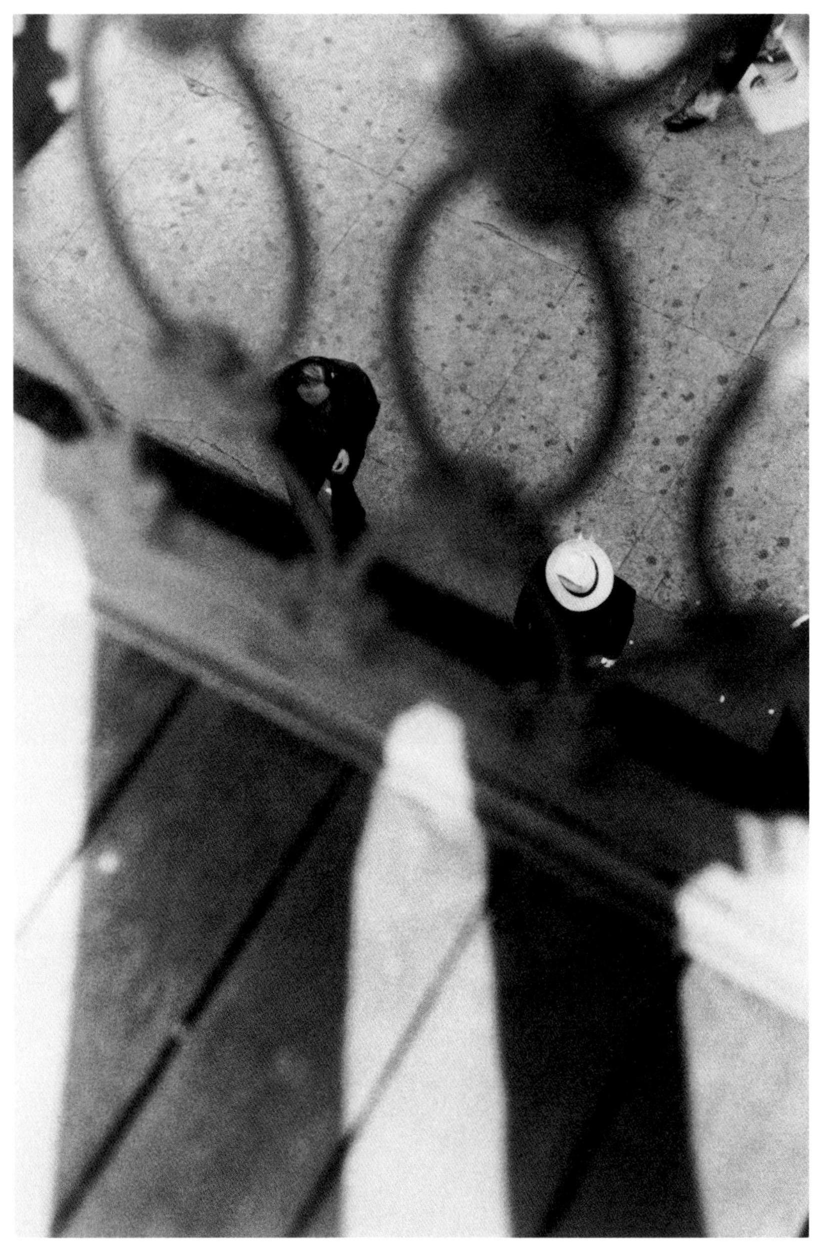

From the El with Bob Weaver, c. 1955

Boy, c. 1960
Accident, c. 1955

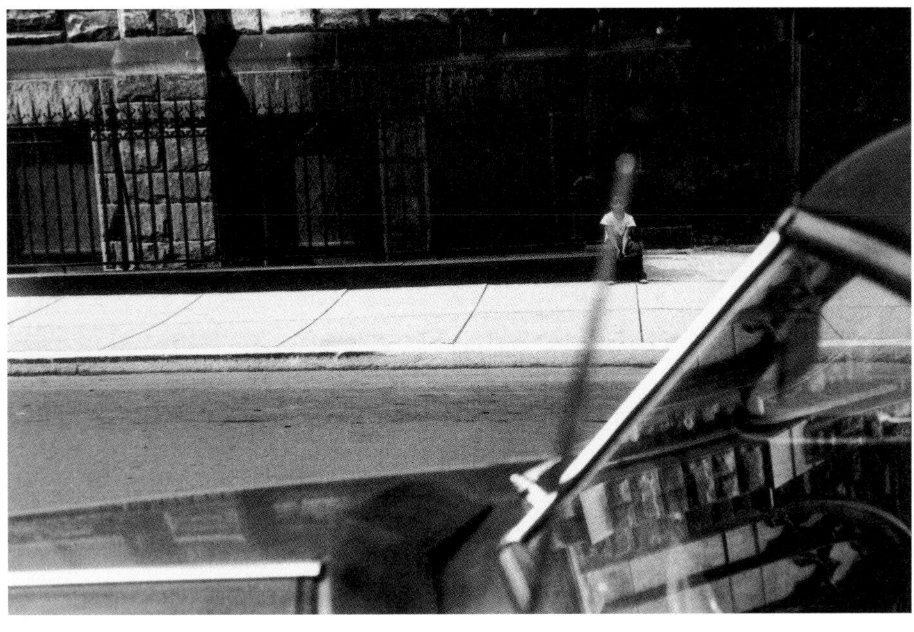

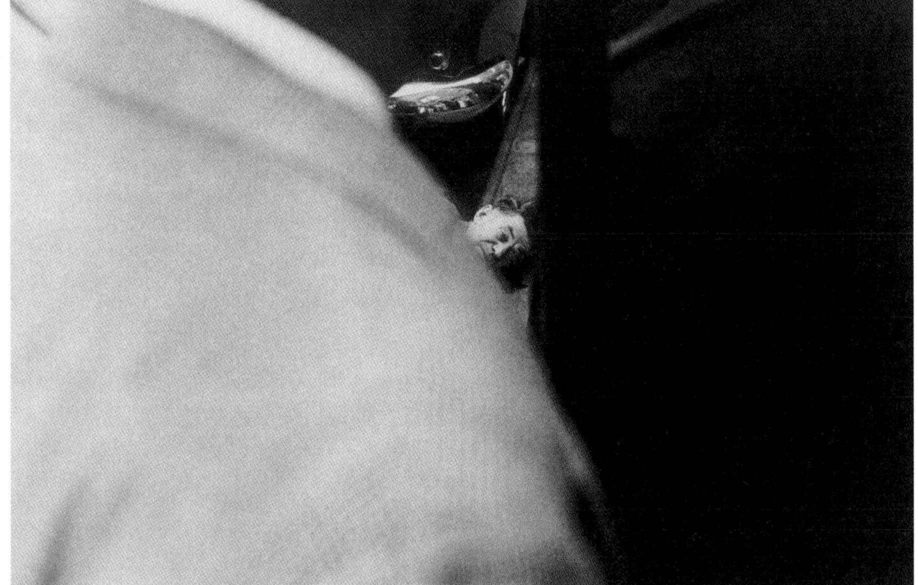

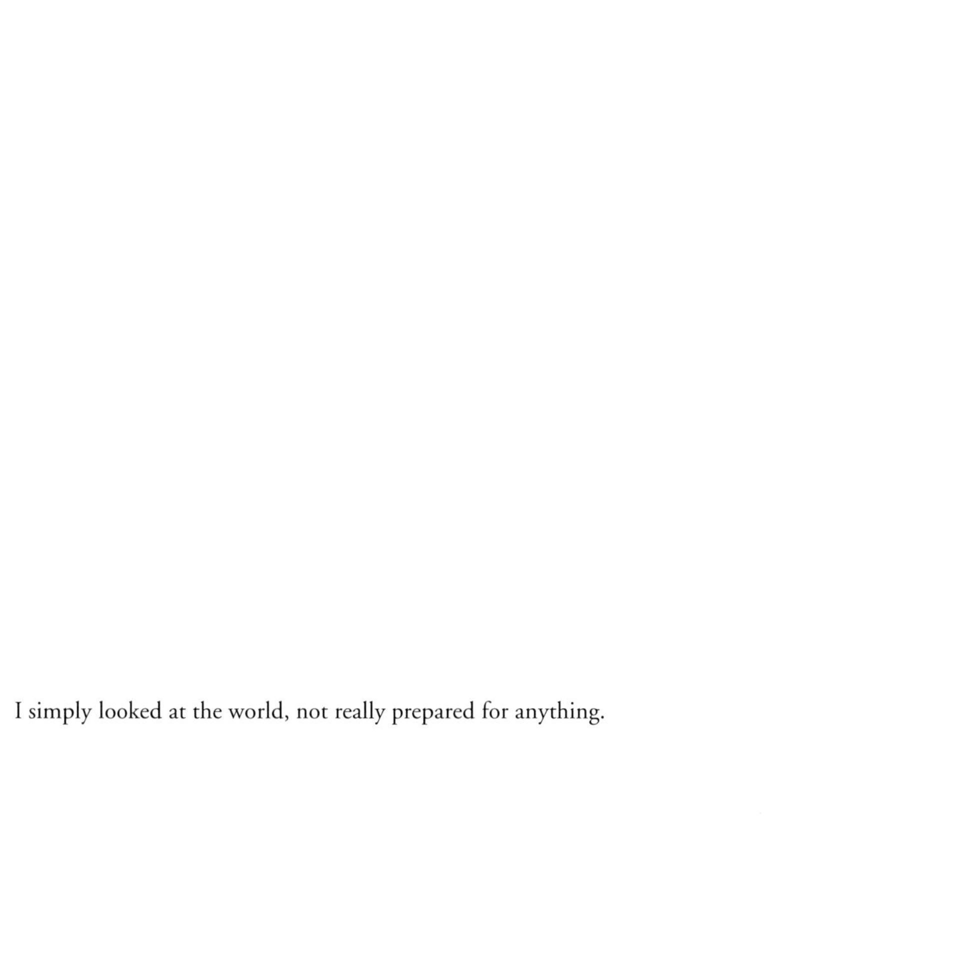

I simply looked at the world, not really prepared for anything.

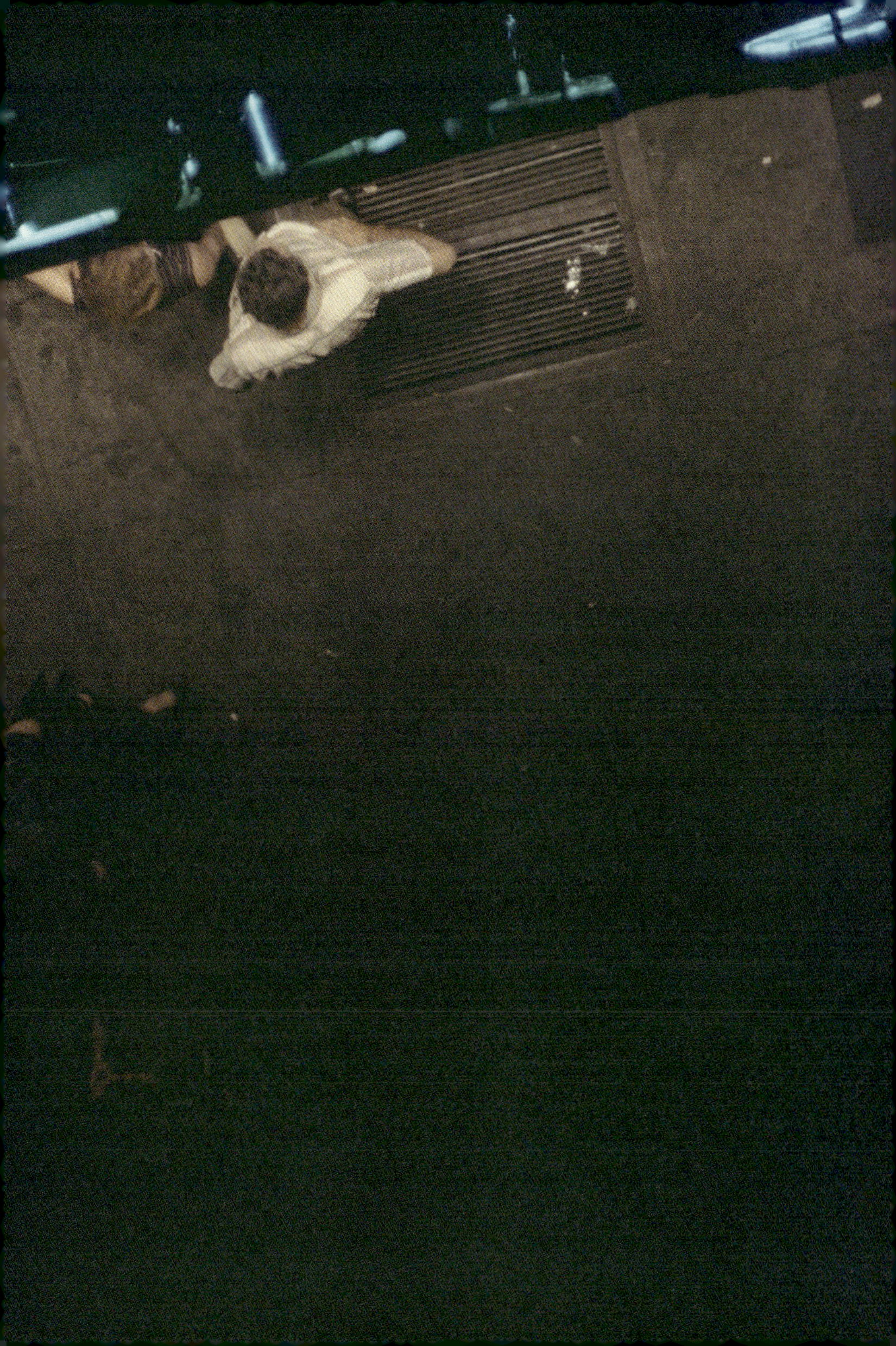

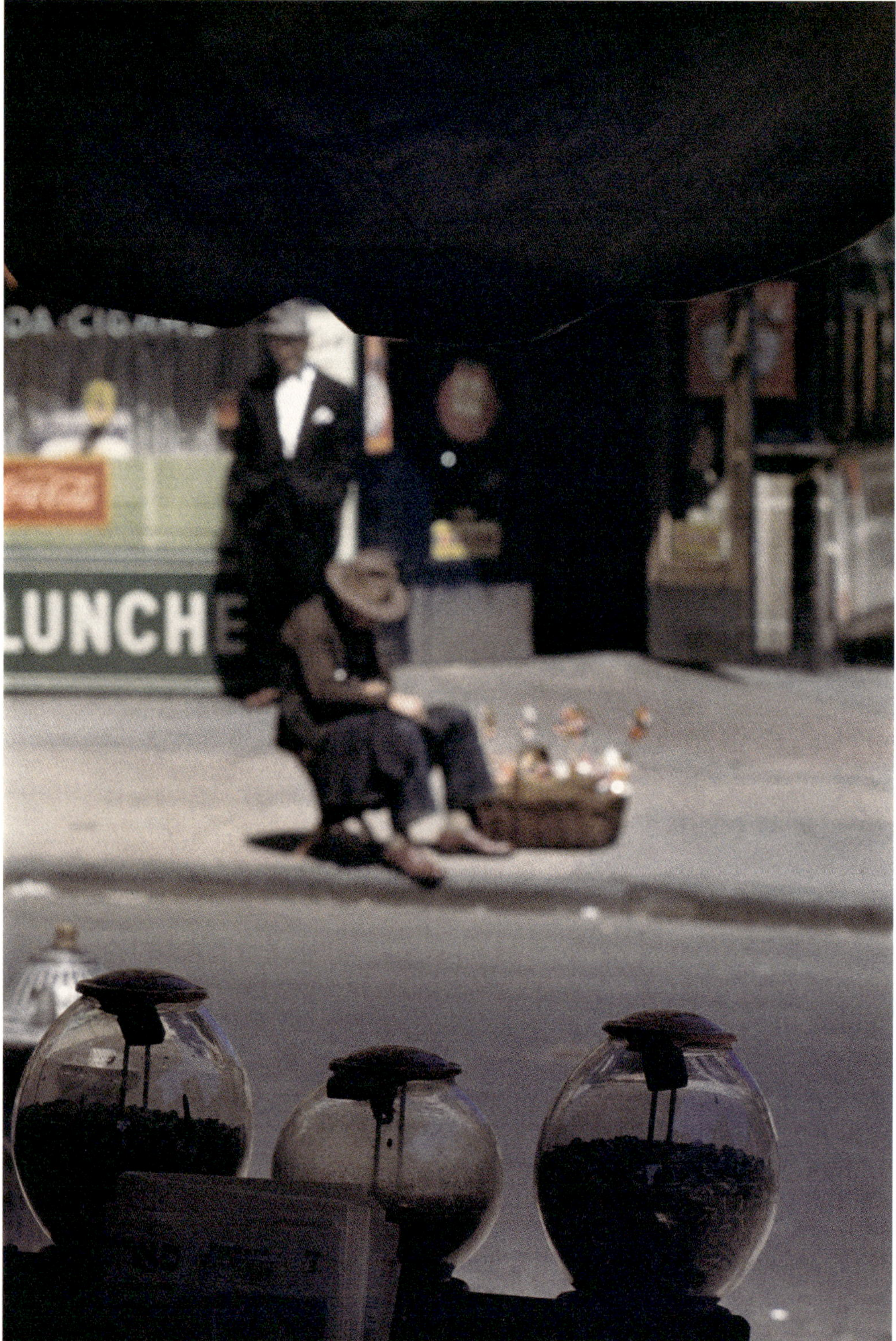

CIGAR
Coca-Cola
LUNCHE

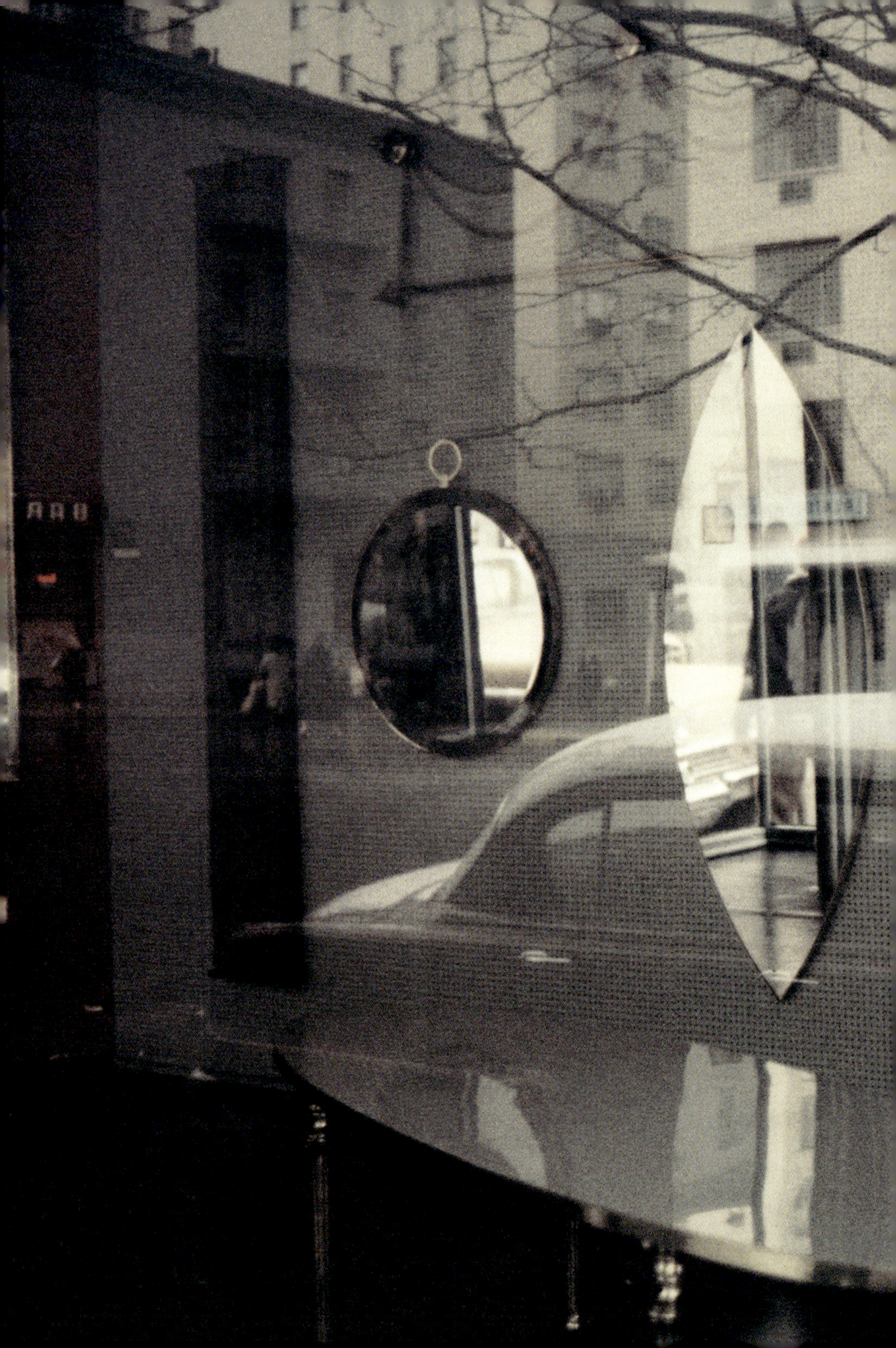

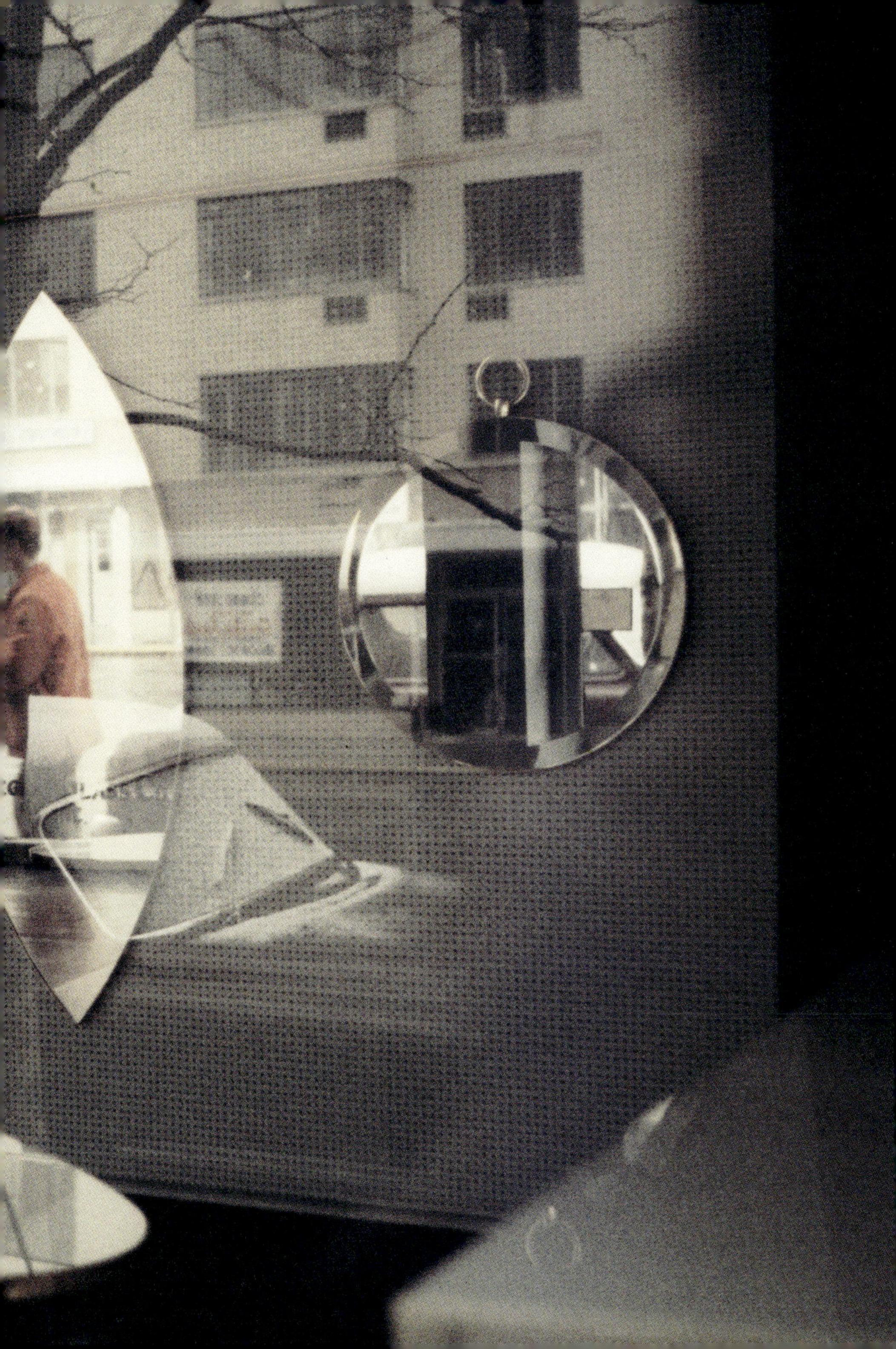

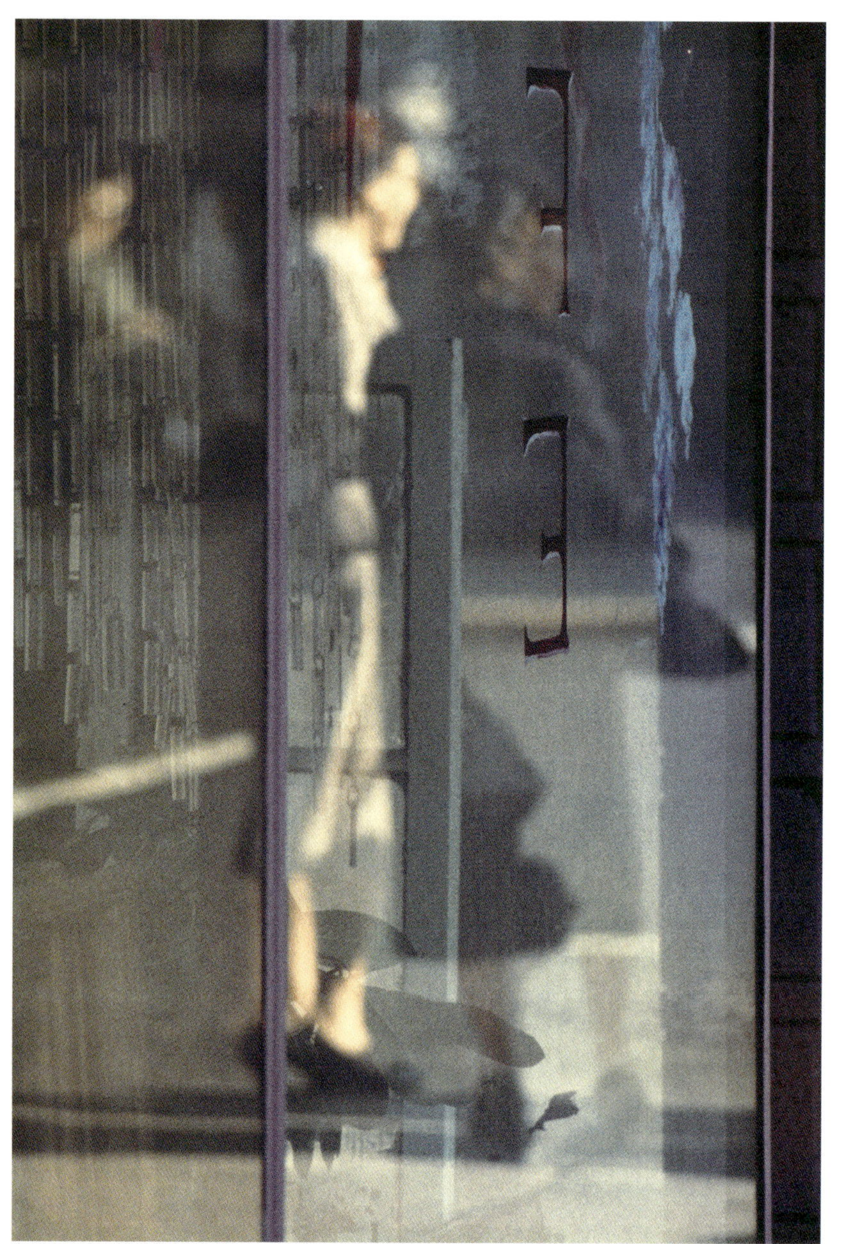

Walking, 1956

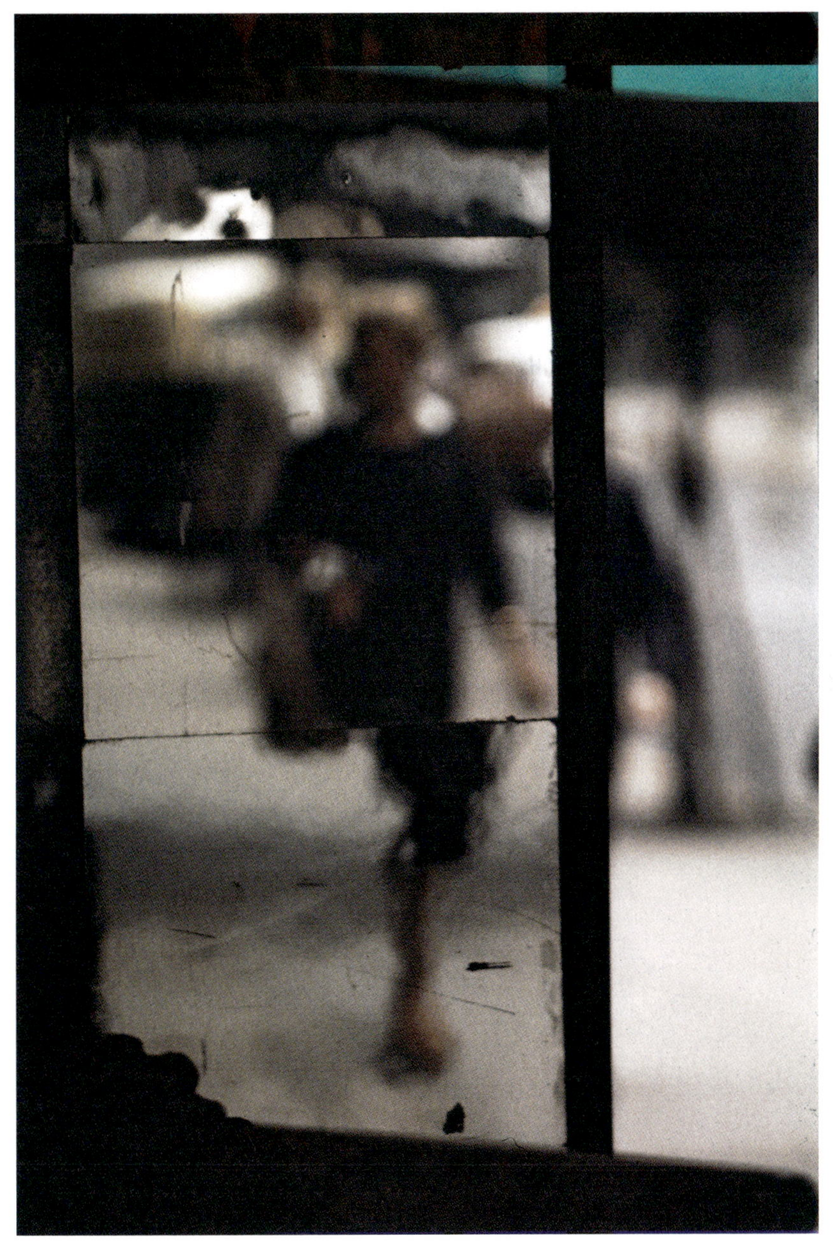

Shopper, 1953

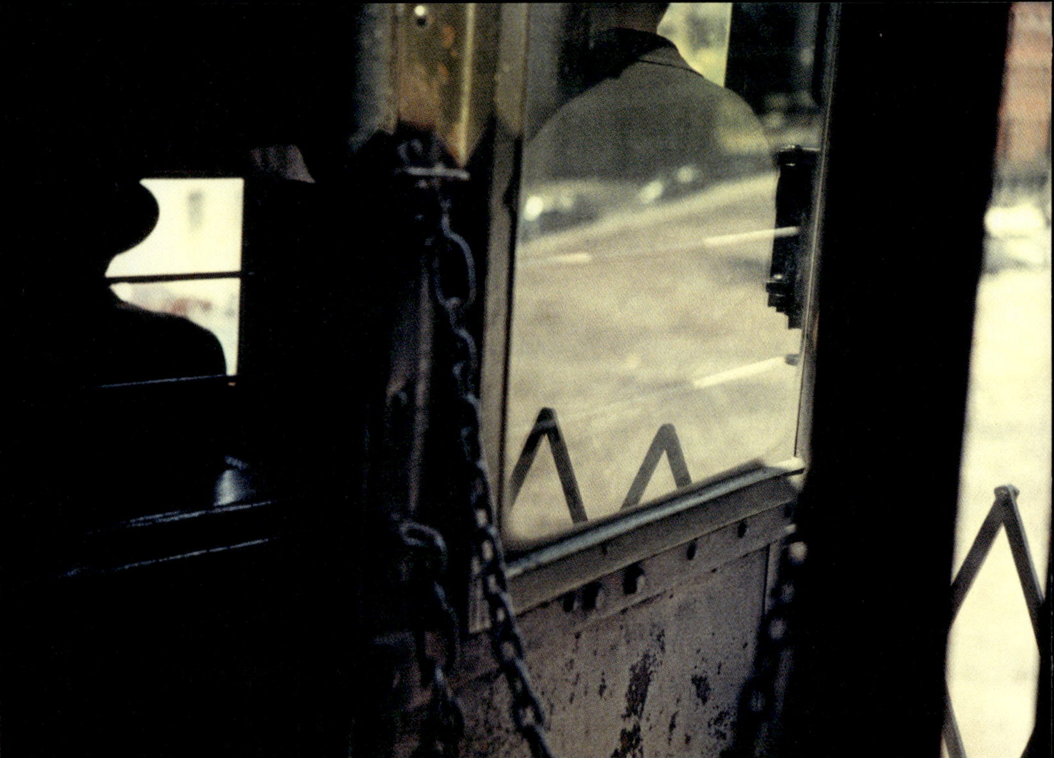

On the El, 1958

Man Reading, 1957

pp. 144–145 Boy, c. 1950

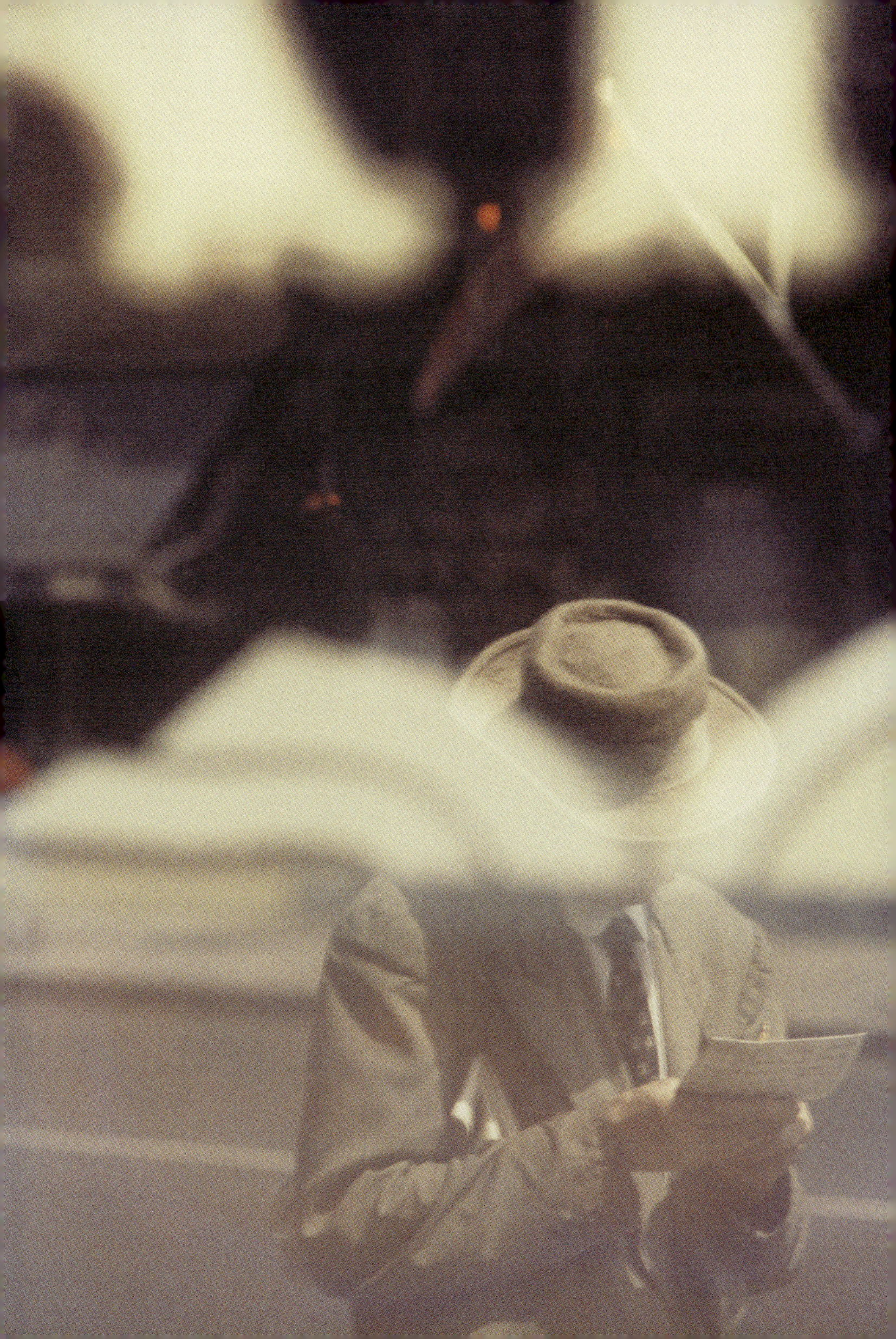

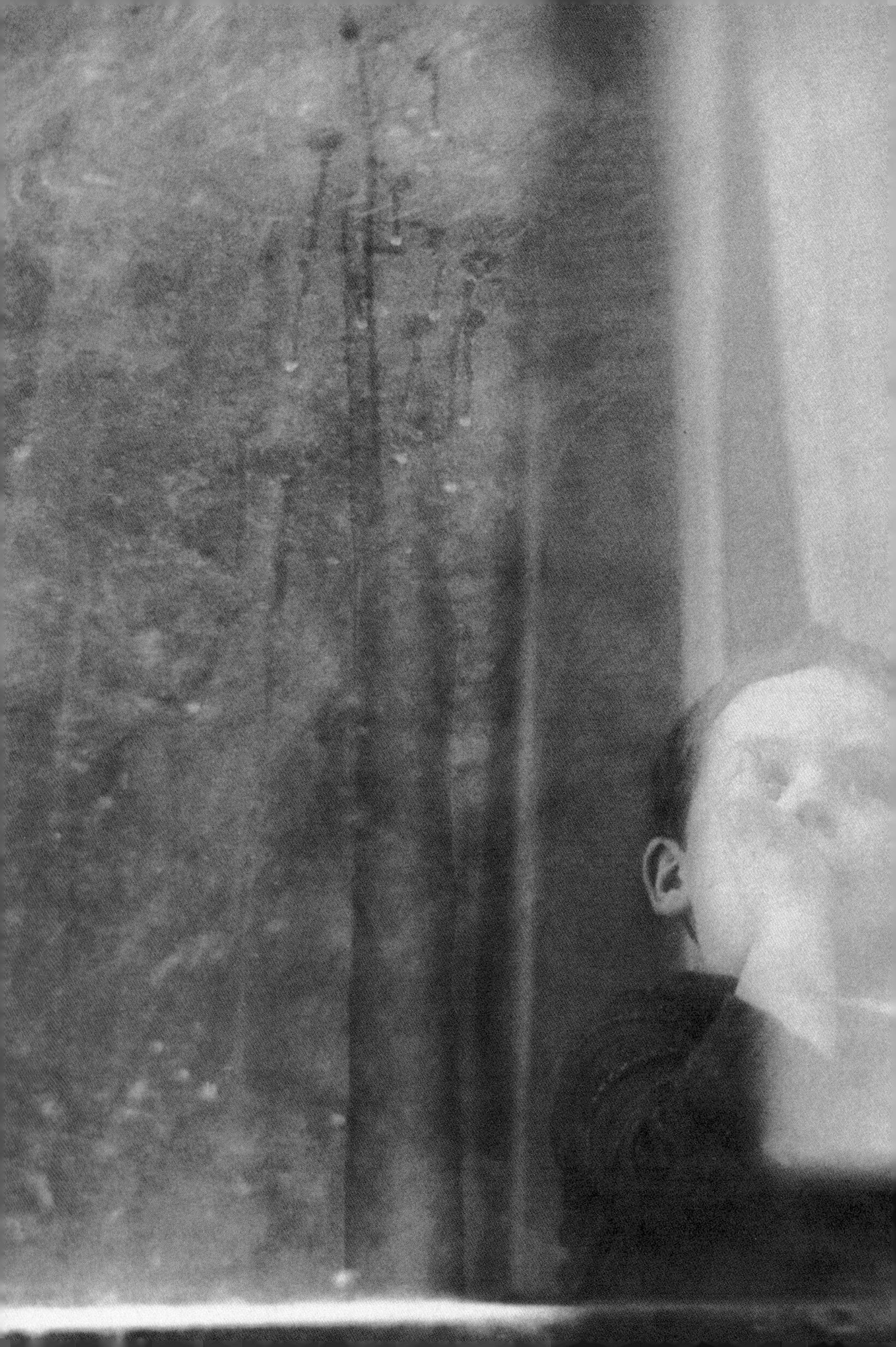

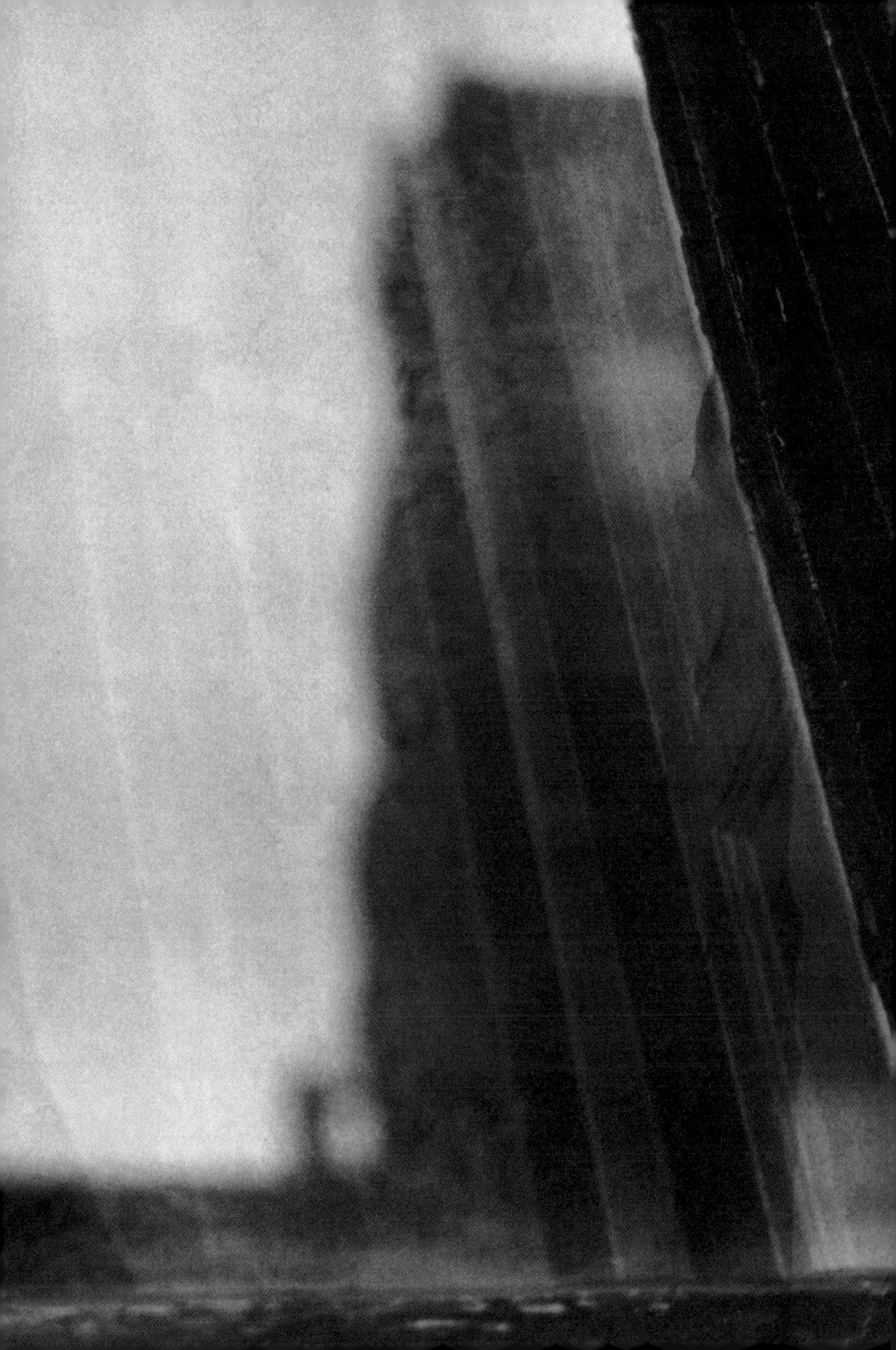

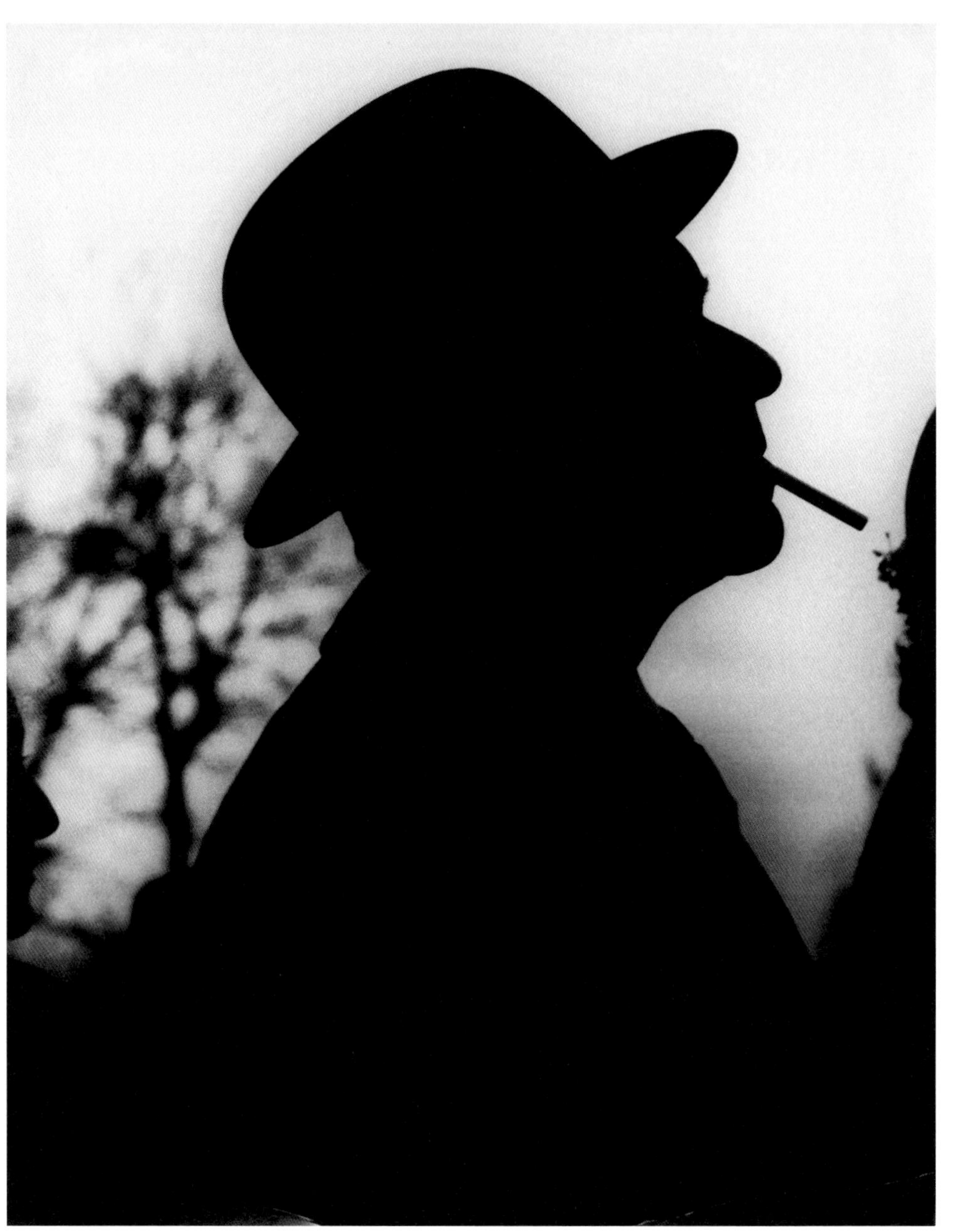

From *Wedding as a Funeral*, c. 1951

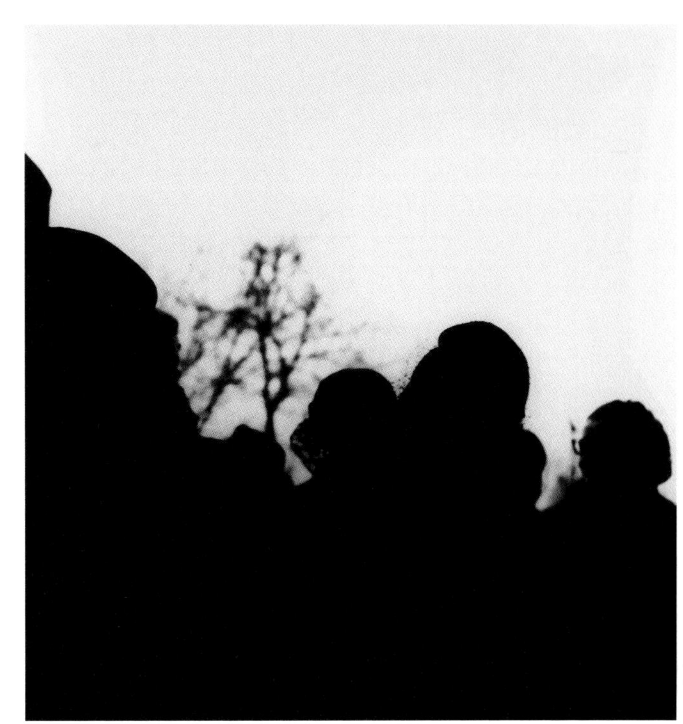

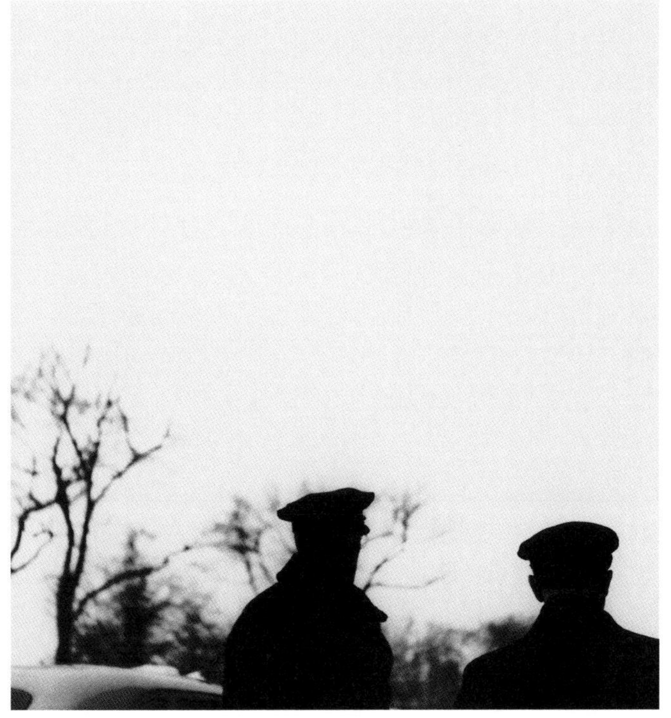

I spent a great deal of my life being ignored.
I was always very happy that way.
Being ignored is a great privilege.

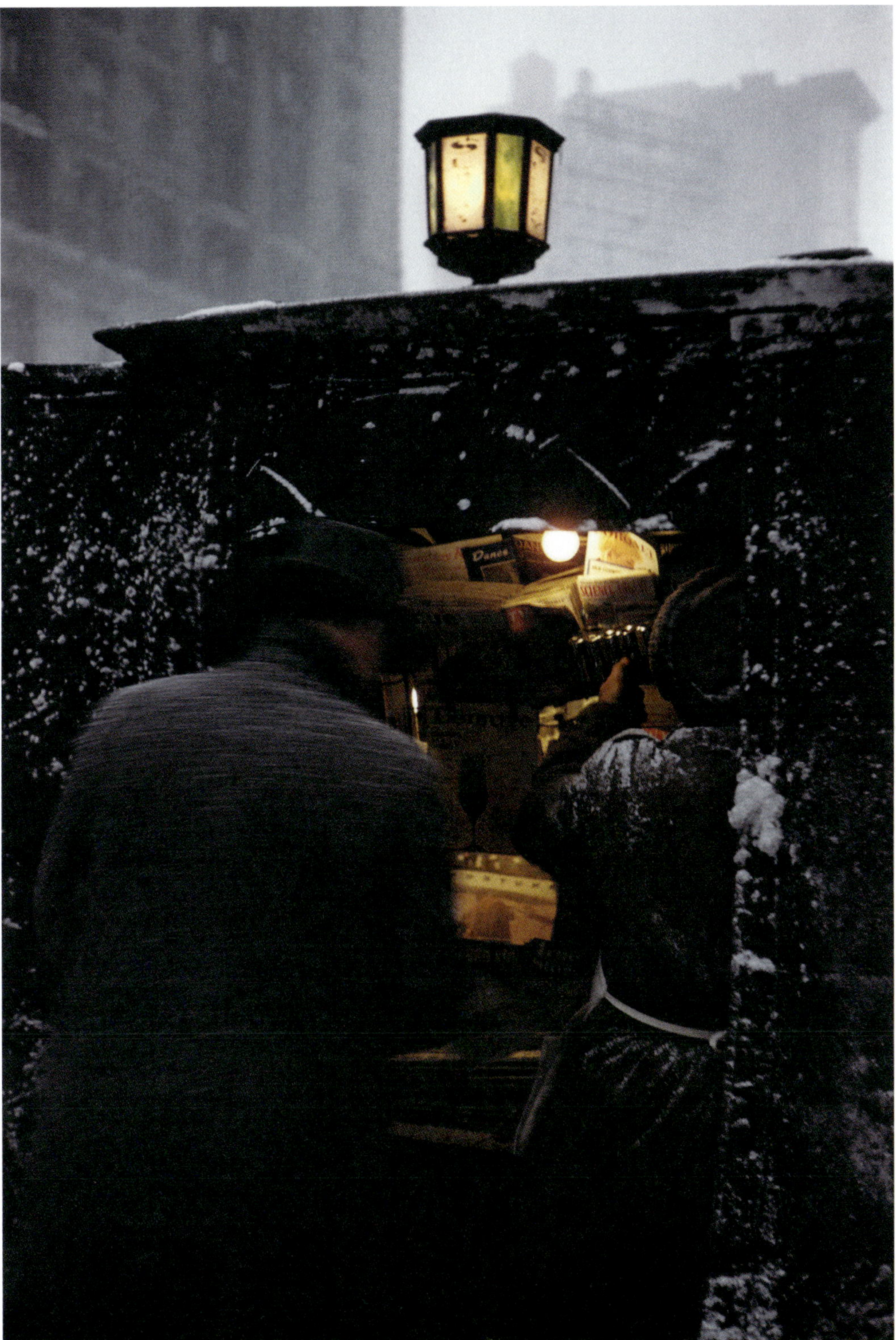

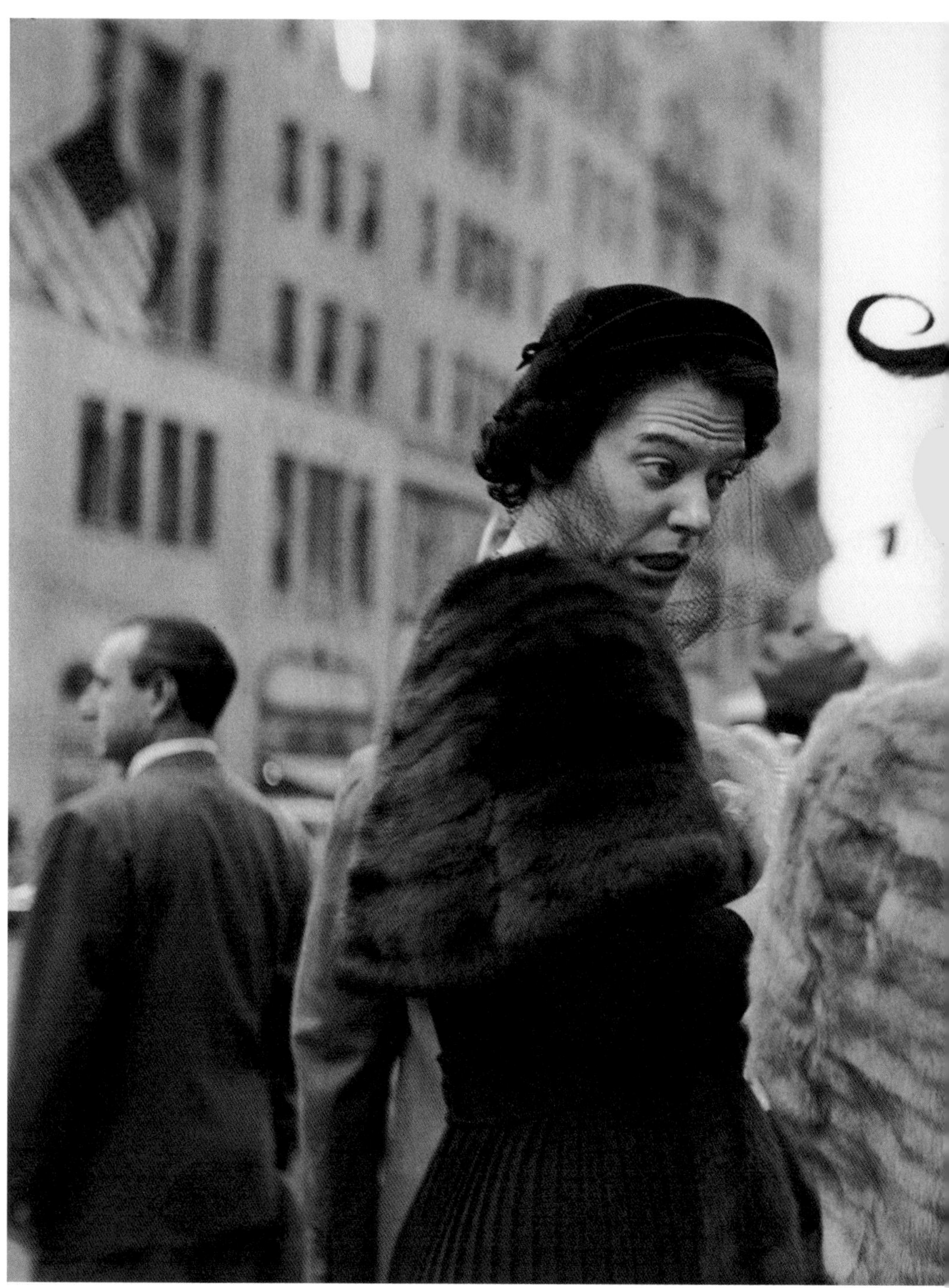

Hat, c. 1952

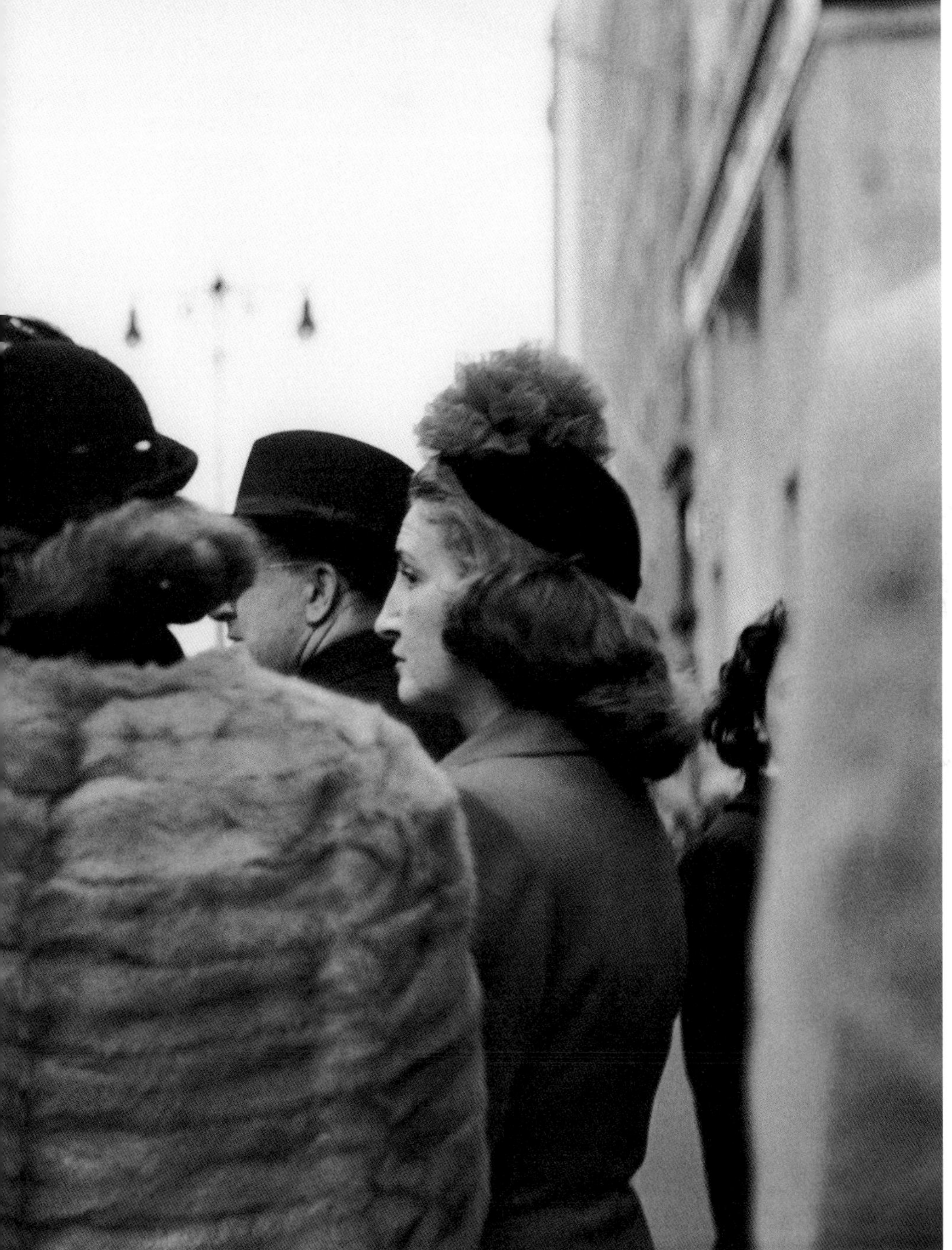

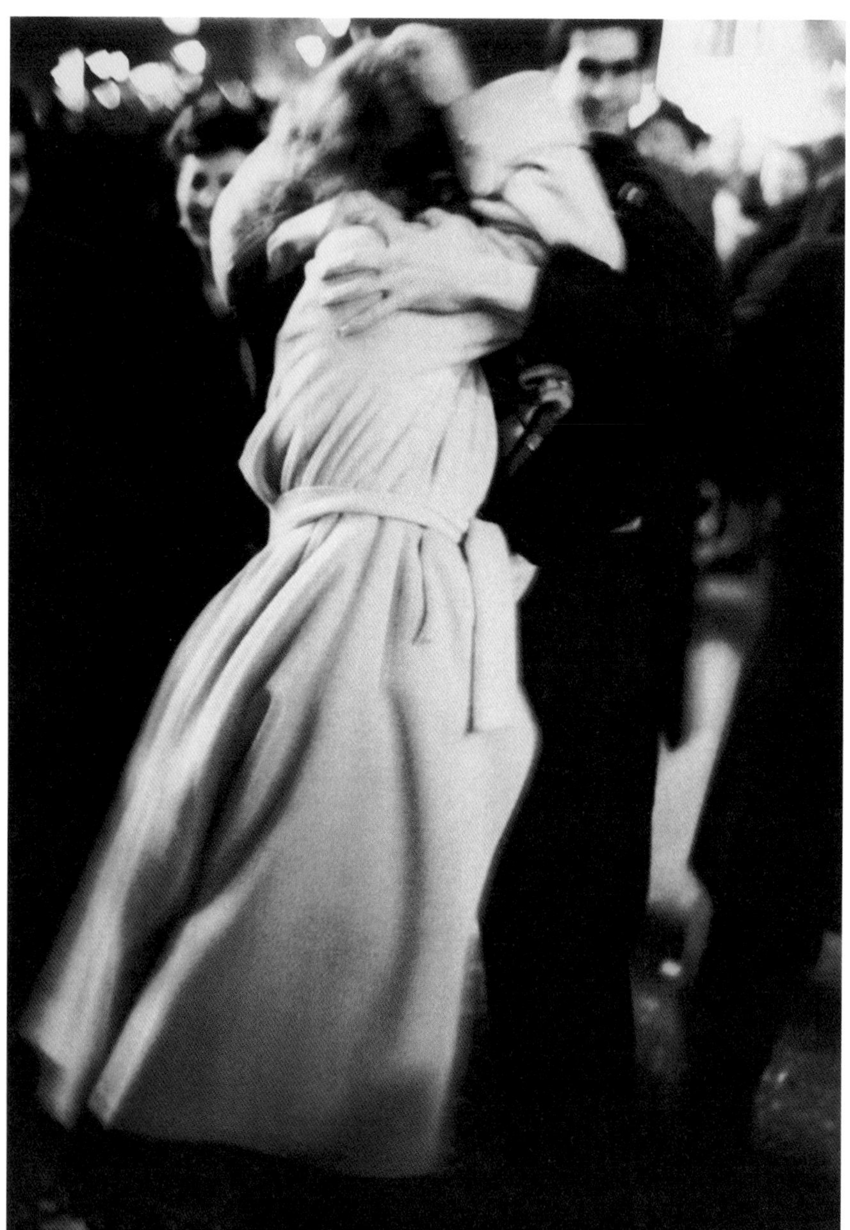

New Year's Eve, 1952–53   Movie House, c. 1952

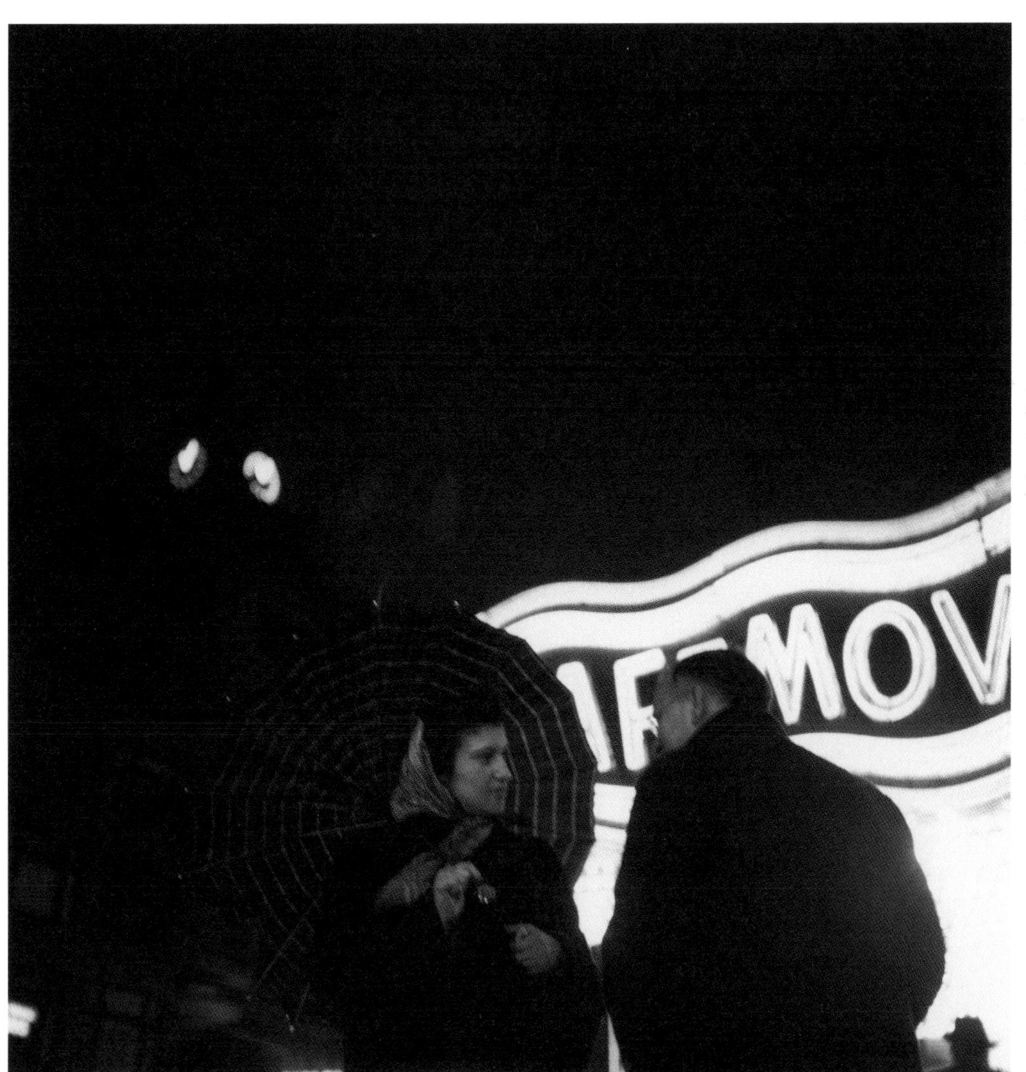

MOV

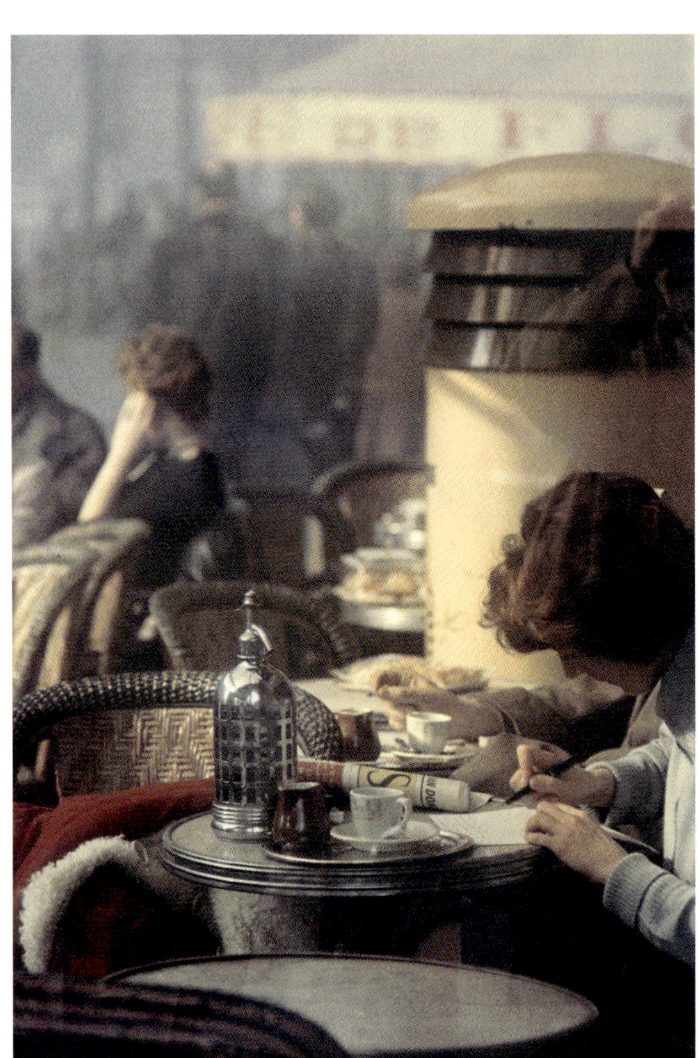

Paris, 1959

Waiter, Paris, 1959

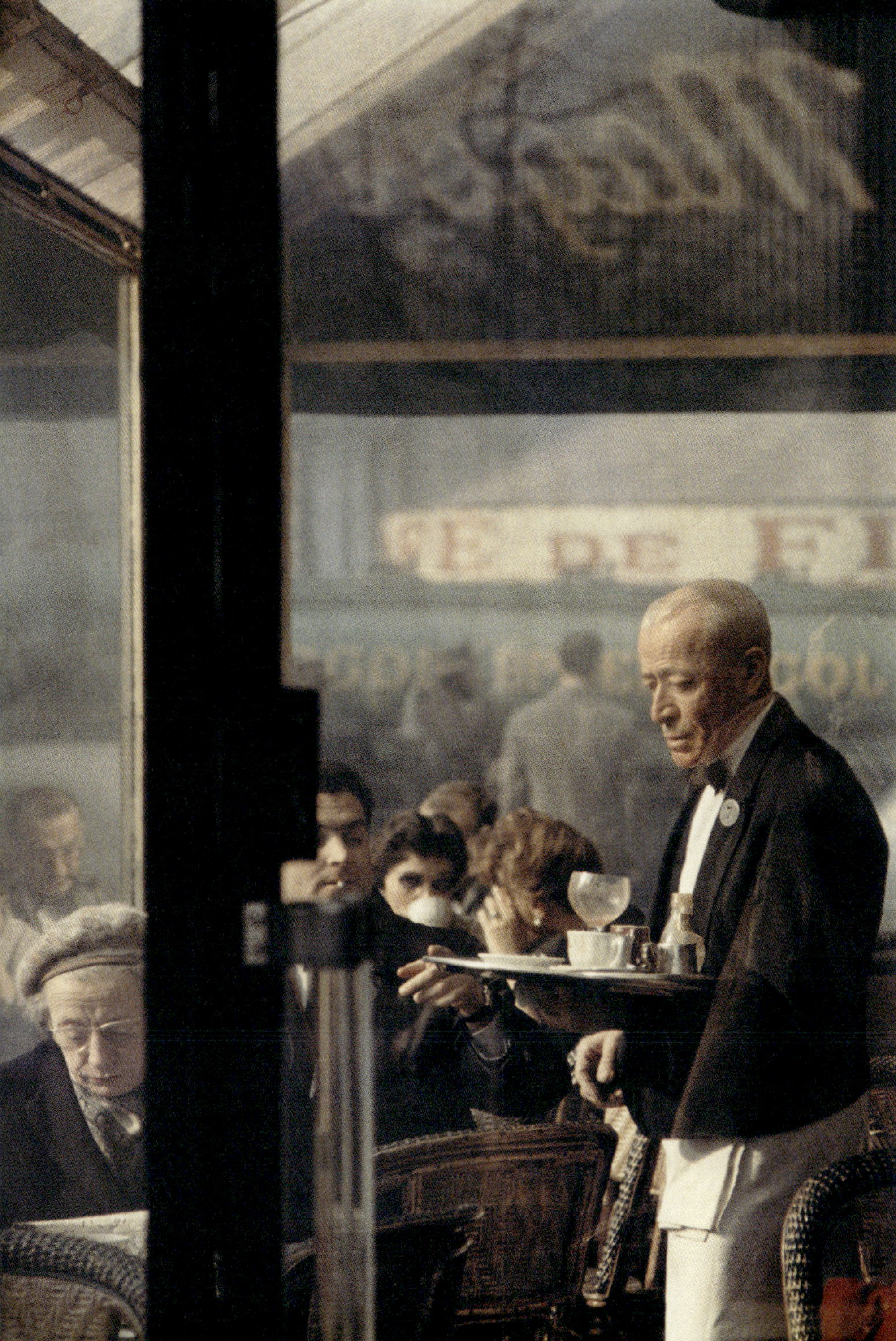

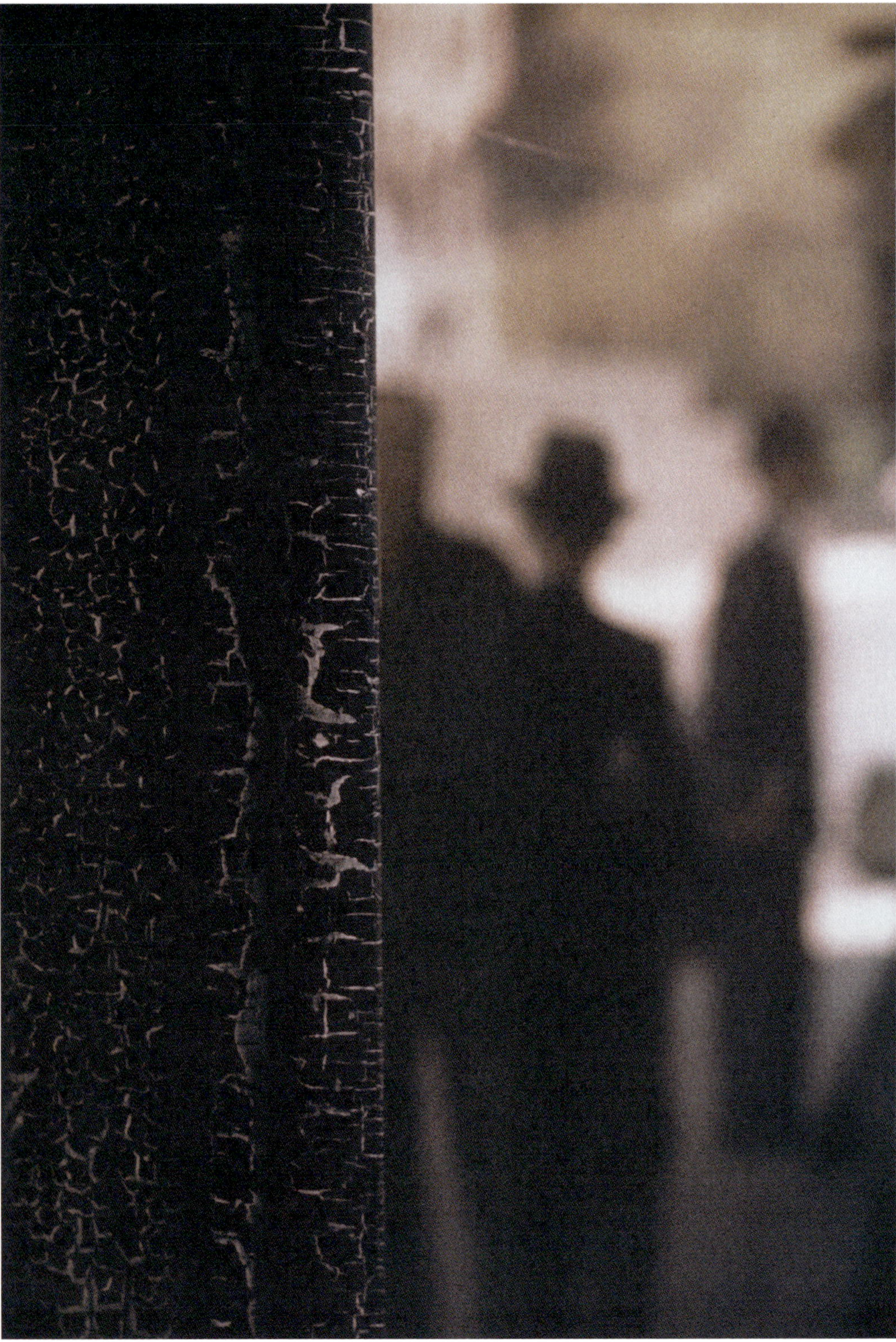

I don't attach as much importance to sequencing (in an art book, for example) as other people do. To me the content is more important.

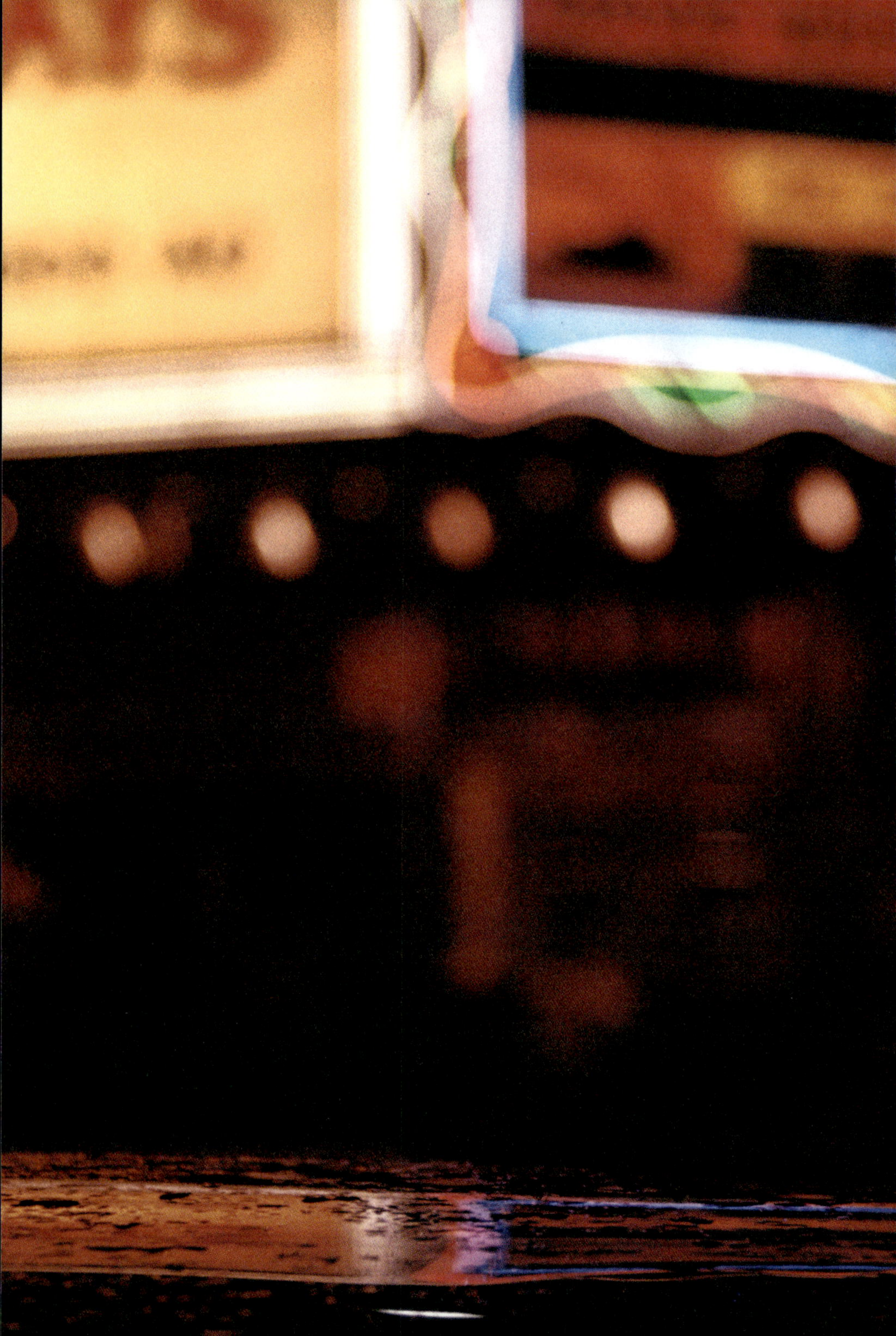

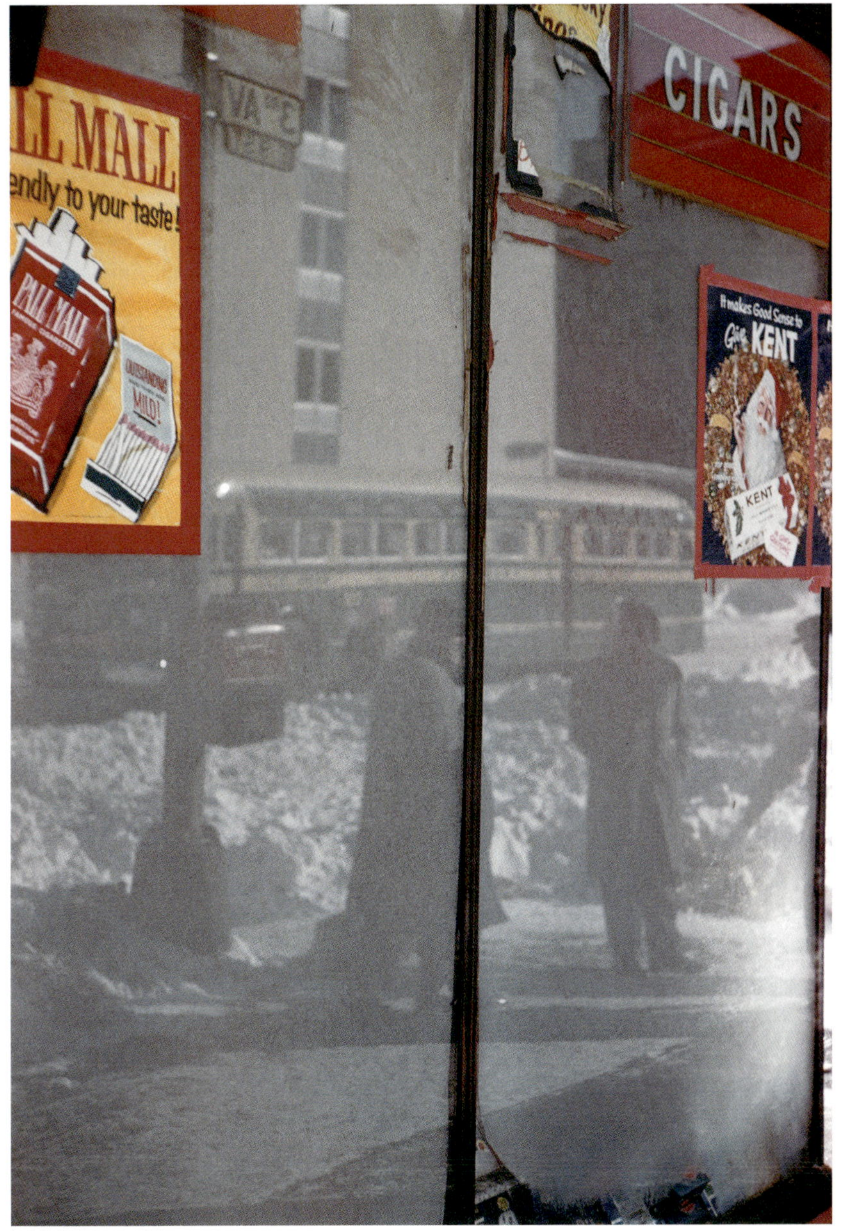

Times Square, 1950s   Snow Scene, 1958

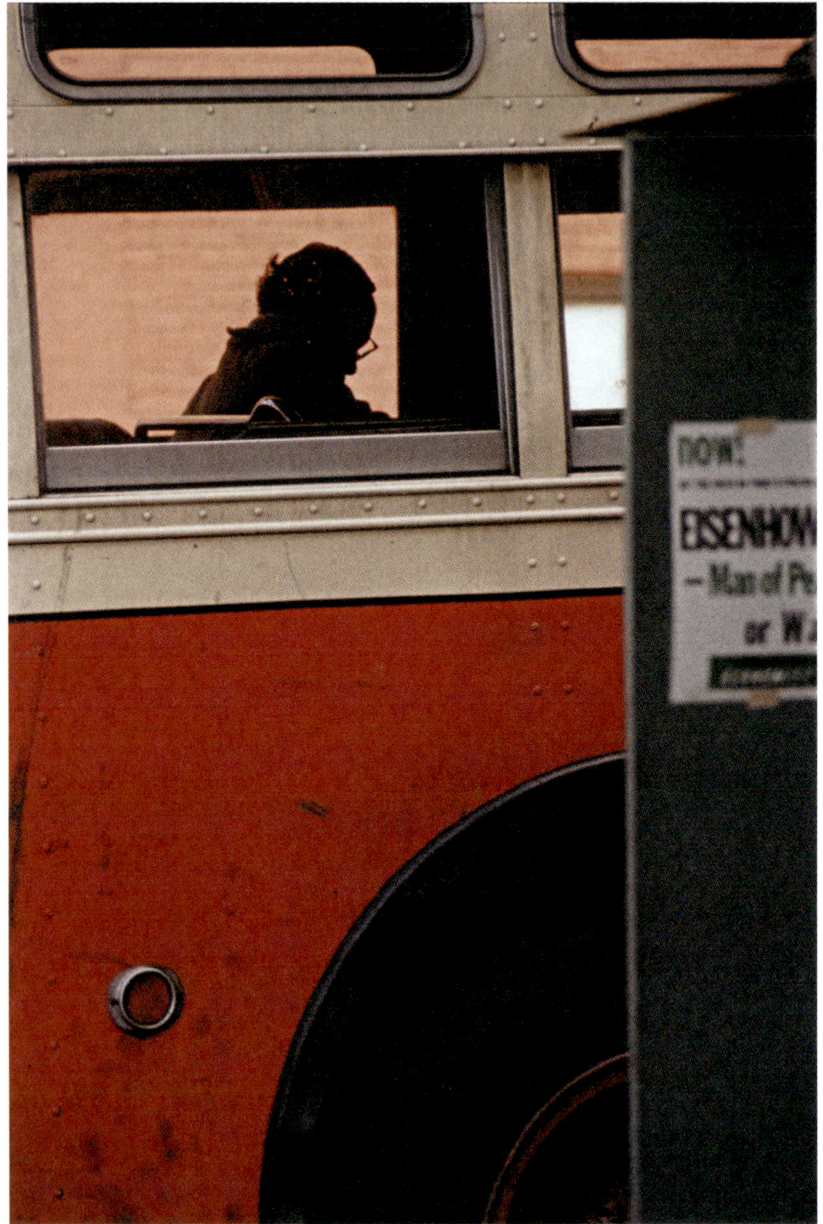

I'm supposed to be a pioneer in color.
I didn't know I was a pioneer, but I've been told I'm a pioneer.
I'll just go ahead and be a pioneer!

Bus, 1954

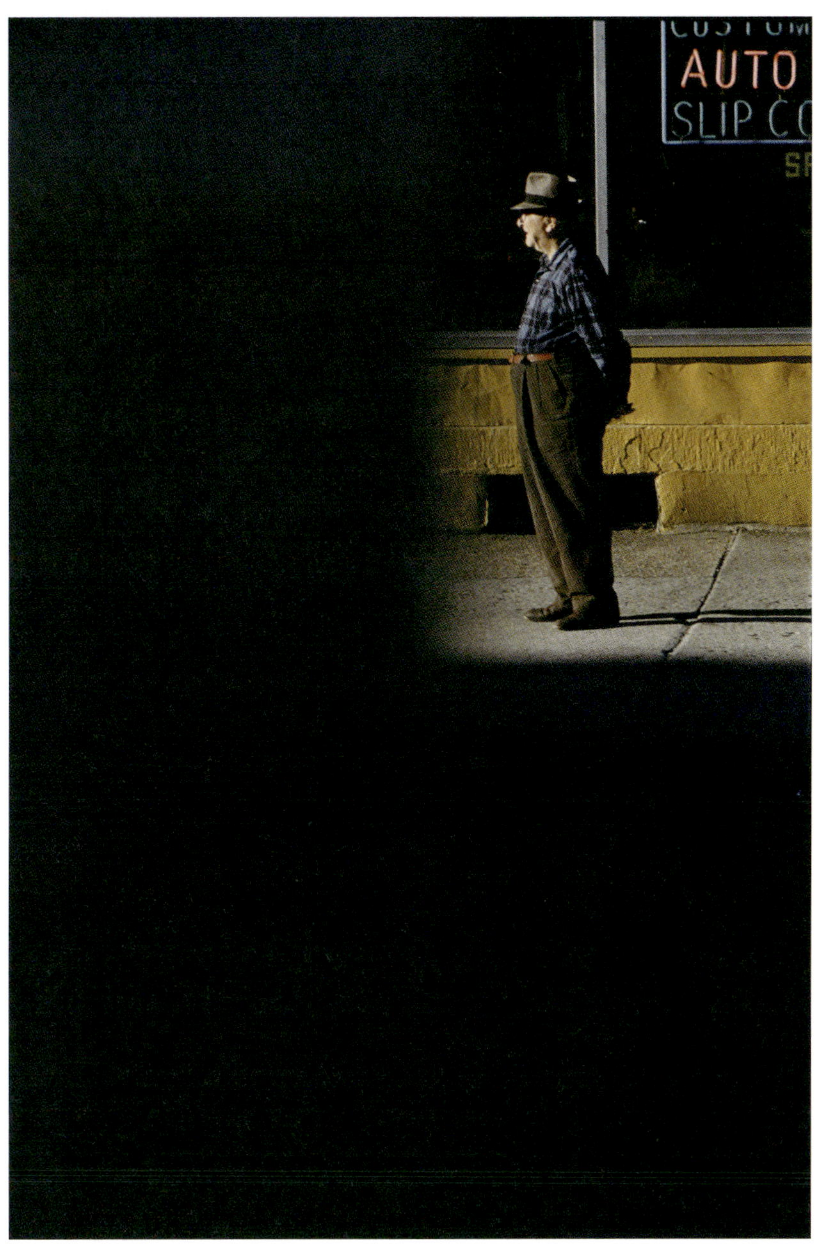

Auto, c. 1960

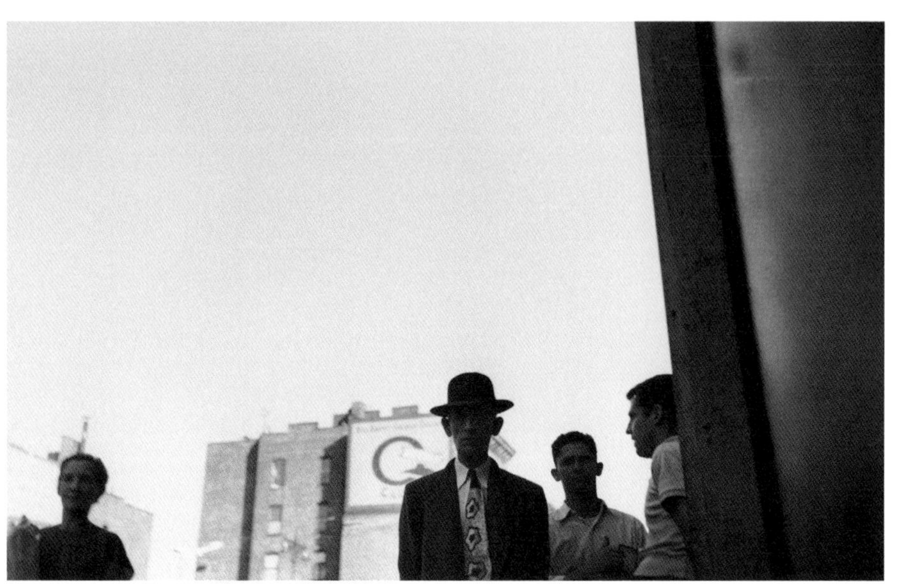

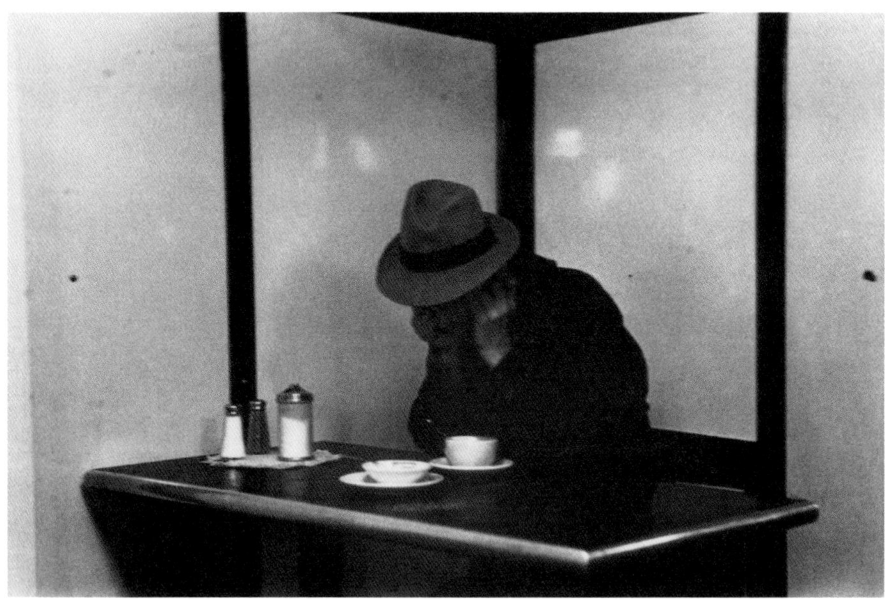

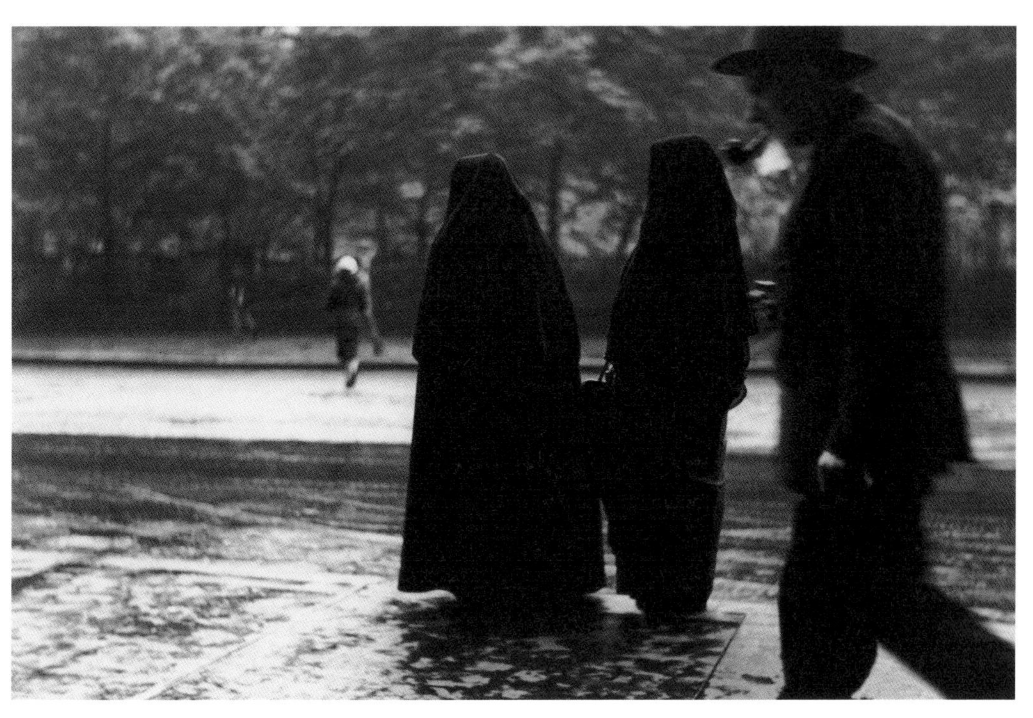

Man with Tie, c. 1949
Thanksgiving, c. 1950   Untitled, 1950s

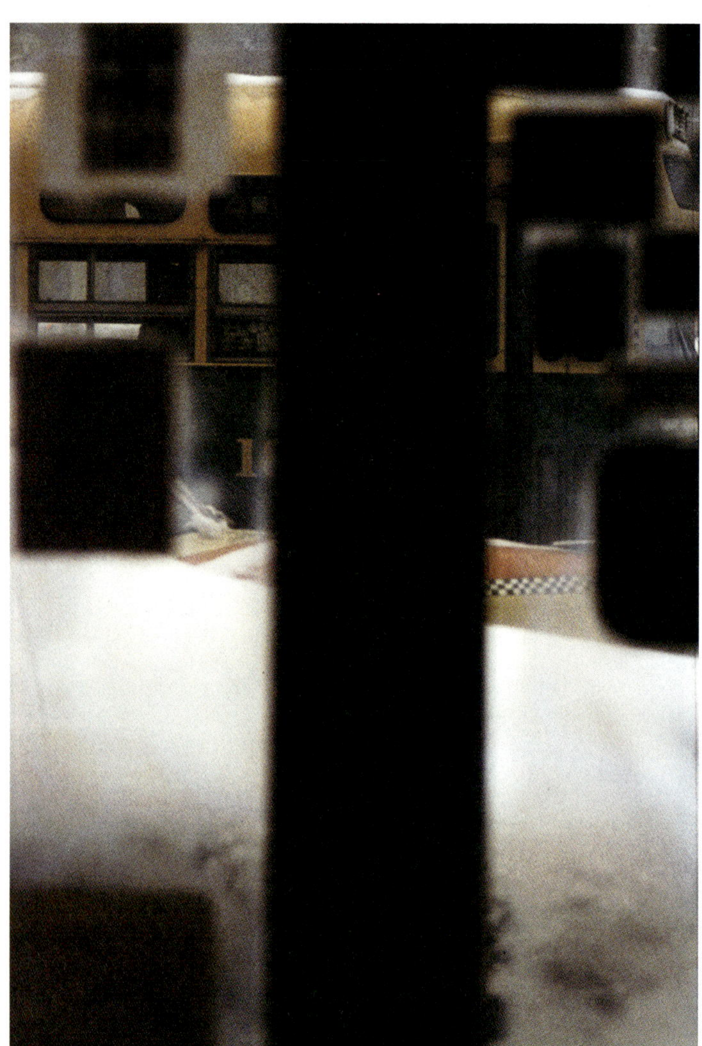

Snow Window, 1959

Street Scene, New York, 1958

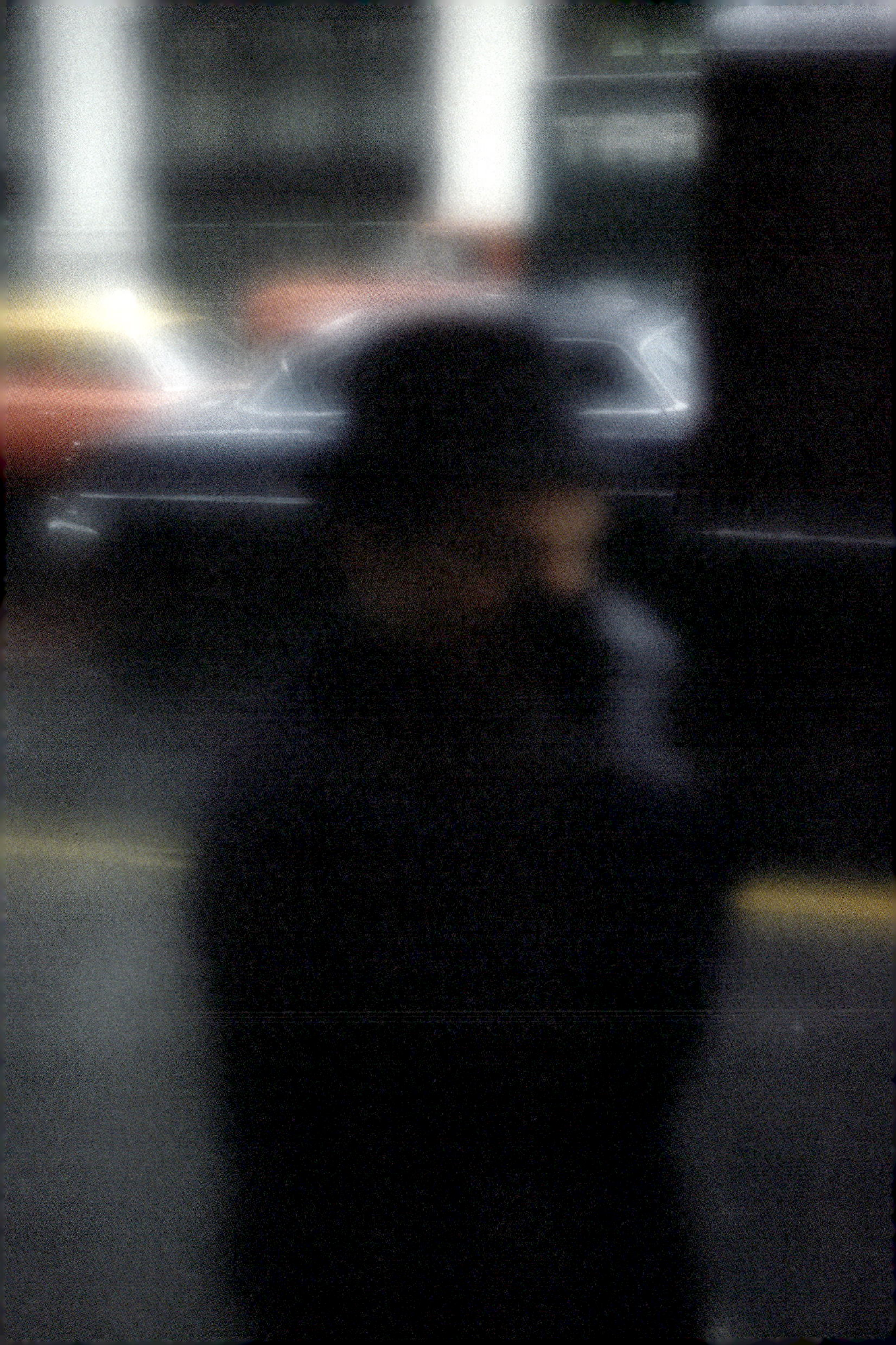

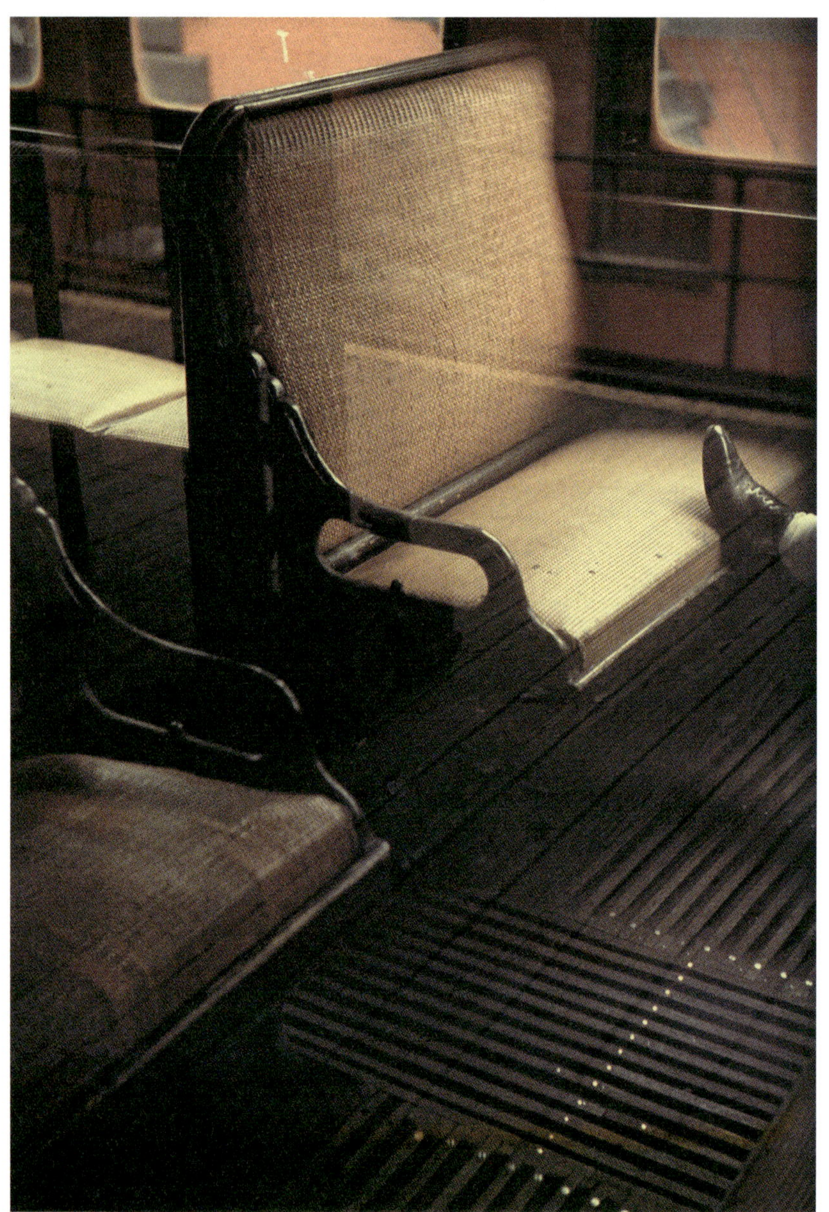

Foot on El, 1954

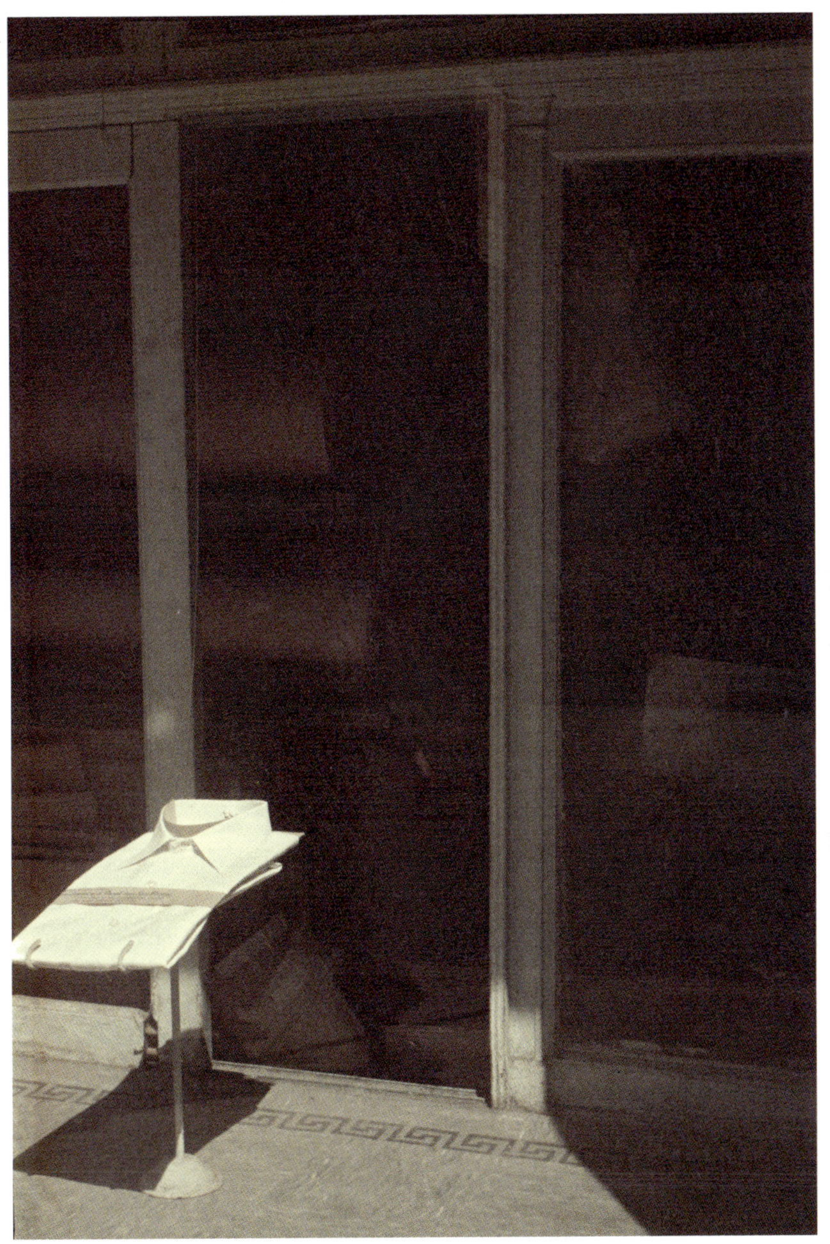

Shirt, 1948

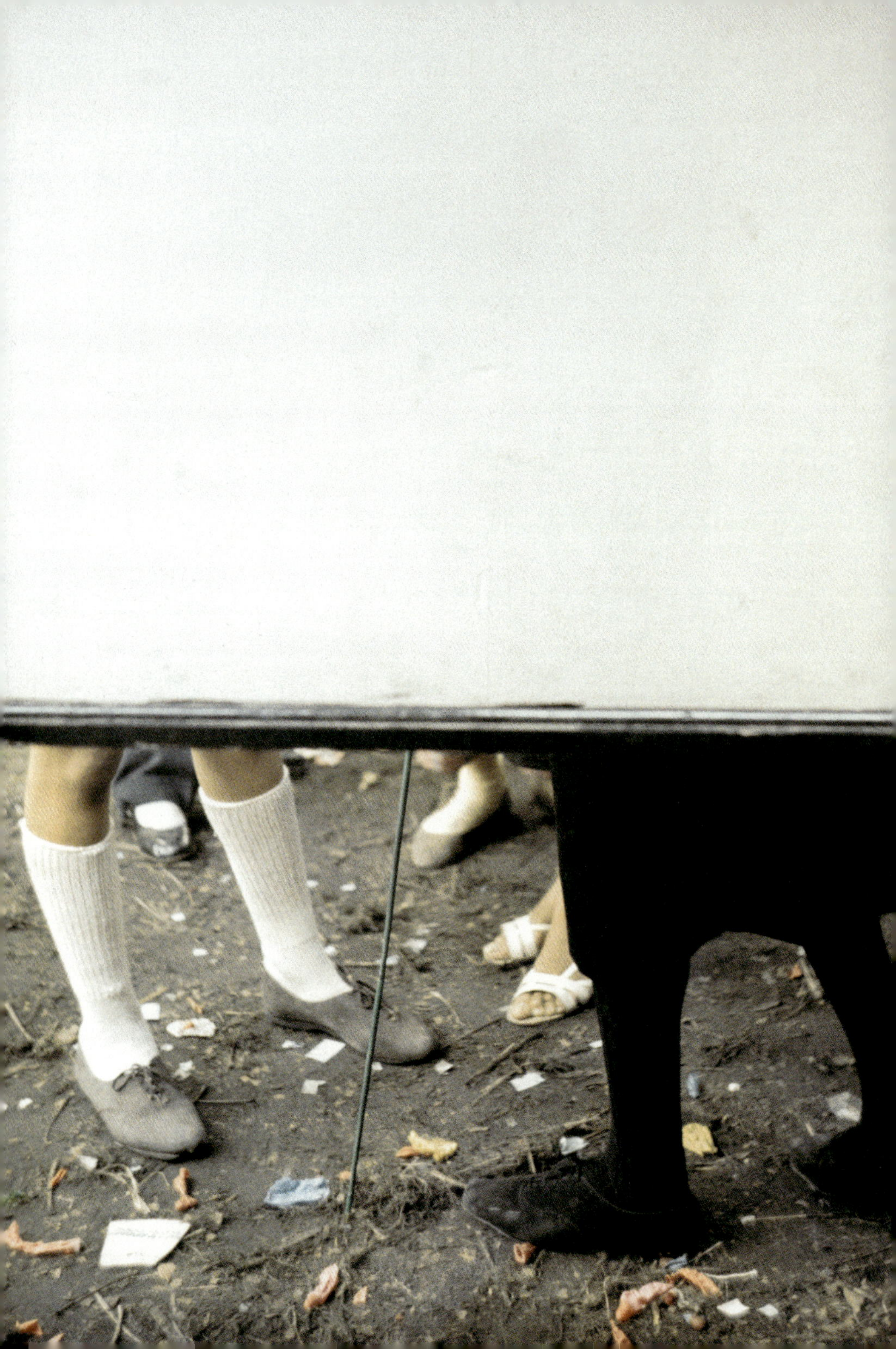

The history of photography keeps changing
as one learns more about hidden and unknown things.

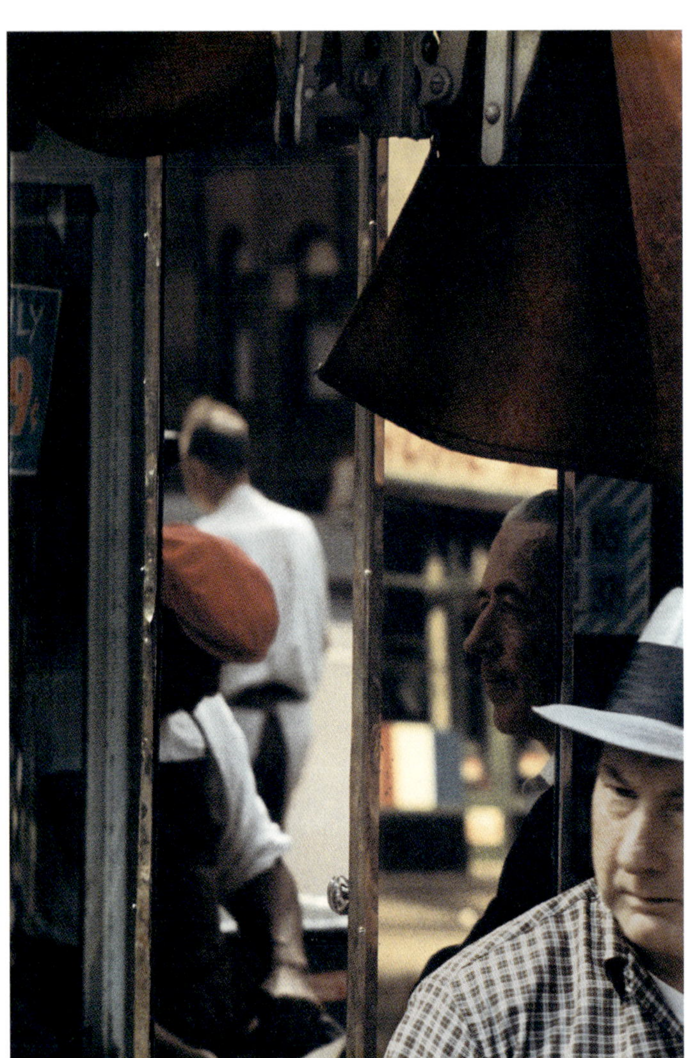

Reflection, 1958

White Circle, 1958

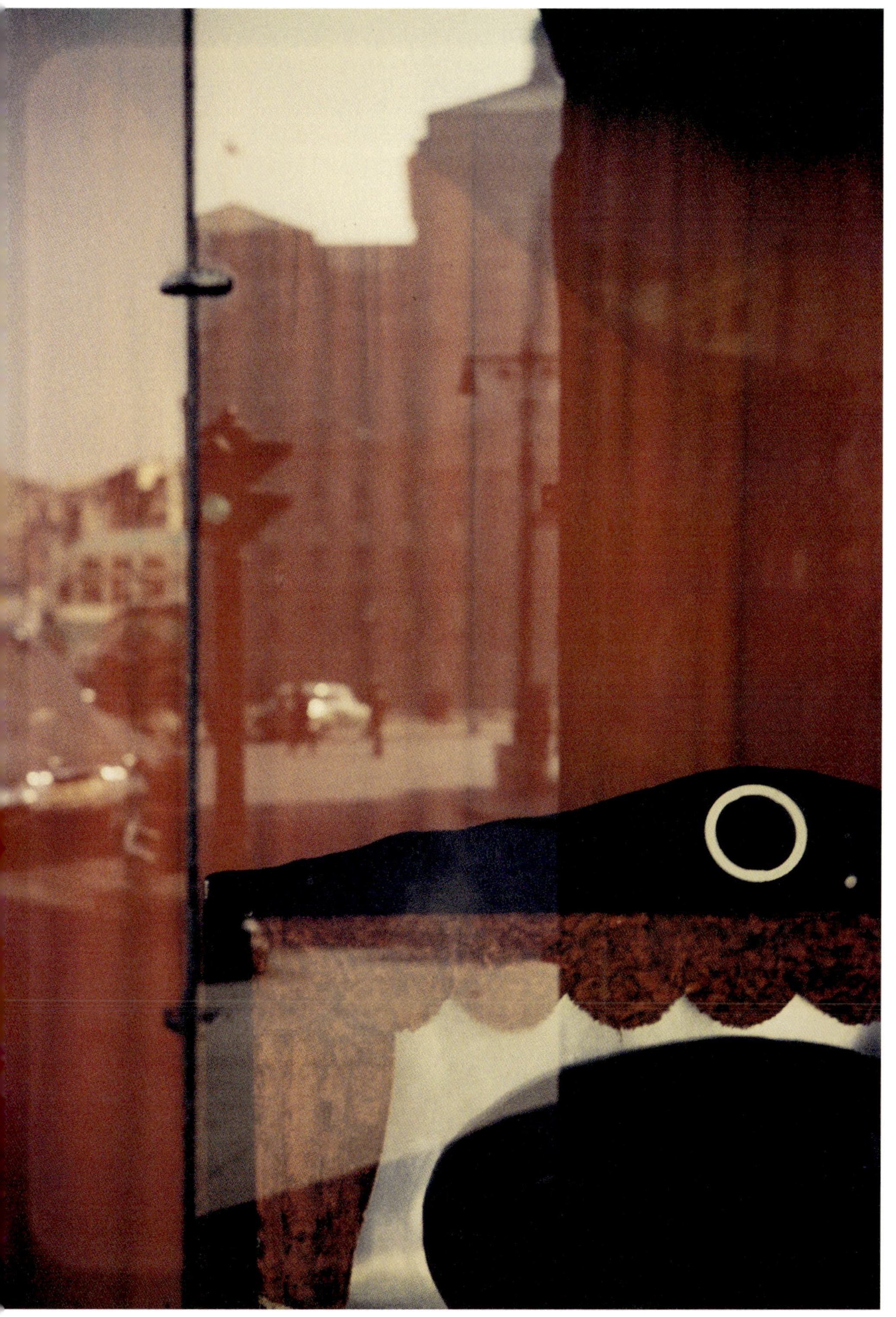

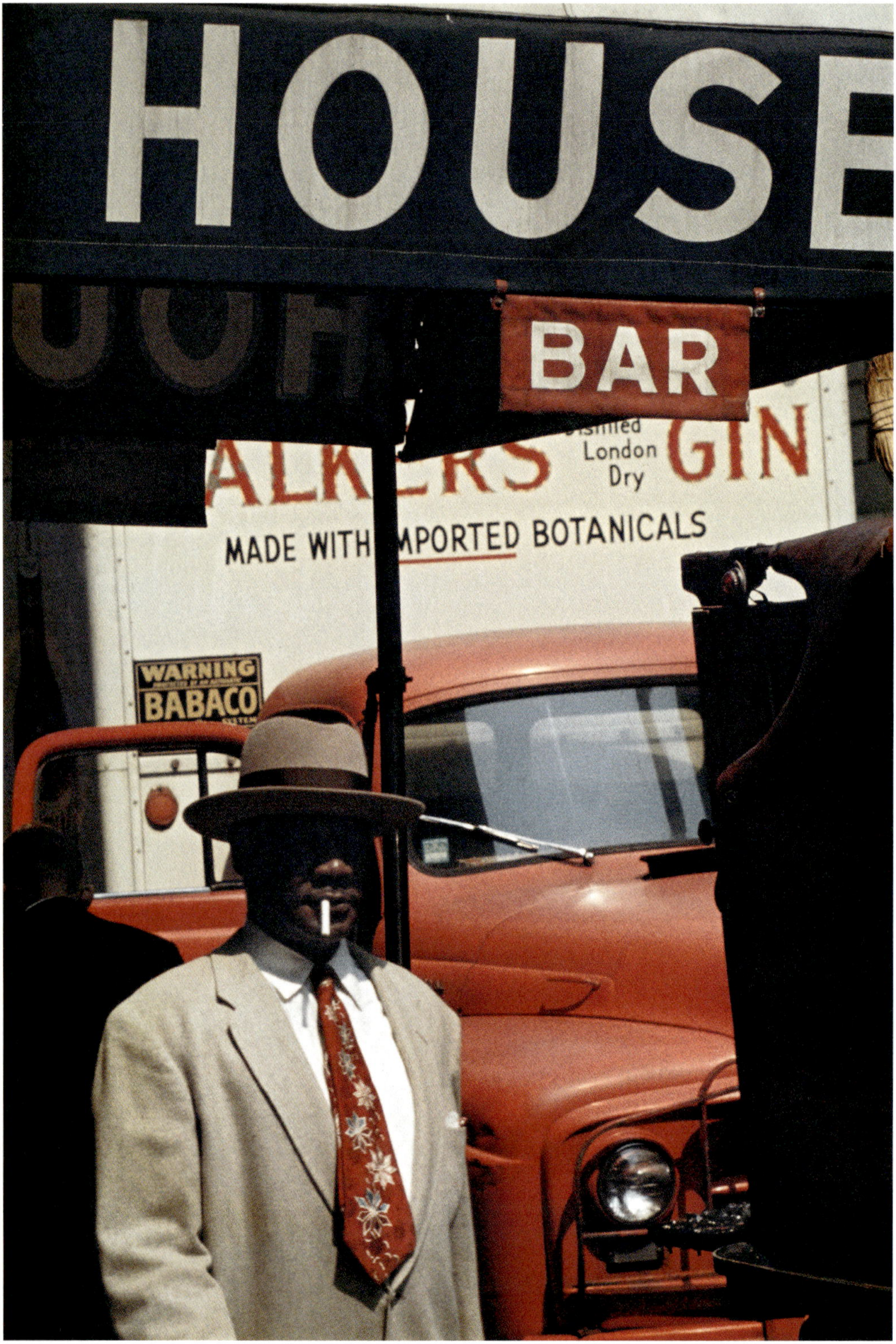

HOUSE
BAR
ALKERS
London
Dry
GIN
Distilled
MADE WITH IMPORTED BOTANICALS
WARNING
BABACO

Harlem, 1960

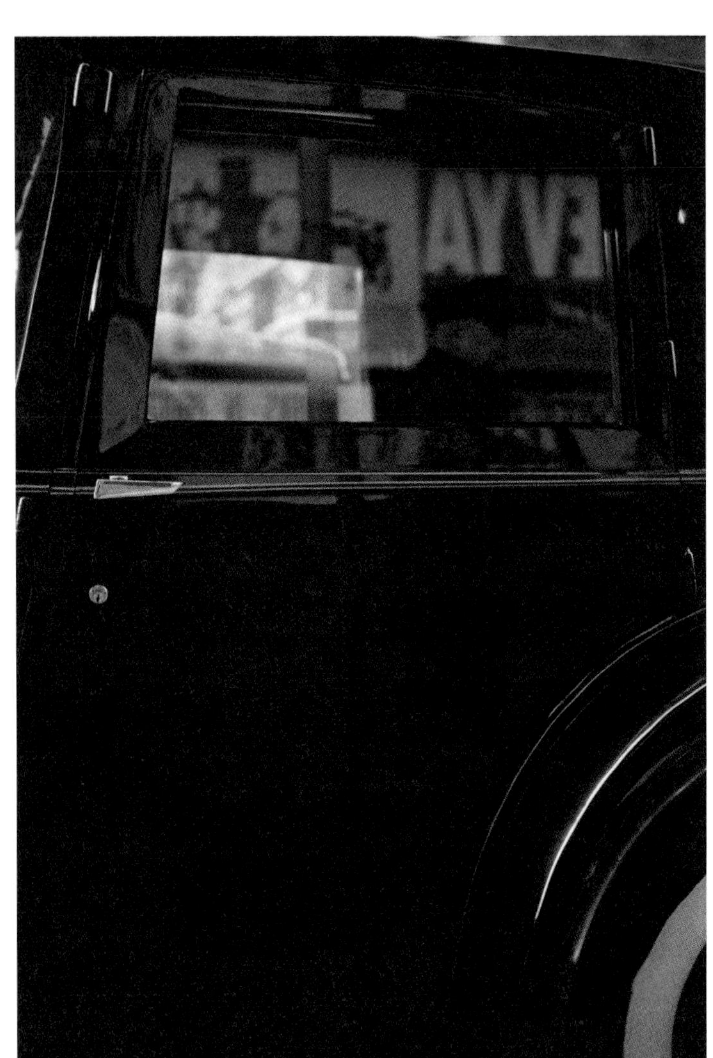

Chauffeur, 1955

Bus, Spain, c. 1959

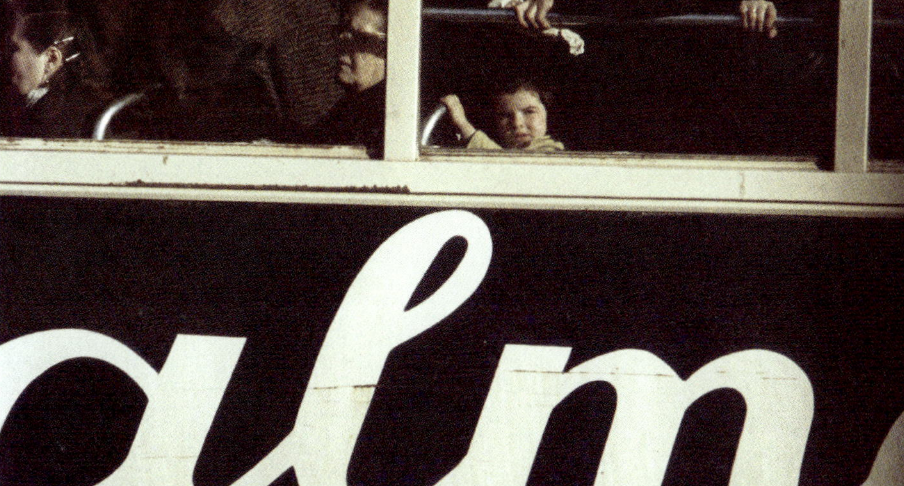

alma

I liked color even though many photographers
looked down on color or felt it was superficial or shallow.

BROADWAY
STAGE HITS
ST. PLAYHOUSE
XMAS THEAT
2 WEEKS DEC 26
HOLIDAY IN PAR

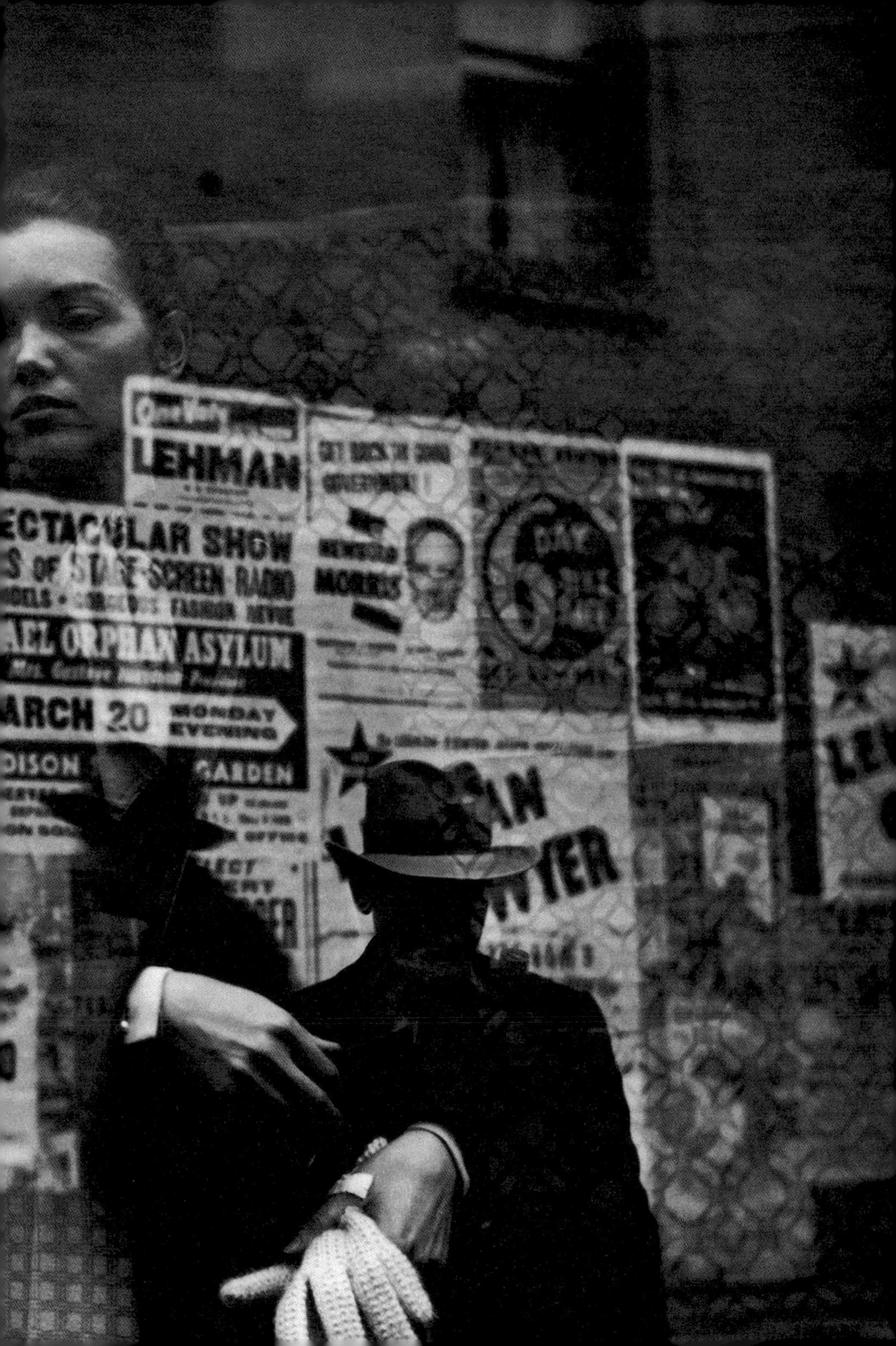
LEHMAN
ECTACULAR SHOW
S OF STAGE·SCREEN·RADIO
AEL ORPHAN ASYLUM
ARCH 20 MONDAY EVENING
DISON GARDEN
AN
TER
LEH

I find it strange that anyone would believe that the only thing that matters is black and white.
It's just idiotic. The history of art is the history of color.
The cave paintings had color...

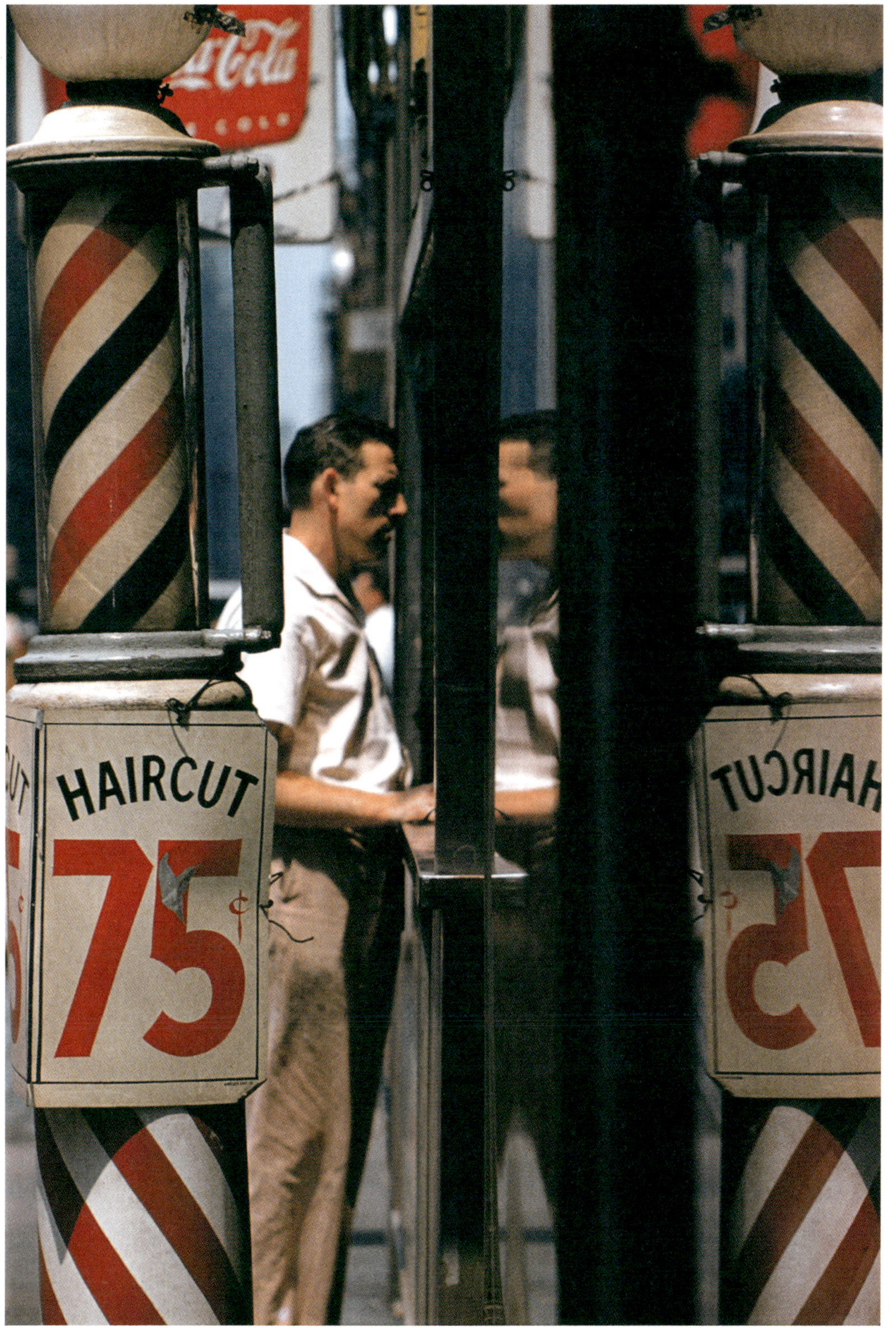

Coca Cola
HAIRCUT
75¢
HAIRCUT
75¢

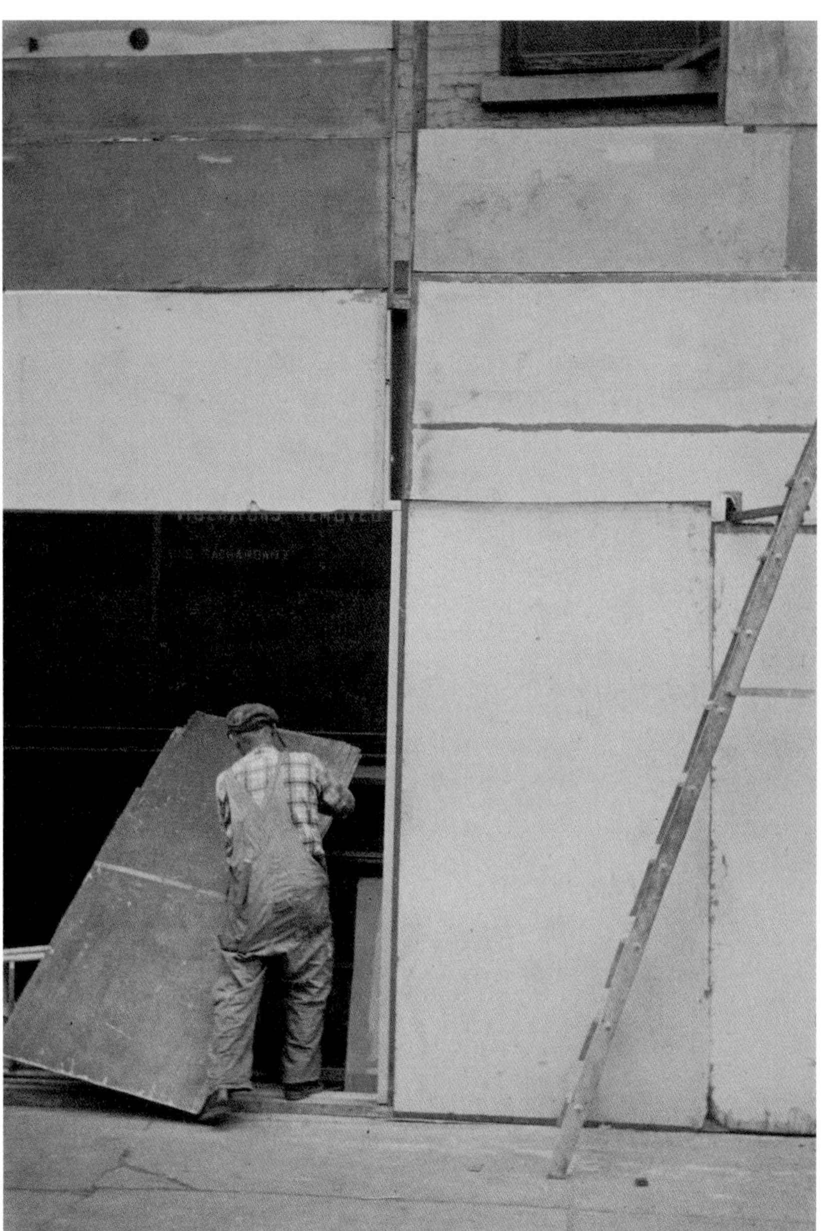

Mondrian Worker, 1954

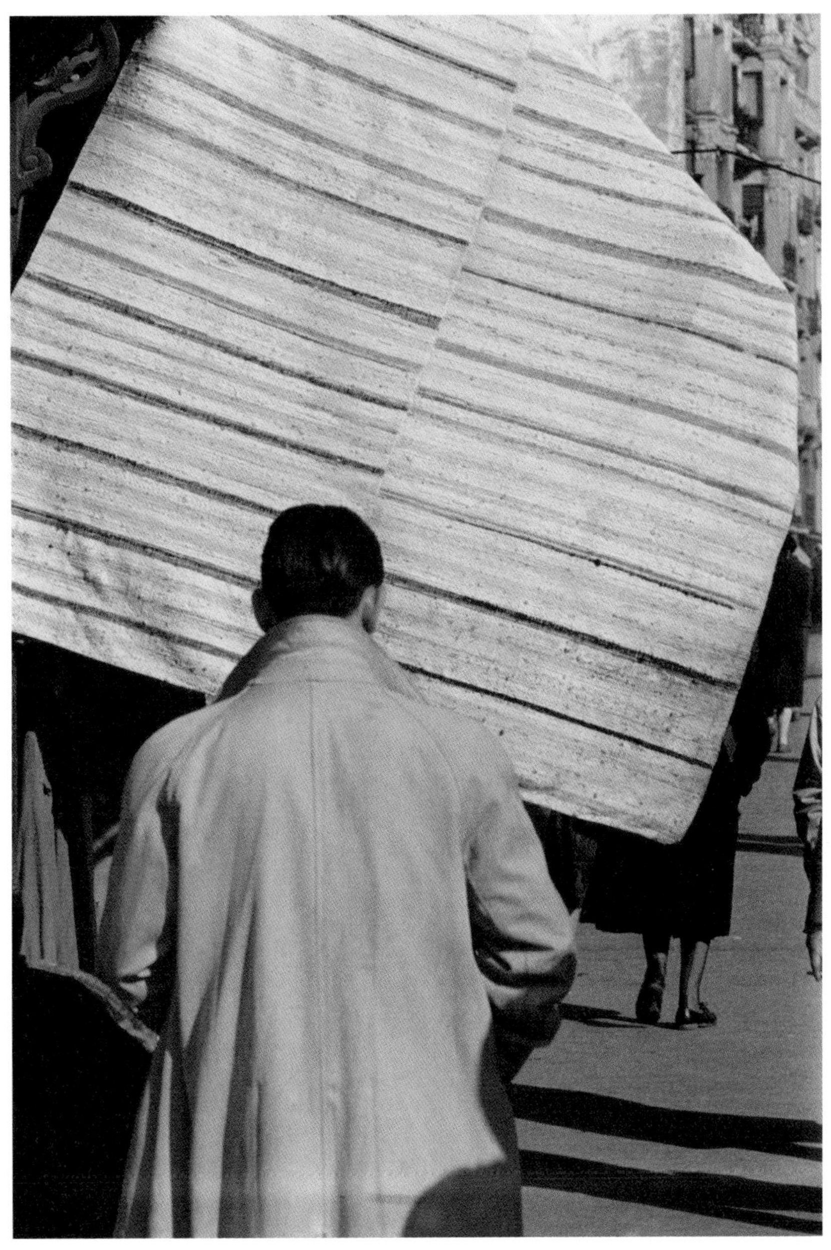

Spain, 1959

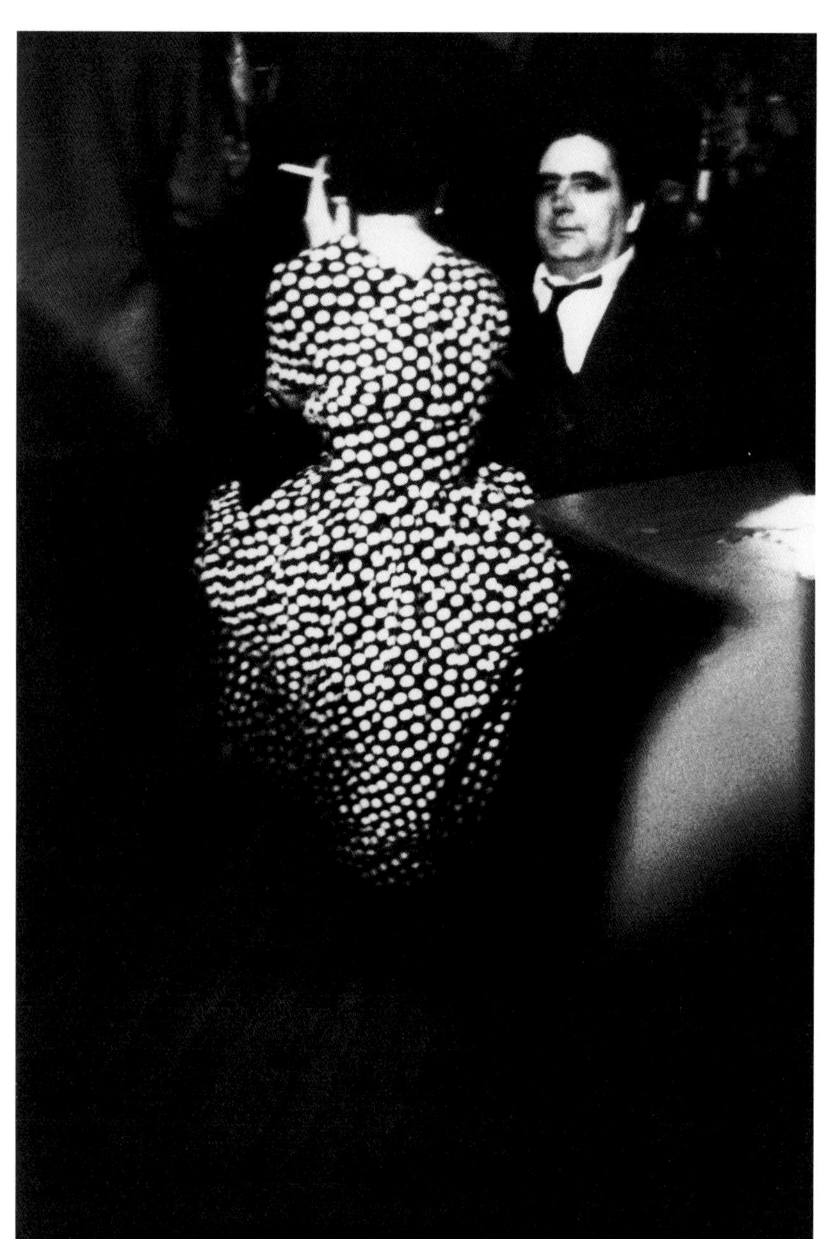

Party, c. 1953   Untitled, c. 1950

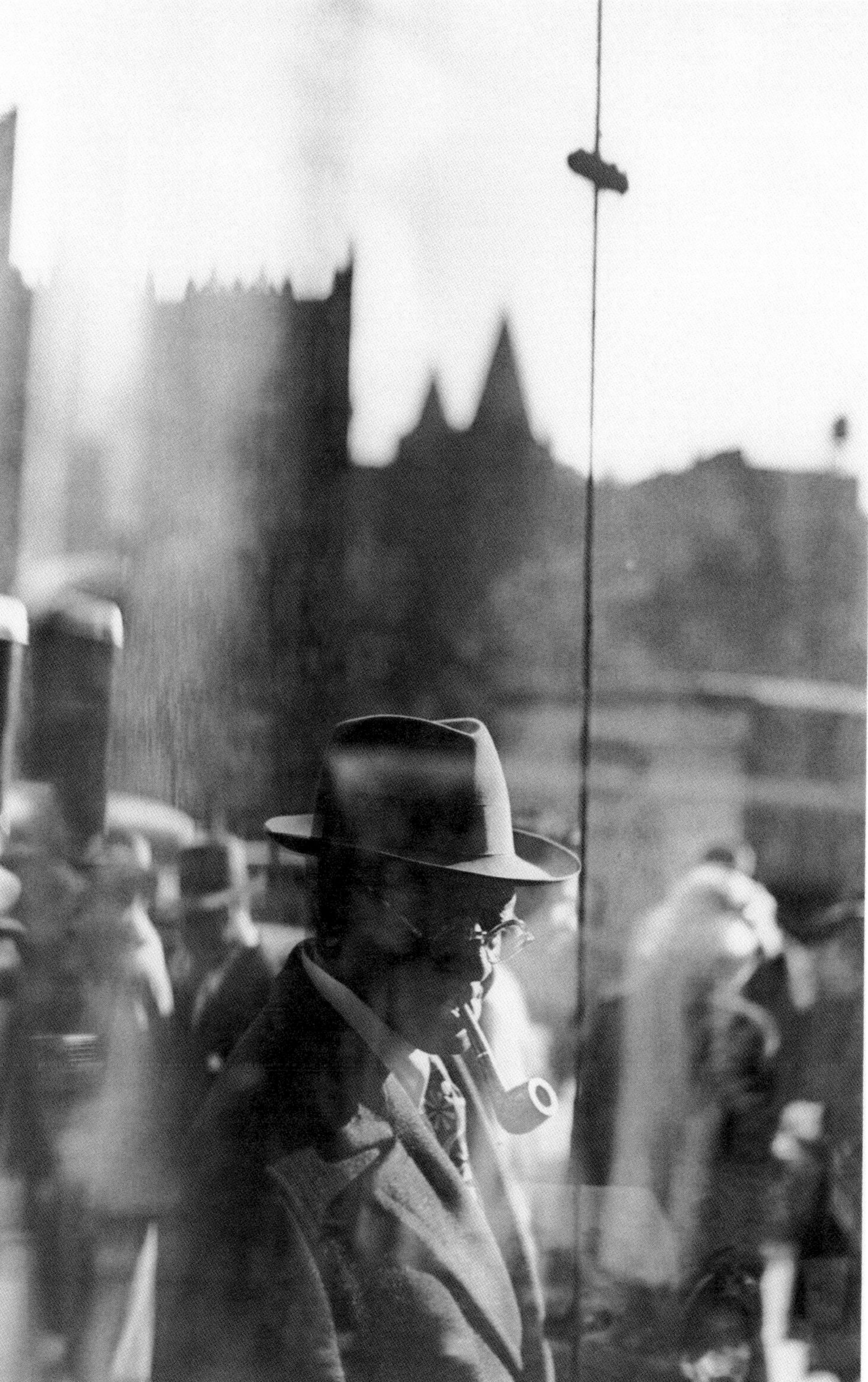

I always assumed I would just slip into oblivion.

Street Scene, 1953

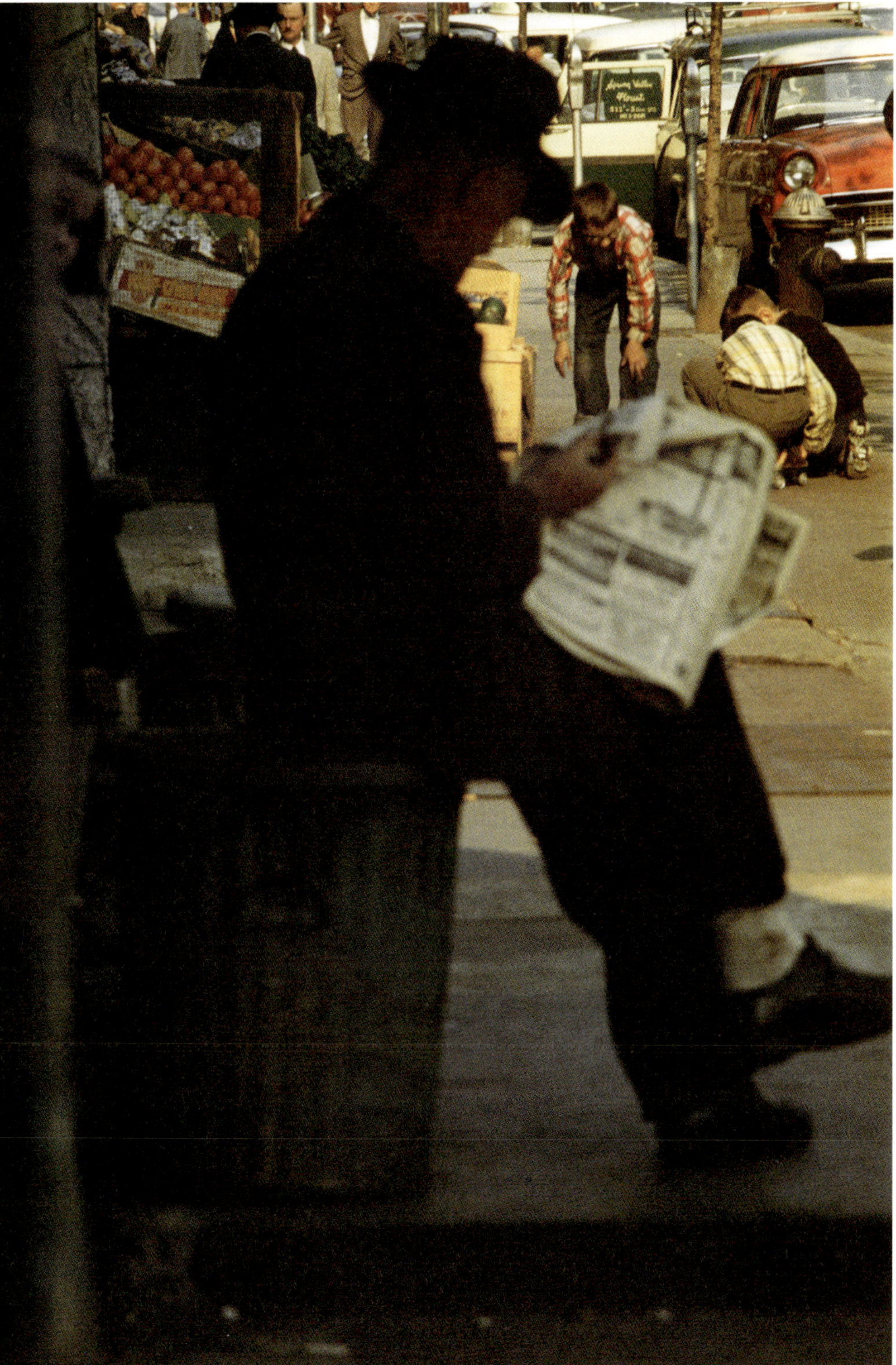

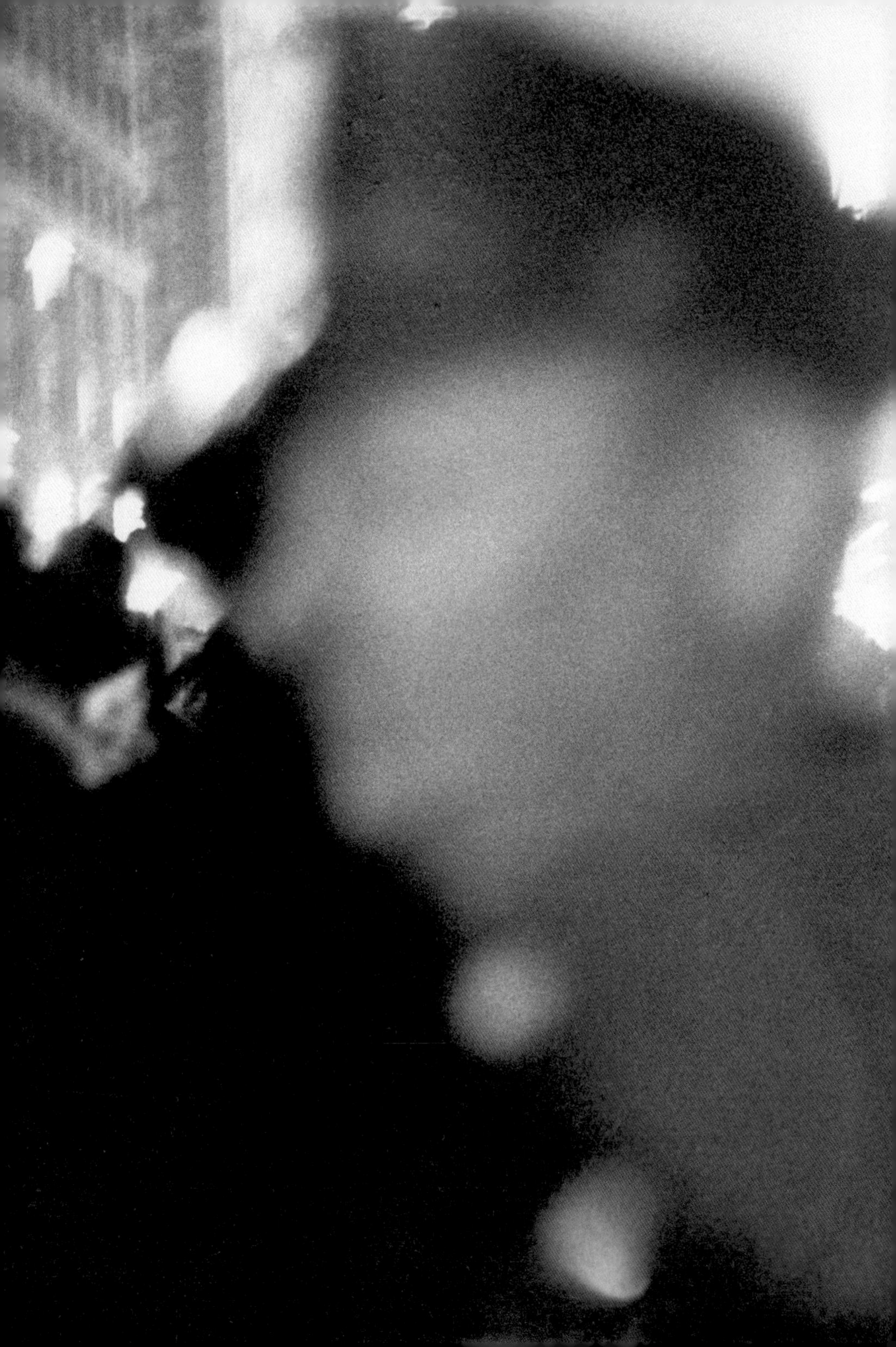

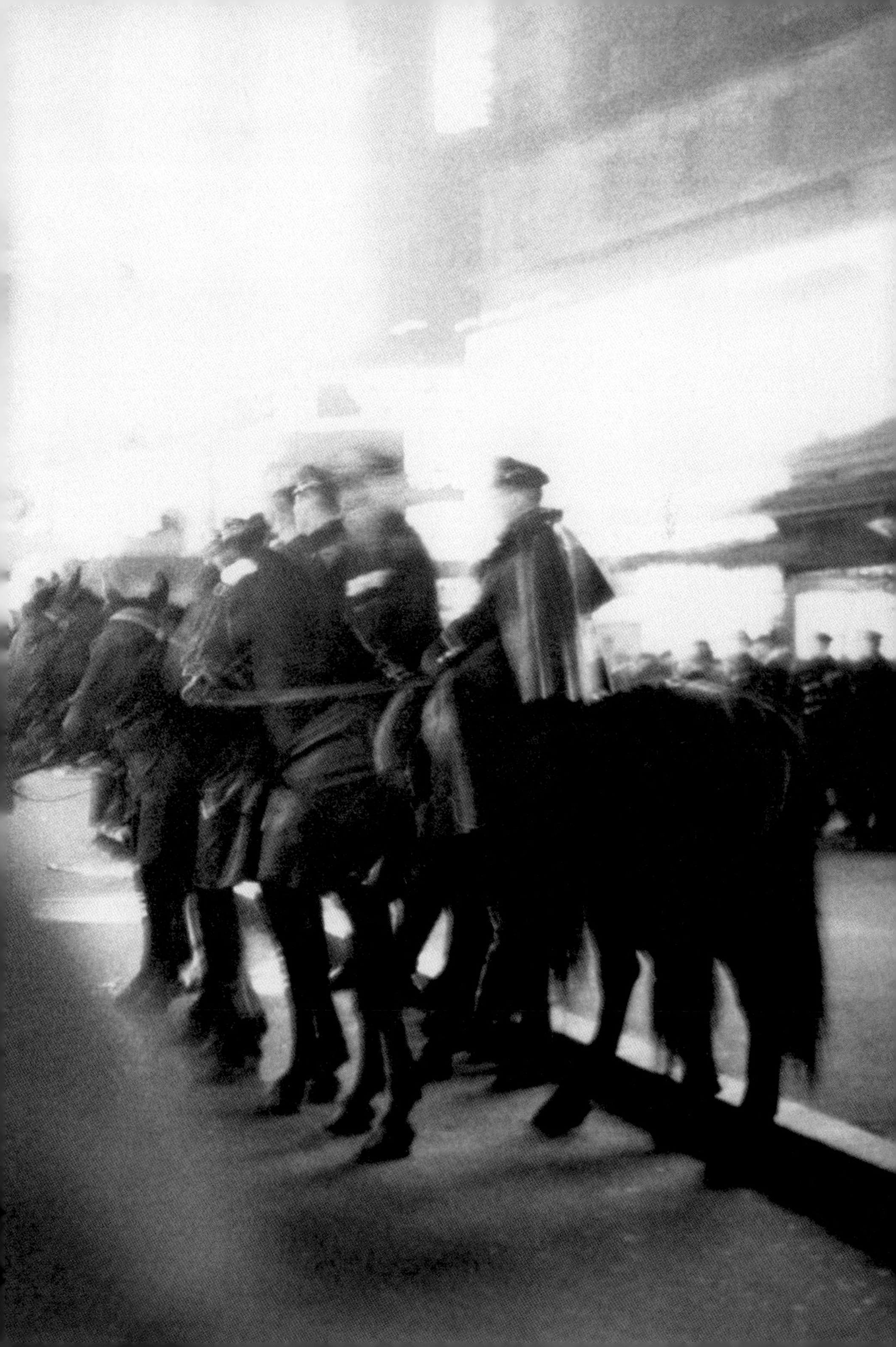

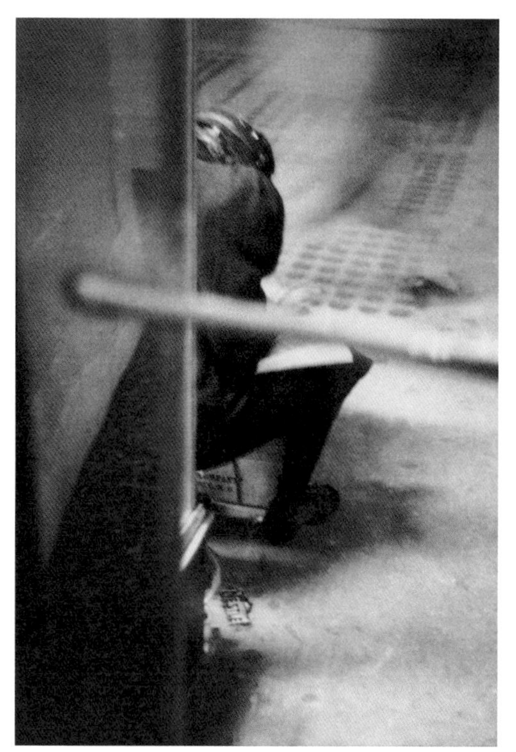

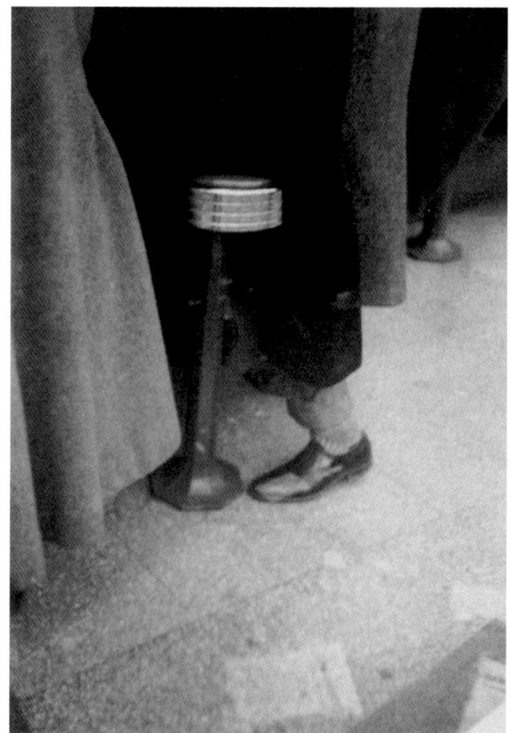

    Subway Lady, c. 1958   L&M, c. 1958   Hands, c. 1954

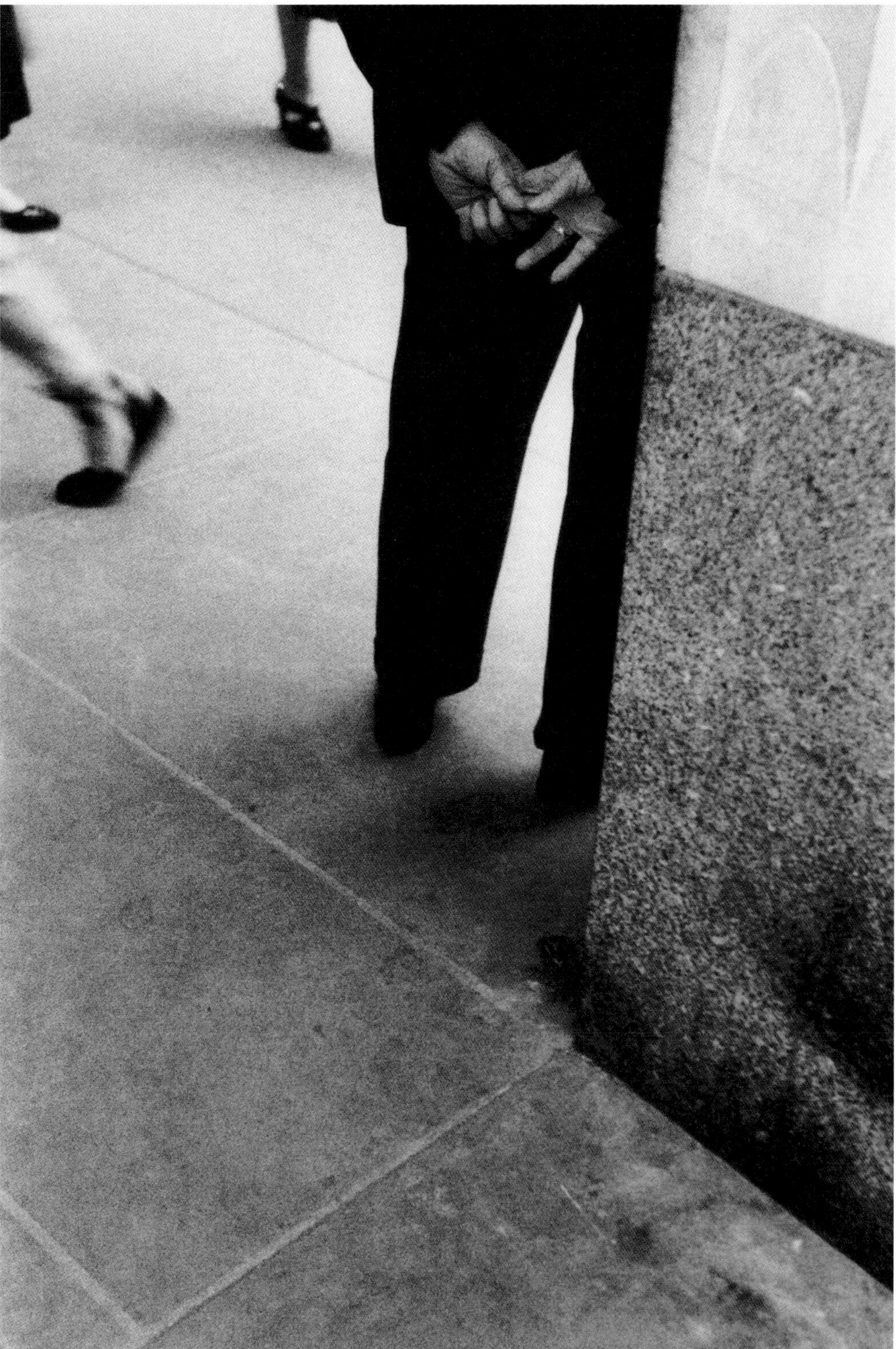

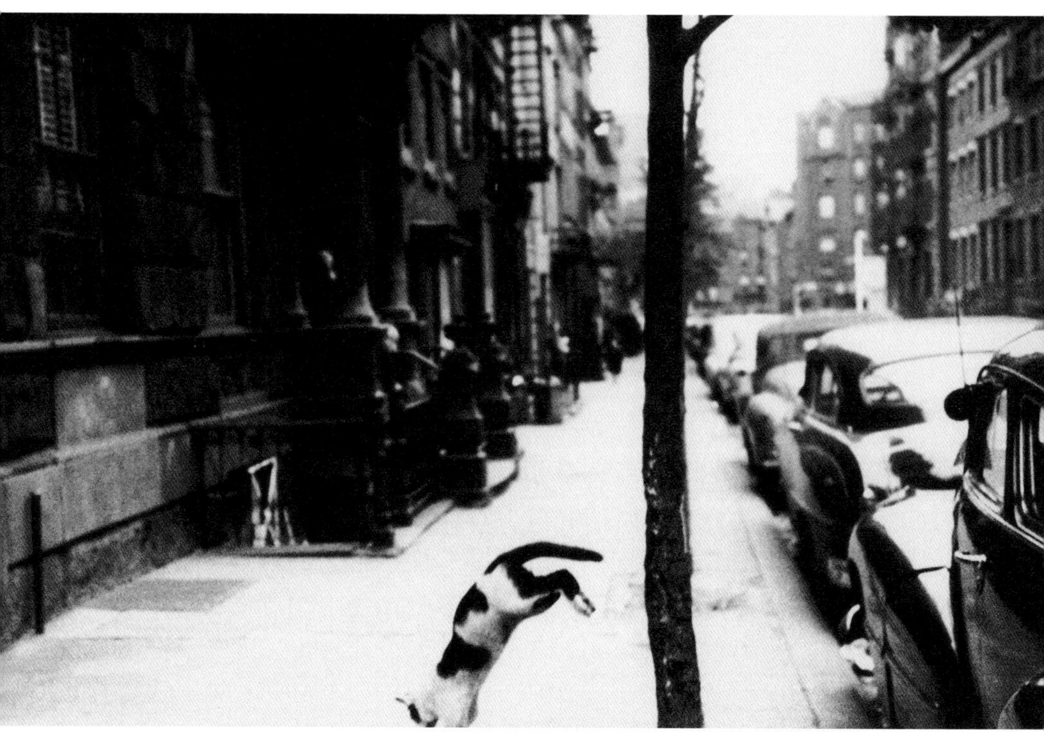

Max Kozloff said to me one day, "You're not really a photographer.
You do photography,
but you do it for your own purposes—your purposes are not the same as others'."
I'm not quite sure what he meant, but I like that. I like the way he put it.

Perry Street Cat, c. 1949

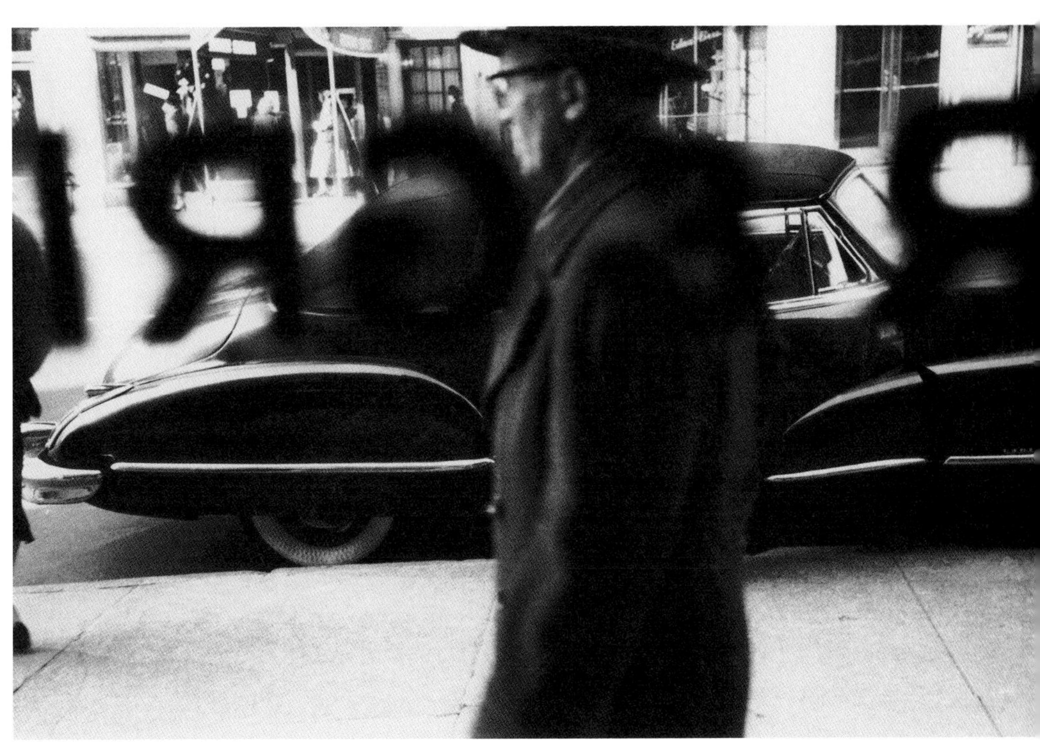

Untitled, 1950s

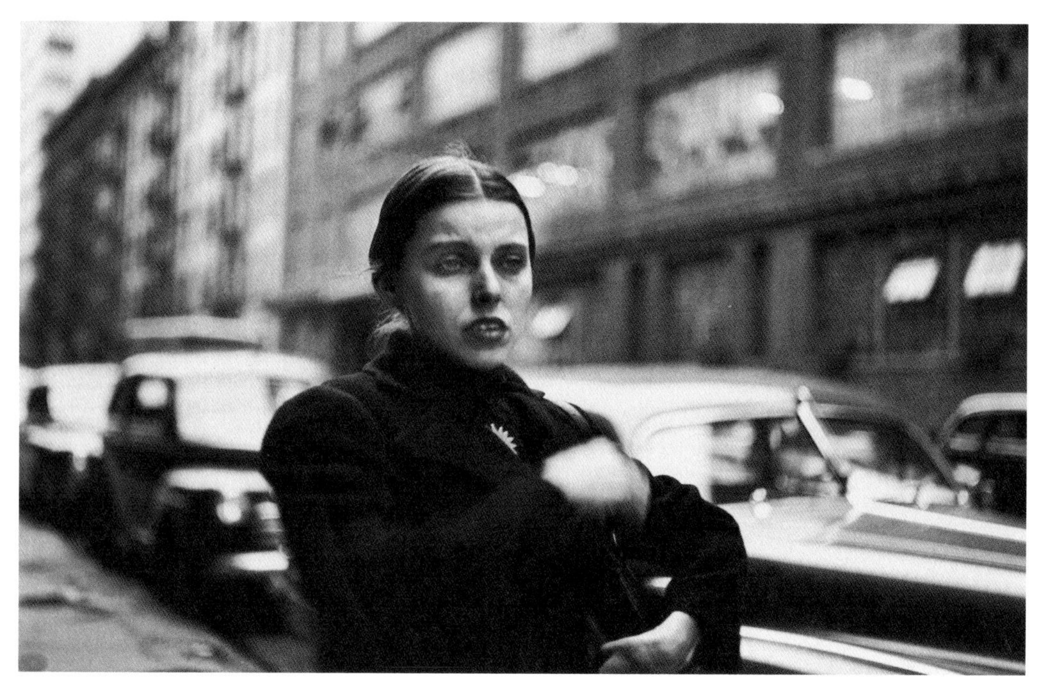

Evelyn, c. 1948

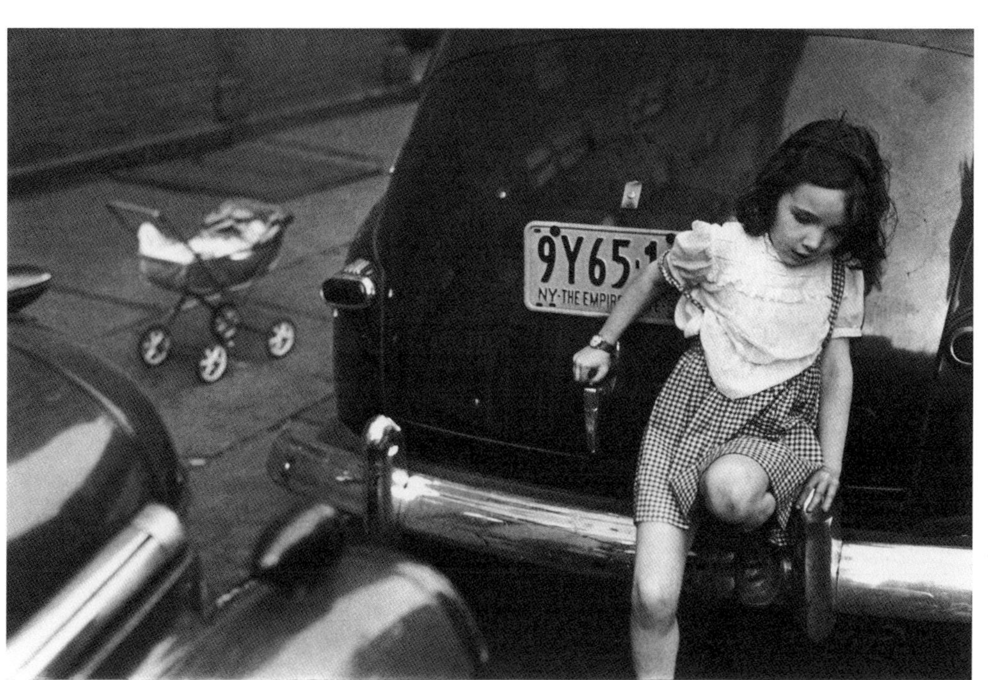

Girl, c. 1953

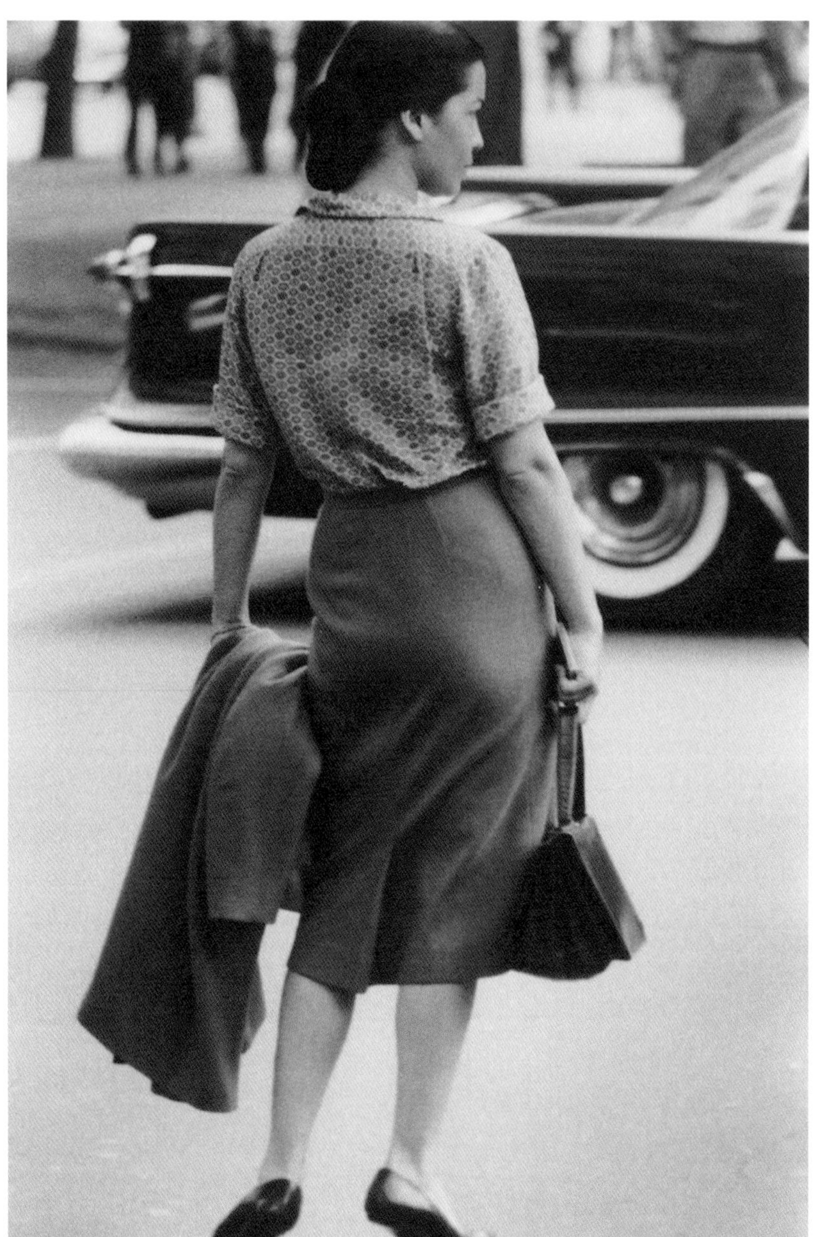

   Untitled, 1950s   Sunday Morning at the Cloisters, c. 1947

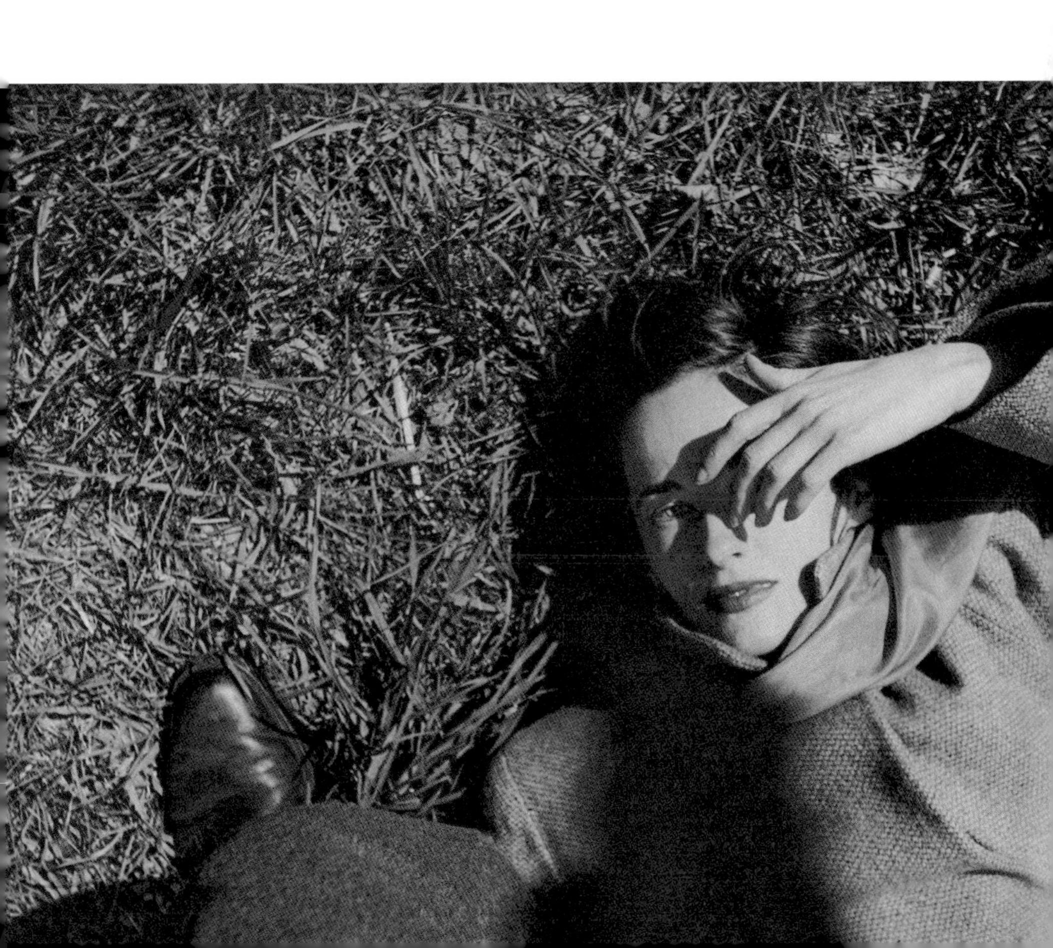

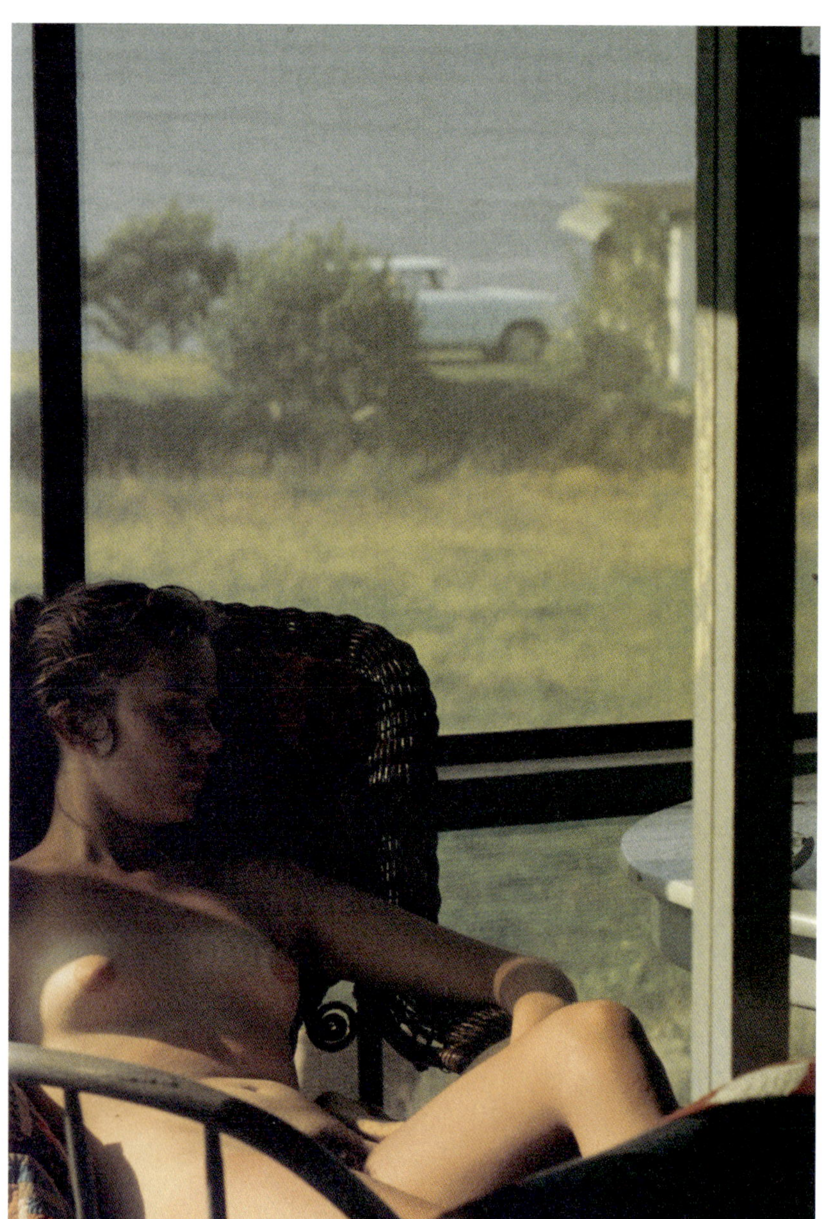

Lanesville, 1958

Woman Waiting, 1958

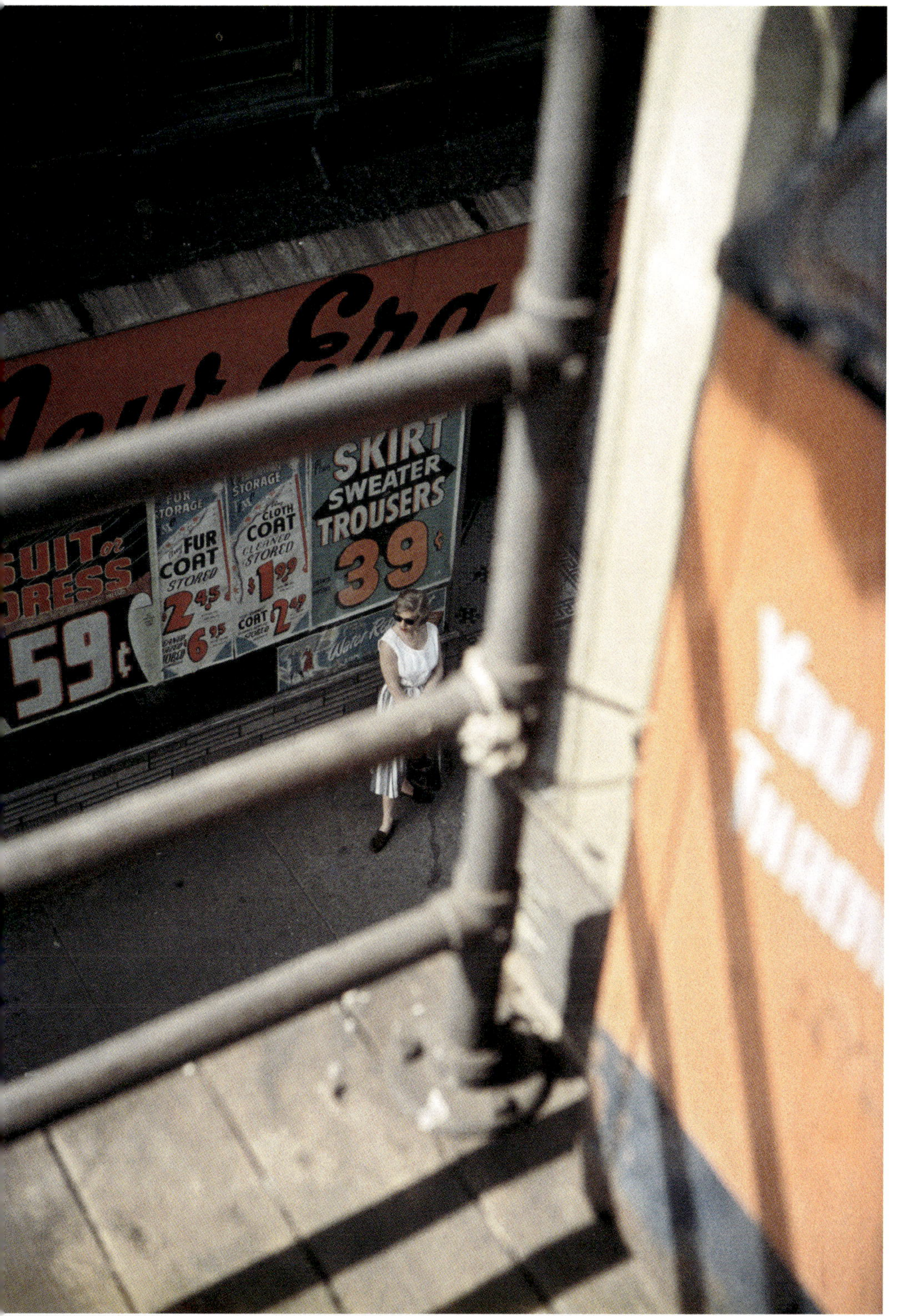
New Era
SKIRT
SWEATER
TROUSERS
39¢
FUR
STORAGE
STORAGE
FUR
COAT
STORED
2 45
CLOTH
COAT
CLEANED
STORED
1 99
COAT
STORED
2 49
6 95
SUIT or
DRESS
59¢
Water R

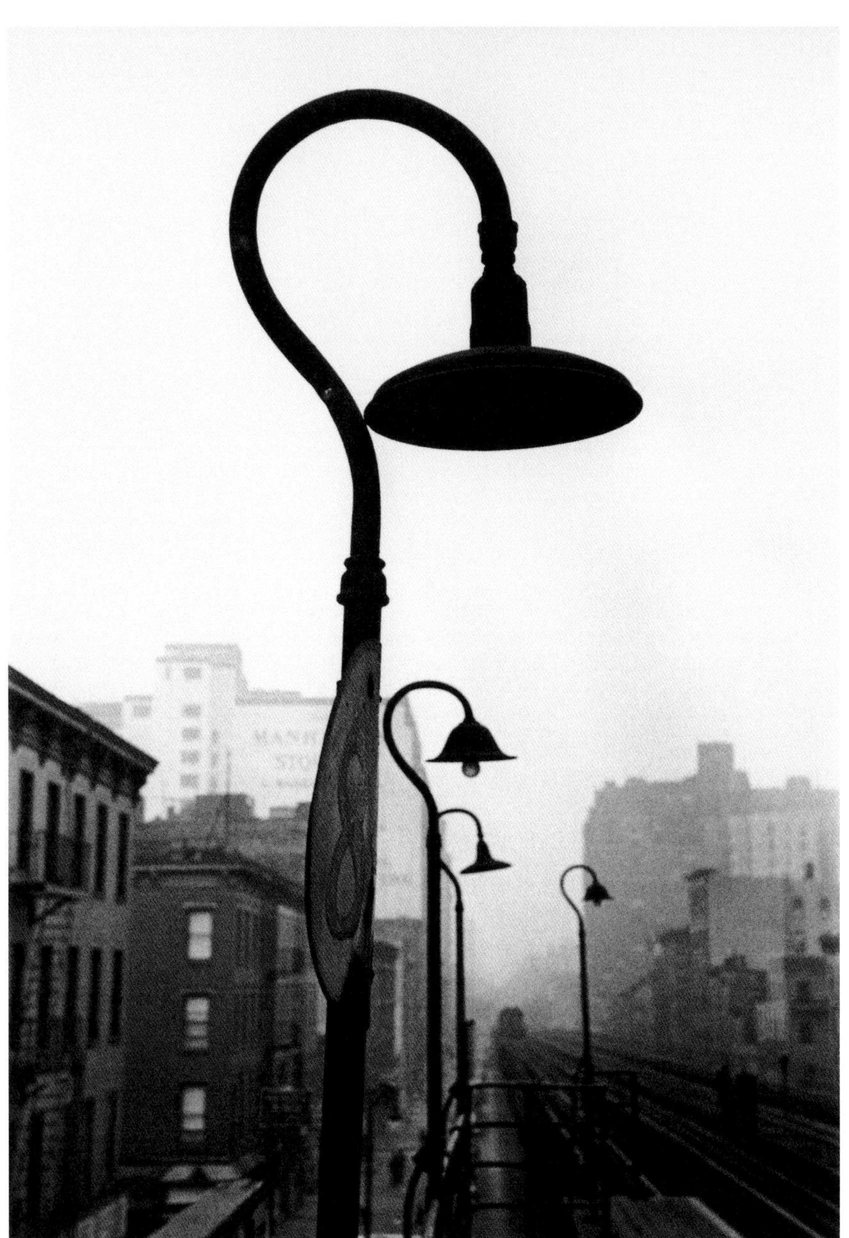

A Walk with Bob, c. 1954

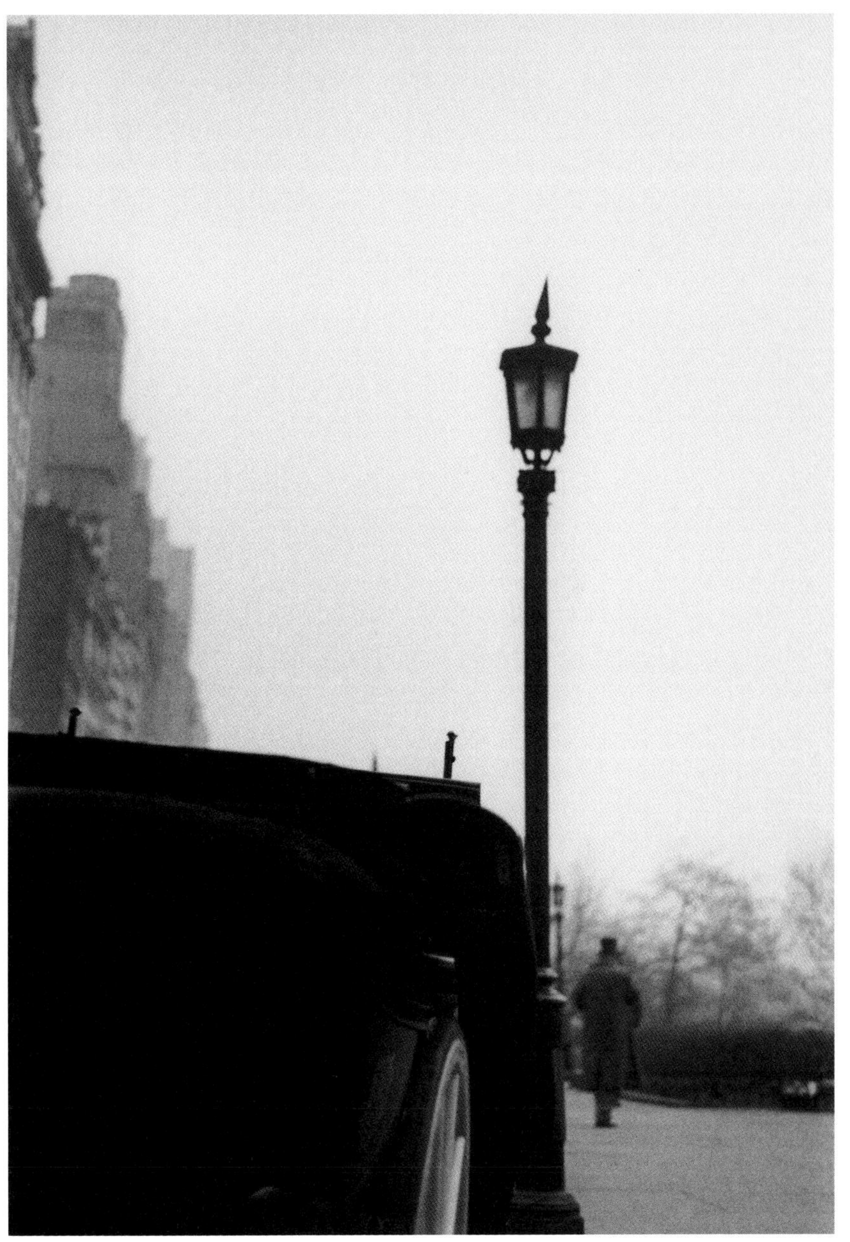

Lamp, 1950s

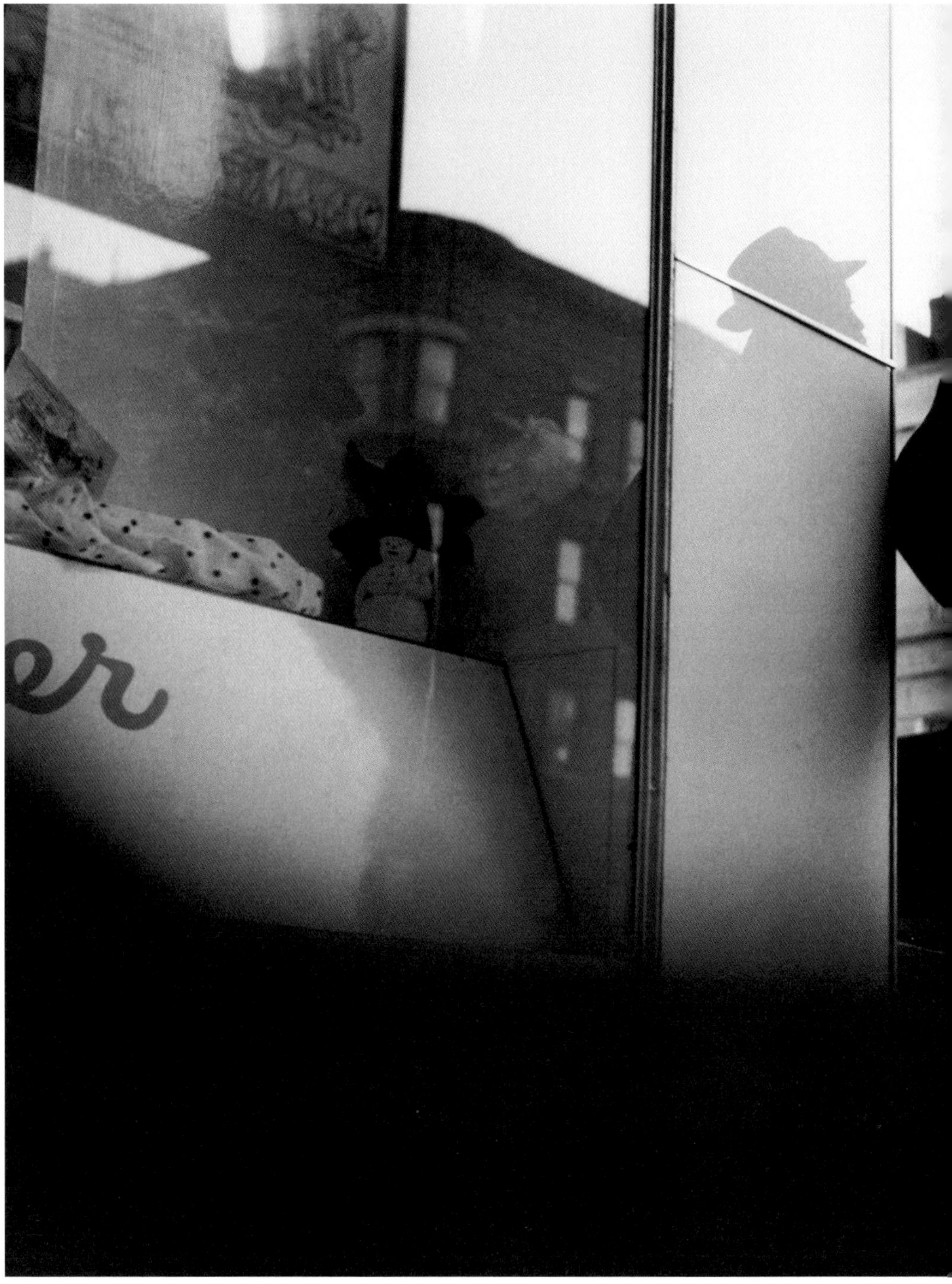

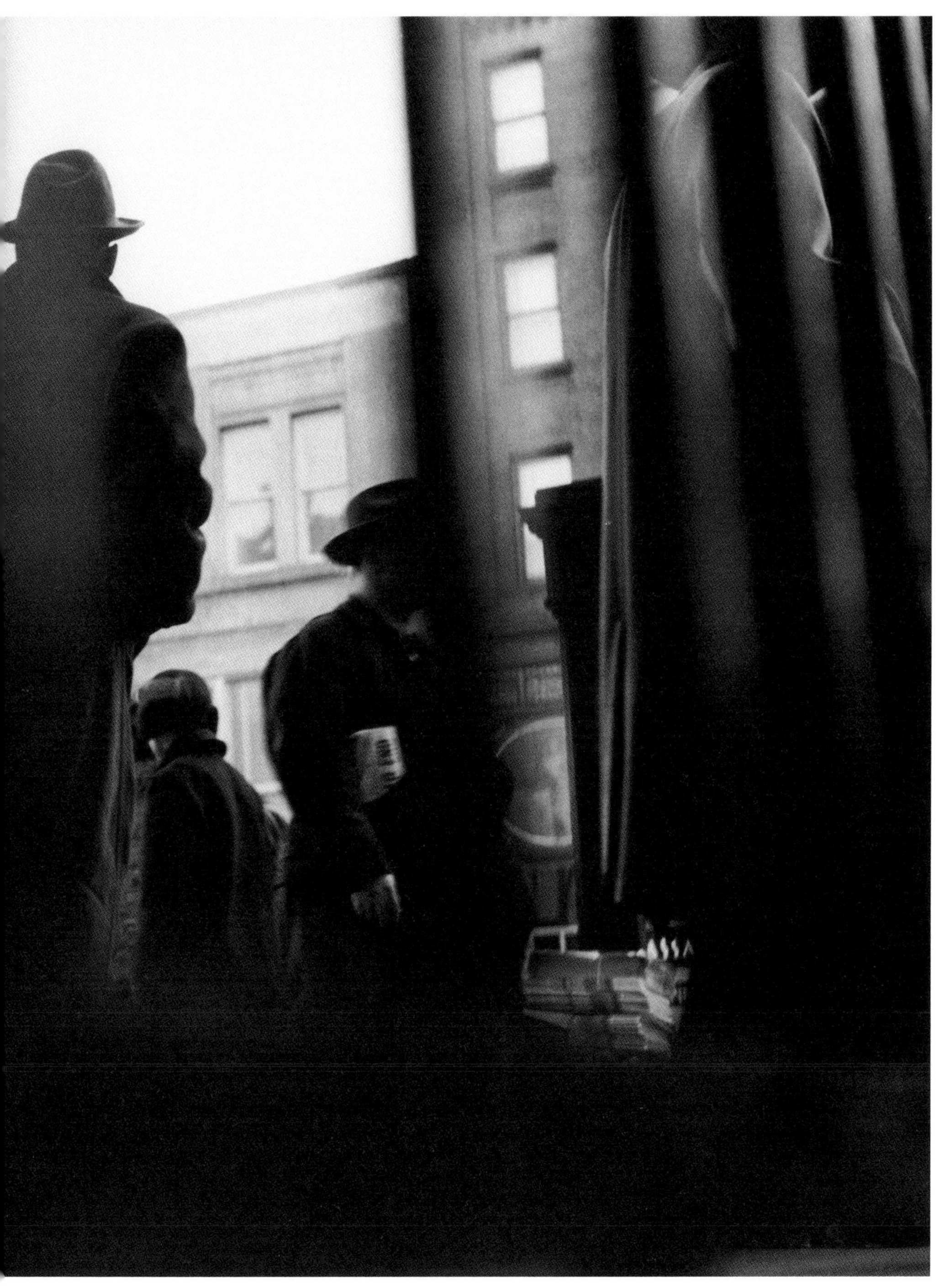

Untitled, 1950s

Life is full of unused opportunities
or, as my friend Henry used to say,
"Saul, you have a talent for avoiding opportunities."

Barbara Dressing, c. 1951

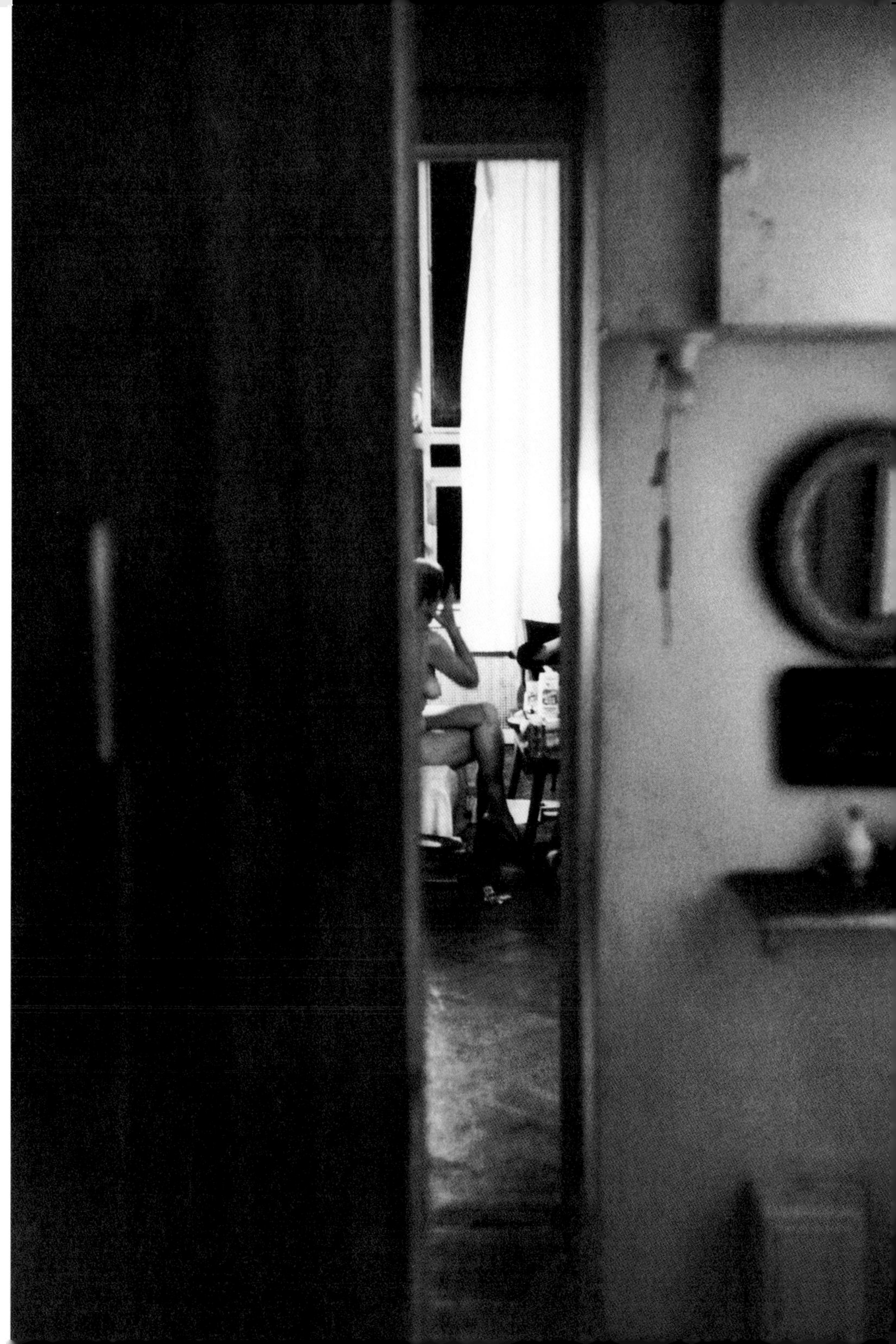

I've never been overwhelmed with a desire to become famous.
It's not that I didn't want to have my work appreciated,
but for some reason—maybe it's because my father disapproved
of almost everything I did—in some secret place in my being
was a desire to avoid success.

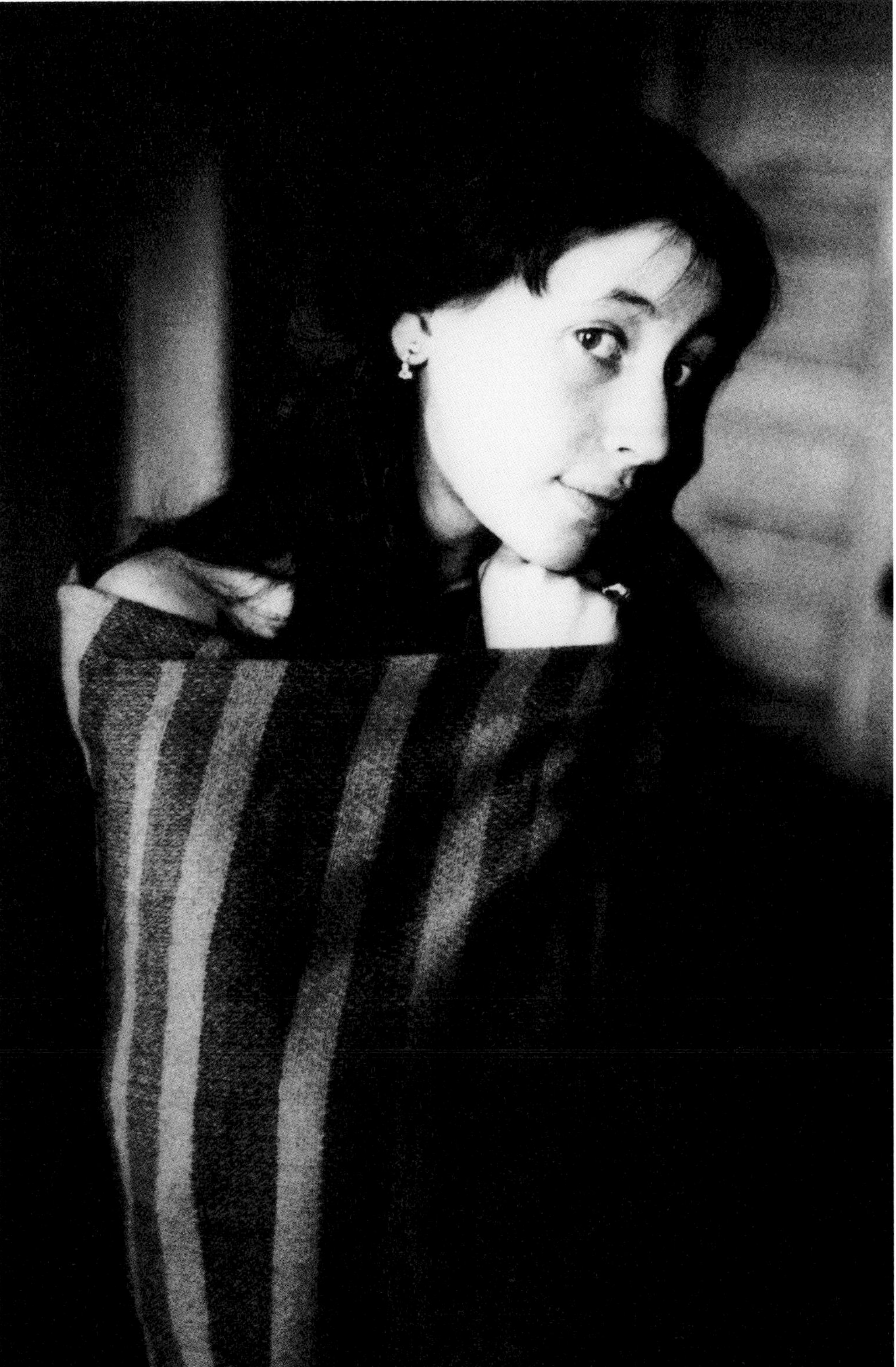

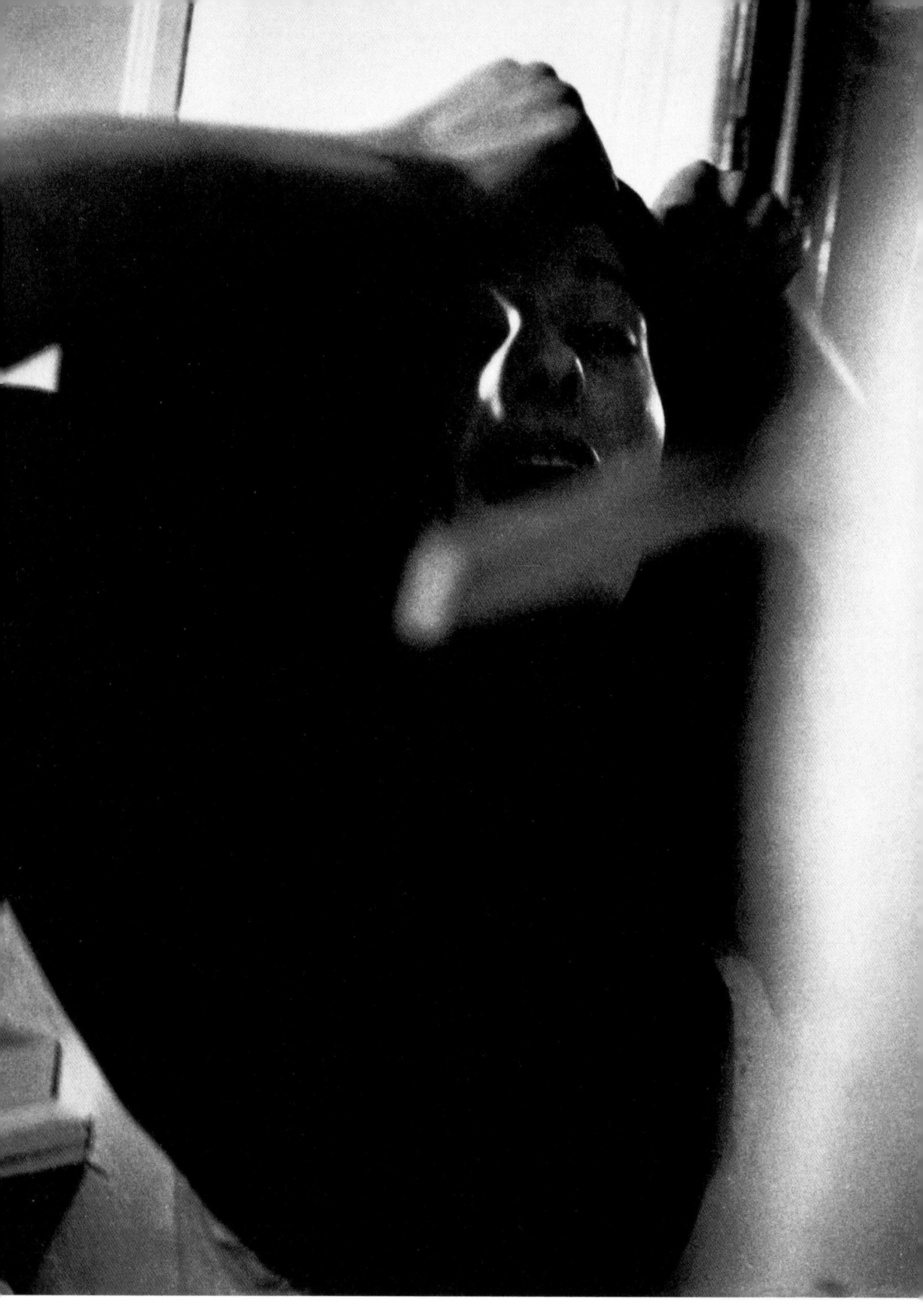

Kim, c. 1947

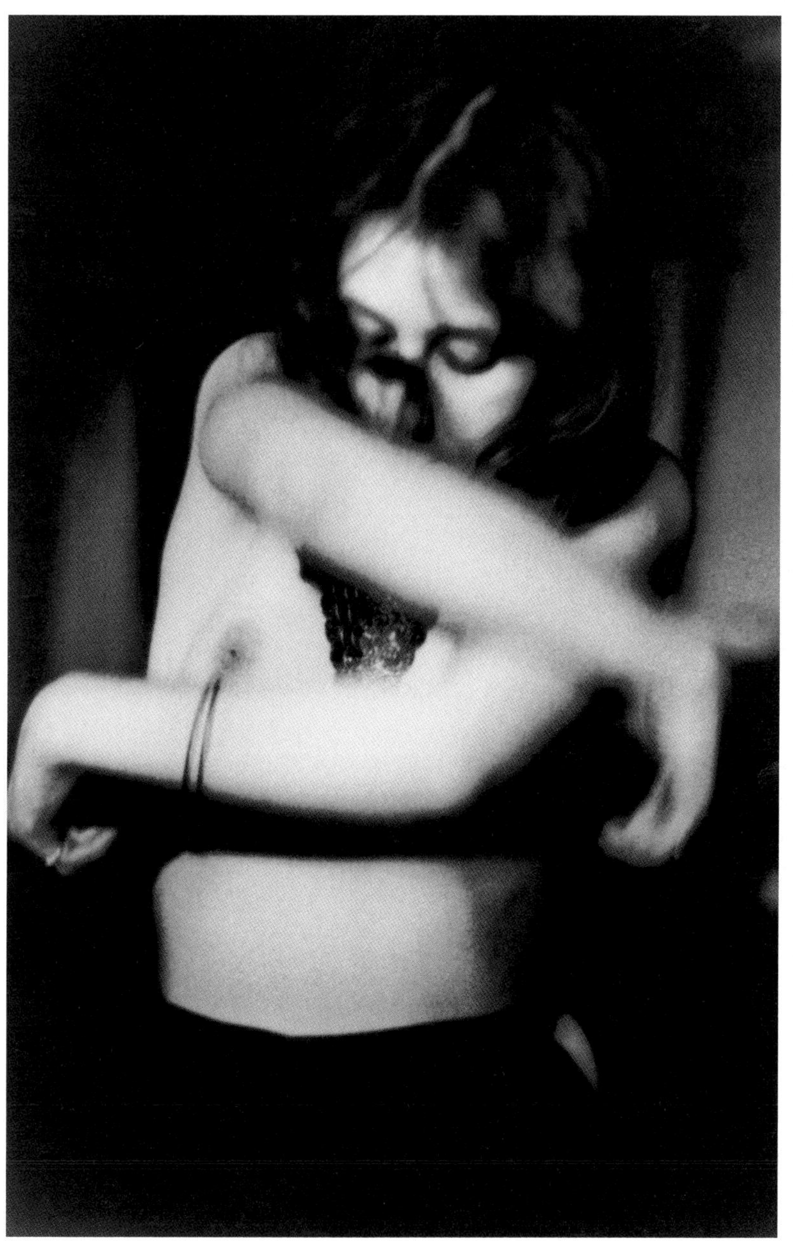

Inez, c. 1947

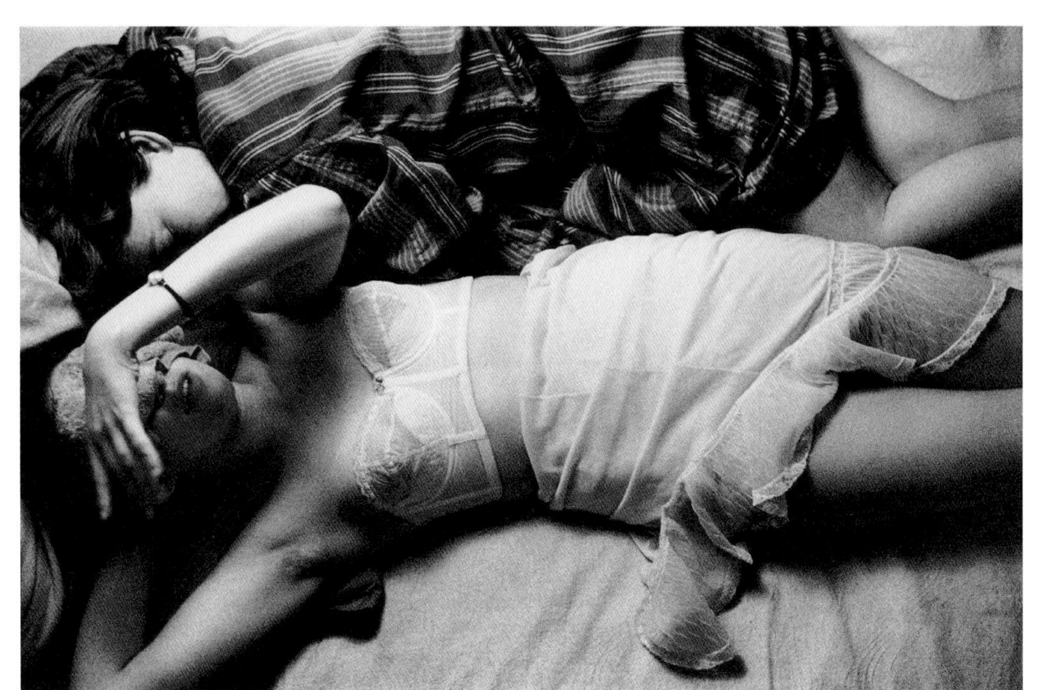

Barbara and Bettina, c. 1950

Inez, c. 1947

p. 216 Barbara, c. 1955

p. 217 Untitled, 1950s

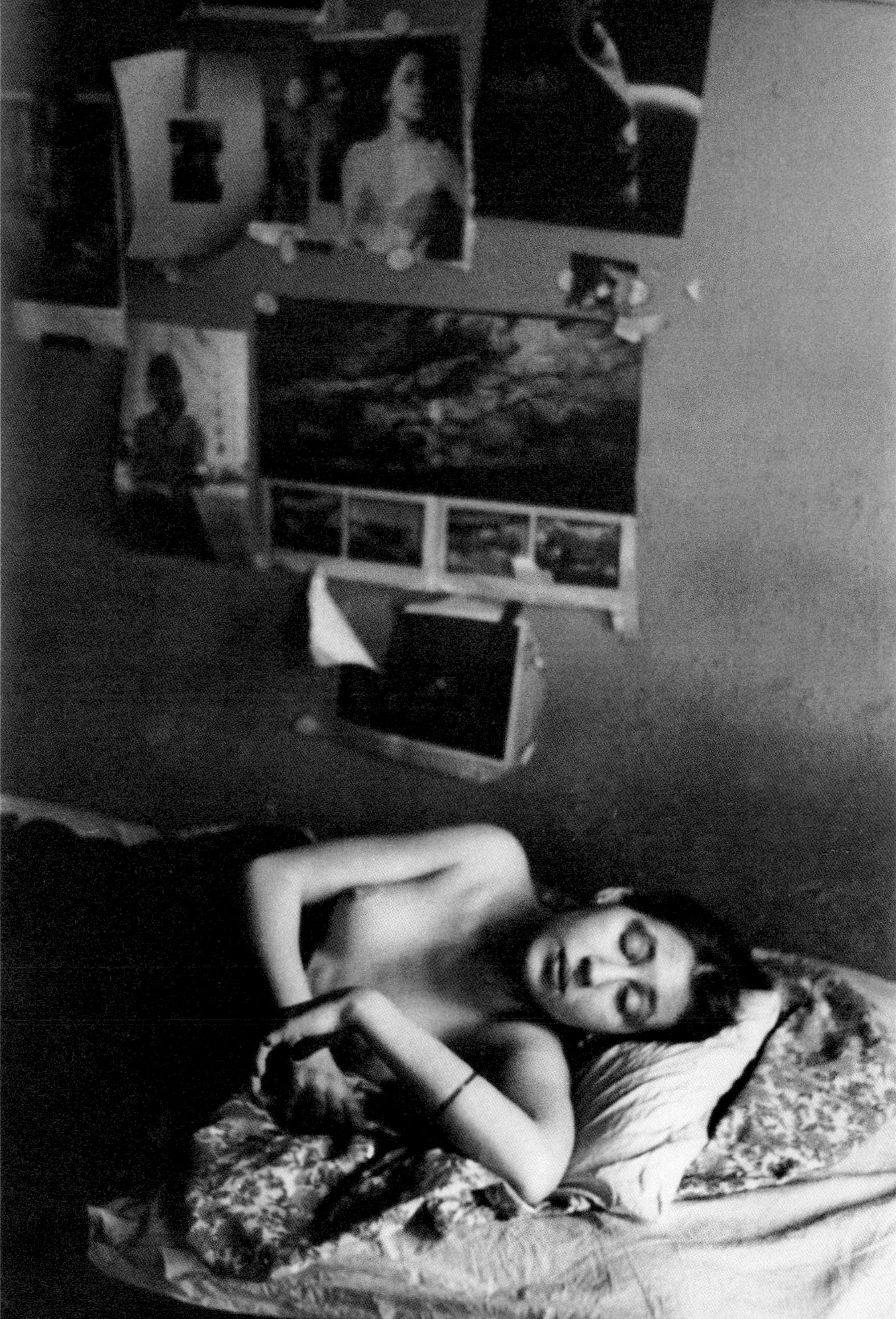

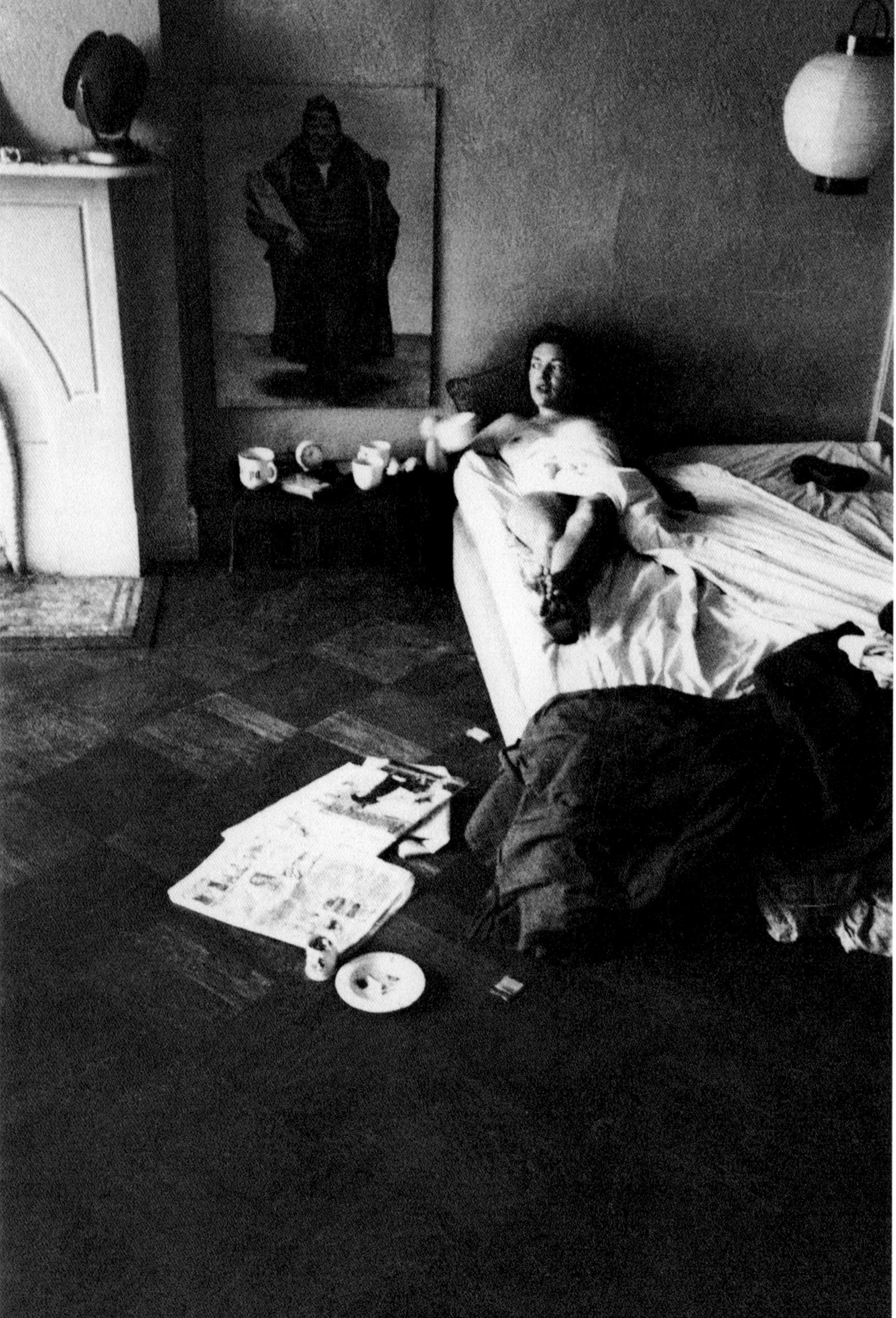

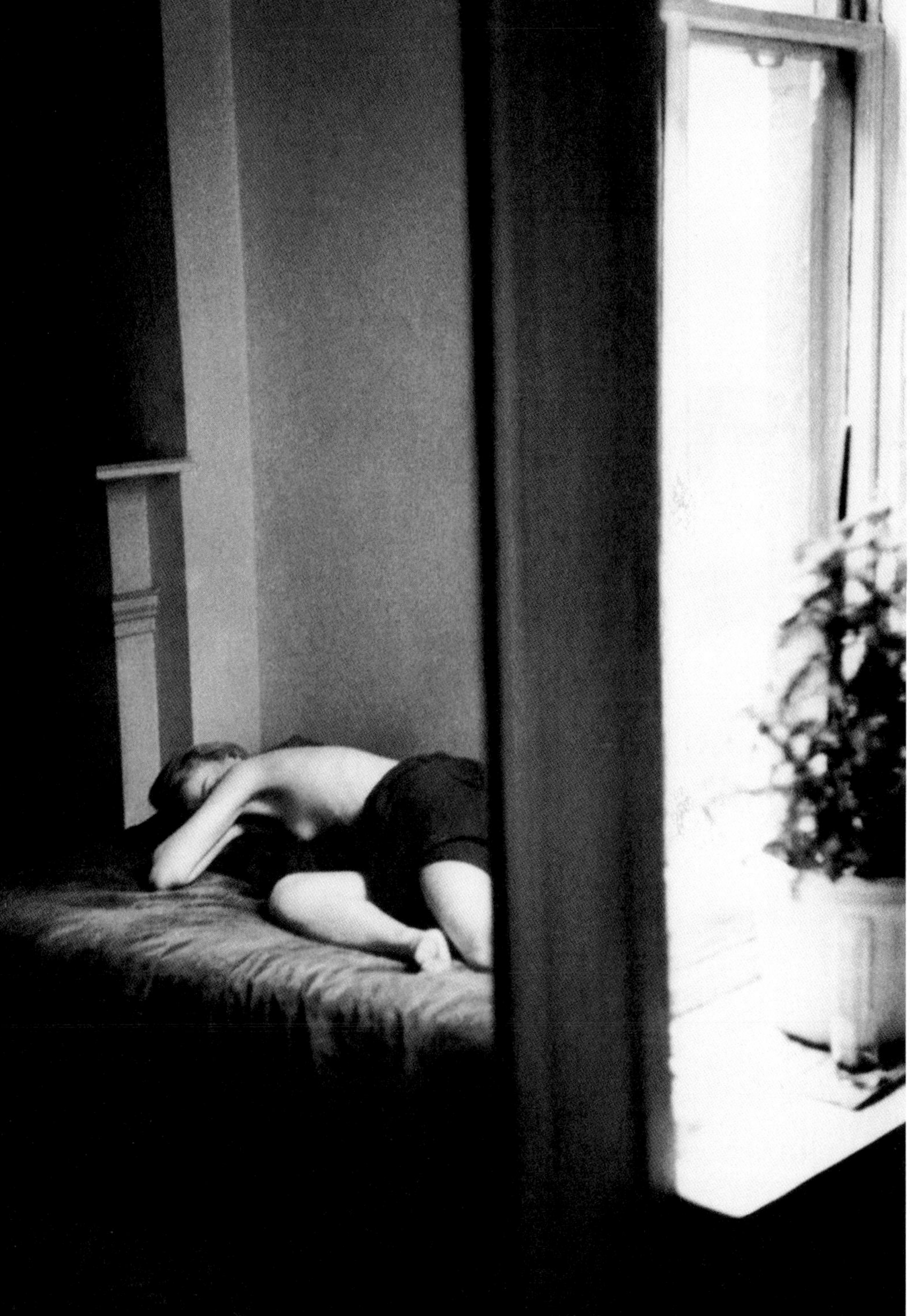

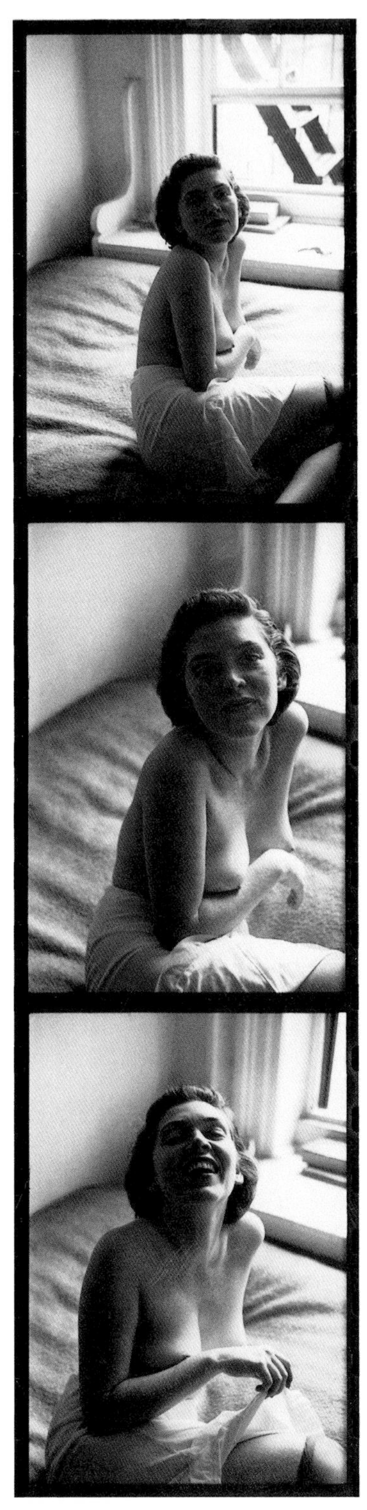

However unruly they may at first appear,
things are given a new logic by the rhythms and accords created for them within the frame.

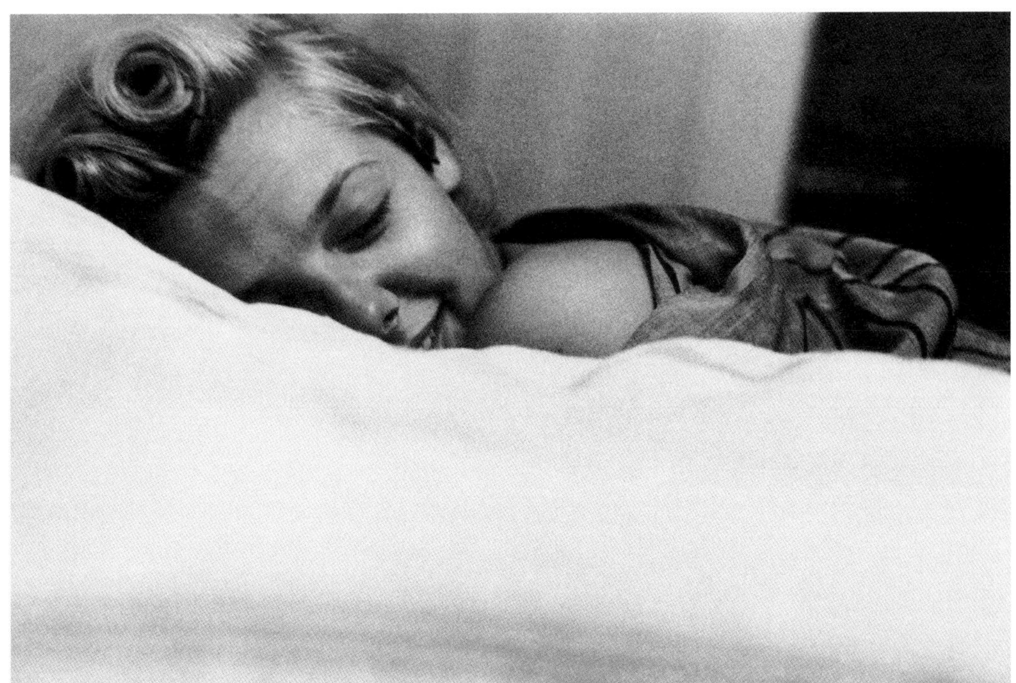

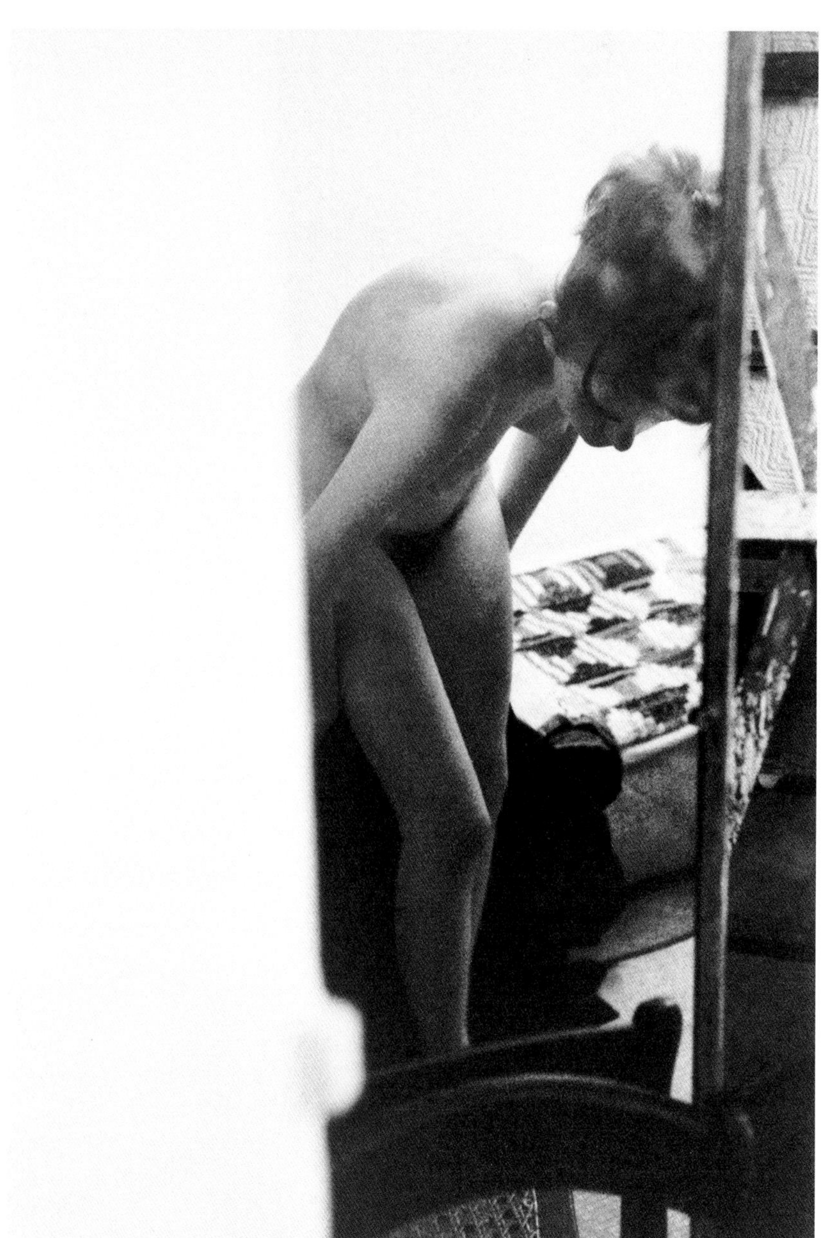

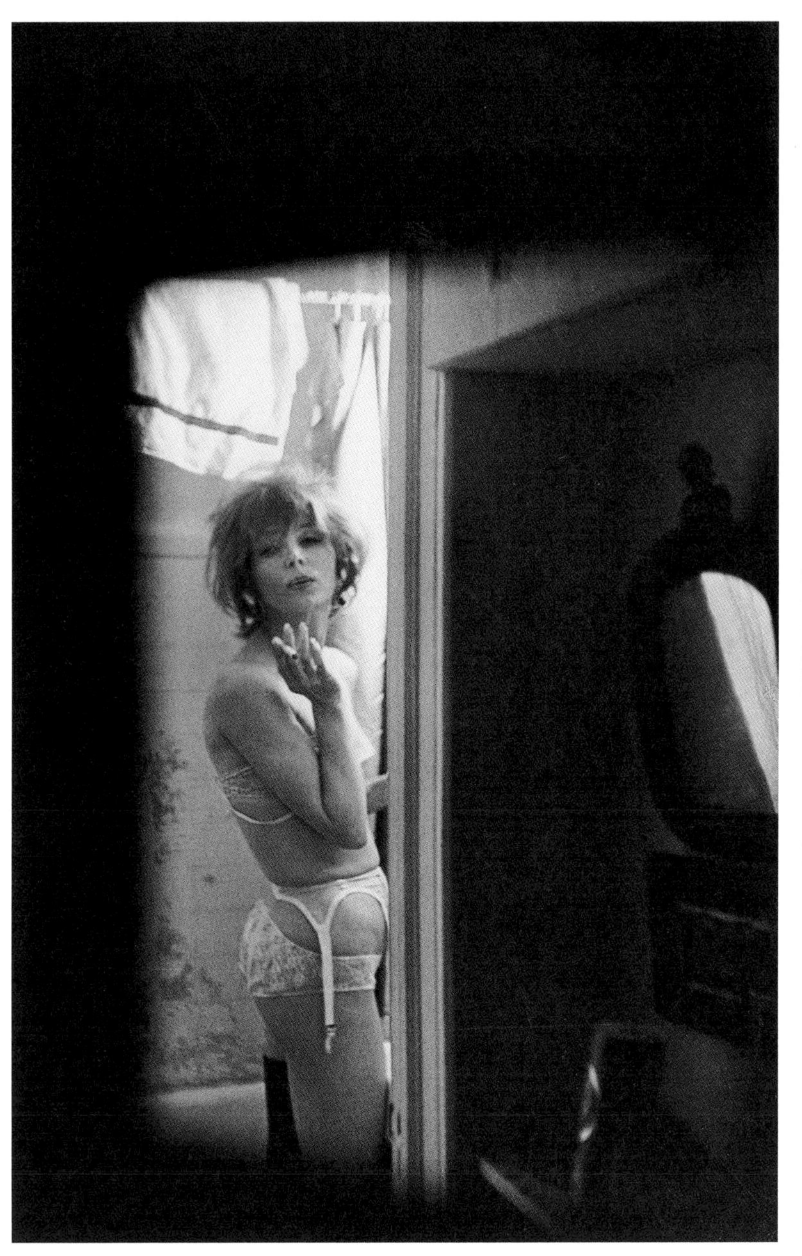

Soames, c. 1962

p. 222 J., c. 1958

p. 223 Barbara, c. 1955

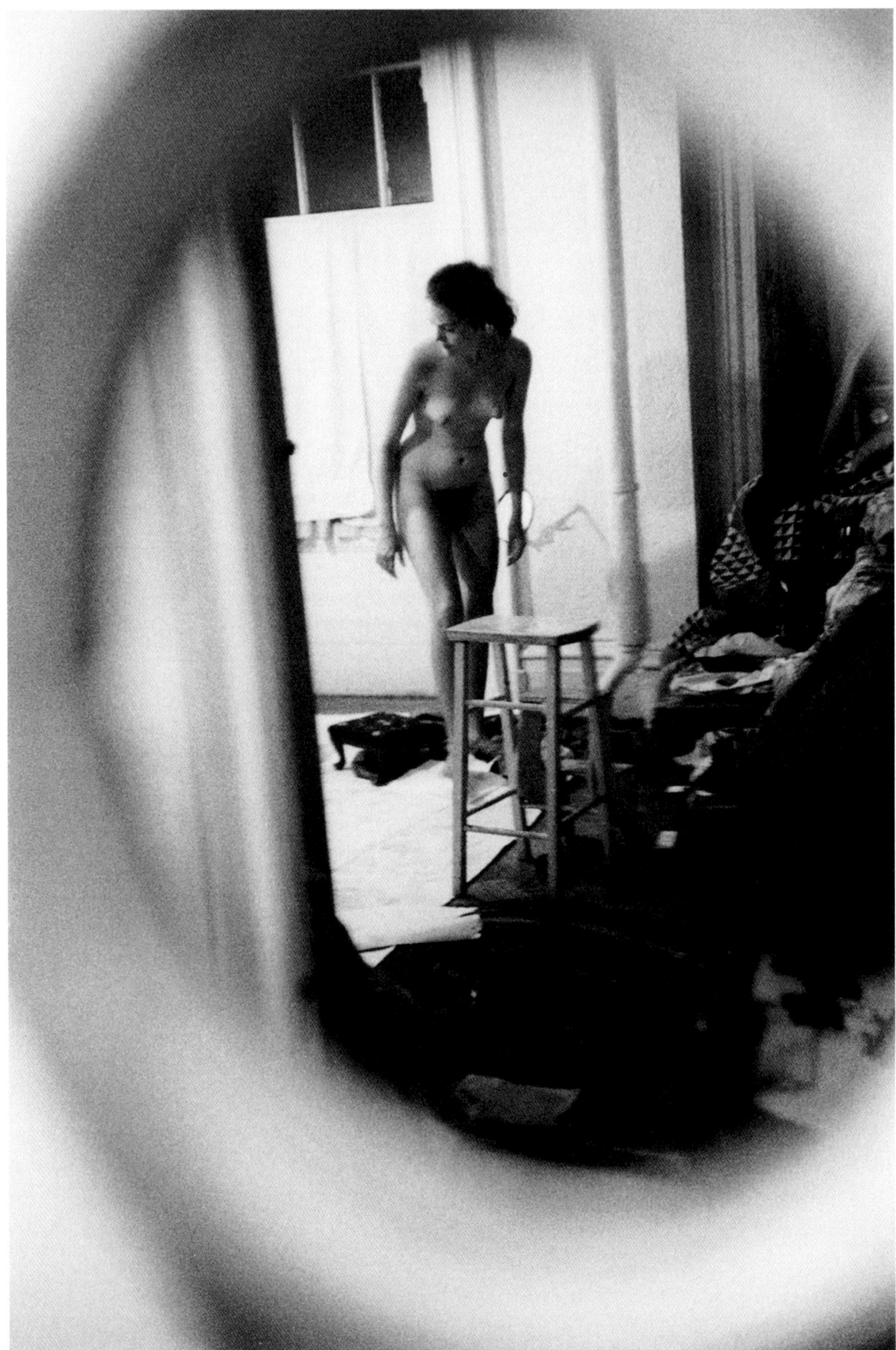

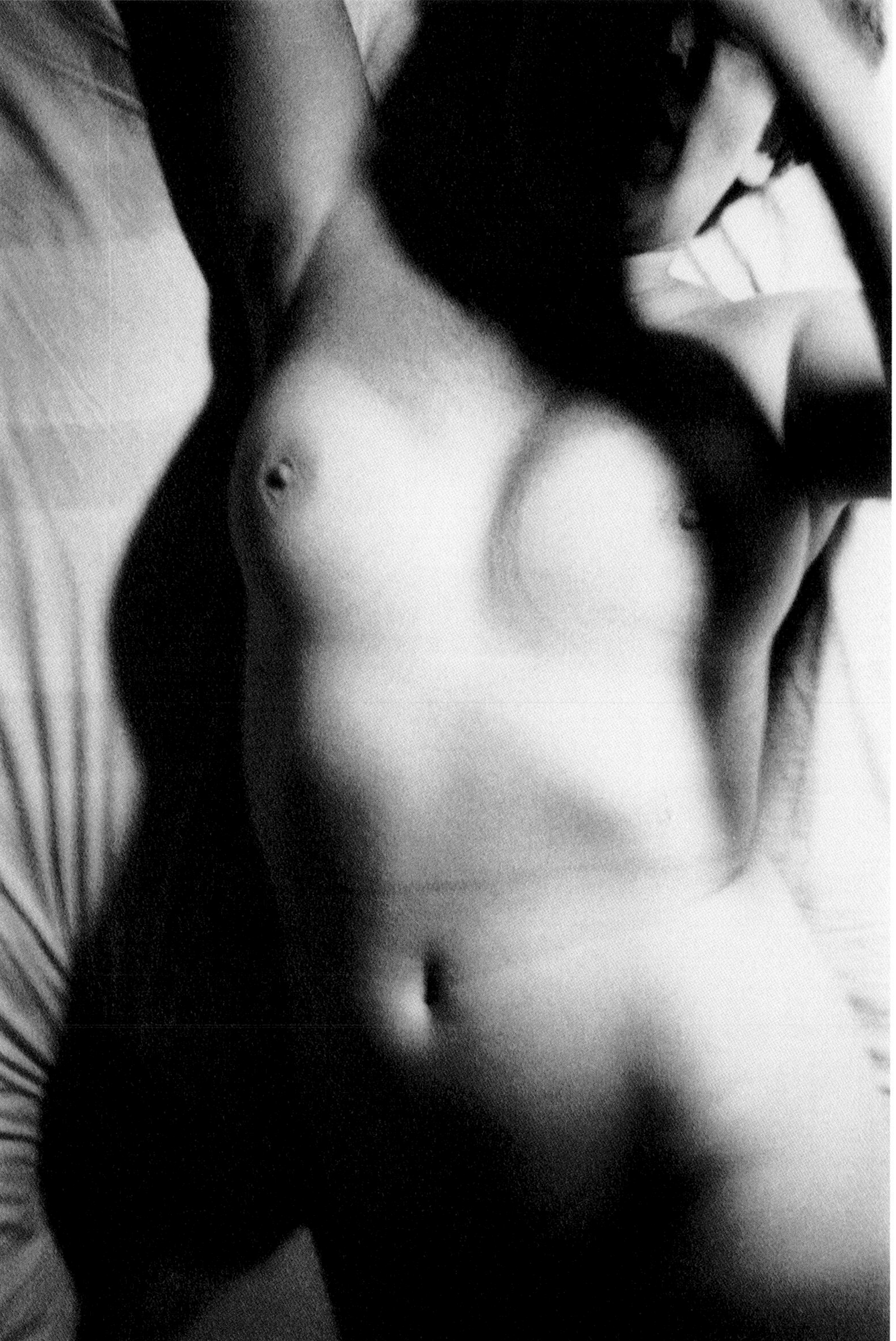

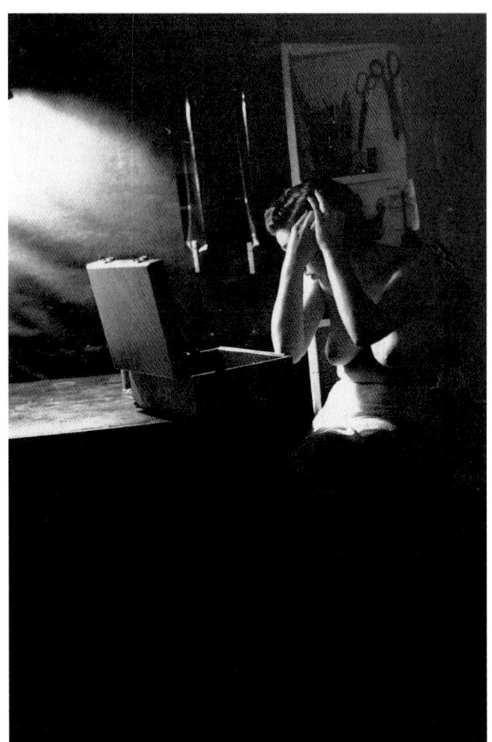

Barbara, c. 1950

Soames, c. 1960

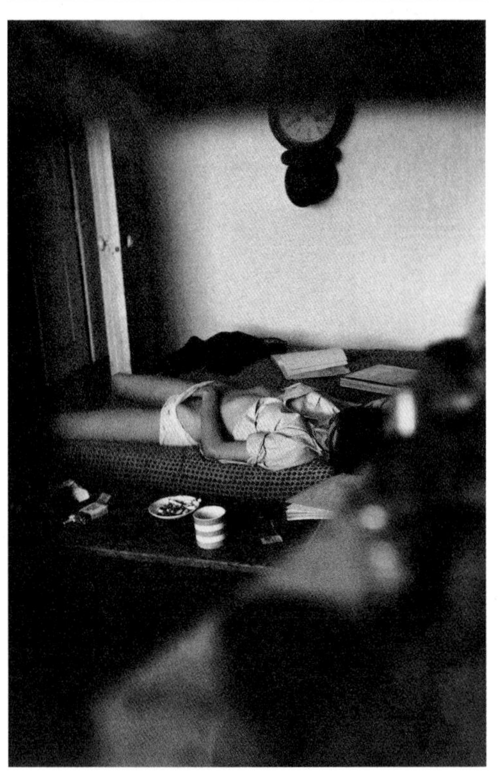

Soames, c. 1962

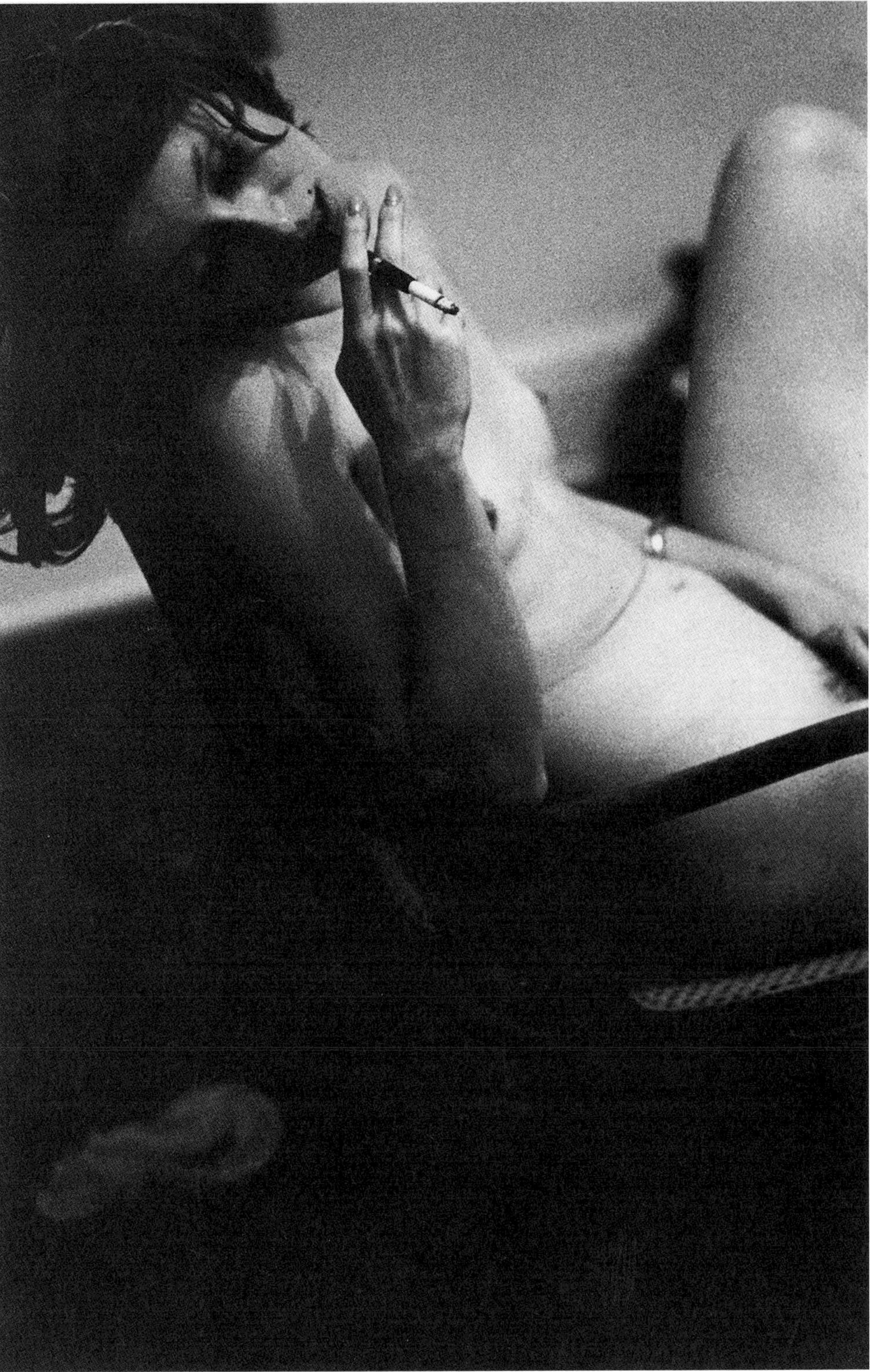

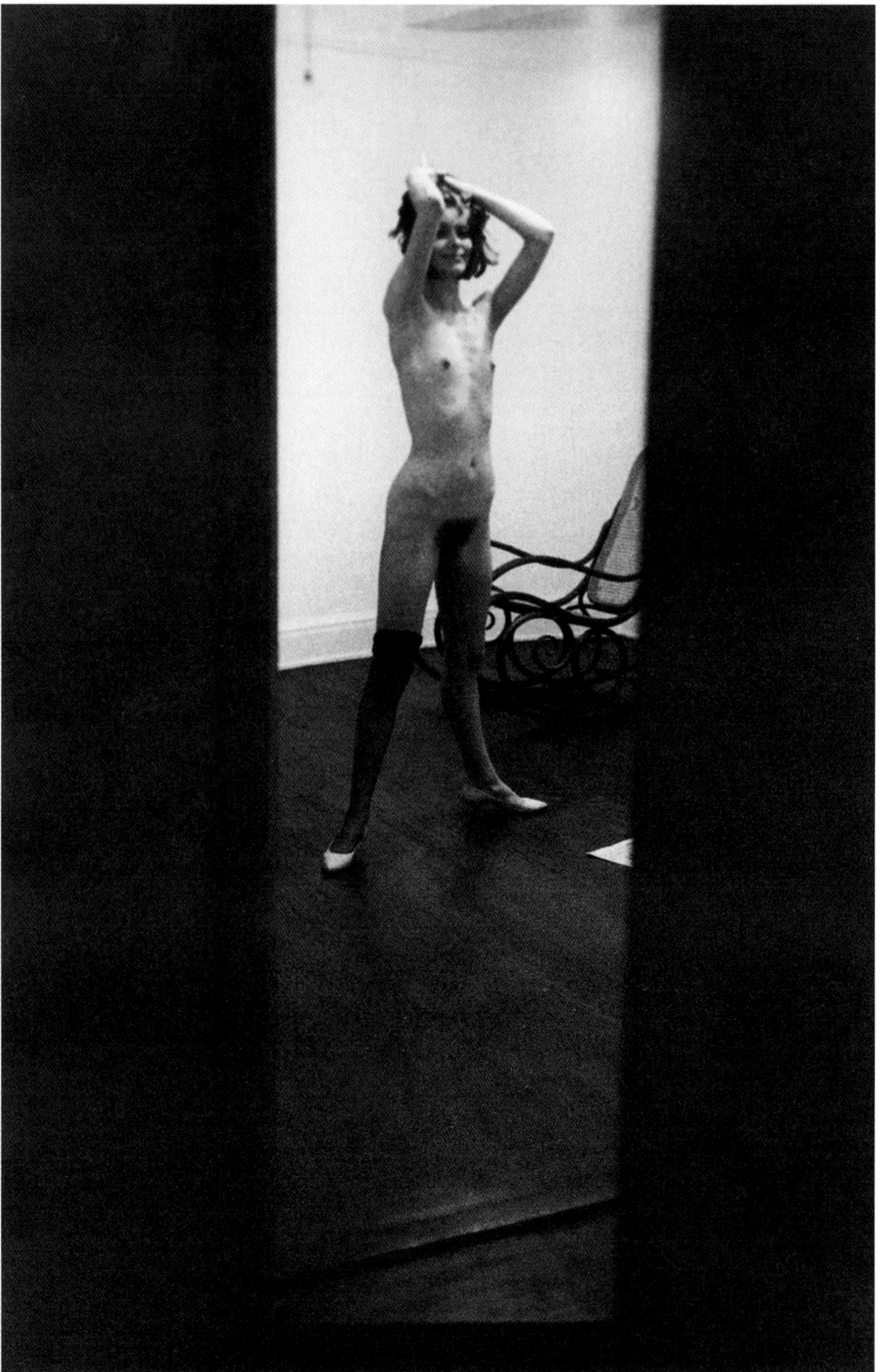

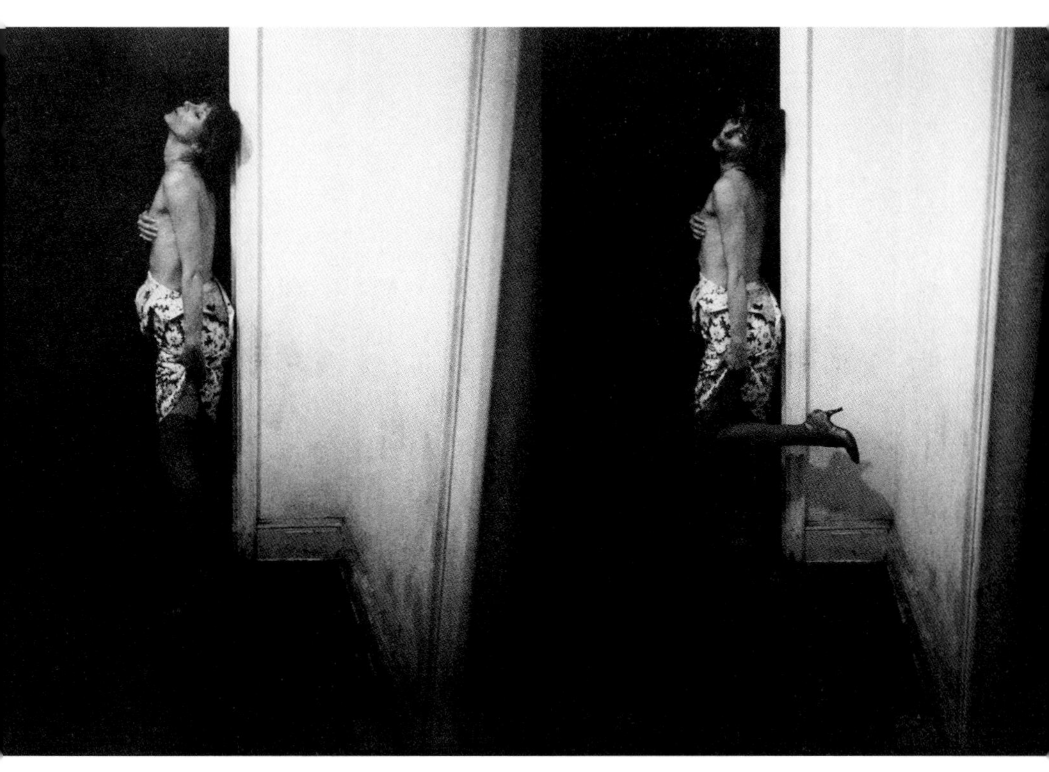

Soames, c. 1962

Soames, c. 1962

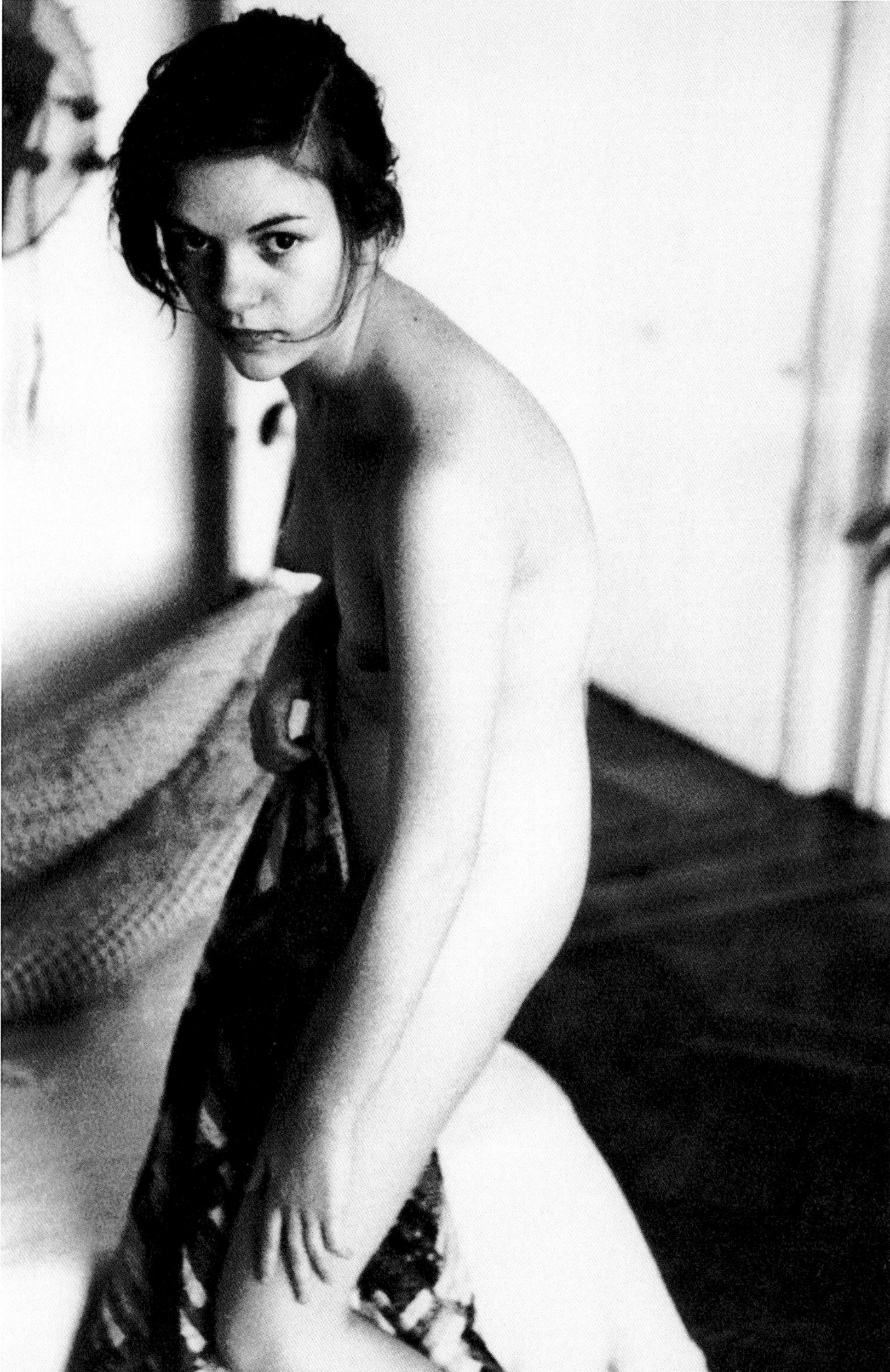

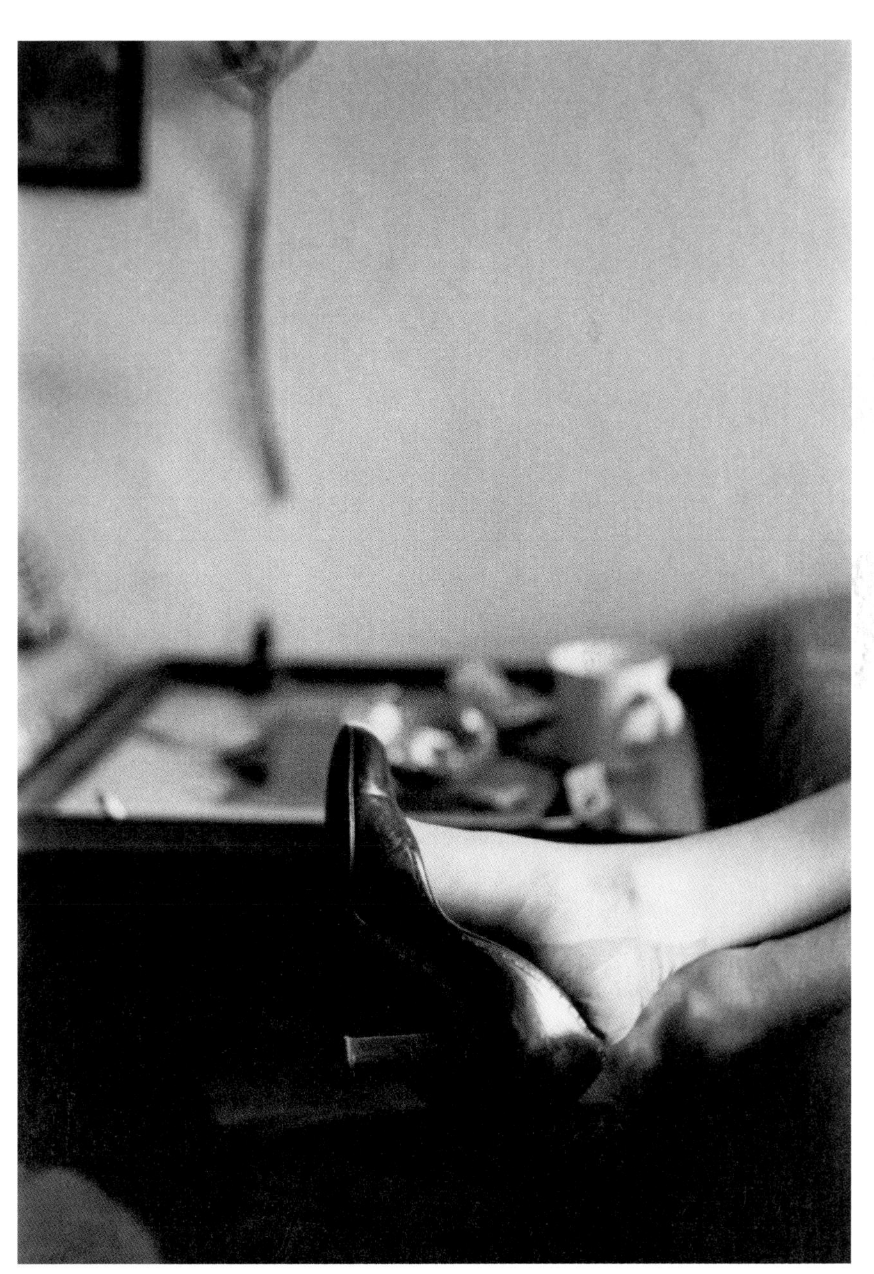

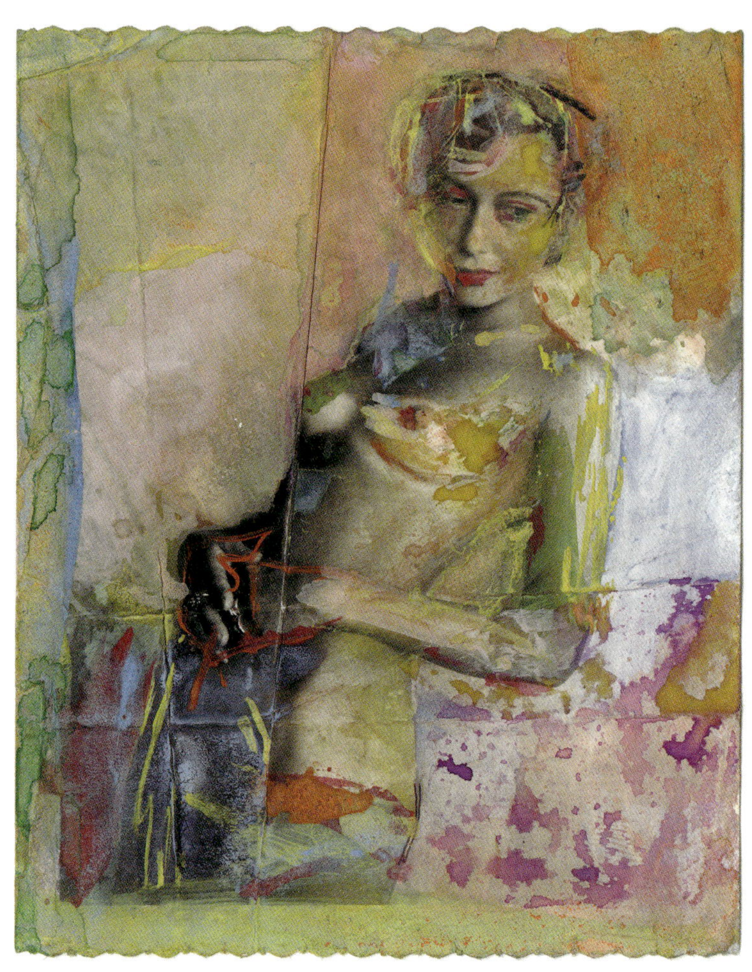

Lynn, printed 1950s, painted c. 1990
Gouache, casein and watercolor on gelatin silver paper

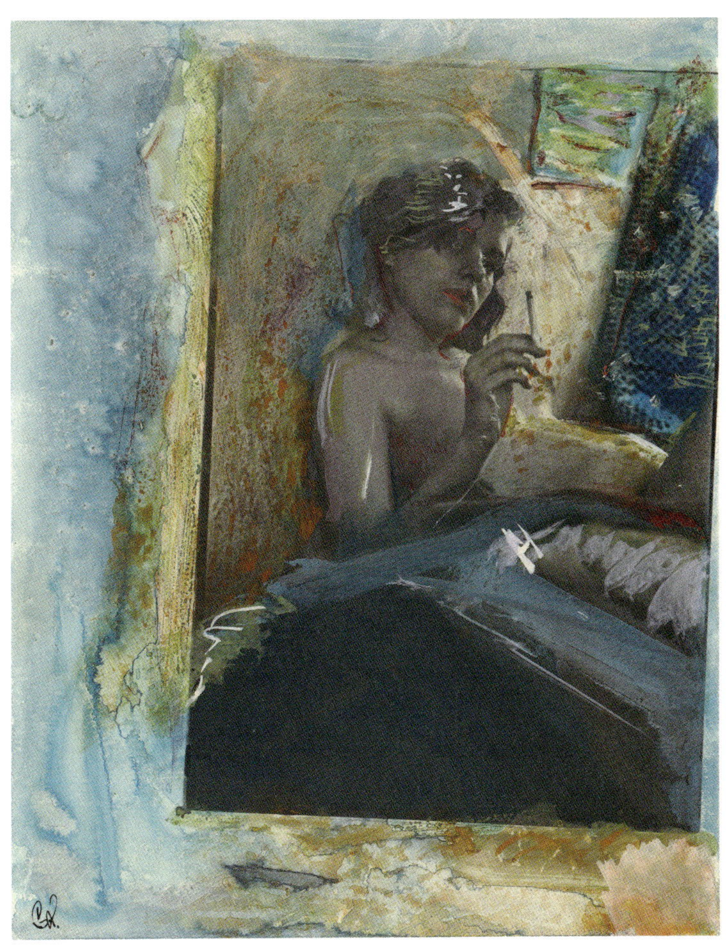

J., printed 1950s, painted c. 1990
Gouache, casein and watercolor on gelatin silver paper

p. 232 Barbara, c. 1954
p. 233 J., c. 1958

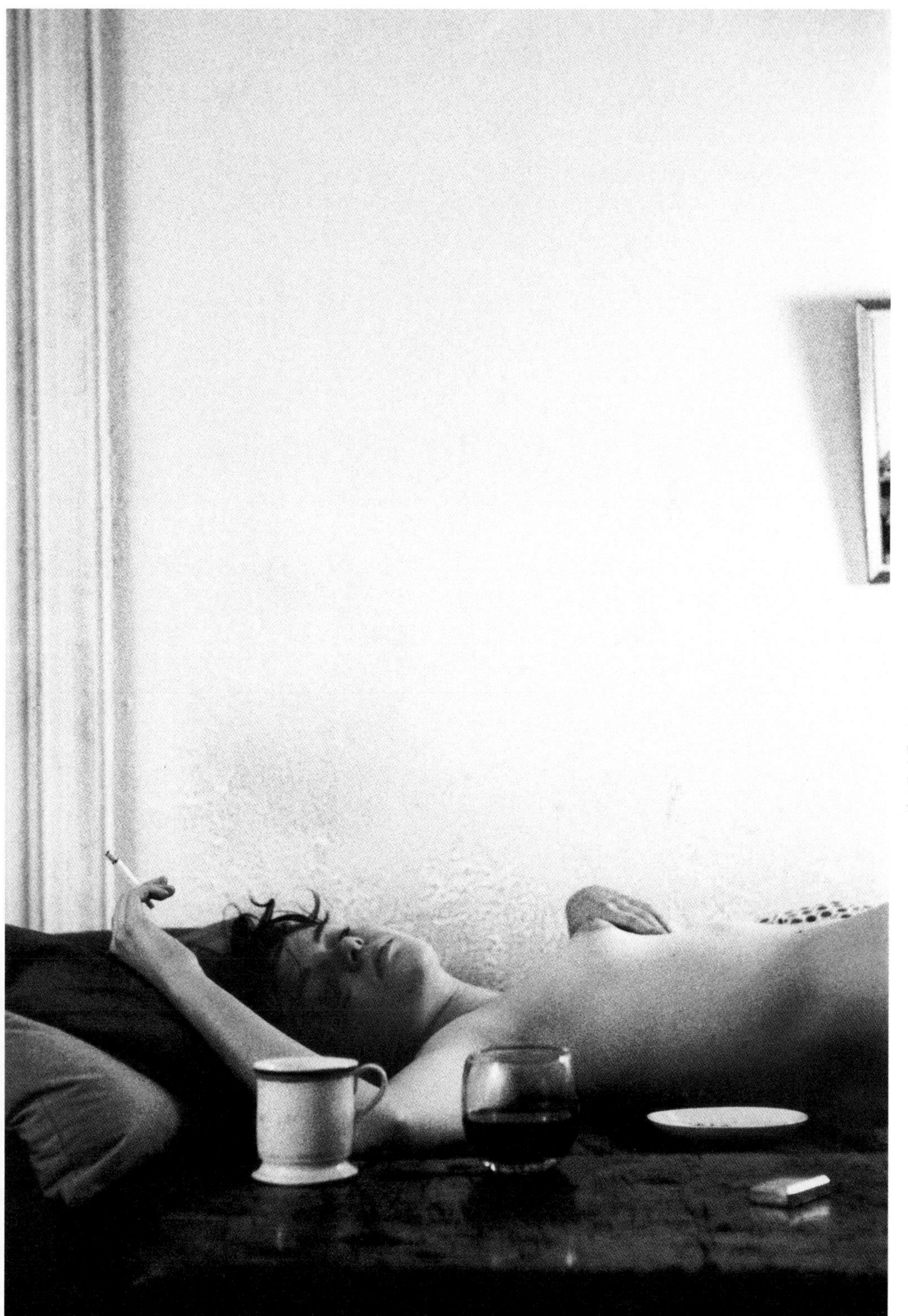

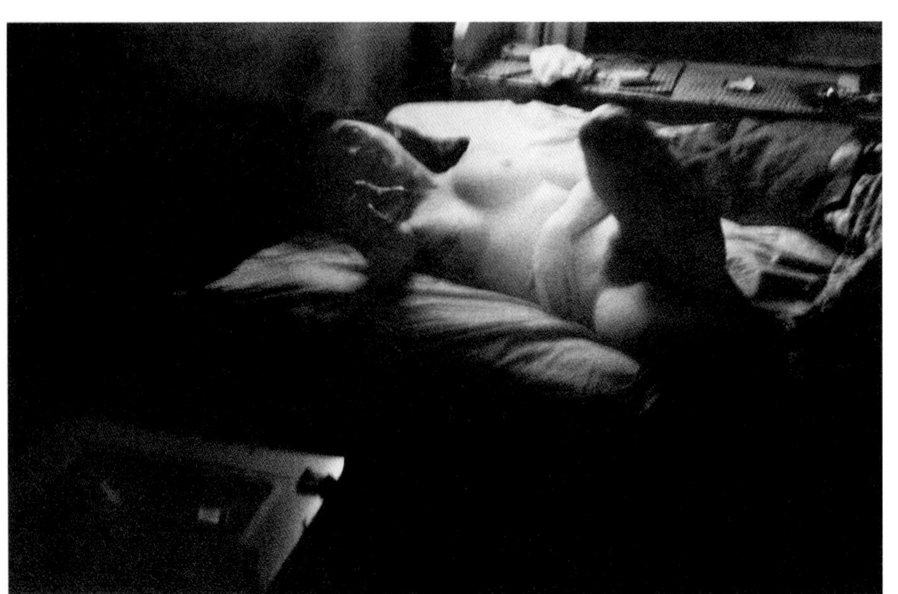

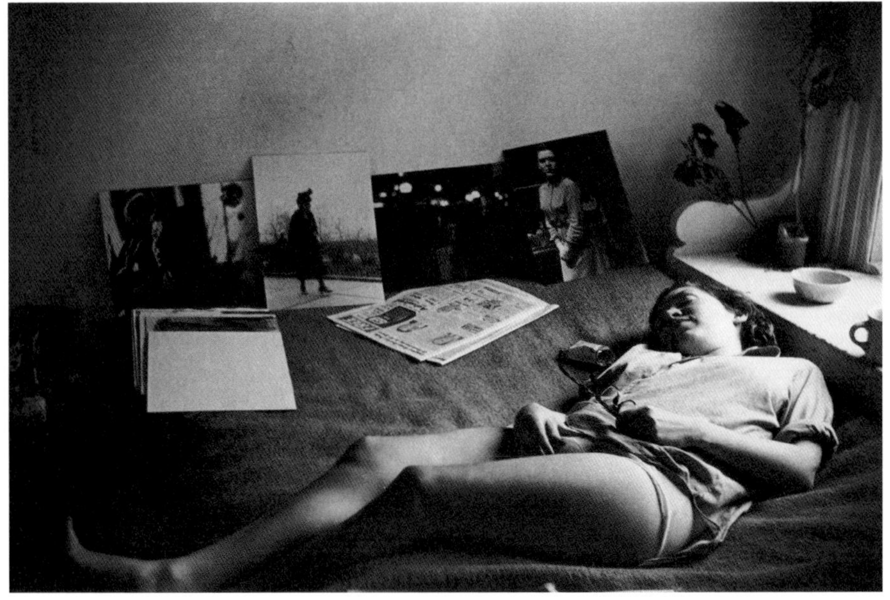

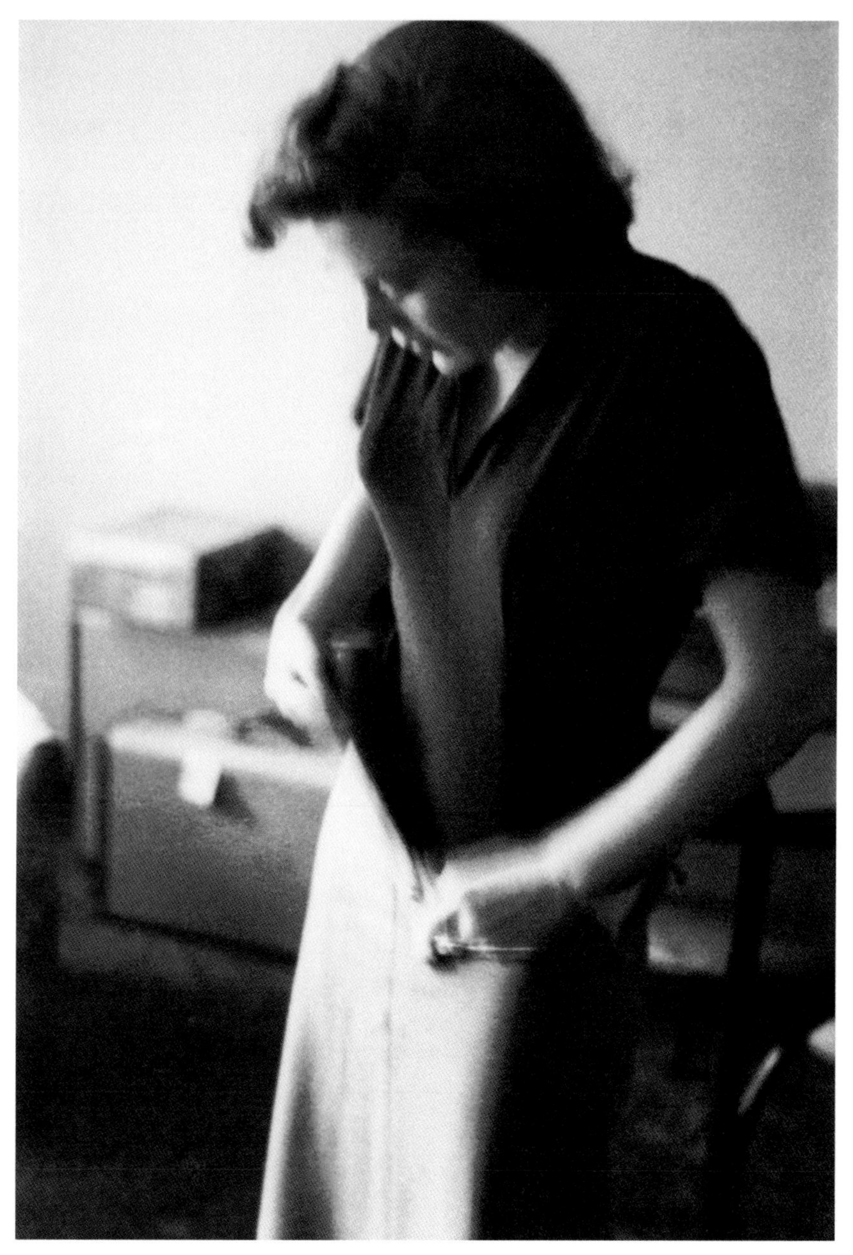

Barbara, c. 1950

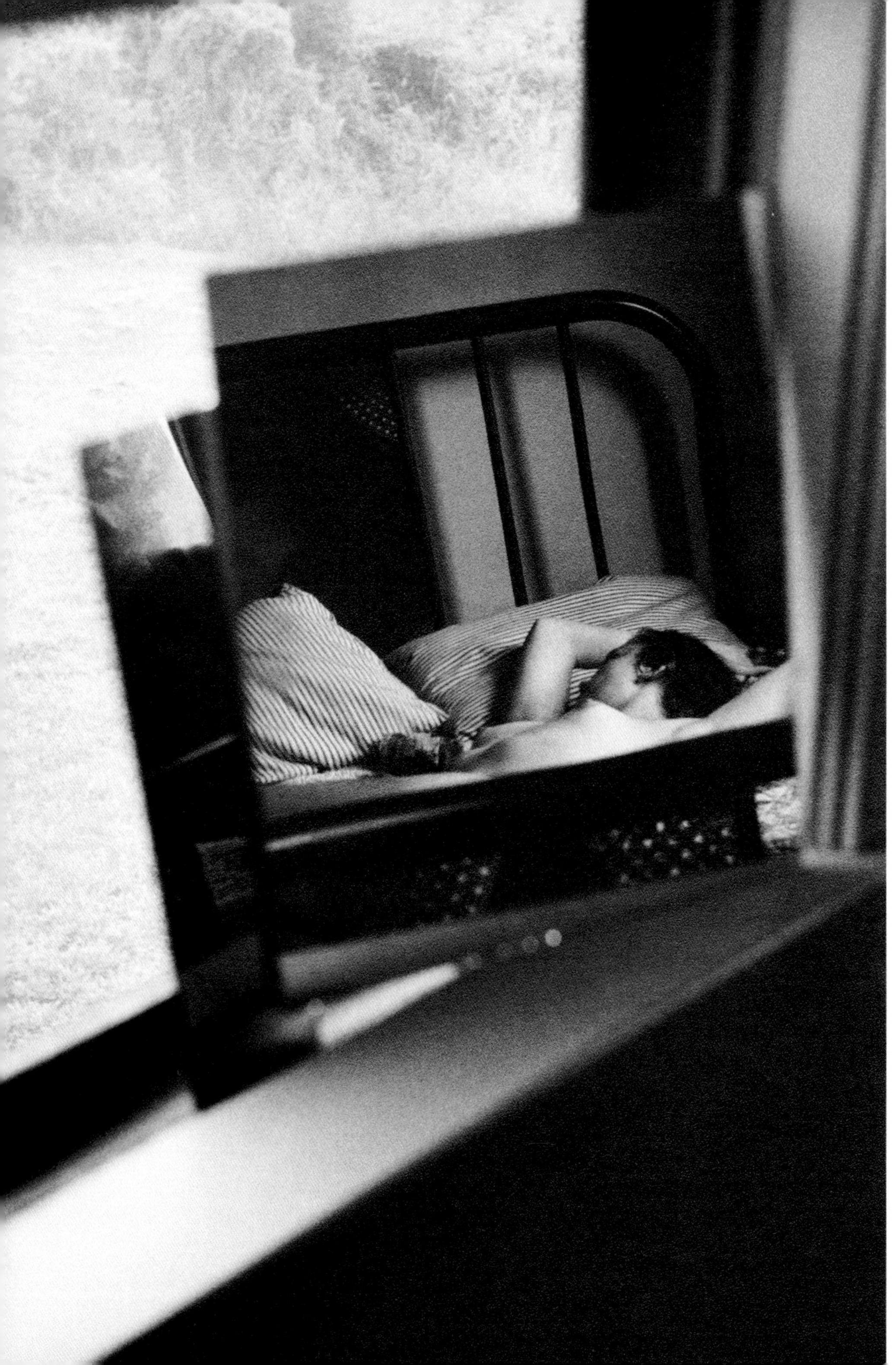

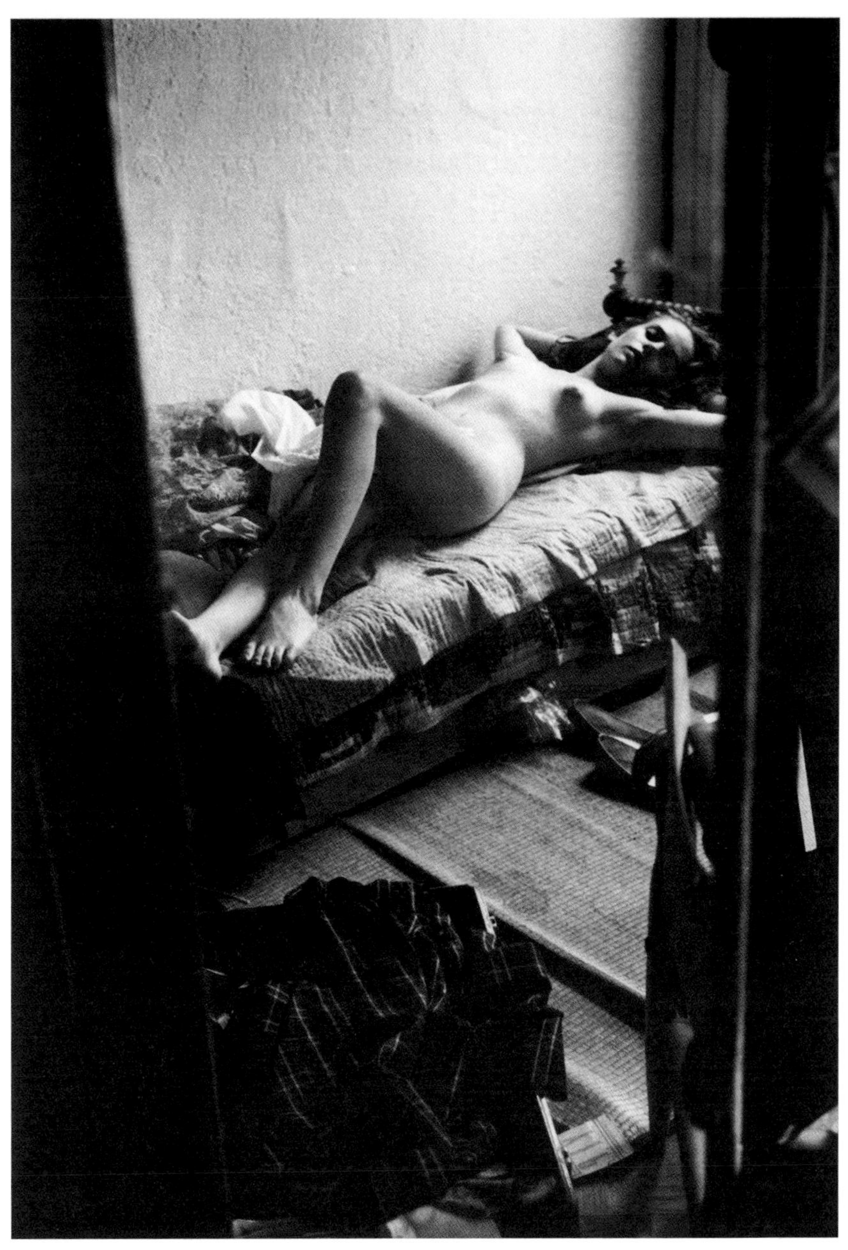

J., c. 1958

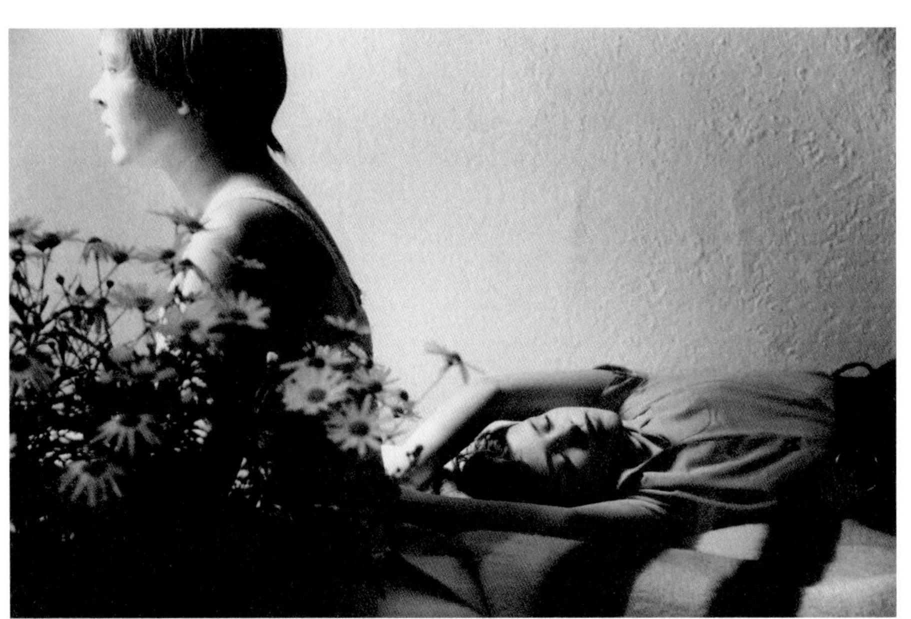

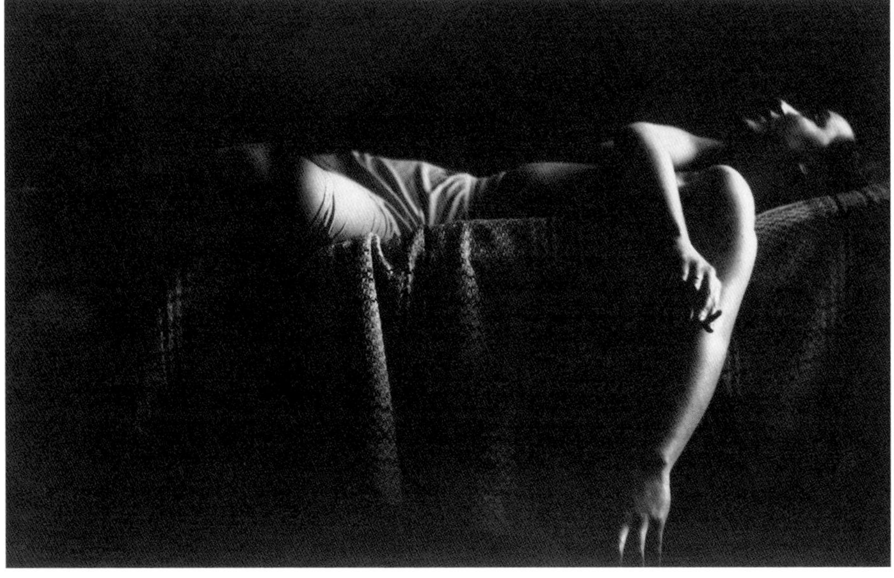

Barbara and J., c. 1950
Marianne, c. 1947

Fay, c. 1946

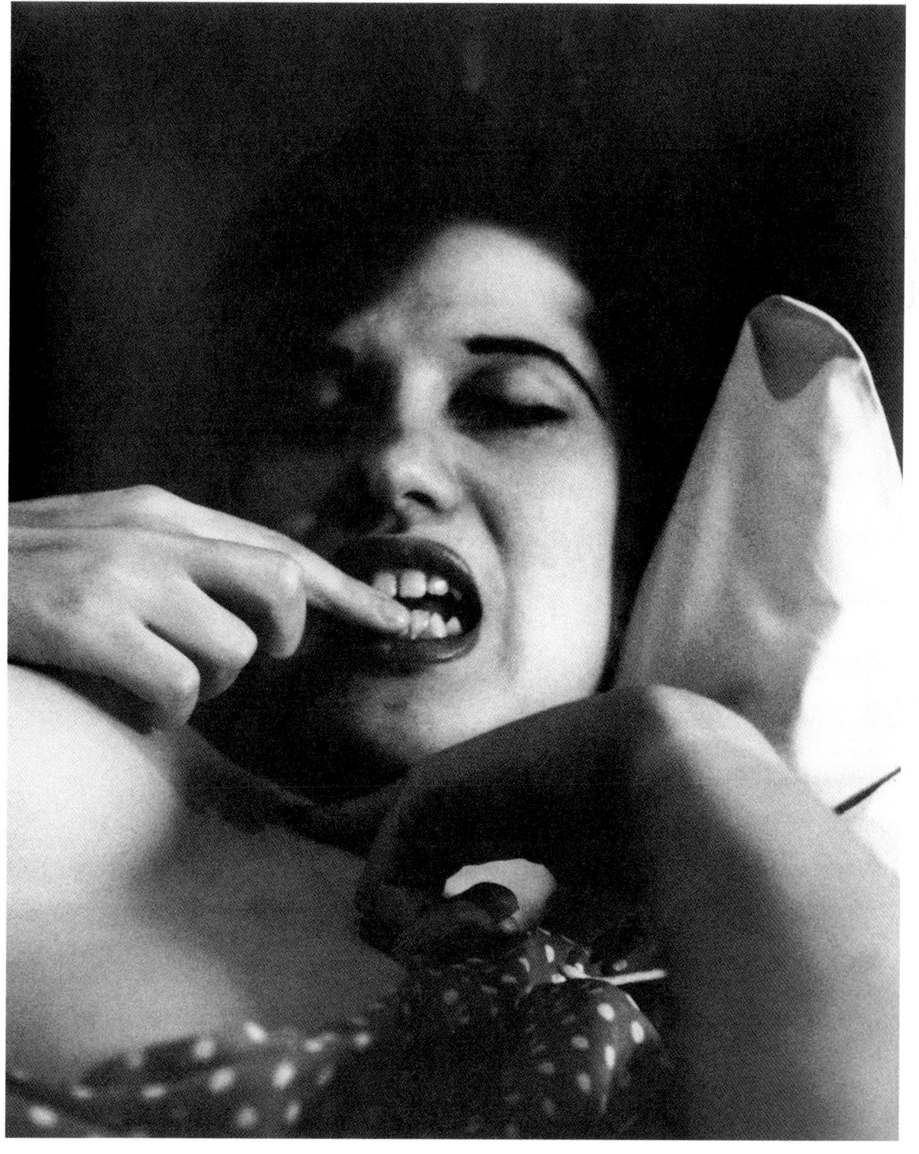

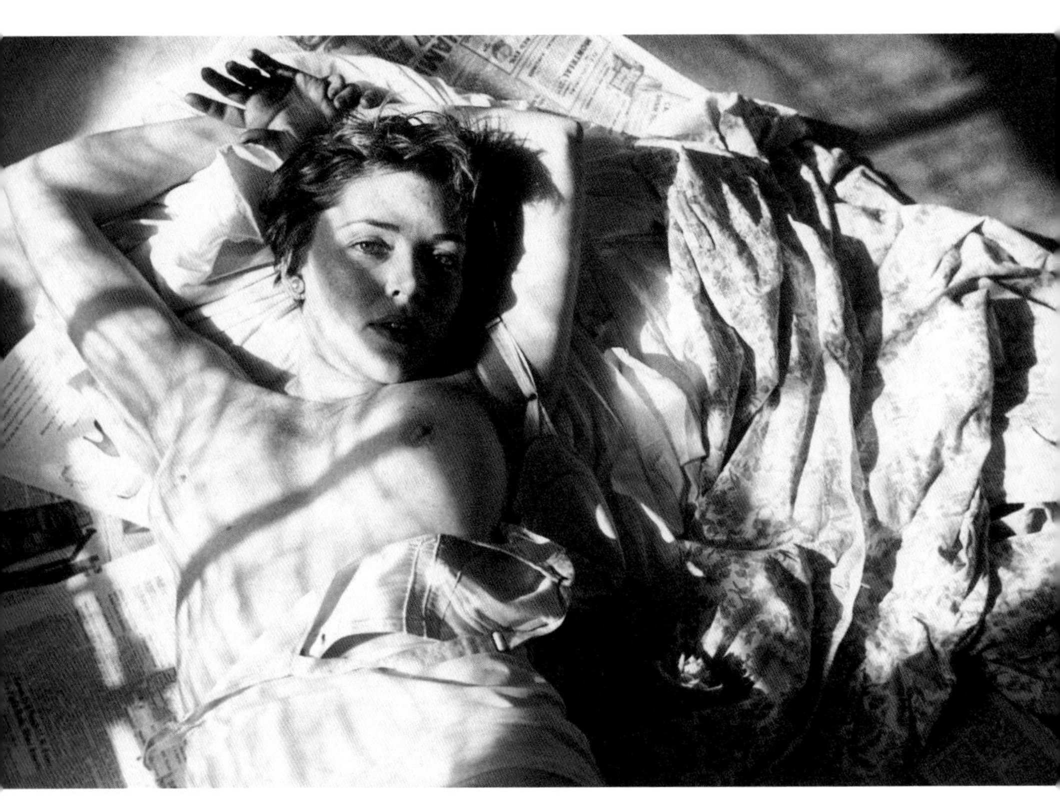

Barbara, c. 1951

J., c. 1958

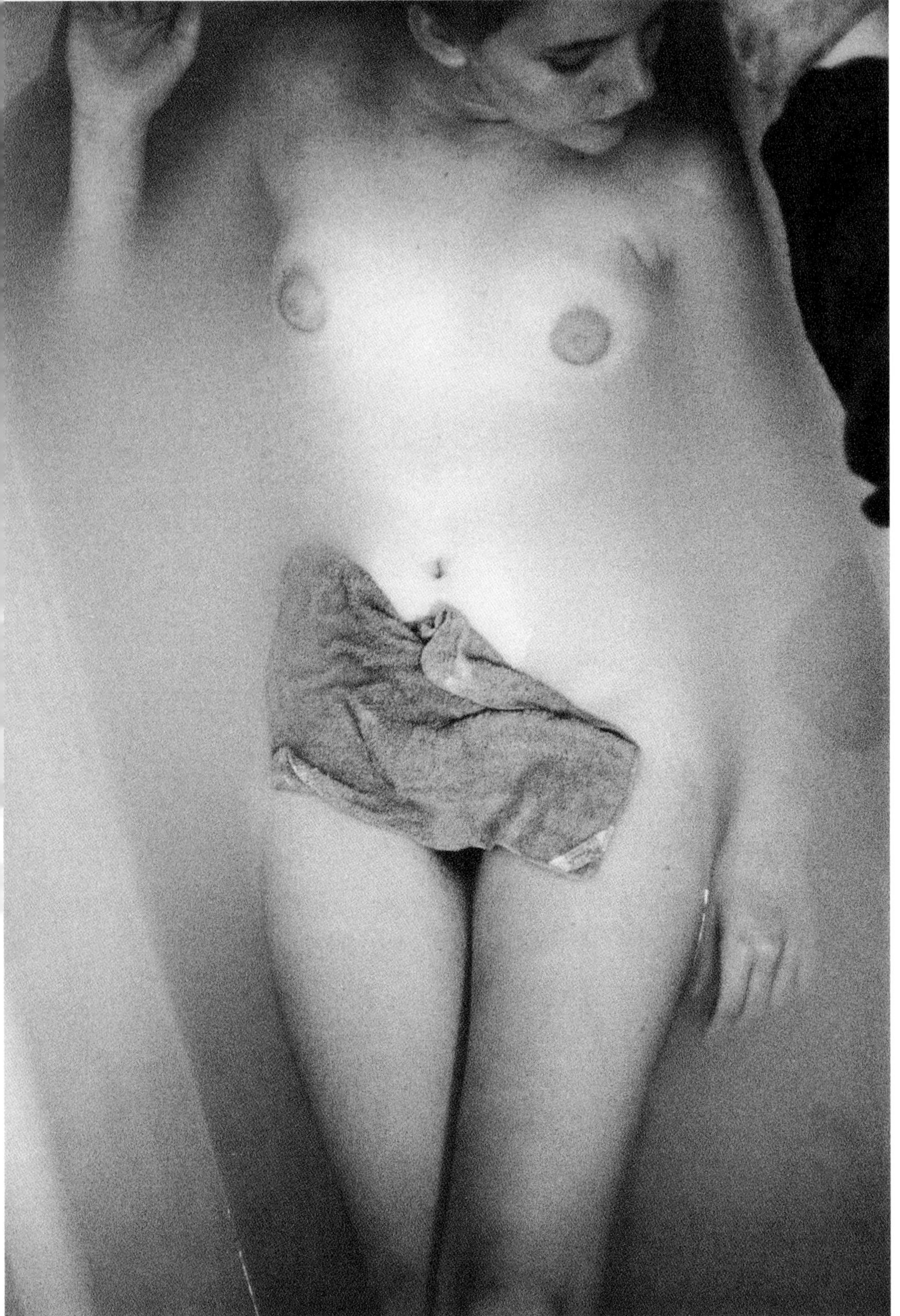

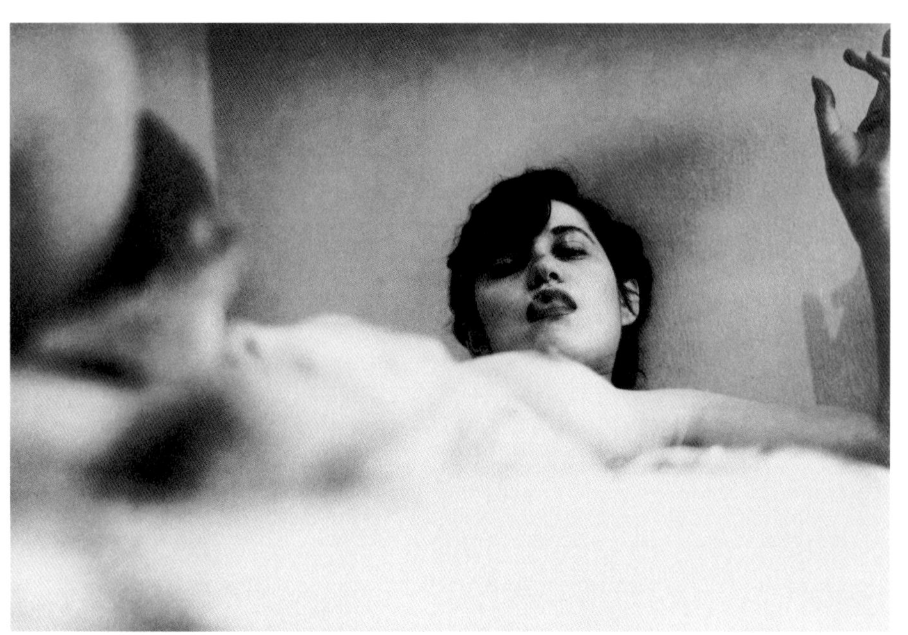

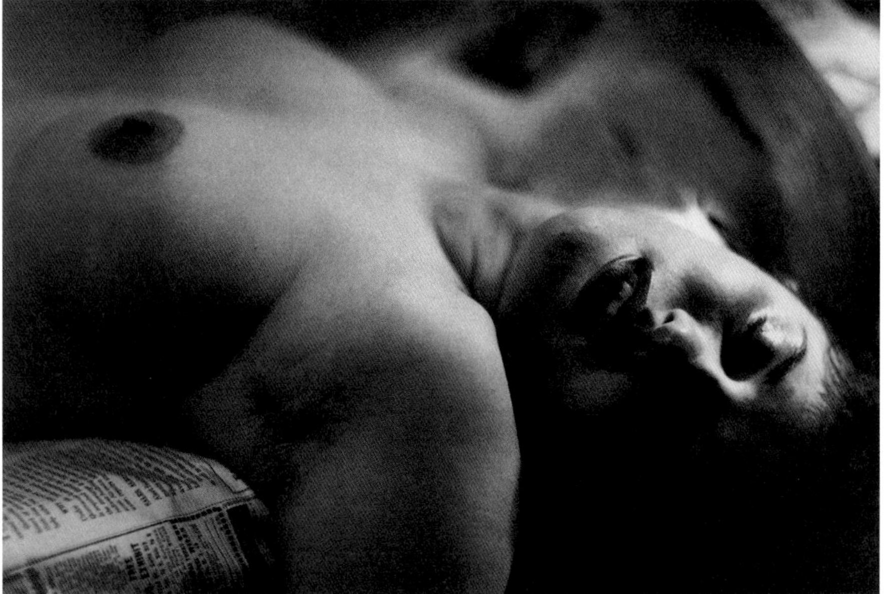

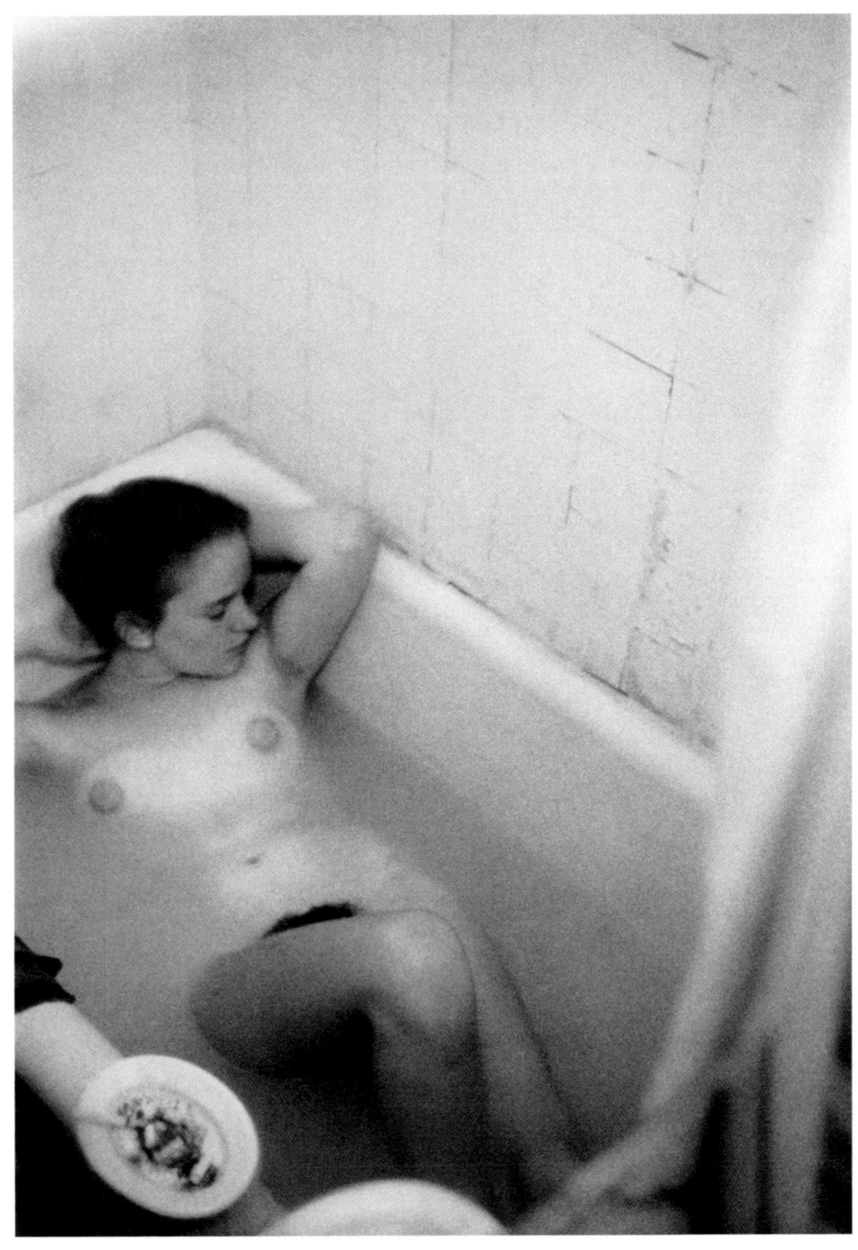

Fay Smoking, 1946
Fay, c. 1946   J., c. 1958

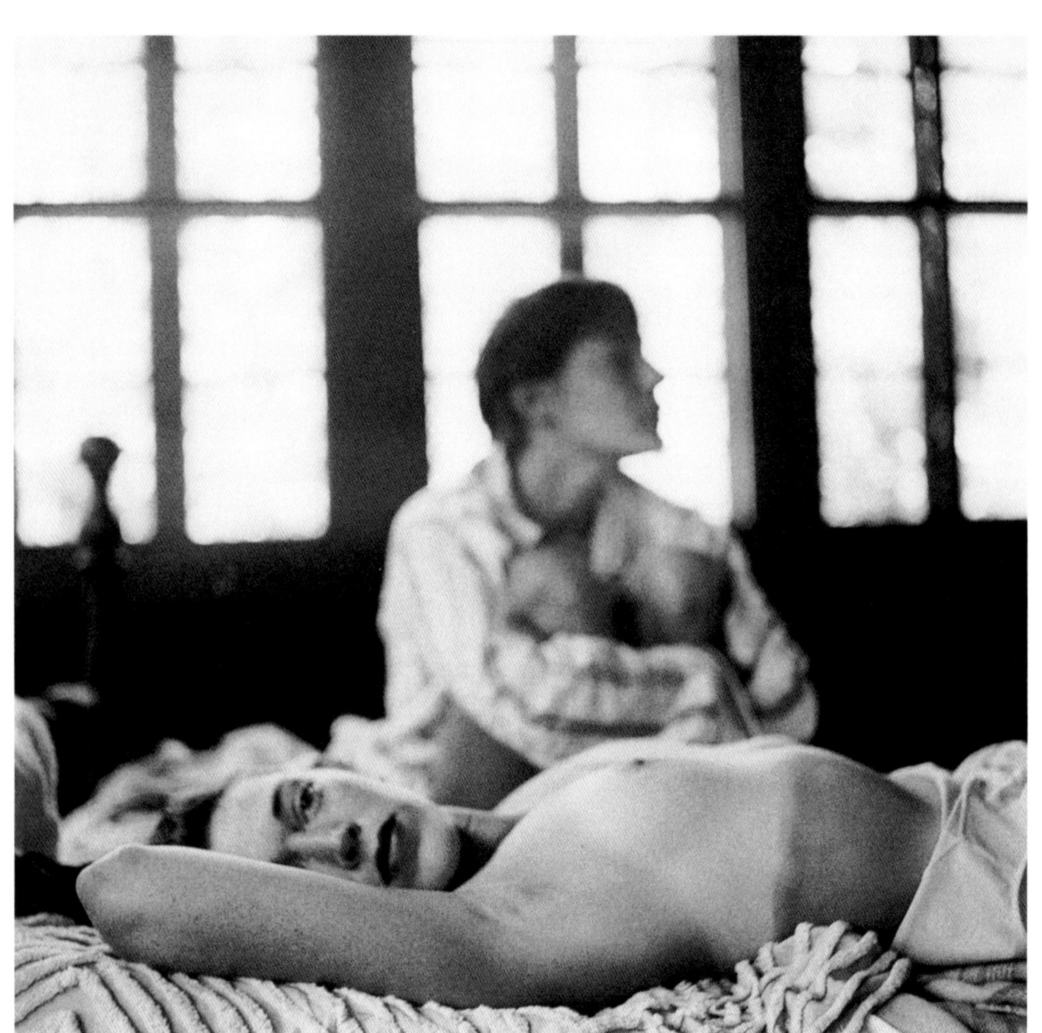

   Barbara and Bettina, c. 1950   Untitled, 1950s

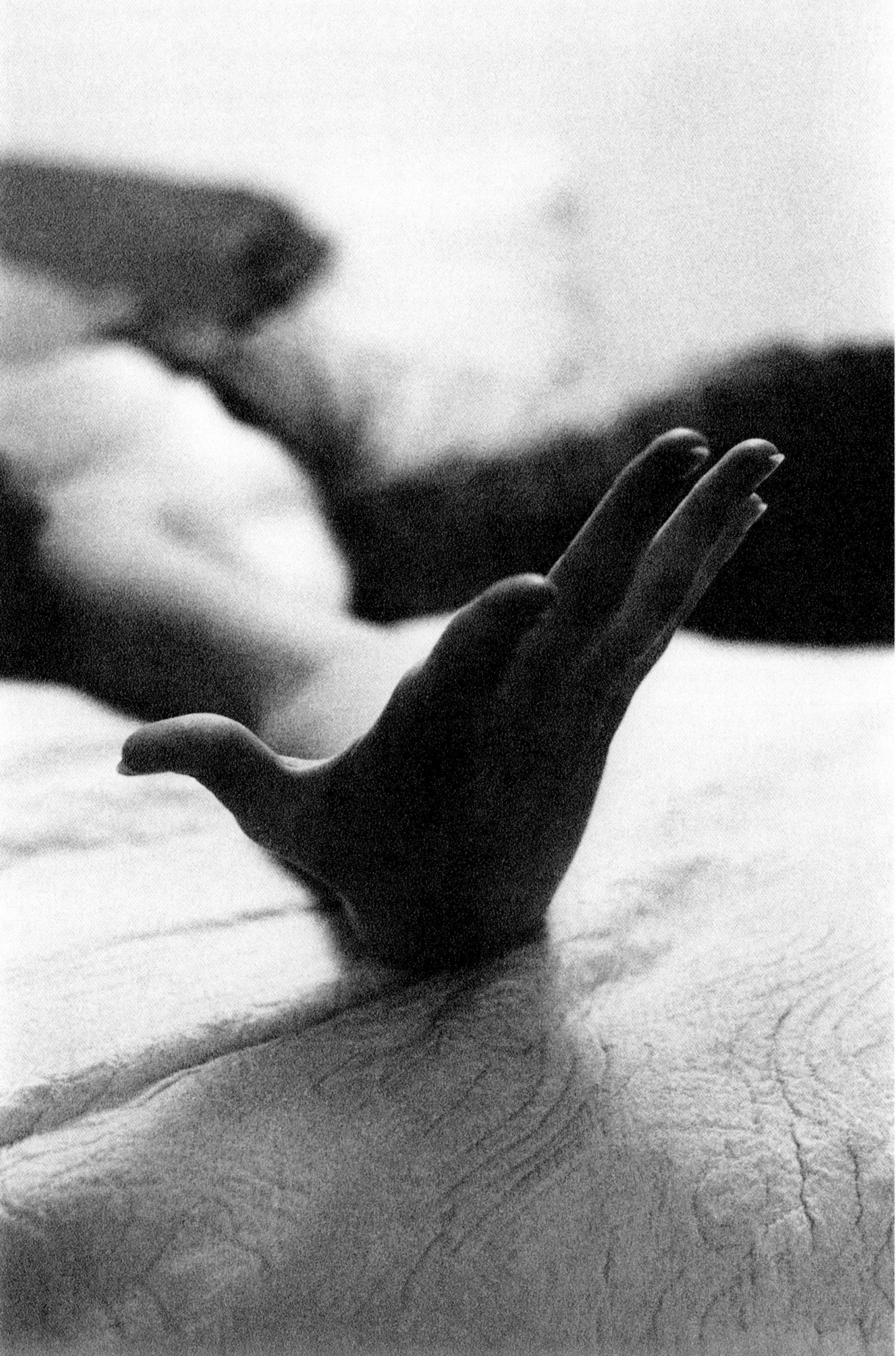

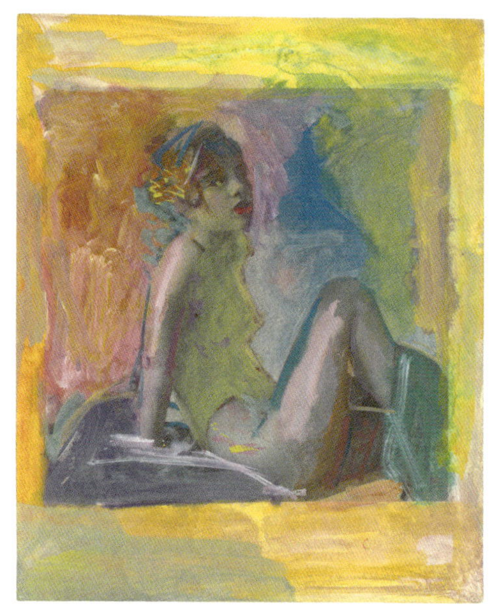

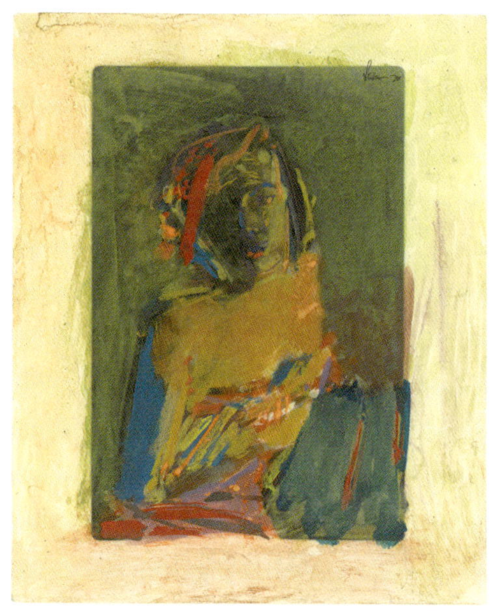

J., printed 1950s, painted c. 1990. Gouache, casein and watercolor on gelatin silver paper
Untitled, printed 1950s, painted c. 1990. Gouache, casein and watercolor on gelatin silver paper

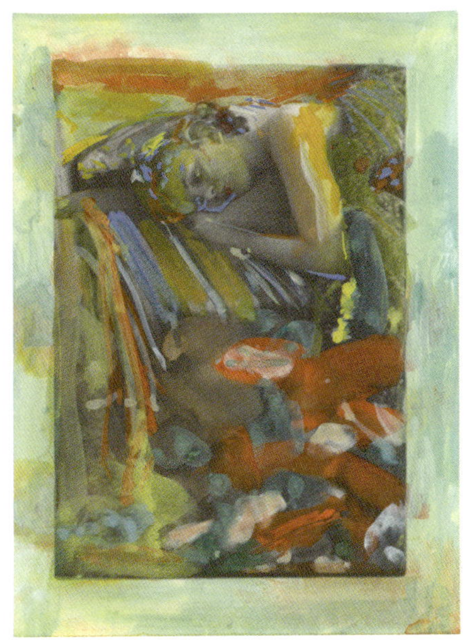

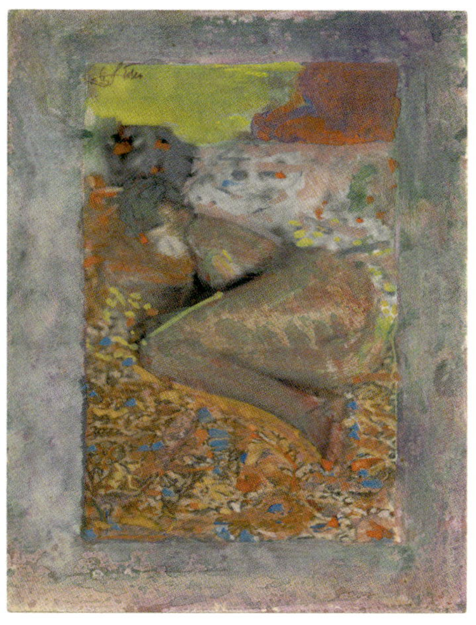

Untitled, printed 1950s, painted c. 1990. Gouache, casein and watercolor on gelatin silver paper
Untitled, printed 1950s, painted c. 1990. Gouache, casein and watercolor on gelatin silver paper

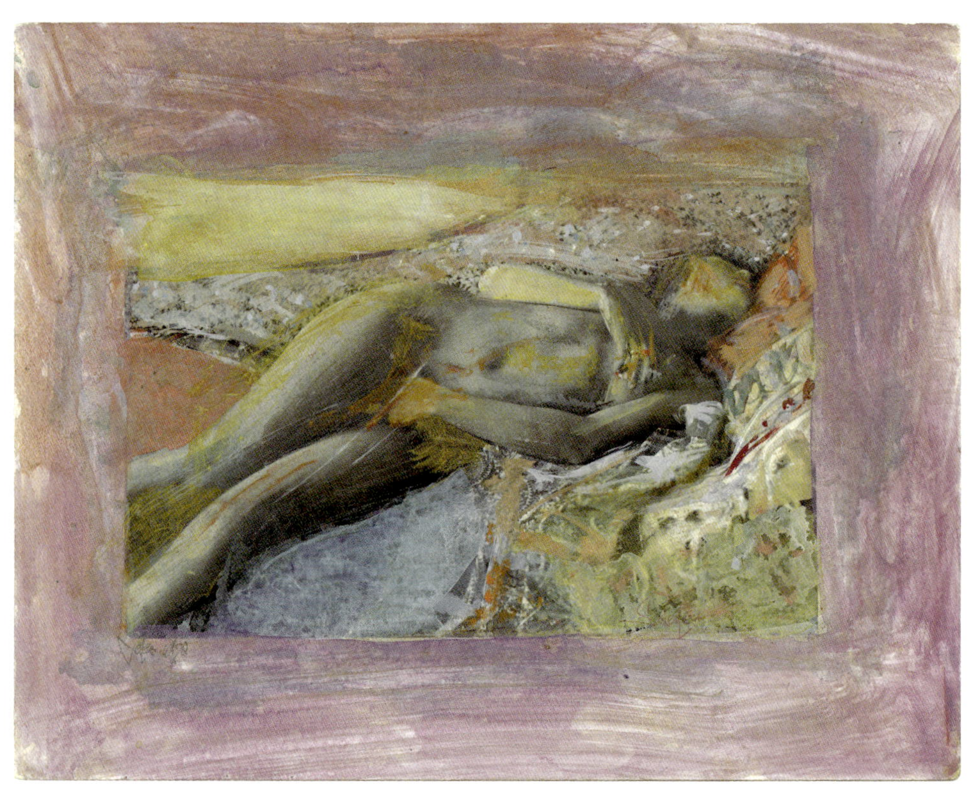

Untitled, printed 1950s, painted c. 1990. Gouache, casein and watercolor on gelatin silver paper

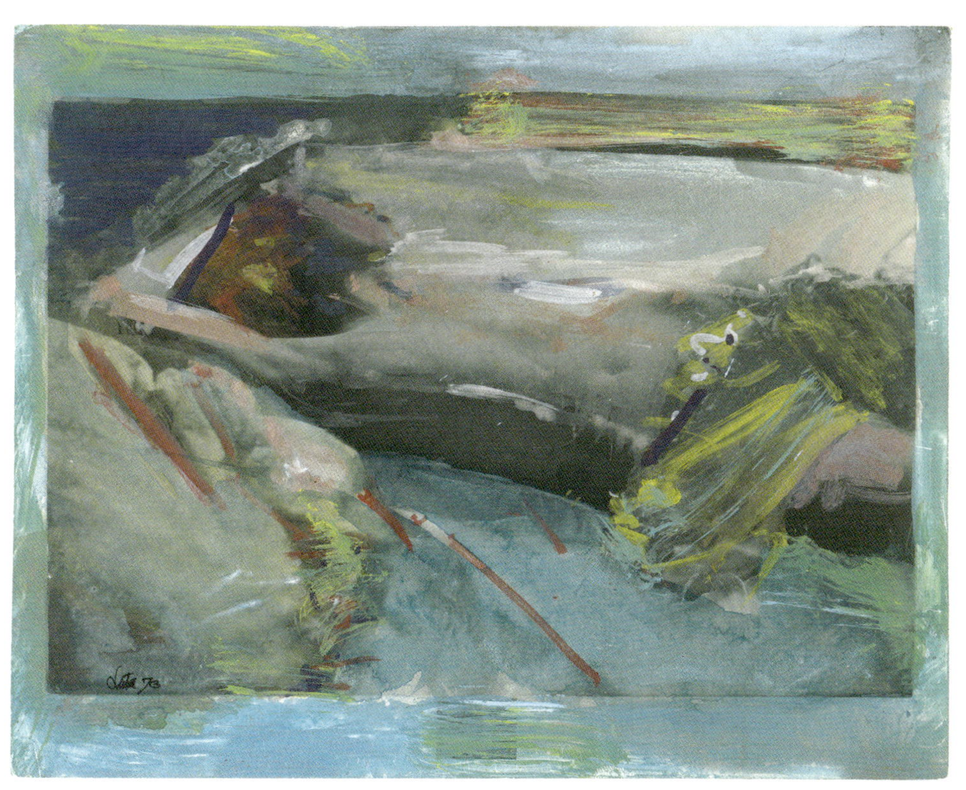

Untitled, printed 1950s, painted c. 1990. Gouache, casein and watercolor on gelatin silver paper

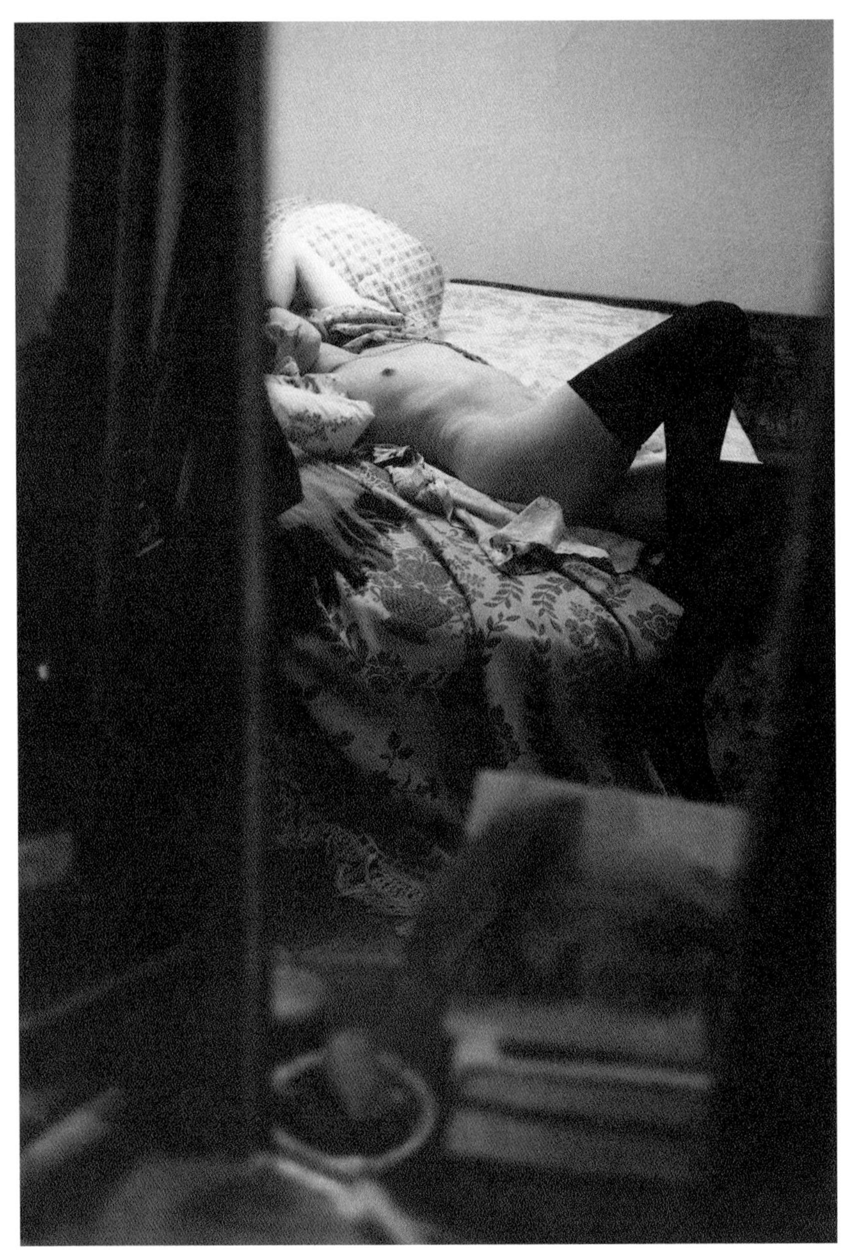

J., c. 1958

Soames, c. 1960

Kim, c. 1946

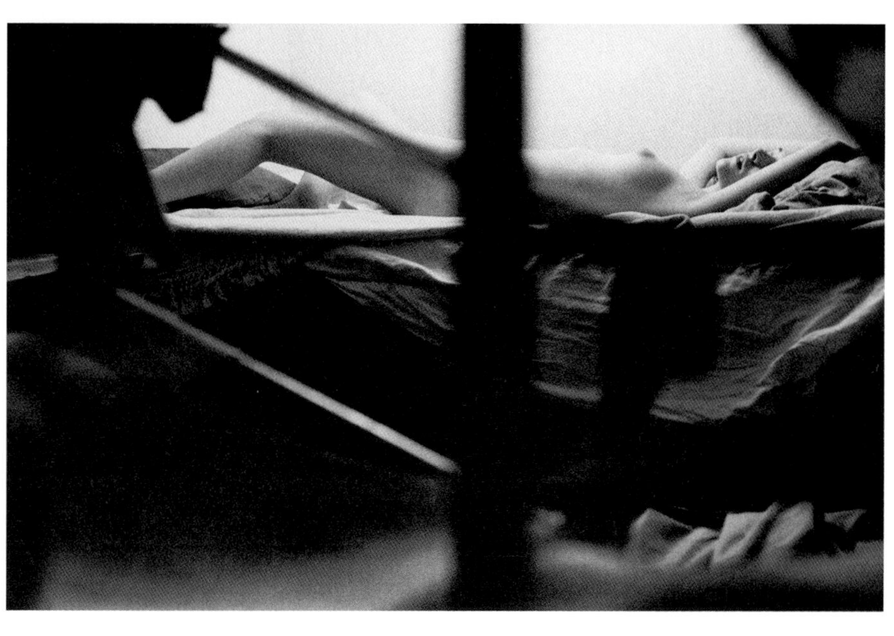

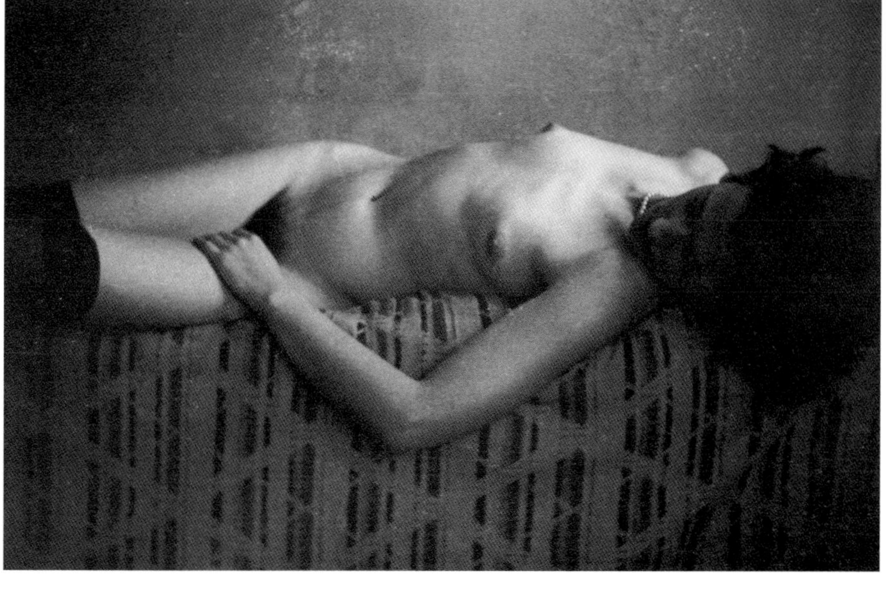

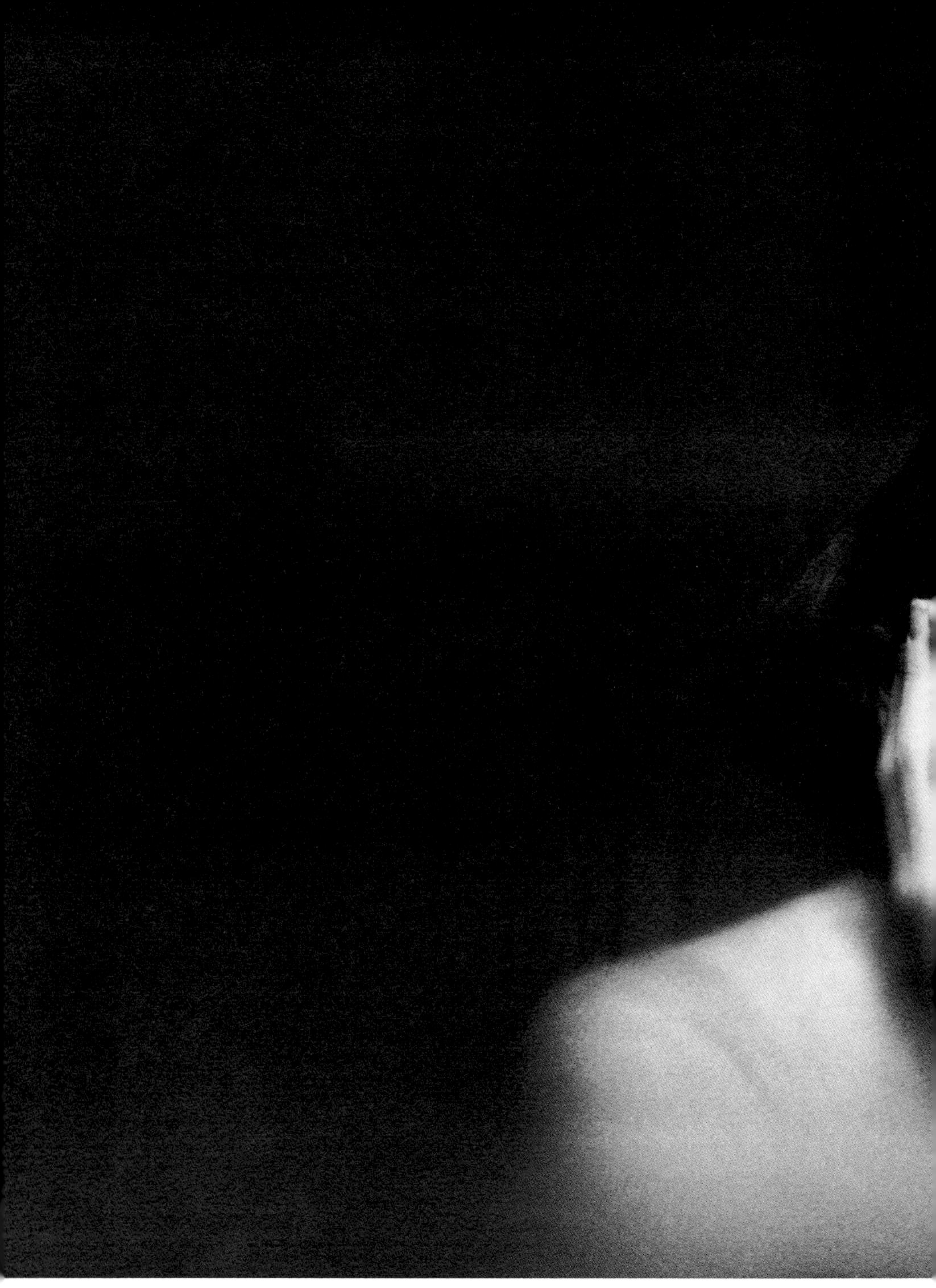

Jean Pearson, c. 1948

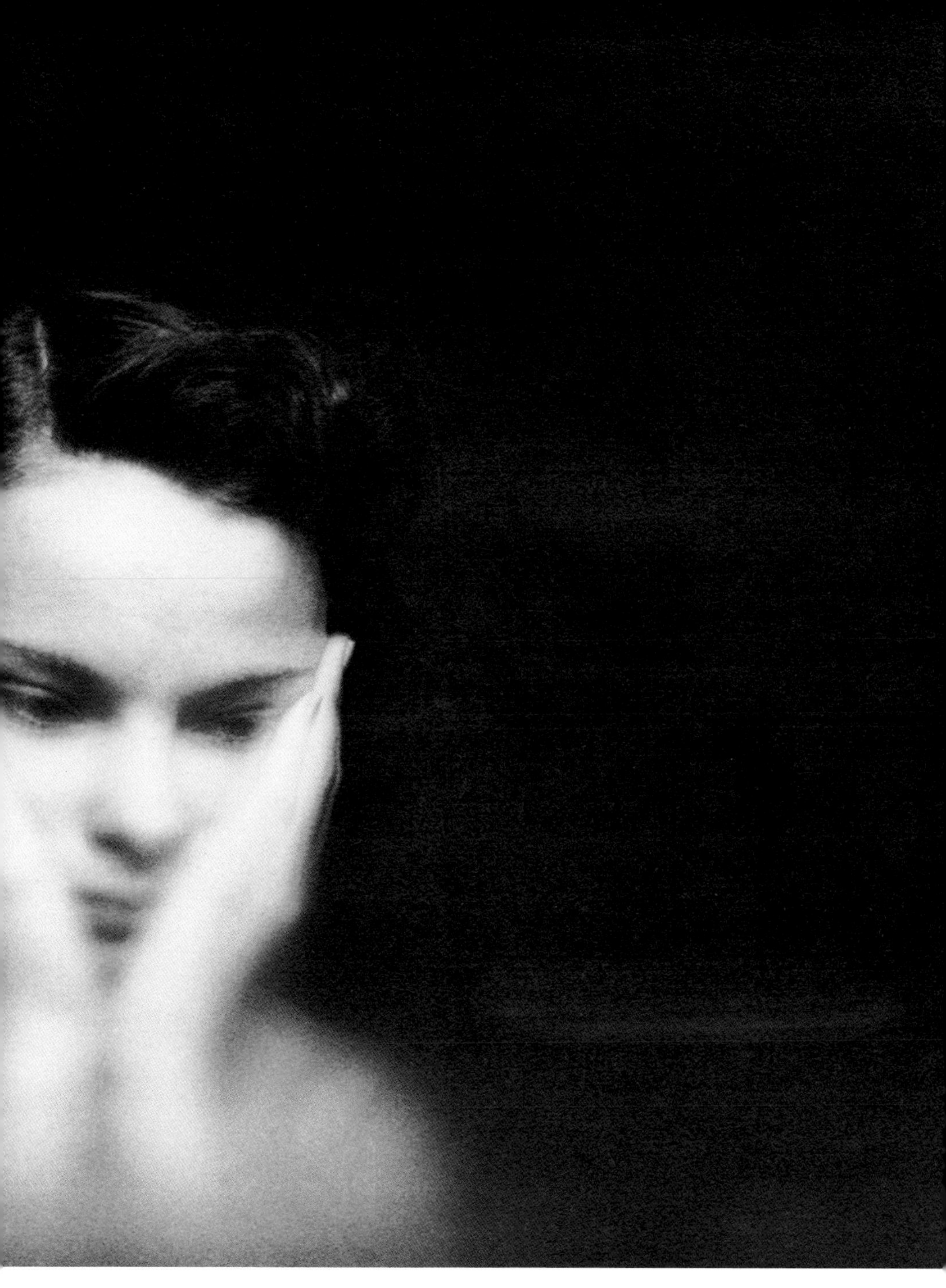

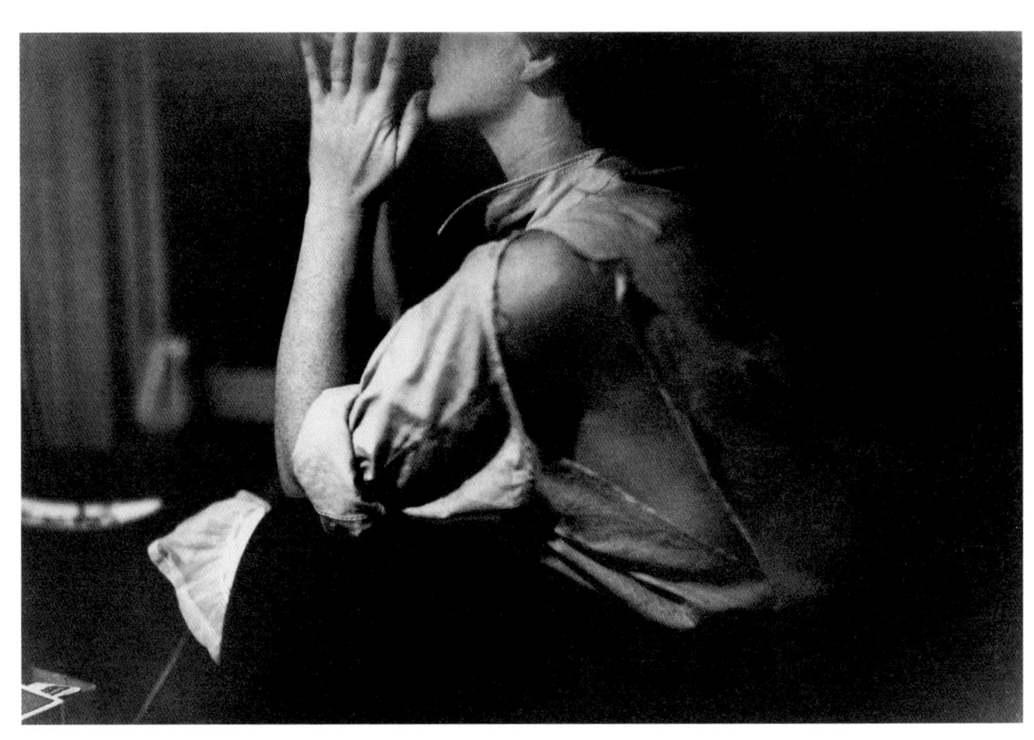

Barbara, c. 1950

Soames, c. 1969

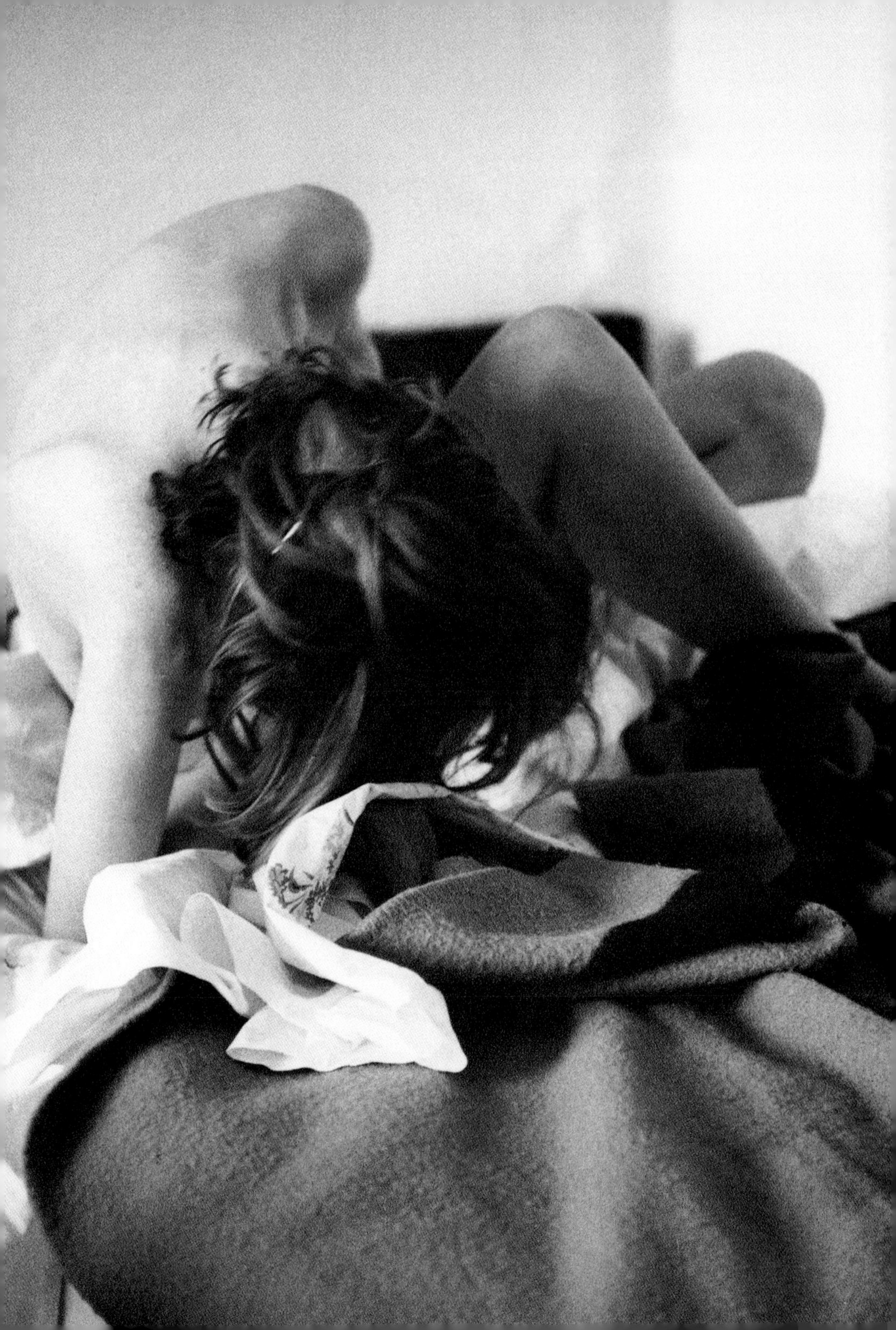

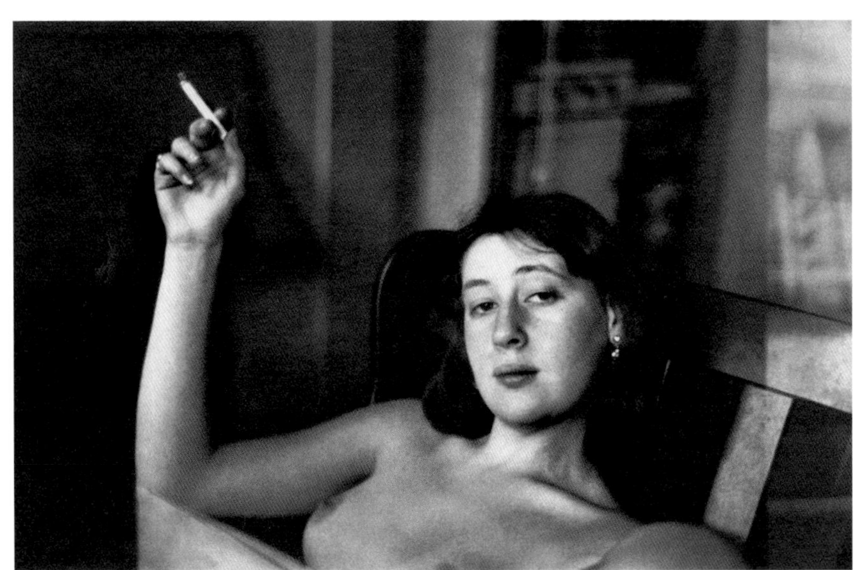

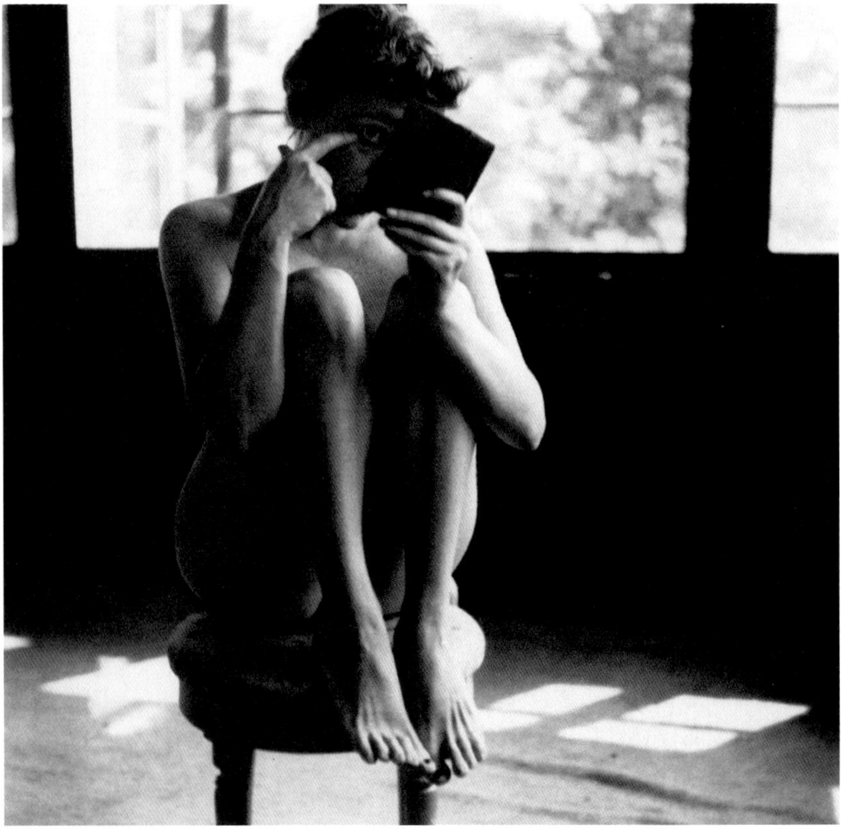

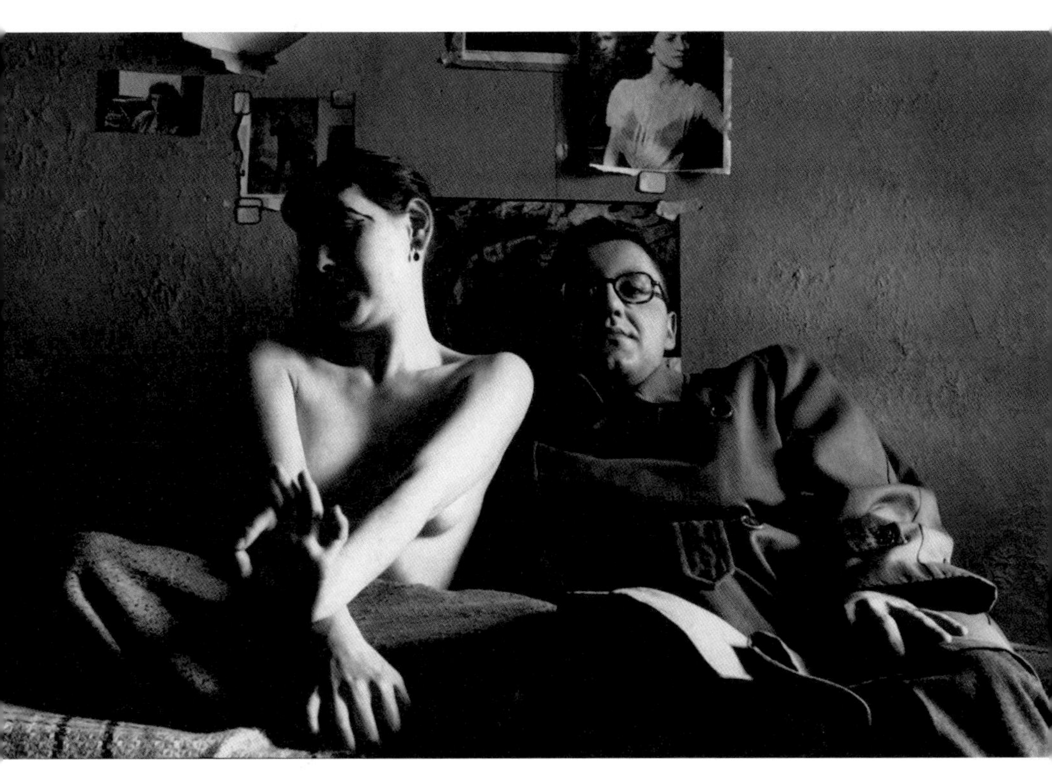

Inez, c. 1947
Barbara, c. 1950

Self-portrait with Inez, c. 1947

The past few years,
I have been doing what I call kitchen paintings.
I get the little boards that they put between the bottles
when you buy wine, and I make acrylic paintings.
I wake up in the middle of the night and do one
of these paintings while I'm heating the water for my coffee.

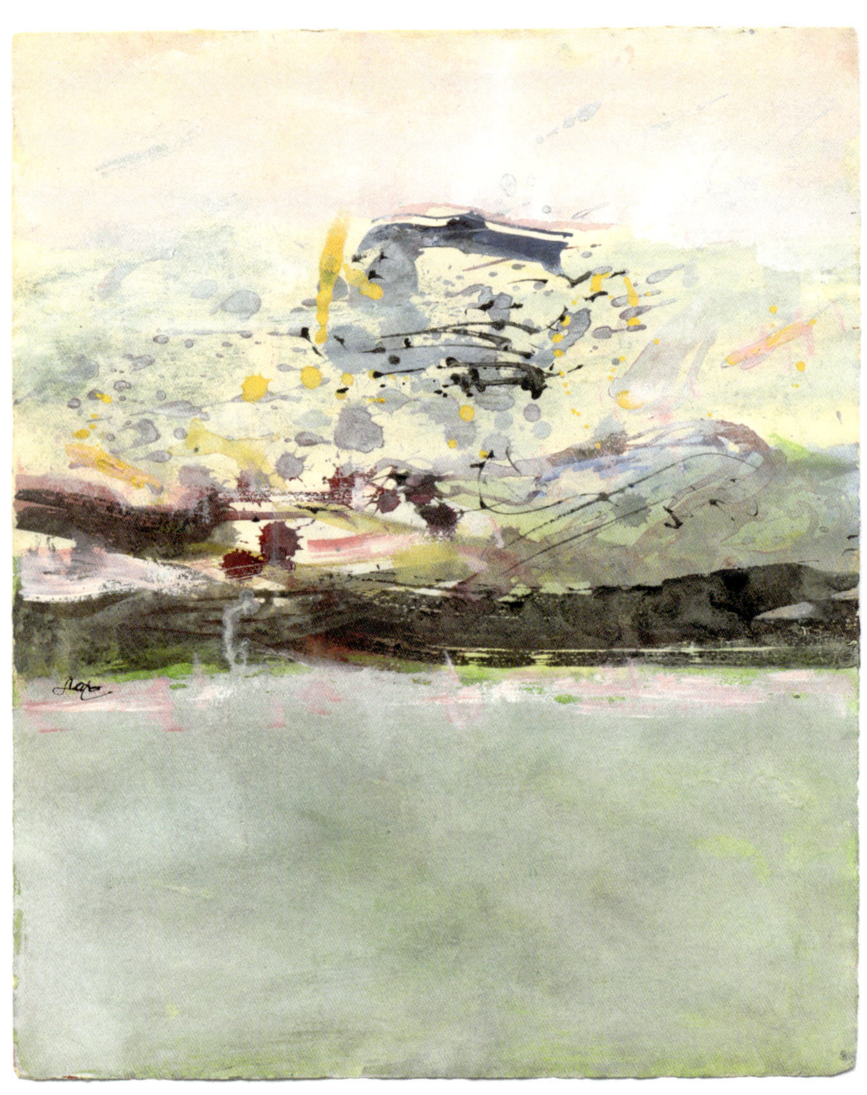

Untitled, undated. Gouache, casein and watercolor on paper

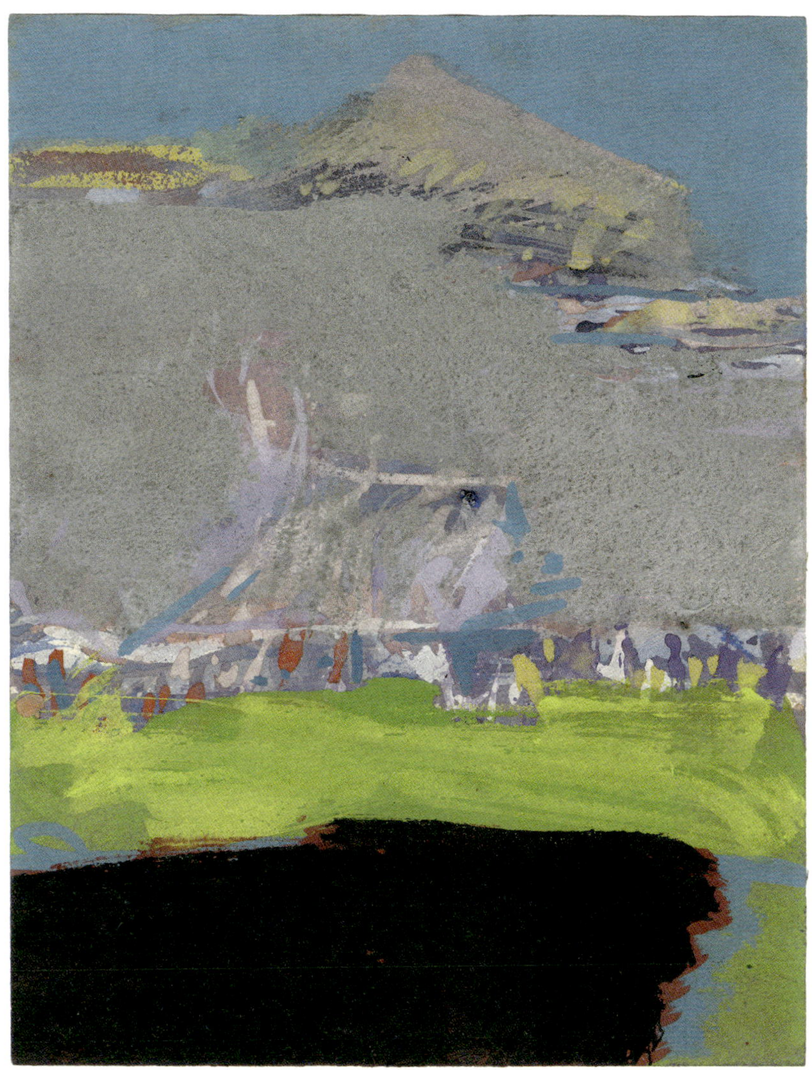

Untitled, undated. Gouache, casein and watercolor on paper

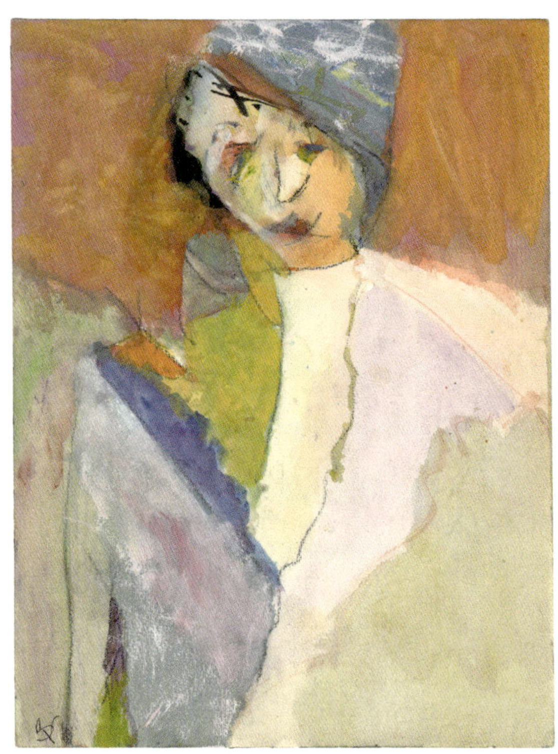

Jean, c. 1960
Gouache, casein and watercolor on paper

Untitled, 1960s
Gouache, casein and watercolor on paper

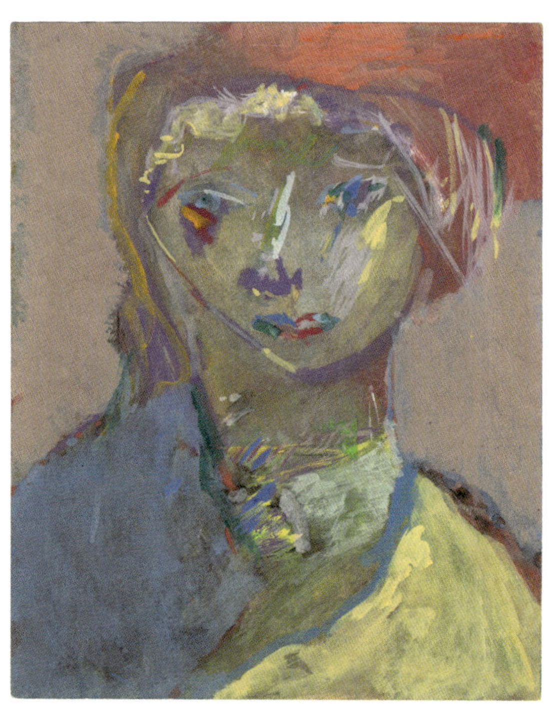

Untitled, undated
Gouache, casein and watercolor on paper

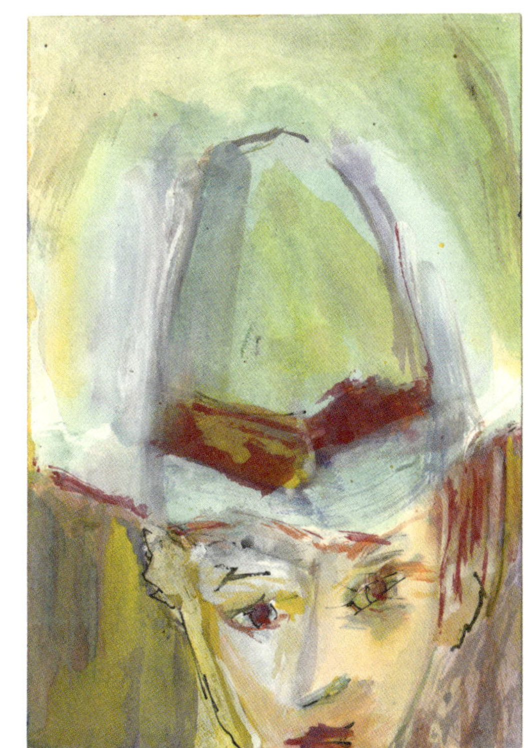

Untitled, undated
Gouache, casein and watercolor on paper

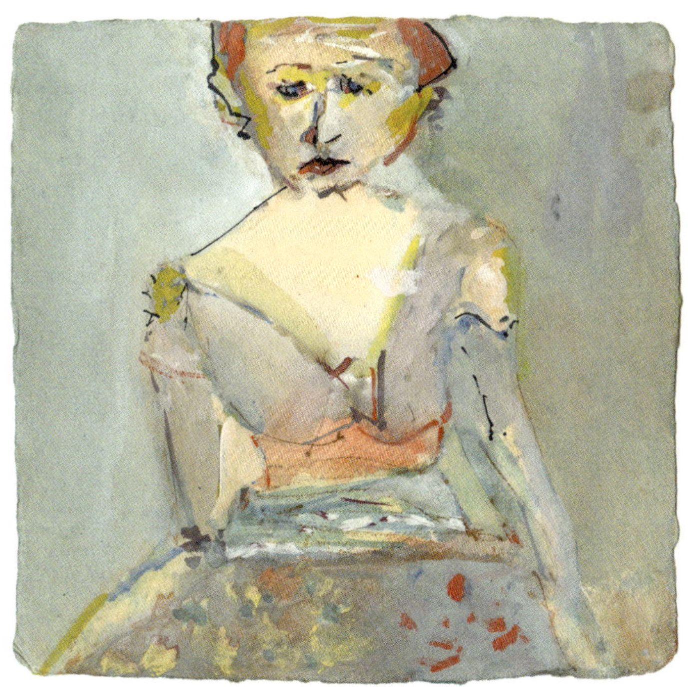

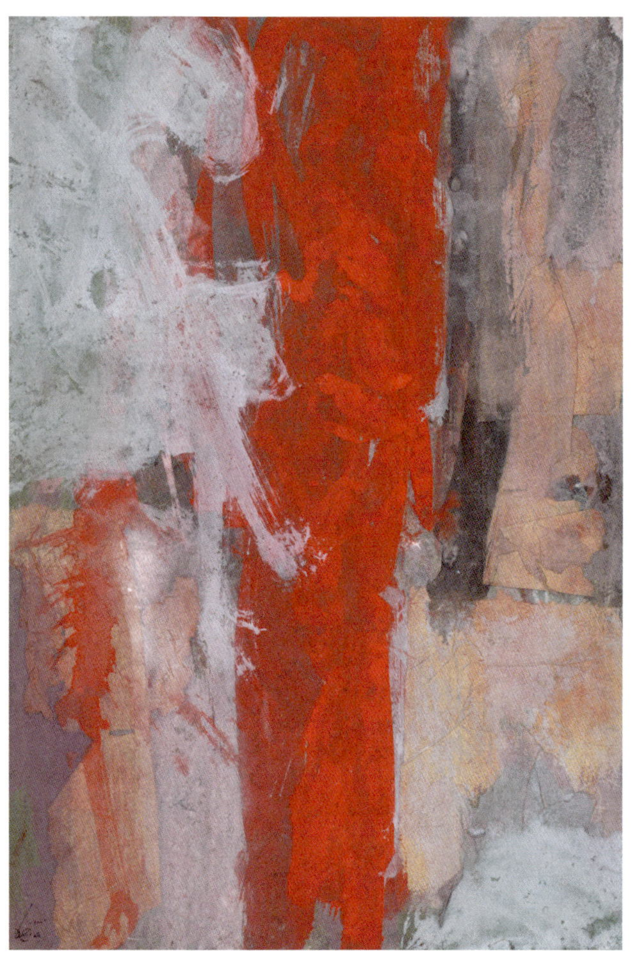

Untitled, undated. Gouache, casein and watercolor on paper

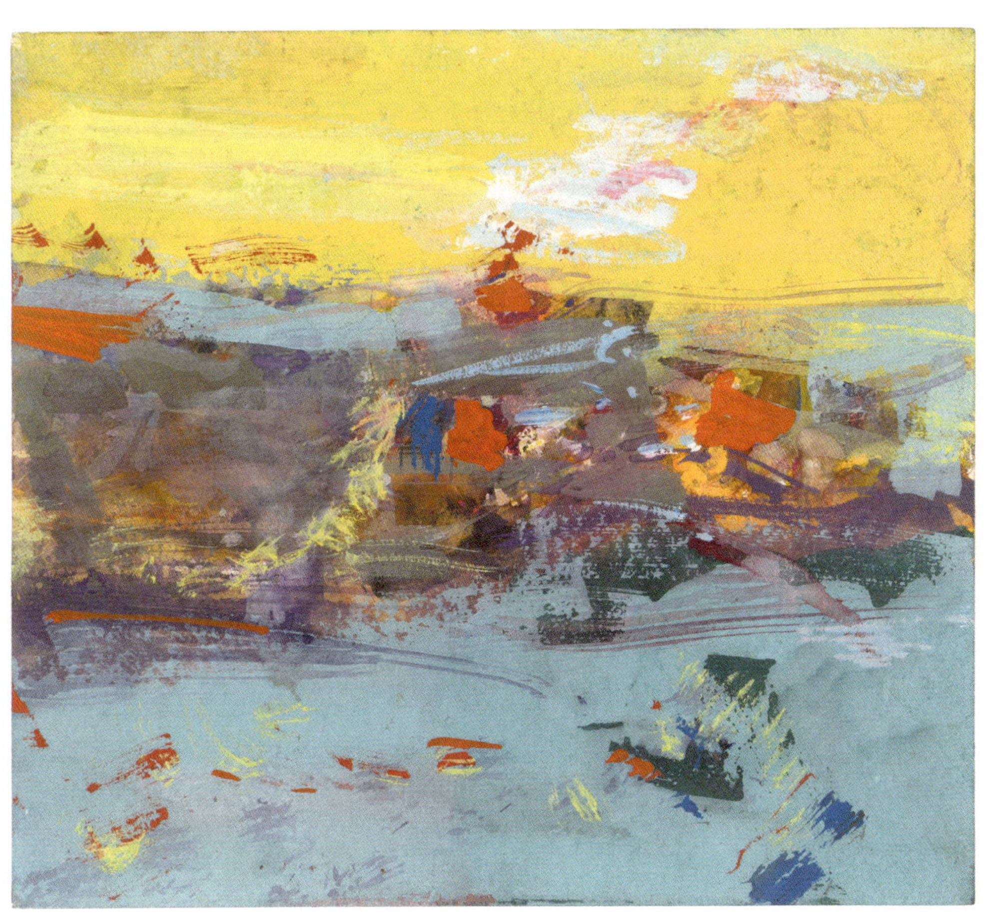

Untitled, 1964. Gouache, casein and watercolor on paper

Untitled, undated. Gouache, casein and watercolor on paper

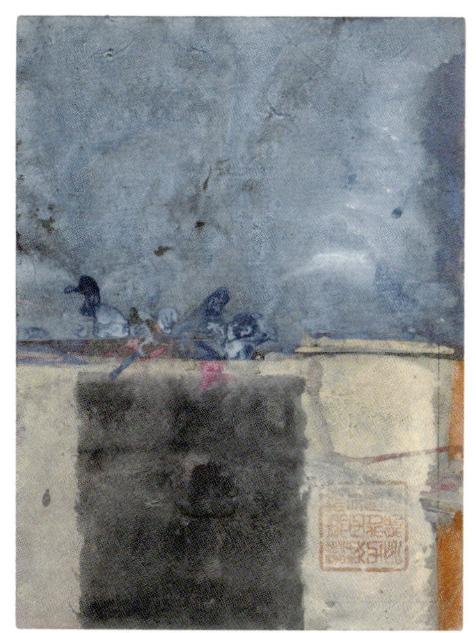

Untitled, undated
Gouache, casein and watercolor on paper

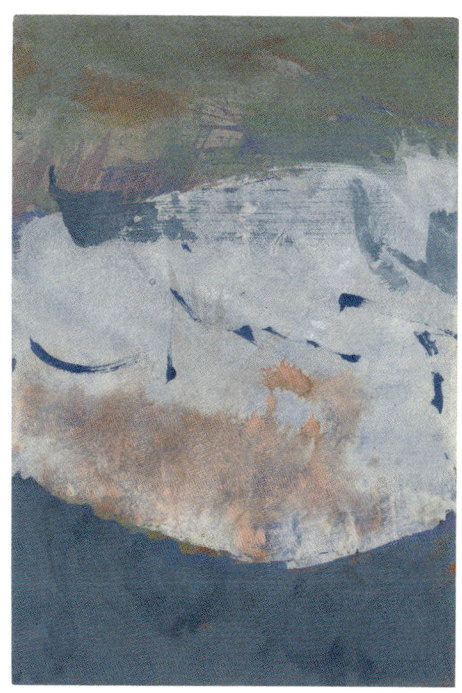

Untitled, undated
Gouache, casein and watercolor on paper

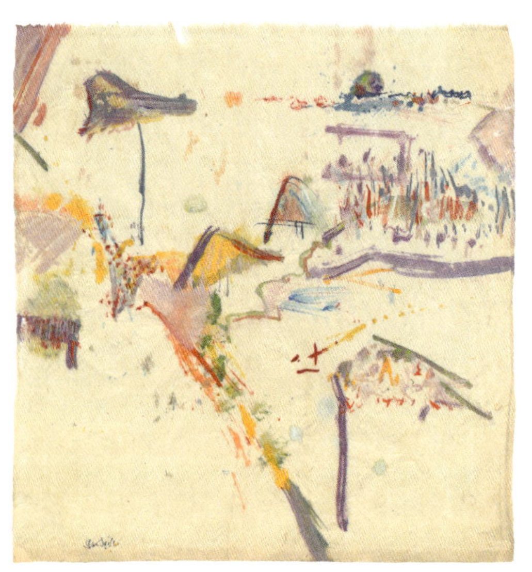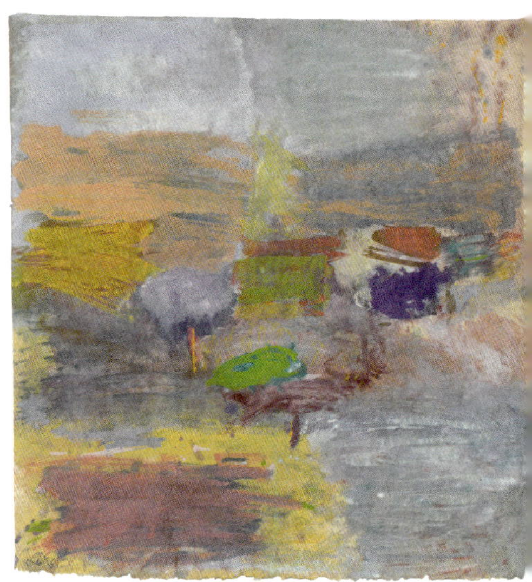

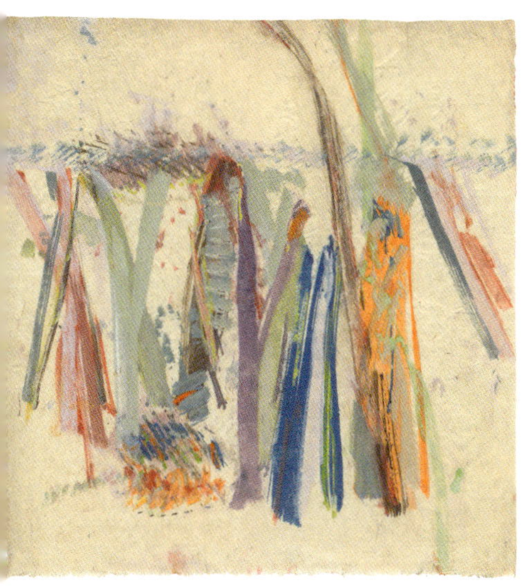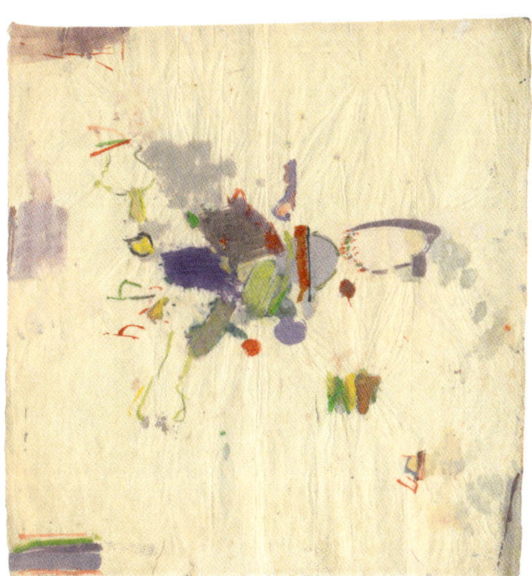

Untitled, c. 1975–87. Gouache, casein and watercolor on Japanese tissue paper

Saul Leiter's studio, New York

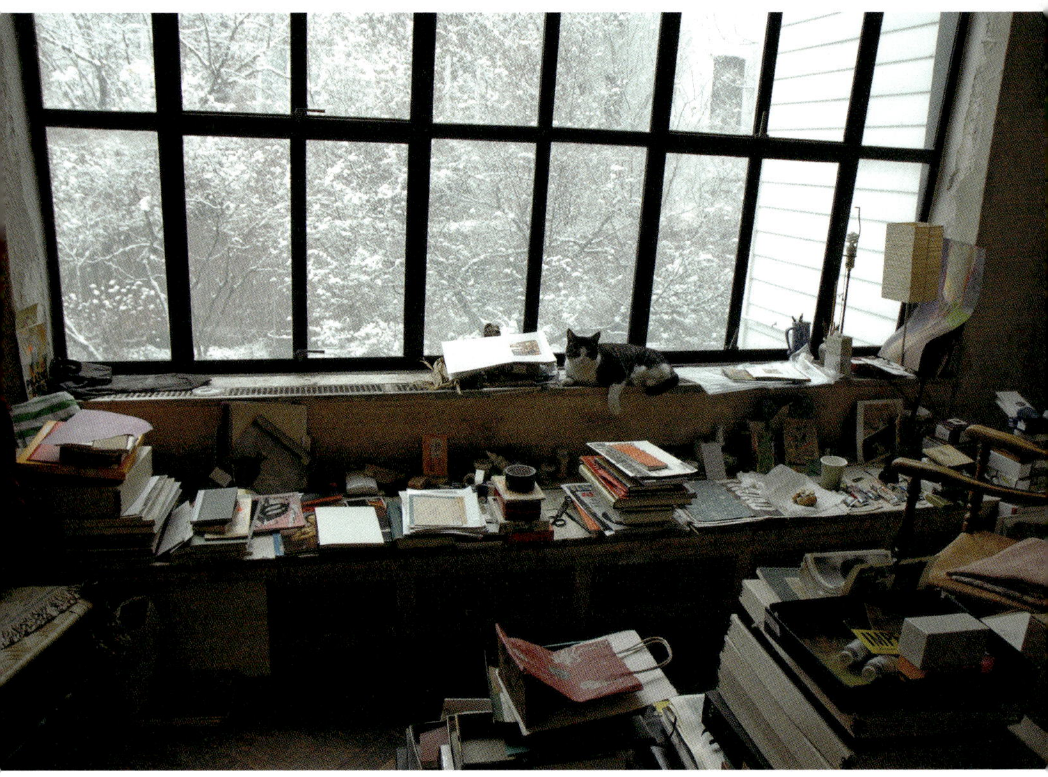

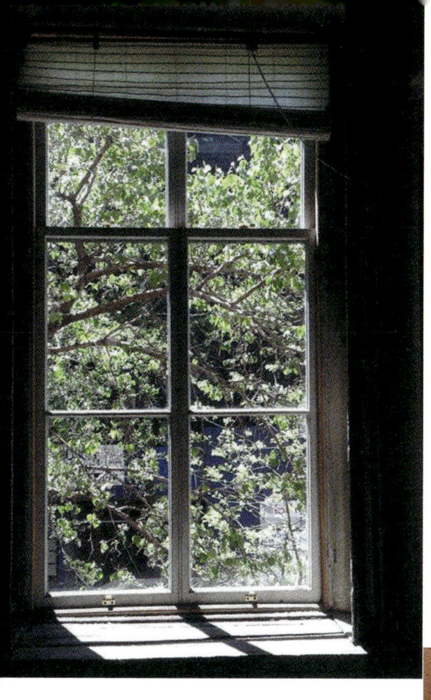

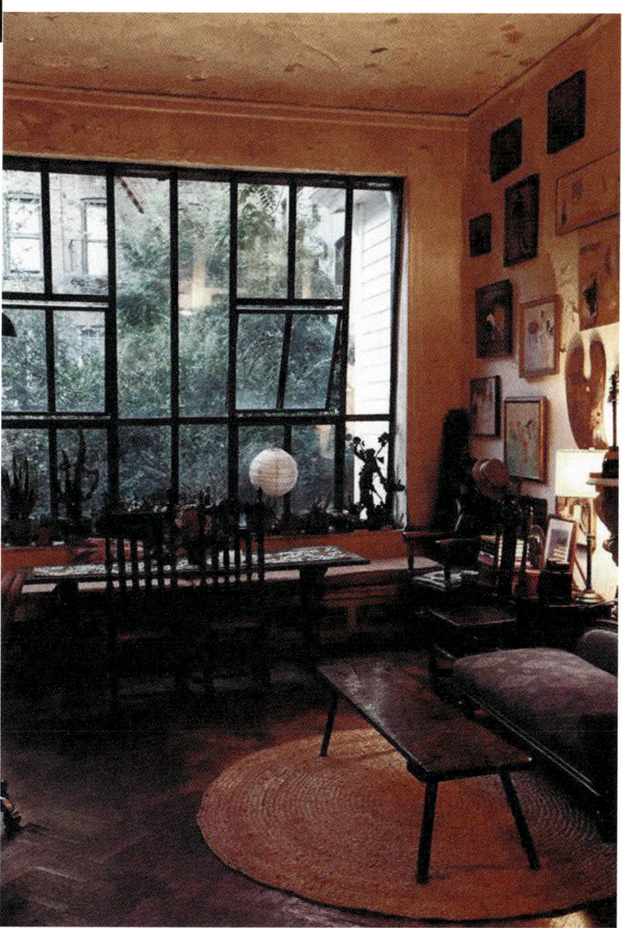

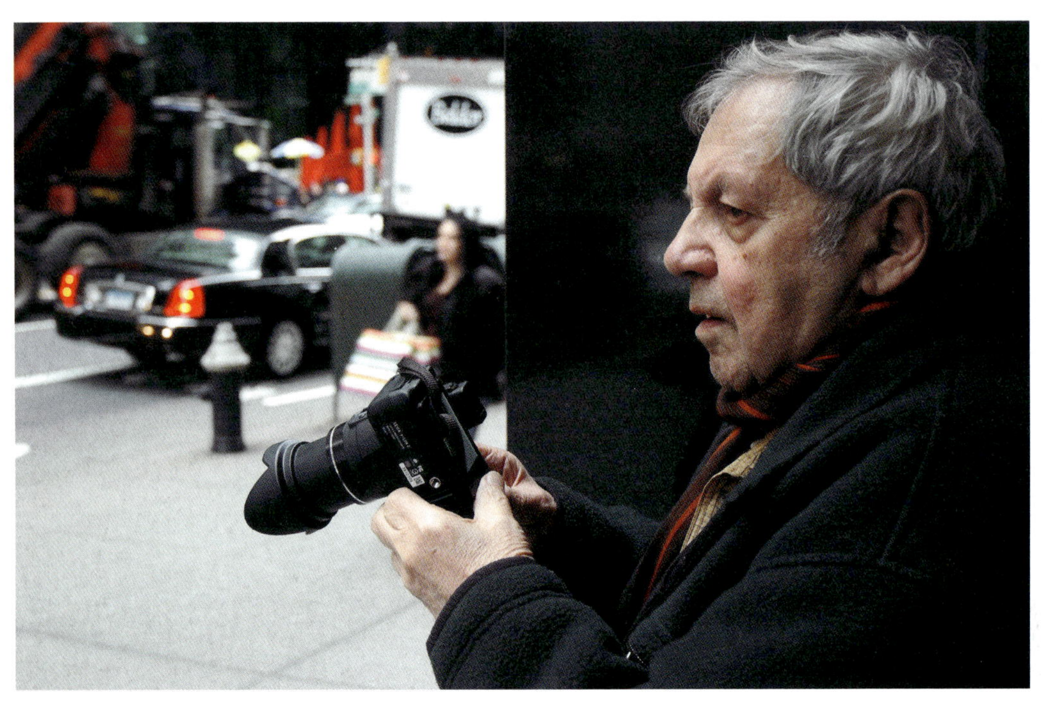

Saul photographing on East 57th Street, New York by Margit Erb, 2010

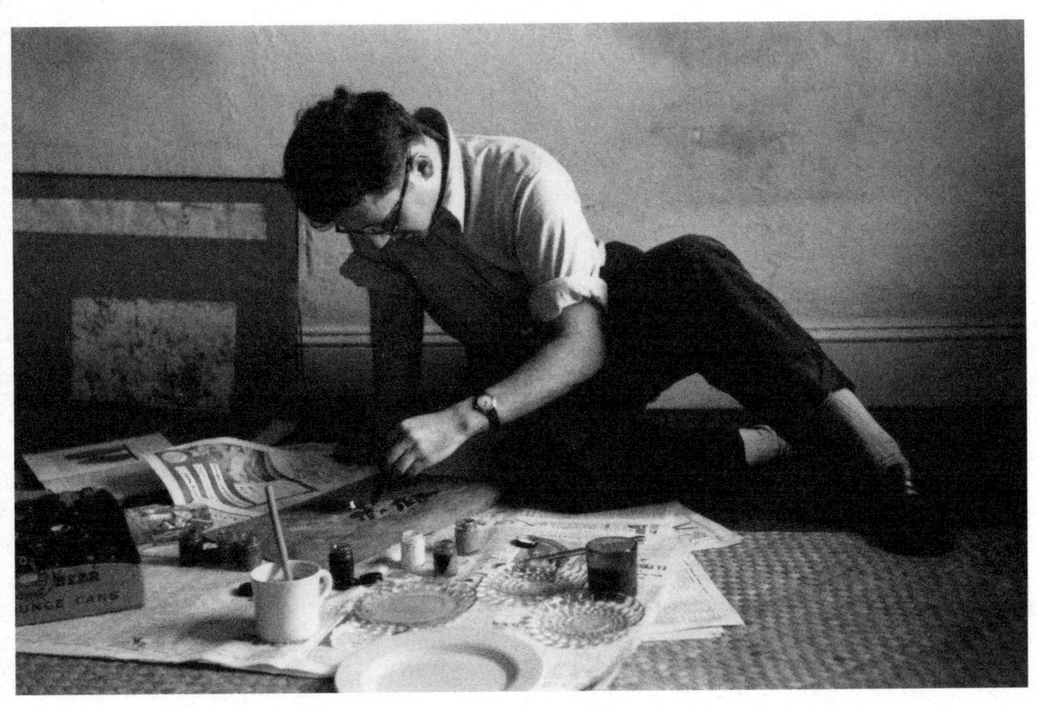

Self-portrait, c. 1946

The Painter in Saul Leiter

Margit Erb Director, Saul Leiter Foundation, New York

In the spring of 2009, Saul Leiter and I unearthed a large black portfolio from under a heap of items in his bedroom. We gently laid the creaky old case on the bed and Saul opened it, revealing a number of watercolors he'd painted on tissue. The paintings were abstract but boldly took on impressions of windows, landscapes, and planetary outbursts. The paper was Japanese tissue and therefore translucent and fragile. As Saul held up each sheet, the room's soft light illuminated the textured paper; the painted hues changed each time the light hit, and the dabs and strokes of paint turned three-dimensional. The lightweight pages, caught by a slight draft, lifted away from us as if with the desire to float upward. For me this magical discovery was like stumbling into a painted paradise. I was elated and in awe. For Saul it was more like being reacquainted with old friends.

In this volume, the Saul Leiter Foundation is pleased to offer an expansive selection of photographs and paintings from the artist's archives, including some of those works on Japanese tissue. The book was originally created in Japan to accompany the exhibition *Photographer Saul Leiter: A Retrospective*, which opened in April 2017 at the Bunkamura Museum of Art in Tokyo and then traveled in Japan and South Korea, displaying Saul's achievements in painting alongside his groundbreaking photographs—a mix of iconic images and fascinating new discoveries. It was fitting that the show began its journey in Japan, a country whose art Saul greatly admired and followed his whole artistic life.

Beginning as a young man, sneaking into the library at the University of Pittsburgh and launching himself on a personal voyage through the history of art— through Europe, Asia, and beyond—Saul was always on an unorthodox journey. In 1946, at age 22, he quit rabbinical school and moved to New York City. Like an alien he landed there with only the thought that he would be a painter. Despite his fame as a photographer, Saul never stopped thinking of himself as a painter. He worked every day and created thousands of pieces. Incredibly, Saul's entire painting career is almost completely intact today. I am delighted that the time has come for the world to see Saul as a painter as well as a photographer, and I'm thrilled that a Japanese audience played a part in this.

This exhibition was first imagined with Pauline Vermare in a conversation over coffee at New York City's International Center of Photography. Both lovers of Japanese art ourselves, we believed we could bring Saul's work to Asia and find a unique kinship with audiences on the other side of the world. As shown in her essay in the book, Pauline's contribution to the understanding of Saul's Japanese and French influences has been huge in our further comprehension of his complete oeuvre. Yet, at the same time, Saul's art reaches across international boundaries and is truly universal, as we hope you'll agree as you look through this special edition of *All About Saul Leiter*.

Margit Erb Biography

Margit Erb is the founder and director of the Saul Leiter Foundation, which is dedicated to preserving Leiter's art and legacy. Starting in 1996 she closely assisted Leiter for more than 18 years. She has worked on many books for the artist, including *Early Color* (2006), *Early Black and White* (2014), and the upcoming *In My Room*. In 2012 she helped produce the exhibition *Saul Leiter: Retrospektive* at the House of Photography, Deichtorhallen, in Hamburg. She is a coproducer of the film *Saul Leiter: In No Great Hurry* (2013). Today she maintains Leiter's archive in his former studio in Manhattan's East Village. She is currently working on a digital catalogue raisonné and several upcoming publications on Leiter's art.

The New York Nabi

Pauline Vermare

Curator of *Photographer Saul Leiter: A Retrospective* exhibition at Bunkamura Museum, Tokyo, 2017

"Sometimes I wake up in the middle of the night and I open a book by Matisse, Cézanne, or Sôtatsu…"[1]—Saul Leiter

Saul Leiter spent over sixty years of his life and took most of his photographs in New York City's East Village, near Saint Mark's Place. Over the past years, the neighborhood has become strikingly Japanese, filled with izakayas, sobayas, ramen restaurants, and Japanese specialty supermarkets. It seems very fitting. Indeed, I've always sensed a closeness to Japan in Saul's work: the photographs in the snow; the women under their umbrellas; the improbable perspectives and revolutionary compositions reminiscent of Japanese woodblocks, *ukiyo-e*; and the presence of the seasons and the verticality of the compositions evoking Japanese scroll paintings, *kakejiku*; the *wabi-sabi* aesthetics of his most abstract work, a melancholy adoration of the unfinished, the imperfect. There is a *"mono no aware"* beauty to these photographs, in the color work especially—an acute awareness of the beauty of the transient, of the ephemeral, which might explain, in part, their magical and poetic essence.

Leiter's photographs were included in a group show at the Tokyo National Museum of Modern Art in 1953, but it was really in 2015, with the Japanese release of Tomas Leach's documentary film *In No Great Hurry*, that the Japanese public met the artist and his work for the first time. With the exhibition *Photographer Saul Leiter: A Retrospective*, we very much hoped to continue and expand the conversation that Leach initiated in his very thoughtful film.

If compared to Japanese photographers, Leiter's work would be close to that of Shôji Ueda or Masao Yamamoto, evoking the same poetic grace and delicateness. Saul had an eye, a painterly eye, for the fleeting moment, for the seemingly banal, and for intimate moments of daily life. His atelier actually looked very much like a traditional Japanese house—the dark wood, the spectacularly tall glass window letting in the northern light, the very Japanese garden outside. The windows always held traces of dust and rain. As Jun'ichirô Tanizaki wrote in *In Praise of Shadows*, "We love things that bear the marks of grime, soot, and weather, and we love the colors and the sheen that call to mind the past that made them."[2]

Saul's studio was filled with a myriad of little Japanese straw brushes that he would use to dust his cameras and boxes. Two framed etchings by Koryûsai were hanging on the walls. The studio had the warm feel of legendary art collector Albert Barnes's house, near Philadelphia, where paintings by Picasso, Degas, Matisse, Bonnard, and Vuillard hang from floor to ceiling and above every door. A painter himself, Leiter admired Vermeer, Matisse, Degas, Vuillard, and, above all, Bonnard. These artists—particularly Bonnard, with his unique tenderness—had a visible influence on Leiter's work.

The birth of Impressionism was directly linked to the birth of photography. The new medium allowed for a detailed representation of reality, liberating some artists and pushing them to explore new subjects—such as *plein-air,* or outdoor scenes, and scenes of ordinary life—along with other ways of painting. The first private exhibition of the Impressionists actually took place in the Paris atelier of the legendary photographer Nadar, on April 15, 1874. Auguste Renoir and Edgar Degas organized the show, which also included the work of Paul Cézanne, Claude Monet, and Georges Seurat. This is when the term *Impressionism* was coined. Saul Leiter, a painter and a photographer, is a direct descendant of this artistic family.

Leiter's style is unique—a rare and beautiful combination of Japanese and French influences runs through his entire body of work, from Hokusai to Bonnard. Indeed, his love for Japanese art might have stemmed, in part, from his passion for the French Impressionists and Post-Impressionists, and from their own love for Japanese arts. *Japonisme* was the term used to describe the fascination with and craving for Japanese aesthetics that arose in the late 19th century, around the time of the Meiji Restoration, which allowed a broader dissemination of Japanese arts in the U.S. and Europe. The main craving was for *ukiyo-e* prints. The Impressionists and Post-Impressionists admired the revolutionary printmaking techniques—the craftsmanship—as well as the radically innovative compositions. Many of them became avid collectors of Hokusai, Utamaro, or Hiroshige.

Both Vuillard and Bonnard were part of a group called Les Nabis ("prophets" in Hebrew); Bonnard's nickname was *"Le Nabi très japonard"*:[3] the very Japanese

Nabi. It is said that Bonnard found in *ukiyo-e* qualities that liberated him from Western conventions of color, form, and composition, and allowed him to create deeply intimate and spontaneous works. It seems that Bonnard's revelations were shared by Leiter, whose work is just as beautifully reminiscent of *ukiyo-e*: the unorthodox and seemingly disproportionate compositions ("Canopy" [p. 59] being the most striking example); the emphasis on shapes; the presence of calligraphy (signs, letters); flat areas of color (often, and perhaps even more powerful in photography, black). Commenting on Leiter's characteristic large blocks of color, the Japanese photo historian Iizawa Kôtarô alluded to the notion of "*ma*," or negative space: the nothingness where, in fact, everything happens.[4] Very much like *ukiyo-e* artists, Leiter was drawn to unusual viewpoints and perspectives (high-angle shots, strong diagonals—the el train providing the most perfect vantage point) and everyday subject matter; other similarities include the ubiquity of women and a fondness for the ordinary (the shoe, the umbrella) and the elements (rain, snow, steam). Saul Leiter was the New York Nabi.

Leiter regularly expressed his love and admiration for Japanese art, and loved to discuss his treasured collection. He would mention Hokusai, Sôtatsu, Hon'ami Kôetsu, Ogata Kôrin.[5] To Saul, calligraphy was "the highest form of art."[6] In the late 1960s, he randomly purchased a batch of Japanese calligraphy paper, about 65 sheets now referred to as "the Japanese tissue portfolio," and painted on every single page over the following years. Some of the paintings are figurative. Others, much more abstract, practically suggest that Saul was trying Japanese calligraphy himself, drawing cryptic characters that looked like kana script.

I asked Margit Erb, the director of the Saul Leiter Foundation, if I could look into Saul's book and music library, to gain more insight into the Japanese artists that moved him so. In his music collection, we found vinyl records of *kabuki nagauta*—a traditional music that accompanied kabuki theater—and many *koto* records. And in Saul's magnificent library, we discovered well over a hundred books dedicated to Japanese literature, poetry, calligraphy, ceramics, painting, and, mostly, *ukiyo-e*. Evidently Saul particularly loved the work of Hokusai. In his collection, garnered primarily at the Strand, his favorite bookstore, on East 12th Street, there were many books on Hokusai, as well as Hiroshige, Harunobu, Utamaro, Kiyonaga, and Sharaku. We also found a few original sewn albums (*fukurotoji-bon*) of original woodblocks, including two rare and stunningly beautiful original Utamaro albums from the late 18th century, sold at Christie's in 1994. Saul owned books on the painters Buson, Sesshu, Zeshin, and Sôtatsu as well. And in the midst of his collection there was a beautiful volume on Corot, who was a role model for the Impressionists. The book, published in 1936 by Atelier-Sha, perfectly embodies the confluence of Saul's Japanese and French inspirations.

We also found dozens of anthologies of Japanese art, such as a series published in 1932 by Seibundo, and a few collected works, including one about "the decadent Suzuki and Oka"[7] and another on "eccentric, non-conformist Japanese artists."[8] Saul owned books on Japanese motifs and ceramics, including the work of Ogata Kenzan; art from the Momoyama and Edo eras; *kakejiku* and Japanese *noh* plays; and Japanese carpentry, architecture,[9] and design (including the amusing title *How to Wrap 5 Eggs: Japanese Design in Traditional Packaging*). There were a few books of haiku as well, and classics of literature such as *The Life of an Amorous Woman*, *The Pillow Book of the Lady Sei Shonagon*, and *Diaries of Court Ladies of Old Japan*. There was also a copy of *The Book of Tea* by Kakuzô Okakura, signed by Saul's great love, Soames Bantry: "To a truly sincere and long abiding lover of tea." (Saul was quite the Balzacian coffee drinker too.) And one photo book: *A History of Japanese Photography (1840–1945)*.[10]

It is worth noting that most of these books were written in Japanese, a language that Leiter did not speak or read, which exemplifies his fondness and admiration for Japanese art. One book in his collection stood out: the catalogue of an exhibition on Hon'ami Kôetsu, the Renaissance calligraphy master, organized by the Philadelphia Museum of Art. Saul dedicated it to his dear friend Margit, and saved a critique of the show by Robert Hughes—"The Subtle Magic of Kôetsu," a title that suits Leiter himself beautifully.[11]

Finally, there were a few books related to Buddhism, and Zen, and a copy of *Edo Satirical Verse Anthologies* by R.H. Blyth,[12] in which Saul added his initials,

"SL," to the opening quote that reads: "Dedicated to Daisetz Suzuki, who taught me not to teach." That sentence evidently spoke to Leiter, a man who chose to be an artist rather than a preacher. Through painting and photography, he transcended the theological nature of his upbringing and ended up becoming another kind of spiritual leader. There is one portrait in his archive where Saul looks strikingly like a Buddhist monk (p. 294). Cartier-Bresson, a Buddhist himself, would often refer to *Zen in the Art of Archery*, a book by the German philosopher Eugen Herrigel published in 1953 with an introduction by the same Daisetz Suzuki, a great thinker who played a very important role in spreading Zen beyond Japan.

This analogy between *kyûdô* and photography is essential in both Cartier-Bresson's and Leiter's work: the focus, and the letting-go. Leiter and Cartier-Bresson were both painter photographers who shared a love of Bonnard and *ukiyo-e*. Cartier-Bresson used to say that photography was like a sketchbook and painting like a meditation. The two men never met, although Leiter did photograph Cartier-Bresson "HCB style," on the fly, in 1959, when the French photographer was shooting in New York City's Chinatown (p. 290). Leiter was too intimidated to approach him. Leiter actually photographed very much like Cartier-Bresson did in the 1930s: with no other intention than to capture a fleeting moment of beauty. They were both very modern men, but they also had the intellectual depth and bohemian ways of 19th-century artists.

Unlike Cartier-Bresson, who turned to photojournalism after the Second World War, Leiter always remained a pure observer, an apolitical eye. That isn't to say that he didn't care about the world—he actually cared very much. But it seems that Saul also lived in accordance with major Zen principles: not attaching any great significance to himself or even his art, and having no defined purpose or intent in life except for being present to the world and always highly aware of its fleeting beauty. No preaching, just looking.

Pauline Vermare Biography

Pauline Vermare is a photography curator based in New York City and the cultural director at Magnum Photos, New York. She was formerly a curator at the International Center of Photography, the Museum of Modern Art, and the Henri Cartier-Bresson Foundation in Paris, where she assisted with Saul Leiter's first European show in 2008. She grew up in France and Japan.

1   *Saul Leiter*, exhibition catalogue, Paris/Gottingen: Fondation HCB/Steidl, 2008.

2   Leete's Island Books, 1977.

3   *Le Japonisme*, catalogue of the eponymous show at the Grand Palais, Paris (RMN, 1988).

4   Conversation with Iizawa Kôtarô at Megutama, Tokyo, for Leiter retrospective at Bunkamura Museum, Tokyo, April 2017; see more in the author's essay "The Subtle Magic of Saul Leiter" in *Saul Leiter: 1950s New York* collotype portfolio (Benrido, 2017).

5   "Photographers Speak," interview with Dean Brierly, April 22, 2009 (http://photographyinterviews.blogspot.com/2009/04/saul-leiter-quiet-iconoclast-saul.html?m=1).

6   Margit Erb, talk at the SVA, New York, March 15, 2016.

7   *The Decadents: Suzuki and Oka*, Tokyo: Kodansha International, 1969.

8   *Extraordinary Persons: Works by Eccentric, Non-Conformist Japanese Artists of the Early Modern Era (1580–1868) in the collection of Kimiko and John Powers*, Cambridge, MA: Harvard University Art Museums, 1999.

9   *The Way of the Carpenter: Tools and Japanese Architecture*, New York: Weatherhill, 1991.

10 Tokyo: Heibonsha/Japanese Photographers Association, 1971.

11 *Time*, October 23, 2000, a rapturous critique of the show then on view at the Philadelphia Museum of Art.

12 Tokyo: Hokuseido Press, 1961.

Photographs that creep up behind you and tickle your left ear

Motoyuki Shibata Scholar and translator of American literature

In 1946, 22-year-old Saul Leiter abandoned his theological studies, and against the wishes of his father, a well-known Talmud scholar, moved from Cleveland to New York to become a painter. In 1952 he took an apartment on East 10th Street in Manhattan, staying there for over half a century until his death in 2013. The same building was home to fellow art-lover and long-term partner Soames Bantry (d. 2002). Then in Leiter's final years, he shared his living space with cat Lemon (not the worthless feline the name might suggest) who in turn acquired another roommate after Leiter's death before passing away in 2016.

At the time Leiter moved there, this district in the east of Manhattan's Downtown was classed as part of the area known as the Lower East Side. And while today the Lower East Side is a totally different place, having become entirely gentrified, back then it was known for its high concentration of immigrants, mainly Germans in the 19th century, and Jews and Italians from the early 20th century onward. As a part of town where people conversed in heavily accented English, or even languages other than English, it was far more closely associated with poverty than affluence.

But from the mid-1950s, around the time Allen Ginsberg and other poets and artists of the Beat Generation moved into the area, the Lower East Side slowly began to change. Fast-forward to the late 1960s and the flowering of the counterculture, and this neighborhood found itself transformed into a nexus of the New York art scene. Andy Warhol lived here and collaborated with musicians, and it was also home to the Fillmore East, seat of 1960s rock, and punk mecca CBGB. The district also broke away, so to speak, from the appellation "Lower East Side," which covered a sizable area, becoming known instead as the East Village and acquiring a reputation as an "arty" neighborhood, in complete contrast to the Lower East Side. And as is inevitably the way in New York, it then rapidly went upmarket. Yet the raw energy of that period of new and exciting culture can, in a way, still be felt there.

The interesting thing about Saul Leiter is that despite living right through these changing times and mingling after a fashion with his artist neighbors, this seems to have had almost no influence on his photography. Even in his photos taken on the streets in the 21st century, though of course the fashions are different, his actual approach to taking photographs is unchanged. A depth that goes beyond capturing local color even as he directs his gaze at street corner minutiae; the free choice of subjects, unbound by considerations of race, gender, or class; bold, determinedly off-center composition; a diversity of mirror images and images shot through glass; and underpinning it all, a sense of humor: these features that distinguish Leiter's photos from those of anyone else did not change in the slightest from the 1950s. And yet, by no means do his photos ever seem dated. His approach is consistently what could only be described as not conservative, not avant-garde, but "Leiter style."

When it comes to pondering this "Leiter style," Martin Harrison, who penned the introduction to *Early Color* (Steidl, 2006), the book that ignited a reappraisal of Leiter's work, has said that rather than looking at Leiter alongside other photographers, a more valid approach would be to group him with the "intimiste" painters, who preferred to depict familiar scenes, artists such as Bonnard and Vuillard, of whom Leiter himself was a fan. As an extension of Harrison's idea, here I would like to consider Leiter's work in connection with American poetry.

Thinking of poetry that is also thematically close to the series of photos Saul Leiter took in New York, first to spring to mind are Frank O'Hara (1926–1966) and Charles Reznikoff (1894–1976), who created poetry out of their daily perambulations around New York streets.* These two wrote most of their New York poems in the 1950s and '60s, overlapping almost exactly with the period when Leiter was taking the majority of his photos of the city. O'Hara was also a curator at MoMA, and a central figure in the New York School (an informal gathering of poets, painters, and other artists), while Leiter's photos can be found in Jane Livingston's *The New York School: Photographs 1936–1963* (1992), so it is hardly drawing a long bow to link the pair. However, in terms of the actual substance of the poems, Charles

Reznikoff's short, almost snapshot-like verse would appear to have more in common with Leiter's photographs.

> *This Puerto Rican—just an ordinary laborer—*
> *how he goes about his work in the park*
> *jauntily*
> *swinging his rake*
> *like a cane!*
> *[...]*
> *The autumn rains have begun*
> *but are over for the moment;*
> *leaves float*
> *on the pools of water on the pavement.*
> *The lonely walker hears*
> *only the swift motor-cars.*
>
> (From *By the Well of Living and Seeing*
> *and The Fifth Book of the Maccabees* [1969])

Simple use of language, an unobtrusive eye on the city, a teasing tone tinged with affection, dry humor: apart from the use of words, all are elements that could equally apply to Leiter's photography. And unlike O'Hara, who was at the center of the art scene, and like Leiter, Reznikoff was only at last properly recognized in his later years. In real-life terms at least, Reznikoff, who for many years had a job summarizing court records, also resembles Leiter in that there is never any sense of him asserting himself strongly as an artist (although in doggedly publishing verse at his own expense using a second-hand printer for all the years he remained unrecognized, he did differ from Leiter, who never even tried to publish his street photographs).

But taking a step further from the obvious connection with O'Hara and Reznikoff, personally one is tempted to link Leiter's photographs to the poems of Emily Dickinson (1830–1886), who lived out her days quietly in a small Massachusetts town, with hardly any of her work published during her lifetime, but is now viewed as one of America's greatest poets.

Further in Summer than the Birds—
Pathetic from the Grass—
A minor Nation celebrates
Its unobtrusive Mass.

No Ordinance be seen—
So gradual the Grace
A gentle Custom it becomes—
Enlarging Loneliness—

(Untitled, 1865: first two stanzas of a four-stanza poem [Fr 895])

Superficially of course, the combination of peaceful late summer cricket-chirping and rites of the Catholic Mass describes a world completely unlike that captured by the lens of Saul Leiter. Yet surely Leiter's understated boldness in combining in the visual domain real image and mirror image, this side of the glass and the other, has much in common with Dickinson's frequent, audacious overlapping of sacred and profane, the religious dimension and the quotidian, in the domain of words?

Sharing the title of America's greatest poet with Dickinson, needless to say, is Walt Whitman (1819–1892). In contrast to Dickinson, who was self-effacing in both her life and her poetry (though obviously with a core of steel), in Whitman's poems "I" unites with multiple "yous," extending indefinitely until ultimately, statements about the self also become statements about America. The situation that frequently arises in American art—that of correlating the self's concerns directly with those of America—also arises in Whitman's poetry. That two such contrasting poets should appear consecutively in the mid-19th century was a great boon for American poetry.

Moreover, the contrast between Whitman and Dickinson is, I think, similar to that between Robert Frank and Saul Leiter, both photographers who achieved their most important work in the 1950s.

In his poem "I Hear America Singing" (1860), Whitman wrote of a carpenter, a stonemason, a boatman, a mother, and others, in verse that reads like an inventory of love. Robert Frank attempted the same in his photo collection *The Americans* (1958), by photographing people in different states. And for Frank, a Swiss immigrant, producing *The Americans* also resembled a rite of passage in becoming American himself. Here again the self's concern is directly linked to the subject of America.

On the other hand, there are probably no photo books *less* suited to the title *The Americans* than those of Saul Leiter. If Leiter had a job in fashion photography, he took splendid fashion photographs, but the photos he by far preferred to take were those shot walking around his neighborhood, and he did not travel the United States in search of diverse subjects in the manner of Robert Frank (doubtless he found the world diverse enough close to home). For Leiter, just as for Dickinson, "my" concerns were not "America's" concerns. This was a photographer with no desire to amplify his own presence in any sense. Max Kozloff's introduction to a small book of Leiter's work put out by Thames & Hudson also begins with the line, "Saul Leiter told me that he has always found it comfortable to be ignored."

It goes without saying, this is not a question of which approach is better or worse. It is simply that the discovery in the 21st century that just as American poetry is all the richer for having both Whitman and Dickinson, American photography is the richer for having had both Robert Frank and Saul Leiter in the 1950s, which can only be cause for celebration.

In an essay on Leiter in *The New Yorker* (November 27, 2013 issue, later included in the collection *Known and Strange Things*), American writer Teju Cole notes the following exchange in the documentary film *In No Great Hurry: 13 Lessons In Life With Saul Leiter*:

> Leiter: There are the things that are out in the open and then there
> are the things that are hidden, and life has more to do, the real world
> has more to do with what is hidden, maybe. You think?
> Director (off-camera): That could be true.
> Leiter: You think it's true?
> Director: It could be.
> Leiter: It could be very true. We like to pretend that what is public
> is what the real world is all about.

This view that the most precious things are those we cannot see may be an aesthetic old-fashioned enough to put *The Little Prince* to shame, but of greater interest to Cole is the fact that rather than expounding expansively on "his hard-won insight," Leiter still has not stopped doubting himself. "You think?" "You think it's true?" he persists, quizzing the director off-camera. Even when with "It could be very true" he almost reaches a conclusion, he backtracks again with "We like to pretend that what is public is what the real world is all about," thus avoiding, to the end, entirely affirming his own thoughts. On a personal note, as the translator who provided the subtitles for *In No Great Hurry*, the thing I too took most care with was not to give Leiter's words an assertive tone (this would have been difficult if he was a faster talker—obviously with subtitles there is a limit on length, so for a fast speaker, one has no choice but to be assertive, as this uses fewest characters).

According to Teju Cole, this kind of healthy skepticism can also be discerned in Leiter's photographs. I agree. The photos of Saul Leiter neither affirm nor reject the subject, but on each occasion, prepare an original framework and quietly offer it to the viewer, as if, as the man himself says in the film, they were creeping up behind you, and tickling your left ear. Looking at Leiter's photos, it is evident that this is the very way to celebrate the world most beautifully, by having the most fun.

* The author also wrote in issue 61 of *Coyote* (March 15, 2017) about "Walkers of the streets of New York" (Joseph Cornell, the Collyer brothers, Paul Auster, etc.) who, like O'Hara and Reznikoff, had similarities to Leiter.

Motoyuki Shibata Biography

Born 1954 in Tokyo, Shibata is a scholar and translator of American literature, the editor-in-chief of the literary journal *MONKEY,* and a Special Projects Professor at the University of Tokyo, Faculty of Letters. He is the author of *The American Narcissus* (winner of the Suntory Prize for Social Sciences and Humanities; University of Tokyo Press, 2005) and *Cambridge Circus* (Switch Publishing, 2010), among others. He has translated numerous works of contemporary American literature into Japanese, his translation of Thomas Pynchon's *Mason & Dixon* (Shinchosha) winning him the Japan Society of Translators' 2010 Japanese Translation Culture Award. He was responsible for the Japanese subtitles for the film *In No Great Hurry: 13 Lessons In Life With Saul Leiter.*

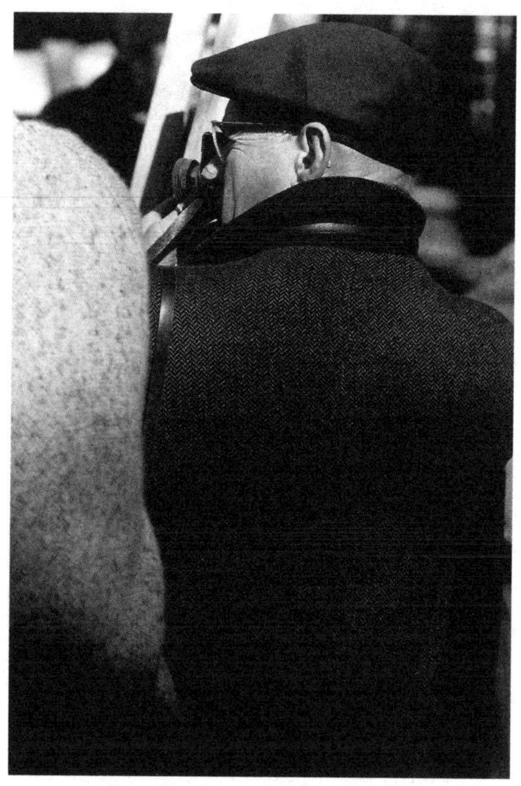

Henri Cartier-Bresson by Saul Leiter, c. 1959

Sources of Saul Leiter quotations

Sam Stourdze interview, *Saul Leiter* (Steidl, 2008): pp. 35, 129

"Saul Leiter's Elegance" by Max Kozloff, in *Saul Leiter*, Photofile series (Thames & Hudson, 2008): p. 219

Saul Leiter: Retrospektive (Kehrer, 2012):

"What His Eyes Can Do" by Adam Harrison Levy: pp. 1, 10, 40

"Saul Leiter's Fashion Photographs" by Vince Aletti: pp. 5, 24, 30, 122

"The Promenader" by Brigitte Woischnik: pp. 92, 108

"Undiscovered Seeing" by Ulrich Rüter: pp. 134, 148, 176

Press release for *Retrospektive* exhibition at Deichtorhallen, Hamburg, 2012: pp. 90, 96, 104, 186

"A Short Interview With Saul Leiter" by David Gibson, *ASX*, 2013: pp. 66, 73, 169

"A Casual Conversation With Saul Leiter" by Phil Bicker, *Time* magazine, February 19, 2013: pp. 81, 157, 160, 180, 194, 207, 210, 259

In No Great Hurry: 13 Lessons In Life With Saul Leiter, directed by Tomas Leach, 2013: pp. 12, 44, 48, 54, 56

Saul Leiter chronology

1923	Born in Pittsburgh, Pennsylvania, on December 3. Parents are Rabbi Wolf Leiter and Regina *née* Goldberg.
1930s	Attends Talmudic Academy in New York City.
c. 1935	Is given a Detrola camera by his mother and begins photographing.
early 1940s	Attends Telshe Yeshiva Rabbinical College, Cleveland.
1944	Paintings exhibited at Ten-Thirty Gallery, Cleveland.
1945	Paintings exhibited at Outlines Gallery, Pittsburgh, and at Gump's department store, San Francisco.
1946	Leaves Telshe Yeshiva Rabbinical College and moves to New York. Befriends Abstract Expressionist painter Richard Pousette-Dart, who encourages Leiter to take photographs.
1947	Attends Henri Cartier-Bresson's exhibition at the Museum of Modern Art. Befriends W. Eugene Smith, who gives him Alexey Brodovitch's book *Ballet*. One of Leiter's paintings is included in *Abstract and Surrealist American Art* at the Art Institute of Chicago. Paintings exhibited at the Butler Institute of American Art, Youngstown, Ohio.
c. 1948	Begins working with color slide film.
1951	*LIFE* publishes his black-and-white series *The Wedding as a Funeral* in its September 3 issue. More work is featured in the November 26 issue of *LIFE* (*Shoes of the Shoeshine Man*).
1952	Moves to New York City's East Village.
1953	Black-and-white photographs are included in *Always the Young Strangers* at the Museum of Modern Art, New York, and in *Contemporary Photography* at the National Museum of Modern Art, Tokyo.
1956	Solo exhibition at the Tanager Gallery, New York.
late 1950	Gives slide talk about color work at "The Club," an art space in the East Village. Exhibits color work at Samuel Kootz Gallery, New York.
1957	Steichen includes twenty of Leiter's color photographs in his slide talk, "Experimental Photography in Color," at the Museum of Modern Art, New York. Henry Wolf, art director at *Esquire*, publishes some of Leiter's fashion photographs.

1958	Begins to photograph for *Harper's Bazaar* when Henry Wolf becomes art director.
1959	Travels to Europe on assignment for *Esquire* to photograph Gina Lollobrigida during the making of *Solomon and Sheba*.
1960–80s	Continues to take fashion photographs and do other commercial work. His fashion work is published in *Harper's Bazaar, Elle, Show, Vogue (UK), Queen*, and *Nova*. His photographs are also included in *LIFE, U.S. Camera, Photography Annual*, and *Infinity* magazines.
1981	Closes commercial studio at 156 5th Avenue.
1991	Fashion work included in group exhibition *Appearances* at the Victoria and Albert Museum, London, with accompanying book by Martin Harrison.
1992, September	Black-and-white work included in Jane Livingston's book *The New York School: Photographs 1936–1963*.
1993–94	Black-and-white photographs exhibited at Howard Greenberg Gallery, New York. Receives funding from Ilford Paper Company to begin printing color work as Cibachromes with Laumont Labs in New York.
1997	Exhibition of color photographs at Howard Greenberg Gallery, New York.
2005	Exhibition *Saul Leiter: Early Color* at Howard Greenberg Gallery.
2006	First monograph *Early Color* is published by Steidl, Göttingen, Germany. First solo museum show at Milwaukee Art Museum.
2008	First solo museum show in Europe at the Henri Cartier-Bresson Foundation, Paris, with accompanying book.
2009	First painting exhibition in over 30 years at Knoedler Gallery, New York.
2013	Saul Leiter dies at the age of 89 on November 26, in New York. The release of the documentary film *In No Great Hurry: 13 Lessons In Life With Saul Leiter*, directed by Tomas Leach. Exhibition at Gallery Fifty One in Antwerp, Belgium, with accompanying monograph *Here's More Why Not*.
2017	First solo exhibition in Japan at the Bunkamura Museum of Art, Tokyo.
2018	Bunkamura show travels to Itami City Museum of Art in Japan and to S Factory in Seoul, South Korea.

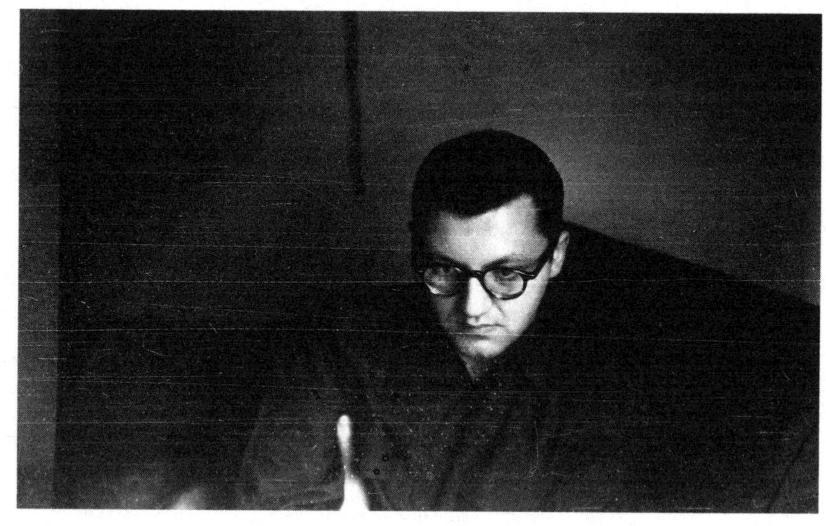

Saul Leiter, Self-portrait, c. 1950

Acknowledgments

The Saul Leiter Foundation gives sincere thanks to the many people whose participation facilitated this book and the traveling exhibition *Photographer Saul Leiter: A Retrospective*. It was especially fortunate that these projects were coproduced with the talented oversight of Masako Sato at CONTACT. The foundation is grateful to the Bunkamura Museum of Art in Tokyo, the Itami City Museum of Art, and S Factory in Seoul for holding the exhibitions. Thanks also for the invaluable contributions from Eriko Kamada (Seigensha), Osamu Ouchi, Motoyuki Shibata, and Kyoko Wada (Goliga). Finally, endless gratitude goes to the Saul Leiter Foundation family, including Robert Benton, Alicia Colen, Gabria Fischer-Shay, Anders Goldfarb, Howard Greenberg, Philippe Laumont, Roger Szmulewicz, Pauline Vermare, and Gregory Wakabayashi, whose continuous efforts helped make these presentations possible.

Margit Erb and Michael Parillo
Saul Leiter Foundation
saulleiterfoundation.org

Photo Credits
Margit Erb pp. 270, 271 (left), 272
Anika Gusick p. 271 (right)

Translated from the Japanese by Pamela Miki Associates (pp. 282–288)

First published in the United Kingdom in 2018 by
Thames & Hudson Ltd, 6-24 Britannia Street, London WC1X 9JD

Reprinted 2018, 2019, 2021, 2022, 2025

Original edition © 2017 Seigensha Art Publishing, Inc., Kyoto
Photographs © 2018 Saul Leiter Foundation
This edition © 2018 Thames & Hudson Ltd, London

Produced by Masako Sato (Contact)
Designed by Osamu Ouchi (nano/nano graphics)
Edited by Eriko Kamada (Seigensha)

All Rights Reserved. No part of this publication may be reproduced
or transmitted in any form or by any means, electronic or mechanical,
including photocopy, recording or any other information storage and
retrieval system, without prior permission in writing from the publisher.

EU Authorized Representative: Interart S.A.R.L.
19 rue Charles Auray, 93500 Pantin, Paris, France
productsafety@thameshudson.co.uk
www.interart.fr

A CIP catalogue record for this book is available from the British Library

ISBN 978-0-500-29453-6
06

Printed and bound in Slovenia by DZS-Grafik d.o.o

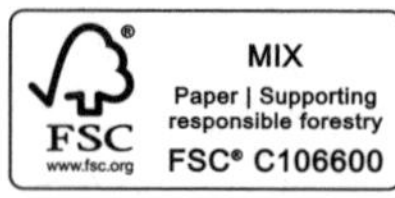

Be the first to know about our new releases,
exclusive content and author events by visiting
thamesandhudson.com
thamesandhudsonusa.com
thamesandhudson.com.au